PROPERTY, POWER, AND AUTHORITY IN RUS AND LATIN EUROPE, CA. 1000–1236

BEYOND MEDIEVAL EUROPE

Beyond Medieval Europe publishes monographs and edited volumes that evoke medieval Europe's geographic, cultural, and religious diversity, while highlighting the interconnectivity of the entire region, understood in the broadest sense—from Dublin to Constantinople, Novgorod to Toledo. The individuals who inhabited this expansive territory built cities, cultures, kingdoms, and religions that impacted their locality and the world around them in manifold ways. The series is particularly keen to include studies on traditionally underrepresented subjects in Anglophone scholarship (such as medieval eastern Europe) and to consider submissions from scholars not natively writing in English in an effort to increase the diversity of Anglophone publishing on the greater medieval European world.

Series Editor

Christian Alexander Raffensperger, *Wittenberg University*, Ohio

Editorial Board

Kurt Villads Jensen, *Stockholms Universitet*
Balázs Nagy, *Central European University*, Budapest
Leonora Neville, *University of Wisconsin*, Madison

Acquisitions Editor

Erin T. Dailey

PROPERTY, POWER, AND AUTHORITY IN RUS AND LATIN EUROPE, CA. 1000–1236

YULIA MIKHAILOVA

British Library Cataloguing in Publication Data

A catalogue record for this book is available from the British Library

© 2018, Arc Humanities Press, Leeds

 This work is licensed under a Creative Commons Attribution-NonCommercial-NoDerivatives 4.0 International Licence.

The authors assert their moral right to be identified as the authors of their part of this work.

Permission to use brief excerpts from this work in scholarly and educational works is hereby granted provided that the source is acknowledged. Any use of material in this work that is an exception or limitation covered by Article 5 of the European Union's Copyright Directive (2001/29/EC) or would be determined to be "fair use" under Section 107 of the U.S. Copyright Act September 2010 Page 2 or that satisfies the conditions specified in Section 108 of the U.S. Copyright Act (17 USC §108, as revised by P.L. 94-553) does not require the Publisher's permission.

ISBN: 9781942401483
e-ISBN: 9781942401490

https://arc-humanities.org
Printed and bound by CPI Group (UK) Ltd, Croydon, CR0 4YY

CONTENTS

List of Illustrations vi

Acknowledgements vii

Introduction 1

Chapter 1. Rus and Latin Europe: Words, Concepts, and Phenomena 13

Chapter 2. Medieval Texts and Professional Belief Systems: Latin,
Church Slavonic, and Vernacular Political Narratives................... 71

Chapter 3. Elite Domination in Rus and Latin Europe: Princely Power
and Banal Lordship 113

Chapter 4. Interprincely Agreements and a Question of Feudo-Vassalic
Relations 153

Conclusions...195

Bibliography..201

Index 221

LIST OF ILLUSTRATIONS

Figure 1. Descendants of Igor and Olga viii

Figure 2. Descendants of Sviatoslav Iaroslavich ix

Figure 3. Descendants of Vsevolod Iaroslavich x

Figure 4. Descendant of Briachislav Iziaslavich. xi

Figure 5. A "castle" in twelfth-century England. 134

Figure 6. A "small town" in twelfth-century Rus 135

Map 1. An approximate territory of Rus, with Novgorod's dependent
 lands, in the twelfth century 129

Map 2. Fortifications on the border with the steppe 136

Note on Genealogical Tables

The genealogical tables (Figures 1 to 4) represent the first nine generations of descendants of Igor and Olga. The tables are not comprehensive. Female members of princely families, except Olga, are omitted, and so are some less significant princes, especially of the later generations. For the eighth and ninth generations, only selected members are included.

For many princes, the dates of births arie unknown; the dates of deaths are known better, although for a significant number of princes they are not known either. The tables provide the dates of the death only; if no date is given, this means that it is unknown. The order in which the brothers' names are listed does not necessarily represent the order of their births. The patrimonial lands are indicated in some cases, when highly relevant in the context of the book. The names of the Kievan princes are given in bold; for the purpose of the tables, the prince is considered "Kievan" even if his tenure in Kiev was brief and/or contentious.

ACKNOWLEDGEMENTS

To the memory of Aleksei Konstantinovich Zaitsev.

I EXPRESS MY gratitude to all who have helped and encouraged me in writing this book. The original impulse that led to this project came out of long-ago conversations with A. K. Zaitsev. I received invaluable support, as well as highly helpful comments and critique from Timothy Graham, Jonathan Shepard, David Prestel, Tania Ivanova-Sullivan, Erika Monahan, Petr Stefanovich, and Charles Halperin. Christian Raffensperger was a constant source of inspiration, and I am very grateful for his invitation to be published in this series. My special thanks to Charles West for his generous comments on the manuscript. I am very grateful to Yury Morgunov, Vladimir Koval, and Inna Kuzina for their help and guidance in the matters of Rus archaeology; special thanks to Yury Morgunov for his generous help with illustrations. The project that led to this book owes much to conversations with Nancy McLoughlin, Susanna Throop, Carol Symes, Anton Gorskii, Paul Hyams Jehangir Malegam, and many other people, including the participants and the audience of the session "Transnational Literary History I: East and West, from Rus to Wales" at the 2012 International Congress on Medieval Studies at Kalamazoo. Special thanks to Jehangir Malegam for many ways he helped me during my stay in the Research Triangle area. I also thank Heidi Madden, Adriana Carilli, Ekaterina Makhnina, and Tatiana Makhnina for their generous help. I would also like to thank Erin Dailey for his constant goodwill and patience, and the anonymous reviewer for the helpful suggestions. Needless to say, I am solely responsible for all errors. I am grateful to all my Moscow Lomonosov University professors, and especially to A. L. Smyshlyev, N. S. Borisov, A. D. Gorskii, and N. V. Kozlova. Finally, a big thanks to my husband and daughters for their patience and unwavering support.

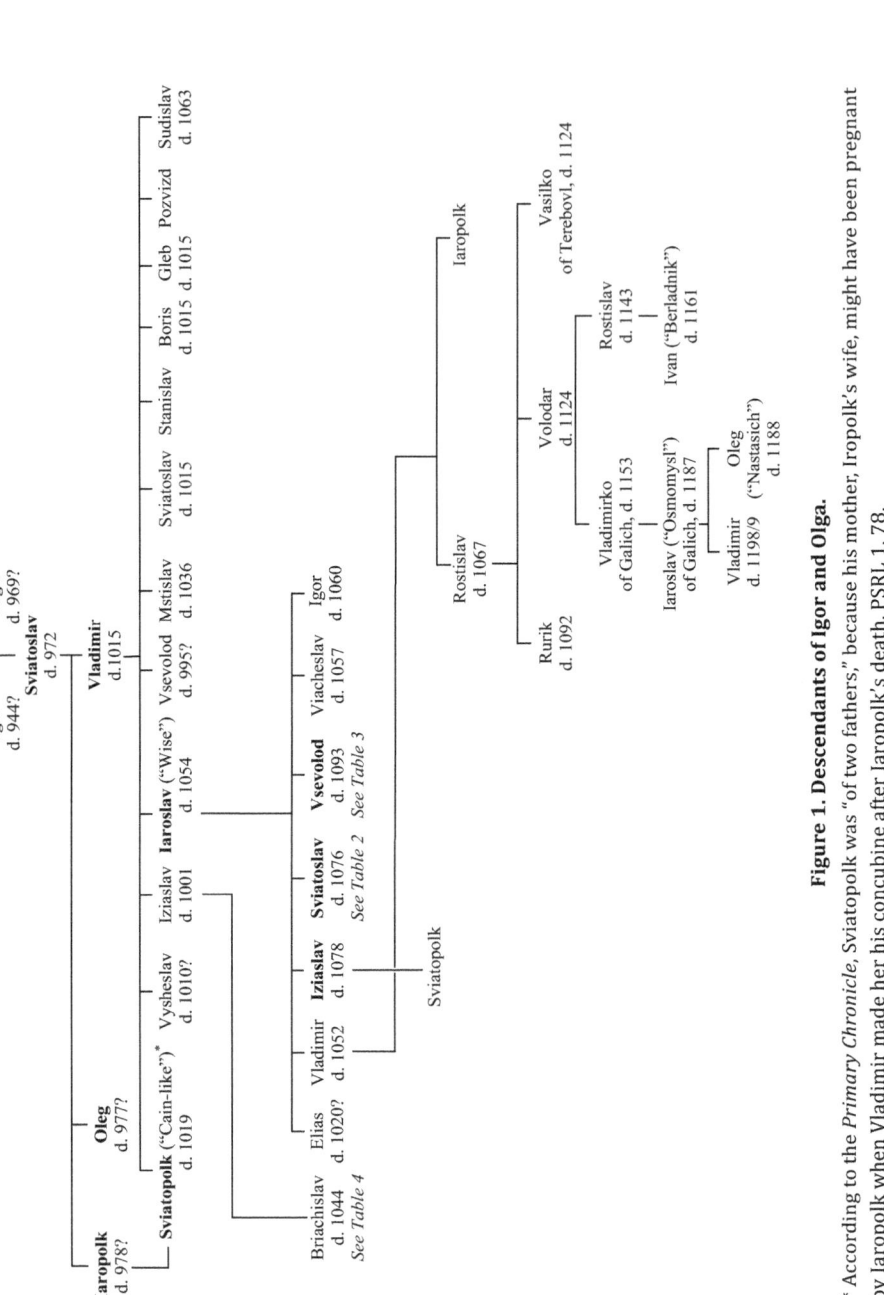

Figure 1. Descendants of Igor and Olga.

* According to the *Primary Chronicle*, Sviatopolk was "of two fathers," because his mother, Iropolk's wife, might have been pregnant by Iaropolk when Vladimir made her his concubine after Iaropolk's death. PSRL 1, 78.

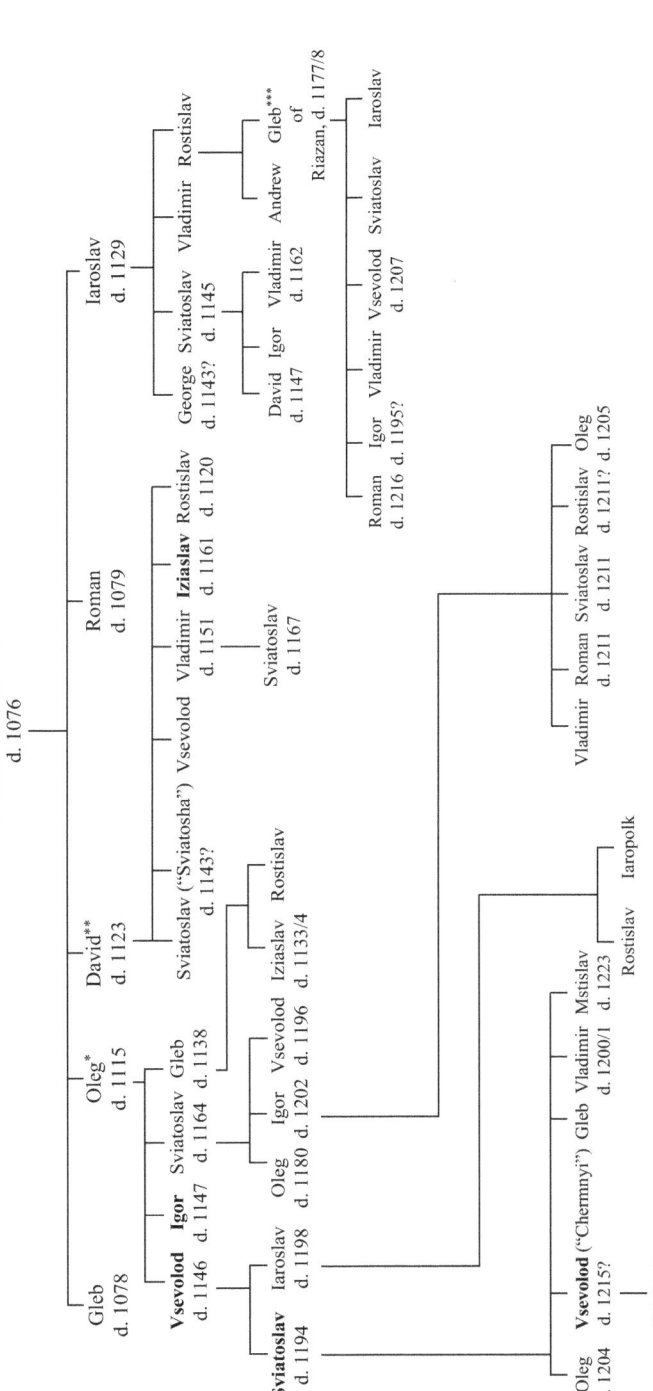

Figure 2. Descendants of Sviatoslav Iaroslavich.

* The founder of the Olgovichi dynasty. ** The founder of the Davidovichi line, sometimes referred to in the sources as part of the Olgovichi dynasty. The Olgovichi and the Davidovichi were based in the Chernigov Land. *** The founder of the Riazan princely line, the father of the Glebovichi, discussed in Chapter 4.

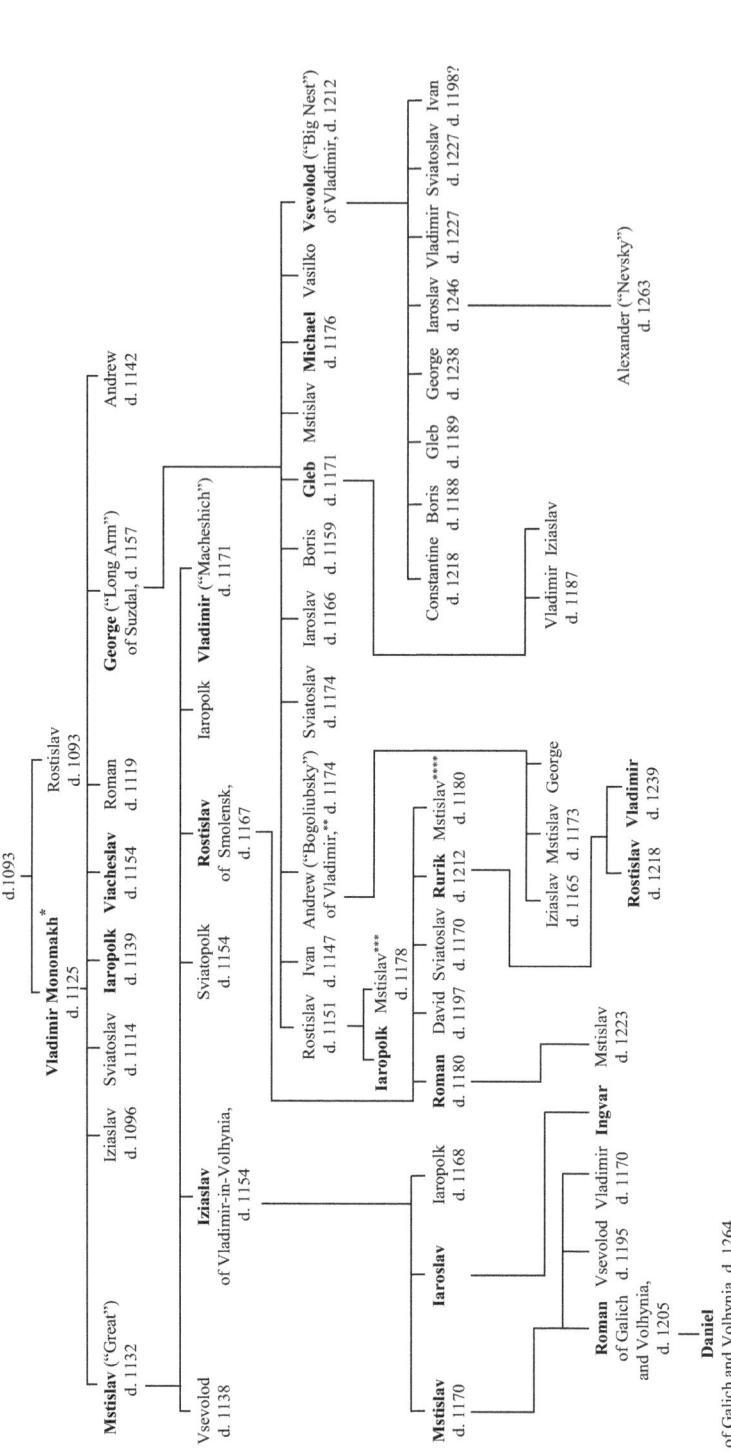

Figure 3. Descendants of Vsevolod Iaroslavich.

* The founder of the Monomakhovichi dynasty. ** Under Andrew and his brother Vsevolod the "Big Nest," Vladimir became the capital of Suzdalia (the original capital was Suzdal). Princes of Vladimir were thus supreme rulers of Suzdalia. *** The Rostislavichi who briefly ruled in Suzdalia after the murder of Andrew Bogoliubsky. **** The Roistislavichi of Smolensk.

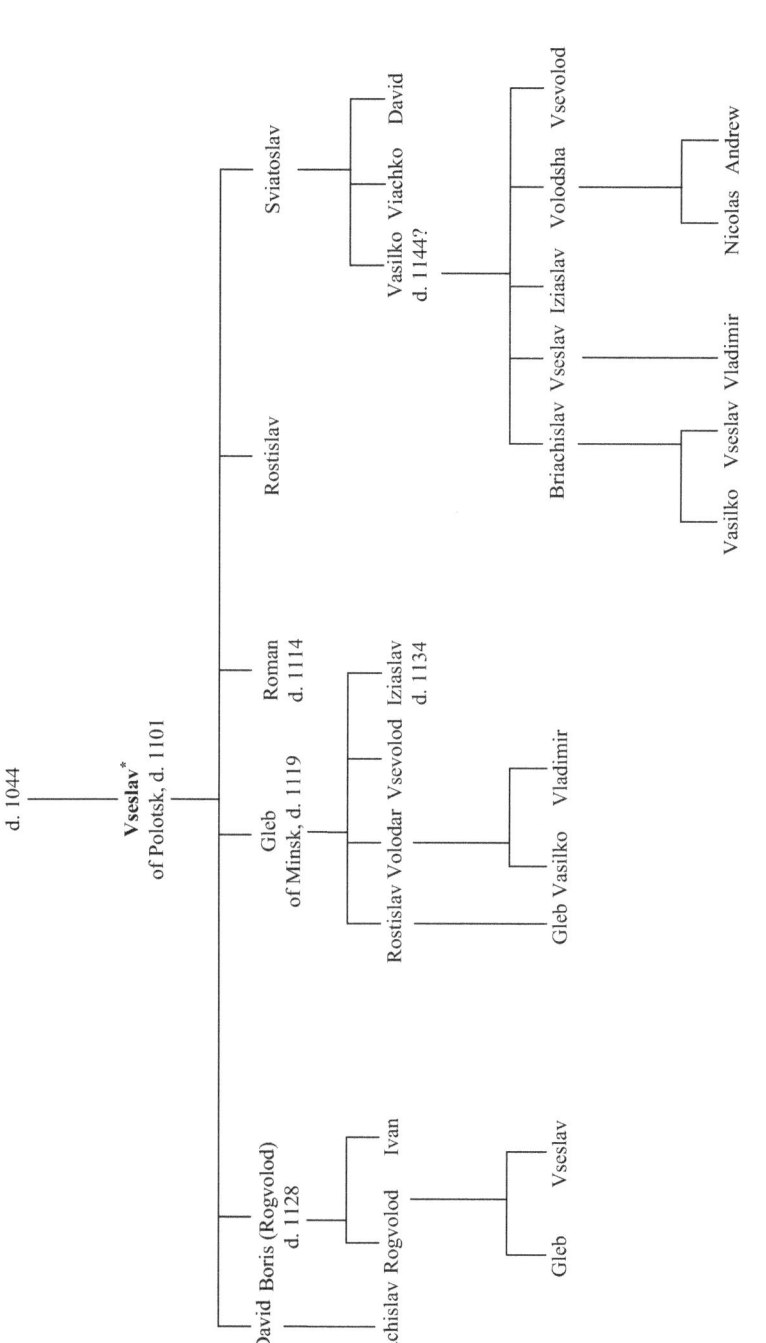

Figure 4. Descendants of Briachislav Iziaslavich.

*Vseslav was briefly made the Kievan prince during an uprising in Kiev in 1068, where he was being imprisoned at the time of the uprising. Princes and other members of the elite never recognized his legitimacy as the Kievan prince, and his descendants never claimed the Kievan throne. PSRL 1, 171–73.

INTRODUCTION

ACCORDING TO THE description of the world and its peoples in the *Primary Chronicle* compiled in Kiev in the early 1100s, when the sons of Noah divided the world among themselves after the flood, the Orient fell to the lot of Shem, the South to the lot of Ham, and Japheth received "northern and western lands." The people of Rus belong to the race of Japheth, and they live in his lot along with other peoples, such as the Swedes, Normans, Angles, Romans, Germans, and Franks.[1] "Rus" is the name used in this book for the medieval polity located in present-day Ukraine, Belarus, and parts of Russia; in Anglophone scholarship, it is also known as Kievan Rus, medieval Russia, and medieval Ukraine.

For a twelfth-century Kievan monk, it appears self-evident that his country belongs to the cultural sphere of the Angles, Romans, Germans, and Franks. To use modern terms, the *Primary Chronicle* describes Rus as part of medieval European civilization. Most modern scholars would not agree. William Chester Jordan expressed a widely accepted opinion when he stated that medieval "Europe was where Latin Christians—Roman Catholic Christians—dominated the political and demographic landscape. A profound divide [...] separated Catholics from Greek or Orthodox Christians."[2] In scholarly literature, Rus has been traditionally presented as part of a "Byzantine Commonwealth," an area dominated by Greek Orthodox Christianity and separate from Latin Europe.[3] Alternatively, some scholars have argued that Rus, a huge polity the size of Charlemagne's empire, was not so much a Byzantine satellite as a world in itself: neither Europe nor Asia, neither East nor West. According to this school of thought, the reception of Christianity from Constantinople isolated Rus from Latin Christendom, but did not create strong ties with Byzantium, which was too distant geographically and too different culturally to become a formative influence. Thus Rus, separated from Byzantium by its geographic location and separated from neighbouring Poland, Hungary, and Scandinavia by its different form of Christianity, followed its own unique path of development. This "unique path" is often invoked to explain the apparent inability of modern Russia, which traces its origins to Rus, to adopt Western institutions and to integrate itself into Europe.[4] Sweeping

---

[1] *Letopis po Lavrentevskomu spisku*, ed. E. F. Karskii. Polnoe sobranie russkikh letopisei, vol. 1, 2nd ed. (Leningrad: Izdatelstvo Akademii Nauk SSSR, 1927) [hereafter PSRL 1], 1–4; *The "Povest' vremennykh let": An Interlinear Collation and Paradosis*, ed. and coll. Donald Ostrowski, with David Birnbaum and Horace G. Lunt, Harvard Library of Early Ukrainian Literature, Text Series 10 (Cambridge, MA: Harvard University Press, 2003) [hereafter PVL], vol. 1, 2–15.

[2] William Chester Jordan, "'Europe' in the Middle Ages," in *The Idea of Europe: From Antiquity to the European Union*, ed. Anthony Pagden (New York: Cambridge University Press, 2002), 75.

[3] Dimitri Obolensky, *The Byzantine Commonwealth: Eastern Europe, 500–1453* (New York: Praeger, 1971).

[4] For a connection between the "special path" of Rus and political developments in modern and contemporary Russia, see, for example, Marshall T. Poe, *The Russian Moment in World History* (Princeton: Princeton University Press, 2003).

generalizations about the alleged profound differences between Rus and Latin Europe are made in the virtual absence of concrete, source-based comparative studies: the last monograph that compared forms of social organization in Rus/Muscovy with the medieval West appeared in 1910.[5]

Recently, Christian Raffensperger challenged the notion of a Byzantine Commonwealth that stood in opposition to Europe, and he argued that the very concept of "medieval Europe" should be "reimagined" in such a way that it includes Rus, which had much more ties with Latin Christendom than was previously believed. While it is hard to dispute the significance of Byzantium for the polities that received Christianity from Constantinople and whose churches were originally organized under the aegis of the Byzantine emperor,[6] it appears that past scholarship tended to exaggerate the degree to which they were separated from Latin Europe.

Raffensperger, and before him Alexander Nazarenko, argued that at least until 1204 Latin and Orthodox Christians did not perceive the divide between them as "profound" and that the lay elites in many cases were hardly aware of any divide at all.[7] Thus, some twenty-first-century historians seem to return to the viewpoint of their twelfth-century Kievan counterpart. I am one of them. One goal of this book is to present Rus as a regional variation of European society.

I seek to achieve this goal through a comparative analysis of representations of power and property relations in high medieval Rusian and Western political narratives.[8] Thus, while other works on the place of Rus in the medieval world discuss its relations with Latin Europe or Byzantium, the focus of this book is a comparison of the inner organization of society in Rus and in the West. It is, of course, impossible to make a source-based comparison of Rus—or of anything else, for that matter—with the "West" in general. For the purposes of my analysis, the best regions are those that, firstly, produced texts typologically analogous to Rusian chronicles, which are the most important source on the social and political history of Rus, and, secondly, produced them in both Latin and the vernacular.

---

5 N. P. Pavlov-Silvanskii, *Feodalizm v udelnoi Rusi* (St. Petersburg: Tipografiia M. M. Stasiulevicha, 1910); reprinted in Russian Reprint Series 21 (The Hague: Europe Printing, 1966).

6 See Jonathan Shepard, "Crowns from Basileus, Crowns from Heaven," in Milana Kaĭmakova, Maciej Salamon, and Małgorzata Smorag Różycka, eds., *Byzantium, New Peoples, New Powers: The Byzantino-Slav Contact Zone* (Cracow: Towarzystwo Wydawnicze Histoira Iagellonica, 2007), 139–60, for a convincing interpretation of some political practices in the Orthodox polities as "a glimpse of that generally elusive concept, the Byzantine Commonwealth" (p. 159).

7 Christian Raffensperger, *Reimagining Europe: Kievan Rus' in the Medieval World*, Harvard Historical Studies 177 (Cambridge, MA: Harvard University Press, 2012); Aleksandr Vasilevich Nazarenko, *Drevniia Rus na mezhdunarodnykh putiakh: Mezhdistsiplinarnye ocherki kulturnykh, torgovykh, politicheskikh sviazei IX–XII vekov* (Moscow: Iazyki russkoi kultury, 2001).

8 Recently, "Rusian" is being increasingly used as an adjective derived from "Rus," as opposed to "Russian" referring to Russia. It has been pointed out that referring to Rus as "medieval Russia," as well as using the term "Russian" in connection with Rus, marginalizes Ukraine and Belarus by creating a false impression that Russia is the exclusive heir of Rus.

I argue that the widespread perception of profound differences in the social and political organization that set pre-Mongol Rus apart from Europe is, in many respects, a product of the nature of the sources. Most Western political narratives before the thirteenth century are in Latin, and they were produced by authors who were influenced by classical literature that medieval *literati* studied as part of their education. The Rusian written culture was much more indigenous. Unlike Western Europe and the Balkans, which had once been parts of the Empire, Rus did not inherit any tradition of classical learning, and its literate elite had little, if any, knowledge of classical languages and literature.

It is in this area that we find an important—possibly, the most important—difference between Rus and Western Europe. As a matter of fact, in this respect Rus differed not just from the West, but from other Eastern Christian polities as well. The role of Latin in Rus was "almost negligible"; the degree to which Greek was known is a subject of debate, but all agree that it was much less than in the Balkan Orthodox polities and that it was in no way comparable to the knowledge of Latin in the West.[9] The language of religion and learning was Church Slavonic, which was created by Byzantine missionaries for the purpose of translating from Greek.

I seek to show that in the "learned" sources written in Church Slavonic, Rus looks like a "normal" European kingdom. The idiosyncratic—or allegedly idiosyncratic—features of its social and political organization are most visible in the texts written in the vernacular East Slavonic and apparently close to the oral political discourse.[10] This is the majority of the Rusian chronicles, all of which apparently are compilations of various extinct texts. Many of these texts are records of disputes; they use direct speech extensively, and occasionally also report the characters' physical location and gestures, for example, "He said, looking at the Holy Mother of God, which is above the Golden Gate, 'It

---

[9] On Latin in Rus, see Simon Franklin, *Writing, Society and Culture in Early Rus, c. 950–1300* (New York: Cambridge University Press, 2002), 106–10. On the degree and the character of the knowledge of the Greek language and of the classical culture in Slavonic translations, see D. M. Bulanin, *Antichnye traditsii v drevnerusskoi literature XI–XVI vv.*, Slavistische Beiträge 278 (Munich: Otto Sagner, 1991); Francis Thomson, *The Reception of Byzantine Culture in Medieval Russia*, Variorum Collected Studies Series (Brookfield: Ashgate, 1999); Simon Franklin, "Po povodu 'Intellektualnogo molchaniia' Drevnei Rusi (o sbornike trudov F. Dzh. Tomsona)," *Russia Mediaevalis* 10 (2001): 262–70; Olga B. Strakhova, review of F. J. Thomson, *The Reception of Byzantine Culture in Mediaeval Russia, Russia Mediaevalis* 10 (2001): 245–61; Franklin, *Writing, Society and Culture*, 101–6, 202–6, 223–28; Franklin, *Sermons and Rhetoric of Kievan Rus'*, Harvard Library of Early Ukrainian Literature, Translation Series 5 (Cambridge, MA: Harvard University Press, 1991), lviii–lxxiv, xcv–cix; Franklin and Shepard, *Emergence of Rus*, 238–43; A. A. Alekseev, "Koe-chto o perevodakh v Drevnei Pusi (po povodu stat'i Fr. Dzh. Tomsona 'Made in Russia')," *Trudy Otdela drevnerusskoi literatury* [hereafter *TODRL*] 49 (1999): 278–95; G. G. Lunt, "Eshcho raz o mnimykh perevodakh v Drevnei Rusi (po povodu stat'i A. A. Alekseeva)," *TODRL* 51 (1999): 435–41; A. A. Alekseev, "Po povodu stati G. G. Lanta Eshcho raz o mnimykh perevodakh v Drevnei Rusi," *TODRL* 51 (1991): 442–45.

[10] The language spoken in Rus is known as "Old Russian," "Old Ukrainian," "Rusian," and "East Slavonic." I follow Franklin in using the latter term (*Writing, Society and Culture*, 84).

is for this most pure Lady together with her Son and our God to judge us in this and in the future life.' "[11]

These features of the Rusian chronicles are important for another goal of this book, which is an exploration of the interplay between the language and genre of the sources and the ways in which medieval authors represent the life of their society. For this purpose, I compare sources that belong to the same, or similar, genres and that have the same, or similar, subject matters, but which are written in different languages and occupy different positions vis-à-vis oral political discourse and high "learned" culture. Hence my choice of Western sources for the comparative analysis offered in this book.

The large-scale advent of the vernacular into the writing of chronicles and histories in continental Europe started in the thirteenth century, when the West saw the rise of central governments, universities, and academic law while Rus was conquered by the Mongols. This period is outside of the chronological scope of this book. The earliest narrative from continental Latin Europe written in what is apparently quite close to the actual spoken language of the time is the already mentioned *Conventum Hugonis* from eleventh-century Aquitaine.[12] Its subject matter is also similar to that of many Rusian chronicle narratives, which display the same three elements—dispute, settlement, and orality—that make the title of the essay on the *Conventum* by its first publisher Jane Martindale.[13] The *Conventum* can be juxtaposed with the Latin chronicle by Adémar of Chabannes written within the same time period and containing an account of the same events from a different perspective.[14]

---

[11] *Ipatevskaia letopis*, ed. A. A. Shakhmatov, Polnoe sobranie russkikh letopisei, vol. 2, 2nd ed. (St. Petersburg: Imperatorskaia archeograficheskaia komissia, 1908); reprinted, Moscow: Iazyki slavianskikh kultur, 1998, with a new introduction by B. M. Kloss and a new index) [hereafter PSRL 2], 431.

[12] First publication: Jane Martindale, "Conventum inter Guillelmum Aquitanorum comitem et Hugonem Chiliarchum," *English Historical Review* 84 (1969): 528–48. Published with a parallel translation in Jane Martindale, *Status, Authority and Regional Power: Aquitaine and France, 9th to 12th Centuries*, Variorum Collected Studies Series (Brookfield: Ashgate, 1997), VIIb. Martindale thinks that, in connection with the *Conventum*, "it is necessary to make some allowance for the possibility that spoken Latin survived in some form—even into the eleventh century," and she notes that "the 'errors' with which the text is studded have many affinities with the 'late' or 'vulgar Latin'." Martindale, *Status, Authority and Regional Power*, VIII, 4, 24; for a review of literature on the language of the *Conventum*, see ibid., VIII, 3–4. Paul Hyams describes the *Conventum* as "a text, which ought perhaps to have been written in the vernacular, Occitan?" Paul Hyams, Introduction to the *Agreement between Count William V of Aquitaine and Hugh IV of Lusignan* at www.fordham.edu/halsall/source/ agreement.asp.

[13] Jane Martindale, "Dispute, Settlement and Orality in the *Conventum inter Guillelmum Aquitanorum Comitem et Hugonem Chiliarchum*: A Postscript to the Edition of 1969," in Martindale, *Status, Authority and Regional Power*, VIII.

[14] *Ademari Cabannensis Chronicon*, ed. P. Bourgain, R. Landes, and G. Pon, Corpus Christianorum, Continuatio Mediaevalis 79 (Turnhout: Brepols, 1999); *The Letters and Poems of Fulbert of Chartres*, ed. and trans. F. Behrends (Oxford: Clarendon Press, 1976), 92.

Many of the other materials for my comparative analysis come from England with its traditions of both vernacular and Latin historiography. Vernacular historiography thrived before the Norman Conquest, when it was produced in Old English, and then again in the twelfth century, when "a new vogue for writing history in Anglo-Norman" appeared more than half a century earlier than a vernacular historical culture began to emerge elsewhere in Latin Europe.[15] The Old English *Anglo-Saxon Chronicle* covers the period when Rus did not yet exist. I concentrate on Norman England, the history of which in the twelfth century is exceptionally well covered by a significant number of Latin historiographical works and by the first post-conquest vernacular chronicle describing contemporary events, known as *Jordan Fantosme's Chronicle*.[16] Not only is it written in a vernacular language, namely the Anglo-Norman variety of Old French, but it also belongs to the same time period as the Rusian chronicles and it discusses a similar subject: a conflict within the ruling strata of society. Even though Fantosme's work is an epic poem while Rusian chronicles are written in the traditional annalistic format, both are vernacular accounts of political struggles in their contemporary societies, and as such are worth comparing.

There is one more region that produced a vernacular historiographical work in the twelfth century. This is Regensburg in Bavaria, where an unknown author wrote the Middle High German *Kaiserchronik* (ca. 1140s–1150s). However, this text does not seem to be a suitable object for a comparative analysis with Rusian chronicles. It is structured as a series of imperial biographies starting with Julius Caesar. Thus, most of the *Kaiserchronik* is devoted to the distant past; it is sometimes described as an early attempt at a world chronicle.[17] A small section at the end of the chronicle describes contemporary events, but, apart from a digression on Godfrey of Bouillon, the author focuses almost exclusively on emperors and bishops and provides very little information about the social organization of the lay nobility.[18] The main subjects of the *Kaiserchronik* have been described as the progress of the Gospel from the heathen to the Christian

---

15 Chris Given-Wilson, *Chronicles: The Writing of History in Medieval England* (New York: Hambledon, 2004), 138.

16 *Jordan Fantosme's Chronicle*, ed. and trans. R. C. Johnston (New York: Oxford University Press, 1981).

17 Graeme Dunphy, "Historical Writing in and after the Old High German Period," in *German Literature of the Early Middle Ages*, ed. Brian Murdock, Camden House History of German Literature 2 (Camden: Boydell and Brewer, 2004), 201–26; Alastair Matthews, *The "Kaiserchronik": A Medieval Narrative* (Oxford: Oxford University Press, 2012), 1–2.

18 Even if "contemporary" is understood in the broadest possible sense as events that took place within a century preceding the time when the *Kaiserchronik* was apparently written, this "contemporary" section starting with Henry IV and ending abruptly in 1147, in the middle of the reign of Conrad III, takes only 748 lines out of the total 17,280 lines of the *Kaiserchronik*. Edward Schröder, ed. *Die Kaiserchronik eines Regensburger Geistlichen*, Monumenta Germaniae Historica, Scriptores Qui Vernacula Lingua Usi Sunt 1 (Hanover: Hahnsche Buchhandlung, 1895), vol. 1, 378–92. For the Godfrey of Bouillon episode, see *Kaiserchronik*, 381–84 (lines 16618–789).

empire and as the *translatio imperii* from Rome to Germany.[19] This imperial agenda sets the *Kaiserchronik* apart not only from Rusian chronicles, but also from the historiography of other regions of the medieval West.

Therefore, the comparative analysis offered in this book leaves out the *Kaiserchronik* and concentrates on the political narratives from Aquitaine and Norman England, the two regions of the medieval West that before the thirteenth century produced texts thematically and typologically comparable to Rusian chronicles and written both in Latin and in the vernacular, or in what can be considered semi-vernacular. I suggest that such a comparison, in addition to situating Rus within the broader context of medieval European history, may also contribute to a debate on feudalism that has been going on among Western medievalists since the 1990s. As a scholar of Rus and, therefore, an outsider to the subject, I enter this complicated and highly charged area with some trepidation.

The absence of feudalism in Rus has traditionally been seen as a fundamental difference that sets it apart from the West. Thus, according to a recent survey of Russian history, the Rusian elite "were not [...] a feudal ruling class, since they did not possess extensive landed estates, but rather small domains and wealthy townhouses. What they levied from the rest of the community was [...] not dues based on ownership of land but rather tribute extorted by superior military power."[20]

In this passage, "feudal" has connotations of what is sometimes described as "Marxist feudalism."[21] Feudalism in its Marxist sense is concerned with the relations between nobles and peasants, while non-Marxist feudalism describes predominantly the relations *within* the noble class. In its original and most restricted meaning, "feudalism" signifies a legal system regulating tenure of land among the medieval elite. A classic definition of this system was formulated by François-Louis Ganshof:

> "Feudalism" may be regarded as a body of institutions creating and regulating the obligations of obedience and service—mainly military service—on the part of a free man (the vassal) towards another free man (the lord), and the obligation of protection and maintenance on the part of the lord with regard to his vassal. The obligation of maintenance had usually as one of its effects the grant by the lord to his vassal of a unit of real property known as a fief.[22]

---

19 Graeme Dunphy, "On the Function of the Disputations in the *Kaiserchronik*," *The Medieval Chronicle* 5 (2009): 77–86; Alexander Rubel, "Caesar und Karl der Große in der Kaiserchronik. Typologische Struktur und die *translatio imperii ad Francos*," *Antike und Abendland* 47 (2001): 146–63.

20 Geoffrey Hosking, *Russia and the Russians: A History*, 2nd ed. (Cambridge, MA: Belknap Press, 2011), 34.

21 See Susan Reynolds, *Fiefs and Vassals: The Medieval Evidence Reinterpreted* (New York: Oxford University Press, 1994), 3, 10–12, 15; Fredric L. Cheyette, "'Feudalism': A Memoir and an Assessment," in *Feud, Violence and Practice: Essays in Medieval Studies in Honor of Stephen D. White*, ed. Belle S. Tuten and Tracey L. Billado (Burlington: Ashgate, 2010), 121–22.

22 François-Louis Ganshof, *Feudalism*, trans. Philip Grierson, 3rd English ed. (New York: Harper, 1961), xvi.

The broad definition of feudalism as a Veberian ideal type formulated by Marc Bloch includes both relations between peasantry and nobility and relations among the nobles. According to Bloch, fundamental features of feudalism are

> [a] subject peasantry; widespread use of service tenement (i.e. the fief) [...]; the supremacy of a class of specialized warriors; ties of obedience and protection which [...] within the warrior class, assume the distinctive form called vassalage; fragmentation of authority; and, in the midst of all this, the survival of other forms of association, family and State.[23]

Societies that had these features formed what Bloch called "the feudal zone," to which Rus did not belong.[24]

Most importantly, as scholars repeatedly pointed out, Rus lacked the type of social relations known as the "feudal contract," unequal, but nonetheless reciprocal, obligations of the lord and the vassal towards each other created by the ritual of homage.[25] These contractual relations, as presented in much of pre-1990s scholarly literature, "befitted what was seen as the uniquely free character of European civilization," in the words of Susan Reynolds.[26] In contrast with Western Europe, the absence of the tradition of a free contract between the superior and the subordinate in Rus—or in the "Byzantine Commonwealth" in general—has been connected with the failure to develop the rule of law and with authoritarian and totalitarian tendencies in Russian history. When the Soviet medievalist Aron Gurevich described Byzantine aristocrats as the emperor's "lackeys looking for a career and a chance to enrich themselves, devoid of personal dignity," his readers easily recognized a covert portrayal of Soviet high-ranking officials. Gurevich explained the *nomenklatura*-like qualities of the Byzantine aristocracy by the fact that "Byzantium knew nothing of the feudal treaty, the loyalty of the vassal or the group solidarity of the peers. [...] It is quite impossible to imagine anything like Magna Carta—a legal compromise between the monarch and his vassals—in a Byzantine setting."[27] An implicit connection between the "feudal" relations among the nobility and

---

23 Marc Bloch, *Feudal Society*, trans. L. A. Manyon (Chicago: University of Chicago Press, 1961), 446.

24 Bloch, *Feudal Society*, 70, 228.

25 For a classic description of "feudal contract," see Ganshof, *Feudalism*, 70–81.

26 Reynolds, *Fiefs and Vassals*, 54. According to Jacques Le Goff, "a system of loyalty" associated with vassalage "was this that would make it possible for hierarchy and individualism to coexist" in modern Europe. Jacques Le Goff, *The Birth of Europe*, trans. Janet Lloyd (Malden: Blackwell, 2005), 59.

27 A. J. Gurevich, *Categories of Medieval Culture*, trans. G. L. Campbell (Boston: Routledge and Kegan Paul, 1985), 128. On the more recent position of Gurevich in regards to the debate about feudalism and on his opinion about *Fiefs and Vassals*, see A. Ia. Gurevich, "Feodalizm pered sudom istorikov, ili o srednevekovoi krestianskoi tsivilizatsii," in *Feodalizm: poniatie i realii*, ed. I. G. Galkova et al. (Moscow: Institut vseobshchei istorii RAN, 2008), 11–51. On the absence of the "feudal contract"— or, indeed, any concept of a contract in Rus and, subsequently, Russia, see Yu. M. Lotman, "'Dogovor' i 'vruchenie sebia' kak arkhetipicheskie modeli kultury," in Lotman, *Izbrannye statii*, 3 vols. (Tallinn: Alexandra, 1993), vol. 3, 345–55. For the widespread opinions about the "feudal contract"

the subsequent development of democracy and the rule of law is also present in the work of the Russian pre-revolutionary scholar Nikolai Pavlov-Silvansky, the only historian who argued for the existence of the "feudal contract" in Rus.[28] It is hardly coincidental that he was a member of the Constitutional-Democratic party that sought to establish Western-style democracy in Russia.[29]

The "feudal contract" is part of the classical concept of European feudalism best represented by the works by Bloch and Ganshof. Since the 1970s this classical concept has come under critique, beginning with the famous article by Elizabeth Brown who argued that the concept of feudalism became too broad and imprecise to be a useful analytical tool; it turned into an artificial construct that distorted realities it purported to describe. She called the historians to end "the tyranny of a construct" and to discard the term "feudalism" as fundamentally misleading.[30] Reynolds further developed Brown's criticisms in her famous *Fiefs and Vassals* (1994), where she argued that the concepts of vassalage and the fief "as they are generally defined by medieval historians today, are post-medieval constructs," and as such they "distort the relations of property and politics that the sources record."[31]

Fiefs and Vassals generated a heated discussion, the ultimate result of which was, paradoxically, a renewal of interest in the subject of feudalism. To be sure, many historians now agree that this term is too nebulous to be useful, and they prefer to talk about "feudo-vassalic relations," that is, relations centred on a land grant made on the condition of the grantee's performance of "honourable" service to the grantor, that is, service not involving manual labour. "Feudo-vassalic relations" appears to be the closest English equivalent of the German *das Lehnswesen*, which Jürgen Dendorfer defines as "the interplay of land grants, vassalage, and the duties resulting from them."[32] Few medievalists heeded Brown's and Reynolds's call to discard all these concepts; instead,

---

in the present-day Russian intellectual milieu see, for example, the site *Historical Personality* at http://rus-history.ru/feodalnaya-razdroblennost-na-r/rossiiskii-feodalizm-bil-osobi.php; Igor Kobylin, *Fenomen totalitarizma v kontekste evropeiskoi kultury* at www.dslib.net/religio-vedenie/fenomen-totalitarizma-v-kontekste-evropejskoj-kultury.html; readers' comments to Vasilii Zharkov, "Zakreposhchennye istoriei," at www.gazeta.ru/comments/column/zharkov/6242617.shtml.

28 N. P. Pavlov-Silvanskii, *Feodalizm v udelnoi Rusi* (St. Petersburg: Tipografiia M. M. Stasiulevicha, 1910), reprinted in Russian Reprint Series 21 (The Hague: Europe Printing, 1966).

29 On a connection between the concept of the "feudal contract" and a liberal political ideology, see Cheyette, "Feudalism," 123.

30 Elizabeth A. R. Brown, "The Tyranny of a Construct: Feudalism and Historians of Medieval Europe," *American Historical Review* 79 (1974): 1063–88.

31 Reynolds, *Fiefs and Vassals*, 2–3.

32 Introduction to *Das Lehnswesen im Hochmittelalter. Forschungskonstrukte—Quellenbefunde—Deutungsrelevanz*, ed. Ürgen Dendorfer and Roman Deutinger (Ostfildern: Thorbecke, 2010), 19, 21, 26. On the difference between the German concepts of *Lehnswesen* and *Feudalismus*, see Levi Roach, "Submission and Homage: Feudo-Vassalic Relations and the Settlement of Disputes in Ottonian Germany," *History* 97 (2012): 355–79, at 356–57. For Reynolds's objections against the validity of the term *Lehnswesen*, see "*Fiefs and Vassals* after Twelve Years," in *Feudalism: New Landscapes of Debate*, ed. Sverre Bagge, Michael H. Gelting, and Thomas Lindkvist (Turnhout: Brepols, 2011), 15–26, at 23.

recent works use them much more carefully than they were used in earlier scholarship. Before the late twentieth-century critique of the classic teaching on feudalism, it was not unusual for historians to postulate the existence of the "feudal contract" every time they saw references to a fief, homage, or any notion that was associated with "feudalism" in historiography. If anyone was described in a medieval text as somebody's *homo* (man), the assumption was that he performed the ritual of homage and entered into a "feudal contract" with the person whose *homo* he was, thus becoming his vassal, even if there was no evidence in the source that this was the case.

Currently, there is general agreement that the words, such as fief, "were used in a variety of contexts and senses in the Middle Ages, so that they seem to relate to rather different phenomena—that is, to different kinds of property entailing different rights and obligations."[33] For Reynolds, this statement is part of her argument that the fief in the sense of a land grant from a lord to a vassal did not exist outside of late medieval legal treaties. However, for a number of scholars, Reynolds's thesis provided a stimulus for a critical re-examination of the sources in order to see if there is, indeed, evidence for the phenomena, the existence of which Reynolds denies.[34] In this sense, "only recently has the process of direct engagement with the kernel of Reynolds's work begun," as Charles West observed in 2013.[35]

The discussion generated by *Fiefs and Vassals* soon intertwined with the debate on the "feudal revolution," which was started by Francophone scholars in the early 1990s. The "feudal revolution" theory goes back to the celebrated study of the society of the Mâcon in Burgundy from the ninth to the twelfth century by Georges Duby. He argued that during a relatively short period in the late tenth to early eleventh century, this region underwent a radical transformation, when the Carolingian system of public order and formalized justice collapsed, and the exercise of justice and administration was privatized by local lords, thus creating a distinctly feudal system.[36] A number of subsequent studies found that various regions at the turn of the first millennium experienced a similar transformation, which was deemed the "feudal revolution," "feudal mutation/transformation," or "mutation of the year 1000." The systematic synthesis of the "feudal revolution" theory was presented by Jean-Pierre Poly and Eric Bournazel in 1980.[37] In the early 1990s, it was challenged by a number of scholars who argued that the change

---

33 Reynolds, "*Fiefs and Vassals* after Twelve Years," 19.

34 Charles West, *Reframing the Feudal Revolution: Political and Social Transformation between Marne and Moselle, c.800–c.1100* (Cambridge: Cambridge University Press, 2013); Steffen Patzold, *Das Lehnswesen* (Munich: Beck, 2012); Roach, "Submission and Homage"; Dendorfer and Deutinger, *Das Lehnswesen*.

35 West, *Reframing the Feudal Revolution*, 200.

36 Georges Duby, *La société aux XIe et XIIe siècles dans la région mâconnaise*, 2nd ed. (Paris: Éditions de l'École des hautes études en sciences sociales, 1971; first published in 1953; reprinted in 1988).

37 Jean-Pierre Poly and Eric Bournazel, *La mutation féodale, Xe–XIIe siècles* (Paris: Presses universitaires de France, 1980); English translation Jean-Pierre Poly and Eric Bournazel, *The Feudal Transformation: 900–1200*, trans. Caroline Higgitt (New York: Holmes and Meier, 1991). For the

was more apparent than real and that features, presented by the "mutationists" as characteristic of the new feudal regime, had existed before the putative revolution.[38]

A number of recent works display what appears to be a reaction against the radical critique of the "feudal construct" in the 1990s. Their authors do not believe that medieval society had a system of institutions as coherent, as ubiquitous, and as clearly defined in legal terms as the classic teaching on feudalism presented it; nonetheless, they tend to see in the High Middle Ages not exactly the classic feudal system, but still "something approximating" it, as Levi Roach put it in an important 2012 article.[39] It appears that the revisiting of the sources, largely inspired by Reynolds, is now bringing back and refining the very concepts of fiefs and vassals that Reynolds sought to annihilate. However, the 1990s movement against "feudalism" left some important legacies beyond reviving an interest in the subject. One of them is Reynolds's objection against the claim of earlier scholarship that feudo-vassalic relations emerged already in the early Carolingian period, in the seventh and eighth centuries. Another is a rejection of the idea that a "feudal regime" emerged suddenly and violently within a few decades before or after the year 1000. It appears that there is an emerging consensus about feudo-vassalic relations developing gradually and slowly over the course of the eleventh and/or twelfth centuries, depending on the region, so that a system "approximating" textbook feudalism can only be seen in the twelfth century, especially in its later part.[40]

If the development of feudo-vassalic relations was already underway in the eleventh century, that is, before universities and the revival of Roman law in Western Europe, academic lawyers could not have played the decisive role attributed to them by Reynolds. In the latest monograph-length contribution to the feudalism debate, Charles West presented feudo-vassalic relations as a long-term unintended consequence of the

---

most recent synthesis of the "feudal transformation" theory, see Thomas N. Bisson, *The Crisis of the Twelfth Century: Power, Lordship, and the Origins of European Government* (Princeton: Princeton University Press, 2009), 22–68, 574. For the significance of Duby's work on the Mâcon for the "feudal revolution" theory, see Thomas Bisson, "The 'Feudal Revolution,'" *Past and Present* 142 (1994): 6–42, at 6. For a somewhat different interpretation of Duby's findings about the Mâconnais region, see Dominique Barthélemy, *The Serf, the Knight, and the Historian*, trans. Graham Robert Edwards (Ithaca: Cornell University Press, 2009), ix, 2–3, 8–9.

38 Dominique Barthélemy, *La société dans le comté de Vendôme: de l'an mil au XIVe siècle* (Paris: Fayard, 1993); Barthélemy, *The Serf, the Knight, and the Historian*; Stephen D. White, "Tenth-Century Courts at Mâcon and the Perils of Structuralist History: Rereading Burgundian Judicial institutions," in *Conflict in Medieval Europe: Changing Perspectives on Society and Culture*, ed. Warren Brown and Piotr Górecki (Aldershot: Ashgate, 2003), 37–68; White, *Feuding and Peace-Making in Eleventh-Century France* (Aldershot: Ashgate, 2005); Fredric L. Cheyette, "Georges Duby's Mâconnais after Fifty Years: Reading it Then and Now," *Journal of Medieval History* 28 (2002): 291–317.

39 Roach, "Submission and Homage," 355, 378.

40 Adam J. Kosto, *Making Agreements in Medieval Catalonia: Power, Order, and the Written Word, 1000–1200* (Cambridge: Cambridge University Press, 2007); Roach, "Submission and Homage"; West, *Reframing the Feudal Revolution*; West, "Lordship in Ninth-Century Francia: The Case of Bishop Hincmar of Laon and his Followers," *Past and Present* 226 (2014): 3–40.

Carolingian reforms. Since the ninth century, the Carolingians "worked to formalize social interaction across the entire social spectrum," which eventually led to a new social formation "that could conventionally [...] be termed feudalism."[41]

The present book poses the question of whether there were some deeper, pan-European processes at work that contributed to the emergence of this new social formation. An analysis of Rusian political narratives offered below suggests that some of them describe relations among members of the elite that are remarkably similar to feudo-vassalic. Arguably, they have not been recognized as such, because the men (all of them are men) entering into these relations belonged to the social stratum described in English as "princes," traditionally considered to be members of an anomalously extended and exceptionally disorganized ruling dynasty. Most studies that have tried to find Rusian analogies to feudo-vassalic relations examine relations between "the prince and the nobles (boyars)."[42] However, information about the boyars in the pre-Mongol period is too meagre to see details of their relations with princes and to reconstruct these relations with any degree of precision.[43] The sources provide a wealth of information about the relations between the princes; however, this information has been studied primarily through the lens of kinship, because for most scholars, Rusian princes are first and foremost members of an extended kin-group (*rod*).

The Soviet historian V. T. Pashuto offered a different view of Rusian princes, treating them not so much as a ruling dynasty but rather as a ruling stratum somewhat analogous to the top nobility in the West. Pashuto never formulated this analogy explicitly; however, he has argued that lesser princes, along with boyars and other categories of nobles, could be "vassals" of other princes, and he has interpreted interprincely relations as "feudal."[44] Following Pashuto, P. P. Tolochko has described relations among the princes as "based on vassalic principles."[45] However, neither Pashuto nor Tolochko explains what

---

41 West, *Reframing the Feudal Revolution*, 8, 260, 263.

42 For a review of literature on "feudalism" in Rus, see P. S. Stefanovich, "Boiarskaia sluzhba v srednevekovoi Rusi," in *Feodalizm: poniatie i realii*, 180–89, at 180–83.

43 An exhaustive analysis of information on boyars can be found in P. S. Stefanovich, "Boiarskaia sluzhba"; Stefanovich, "Boiarstvo i tserkov v domongolskoi Rusi," *Voprosy istorii* 7 (2002): 41–59; Stefanovich, "Religiozno-eticheskie aspekty otnoshenii kniazia i znati v domongolskoi Rusi," *Otechstvennaia istoriia* 1 (2004): 3–18; Petr S. Stefanovič, "Der Eid des Adels gegenüber dem Herrscher im mittelalterlichen Russland," *Jahrbücher für Geschichte Osteuropas* 53 (2005): 497–505. ("Stefanovich" and "Stefanovič" are alternative transliterations of the same name.)

44 V. T. Pashuto, "Cherty politicheskogo stroia Drevnei Rusi," in *Drevnerusskoe gosudarstvo i ego mezhdunarodnoe znachenie*, ed. A. P. Novoseltsev, V. T. Pashuto, and V. L. Cherepnin (Moscow: Nauka, 1965), 11–77. An example of a recent work which, in Pashuto's tradition, describes interprincely relations in "feudal" terms is M. B. Sverdlov, *Domongolskaia Rus: kniaz' i kniazheskaia vlast' na Rusi VI-pervoi treti XIII vv.* (St. Petersburg: Akademicheskii proekt, 2003). Sverdlov provides even less argumentation to support his view of interprincely relations as "feudo-vassalic" than Pashuto does, and no discussion at all of feudo-vassalic relations in the West.

45 P. P. Tolochko, *Kniaz v Drevnei Rusi: vlast, sobstvennost, ideologiia* (Kiev: Naukova dumka, 1992), 178.

they understand by "vassalic principles," and their argumentation is often based on speculations and conjectures. Tolochko's book has been largely ignored, probably both because its argumentation is not entirely satisfactory and because it was published in Ukraine during the time of the disintegration of the Soviet Union. The deficiencies of Pashuto's arguments have been criticized in recent works by Russian scholars who deny that Rusian society had any significant similarities with the West. Even though Pashuto and his followers did not provide sufficient argumentation to support their view of interprincely relations, it appears to me that their suggestion about parallels between the inner organization of Rusian princes and of Western aristocracy deserves further study. This book offers such a study in the form of a comparison of political narratives about Rusian princes, Aquitanian aristocrats, and members of the royal family and nobility in England. I hope that the following chapters will show that such a comparison can yield interesting, and probably unexpected, results.

Chapter 1

RUS AND LATIN EUROPE: WORDS, CONCEPTS, AND PHENOMENA

A COMPARATIVE STUDY of sources written in different languages encounters problems reminiscent of those described by Elizabeth Brown and Susan Reynolds in their critique of the classic theory of feudalism. The two catchphrases capturing the essence of this critique are "the tyranny of a construct," and "the confusion of words, concepts, and phenomena." The confusion, according to Reynolds, results from the way historians typically proceed: first, they employ one *word*, "fief," to translate many different medieval terms; then they define fief as a *concept* of "dependent noble or military tenure." Finally, they assume the existence of the *phenomenon* corresponding to this *concept* every time they see *words* conventionally translated as "fief." This habit of "starting our investigation of phenomena by focusing on particular words" leads to circular argumentation that distorts the realities of the past.

Shedding the habit, however, is not simply a matter of scholarly integrity. Historians behave in this way not necessarily out of prejudice or sloppiness, but because it is often hard to come up with an alternative. Reynolds admits that "historians who work from written sources have to begin with words: they are all we have"; she just calls for thinking hard about what is being discussed (the phenomena) before coming up with generalizations.[1] To avoid generalizations entirely and to adhere strictly to concepts and notions found in medieval texts, one must also avoid the use of any modern language and write in Latin or whichever languages are used in the sources. Indeed, recent works on medieval social and political history contain almost as many words in italics as not: they are peppered with *milites*, *homines*, *fideles*, *suis*, *benefitia*, *feva*, *casamenta*, *castra* and the like, whereas earlier scholarship would have used "vassals," "fiefs," or "castles." Nowadays, historians are careful not to to distort the actual content of their sources by bringing in all the theoretical baggage carried by terms that had been used to describe "feudal society." They know that a *vassalus* was not necessarily a vassal in the textbook sense of the word, and that there is no reason to think that every *homo* did homage and every *fidelis* swore an oath of fealty.

Sticking with the original terminology of the sources may work well for research that concentrates on one linguistic area. Scholars using medieval Latin texts can productively discuss accounts of *homines* receiving *casamenta* and performing, or not performing, *homagium*. When it comes to regions and historical periods where vernacular sources appear alongside Latin ones, the situation gets more complicated, but it is still manageable: many vernacular terms are cognates of Latin, and even Germanic words have conventional Latin correspondents. Scholars may disagree about interpretations of various types of medieval property, but they do agree that *Lehn* corresponds to words such as *fevum* or *fius*.

---

[1] Reynolds, *Fiefs and Vassals*, 12–13.

What happens, however, if we want to compare Latin texts about *milites*, *fideles* and *feva* to documents written in a language unrelated to, and not influenced by, Latin? Apparently, we need to come up with a way to refer to medieval institutions, social groups, or types of property that would be comprehensible to readers not familiar with both languages—in other words, we have to translate. Anyone who, having embarked on a comparative study of sources written in unrelated languages, does not have the luxury of using the original terms, faces a hard choice. One may follow the injunction "not to attempt definitions until after one has looked at usage and thought hard [...] about what may be implied about the notions of the time."[2] This is, undoubtedly, the right way to proceed while comparing a specific phenomenon or institution in two different cultures. However, a rigorous investigation of the usage of the terms involved in a more broad comparison of two societies is unpractical: any conceptual argument would be drowned by pages upon pages of technical discussions. Therefore, general comparative studies usually do not go deeply into the question of terminology, but simply employ conventional translations.

In practice, this means relying on the historiographical traditions out of which the translations were born and, consequently, falling victim to the "tyranny of a construct"— or rather, of multiple constructs. The famous article by Elizabeth Brown, and a number of later works, have traced the rise of "feudalism" as a "tyrannous construct" that came to dominate the scholarship of the medieval West and to distort the realities that it purported to describe.[3] "Feudalism" may have been especially pervasive, but in terms of its power to distort medieval realities, it is hardly unique, as the scholars rising to overthrow its tyranny were to find out. New explanatory frameworks proposed in the wake of the dismantling of the "feudal construct" tend to turn "tyrannical" almost as soon as they become widely accepted.[4] Nor is historiography of the medieval West unique in its tendency to create "tyrannical constructs." In a sense, such constructs are an inevitable by-product of having scholarly terminology.

Every historiographical tradition has its own beloved theoretical models, which simplify messy source material by privileging some aspects of what documents tell us and marginalizing others. Conventional translations of Slavonic social and political terminology carry baggage as heavy as "fiefs," "vassals," and other terms coined by scholars working within the framework of "feudalism"—only, in the case of Slavonic, the baggage is created by different theoretical models, as we shall see. Not only do the conceptual frameworks of Rusian historiography differ from those used by Western

---

2 Reynolds, *Fiefs and Vassals*, 13.

3 Brown, "The Tyranny of a Construct"; Reynolds, *Fiefs and Vassals*; Cheyette, "Feudalism."

4 Paul R. Hyams, "Was There Really Such a Thing as Feud in the High Middle Ages?," in *Vengeance in the Middle Ages: Emotion, Religion and Feud*, ed. Susanna A. Throop and Paul R. Hyams (Farnham: Ashgate, 2010), 151–75; Rees Davies, "The Medieval State: The Tyranny of a Concept?," *Journal of Historical Sociology* 16 (2003): 280–300; West, "Lordship in Ninth-Century Francia," 36, 40; David A. Warner, "Reading Ottonian History: The *Sonderweg* and Other Myths," in *Challenging the Boundaries of Medieval History: The Legacy of Timothy Reuter*, ed. Patricia Skinner (Turnhout: Brepols, 2009), 81–114, at 100–101; Kosto, *Making Agreements*, 12–14.

medievalists, but they have never been scrutinized as closely as "feudalism." In many respects, the scholarship of Rus is still based on unexamined assumptions going back to the nineteenth century.

Timothy Reuter described the historiography of medieval Latin Europe as "a set of parallel universes," where each scholarly tradition—French, German, English, Spanish, or Italian—has its own specific way of looking at things while avoiding eye-contact with the others.[5] From the perspective of a Rus scholar, though, these traditions look like solar systems belonging to the same universe, or even more like planets in one solar system. *Grundherrschaft* may be "not quite the same thing as *seigneurie banale*,"[6] but we do know which German term to juxtapose to which French term while discussing differences between the two traditions. There is thus a common ground, a basis for conversation; whereas if we try to include Rus in this conversation, we would simply not know where to begin. Historiographies of Rus and the medieval West exist in truly parallel universes.

The goal of this chapter is to try to build a bridge between them—or are parallel universes supposed to be connected by a tunnel? Expressed in boring academic, rather than metaphoric, language, this chapter is devoted to creating a context that would make it possible to juxtapose Rus and Latin Europe. And boring it will be, at least in some parts: to establish a common ground between diverse historiographical traditions, it is necessary to engage with such dry topics as terminology and the general outline of the master narrative of Rusian history.

"Kings," "Princes," and "Disintegration"

A comparison between Rus and the West runs into a major problem from the start. Medieval Europe is normally conceived of as a collection of kingdoms. The place of the royal government within the overall socio-political structure varied greatly throughout centuries; scholarly interpretations of the significance of royal power in each given country and time period may be extremely diverse, but "kingship" and "monarchy" as abstractions are undoubtedly among the key concepts of medieval studies. In Rus studies, however, they are conspicuous by their absence.

It is generally believed that Rus did not have a king. Instead, it had "princes," also known in scholarly literature as the Rurikids, whose origin tradition traced to the legendary Scandinavian leader Rurik.[7] The *rex* of Rus, who "belonged to the people

---

[5] Timothy Reuter, *Medieval Polities and Modern Mentalities*, ed. Janet L. Nelson (Cambridge: Cambridge University Press, 2006), 88.

[6] Reuter, *Medieval Polities and Modern Mentalities*, 88.

[7] An alternative transcription is "Riurikids." Some scholars object to the term "Rurikids," because there is no proof that Rurik was historical, and because Rusian princes are not reported to have presented themselves as his descendants. On "Rurikids" (transcribed "Riurikids" in the article) being a scholarly, not contemporary, term, see Donald Ostrowski, "Systems of Succession in Rus' and Steppe Societies," *Ruthenica* 11 (2012): 29–58, at 30–34. On Scandinavians and early Rus, see Jonathan Shepard, "The Viking Rus and Byzantium," in *The Viking World*, ed. Stefan Brink and Neil

of the Swedes," is first mentioned in *The Annals of St. Bertin* under 838;[8] rulers with Scandinavian names based in Kiev, a centre on the middle Dnieper, are documented since the late ninth century; from the mid-900s on, their names become Slavic. Sources also mention tenth-century princes of Polotsk, in modern-day Belarus, apparently unrelated to the house of Kiev, but also bearing Scandinavian names; by the eleventh century their names become Slavic as well. In all likelihood, the princes of Polotsk were Scandinavian leaders who subjugated the population of the area and who in the course of time became assimilated, just as the Kievan dynasty did.[9] By the eleventh century these two lines, and possibly other prominent Scandinavian and local families, intermarried, and it is their progeny that comprised *kniazi*, described in English as "princes" or "Rurikids."[10]

The most well-known Kievan prince is Vladimir, who in 988 converted to Christianity, married a Byzantine princess, and sponsored a mass baptism of the population under his authority. In the traditional narrative of Rusian history, Vladimir and other early princes, although not called "kings," are generally treated as such. Rus before the mid-eleventh century has been presented as—although usually not called—a monarchy: most accounts of Rusian history assume that before 1054 the Kievan prince was the supreme hereditary ruler of the country. Nonetheless, historians would not use the standard word for such a ruler and call him a king.

A good example of terminological problems that emerge as soon as Rus is not so much discussed, but is simply mentioned in passing in a wider European context, is an account of the marriage of Henry I of France in the *New Cambridge Medieval History*: "Henry married Anna, daughter of Jaroslav I, archduke of Kiev. The French kings had been having difficulties [...] in finding brides of suitably elevated status to whom they were nor already related, and a Russian princess (contemporary chronicles called Jaroslav a king) [...] was a welcome if novel solution."[11] Indeed, contemporary Latin sources called Jaroslav, or Iaroslav (r. 1019–1054), *rex Russorum*, and viewed the marriage of his daughter to the *rex Francorum* as a union of two royal families of equal status.[12] Nor was Iaroslav, in this respect, an exception among other Rusian "princes," who were normally

---

Price (Abingdon: Routledge, 2009), 496–516; Fedir Androshchuk, "The Vikings in the East," ibid., 517–42.

8 *Annales Bertiniani*, ed. Félix Grat, Jeanne Vielliard, and Suzanne Clémencet (Paris: C. Klincksieck, 1964), 30–31.

9 PSRL 1, 75–76; Franklin and Shepard, *Emergence of Rus*, 152–53; see also Omeljan Pritsak, *The Origins of Rus*, vol. 1 (Cambridge, MA: Harvard University Press, 1981), 136–37.

10 *Kniazia*, sometimes used as the plural from of *kniaz*, is modern Russian; the East Slavonic form is *kniazi*.

11 Constance Brittain Bourchard, "The Kingdom of the Franks to 1108," in *The New Cambridge Medieval History*, ed. David Luscombe and Jonathan Riley-Smith, vol. 4, pt. 2 (Cambridge: Cambridge University Press, 2004), 125.

12 Christian Raffensperger, *The Kingdom of Rus'*, 77–78. I am grateful to Christian Raffensperger for allowing me to consult a manuscript of his book before it was published. For a review of literature on the translation of *kniaz* see ibid. and A. V. Soloviev, " 'Reges' et 'Regnum Russiae' au Moyen Age," *Byzantion: Revue internationale des études byzantines* 36 (1966), 143–73, at 151–52.

described in Latin accounts as *reges,* and their land as *regnum*.[13] *Rex* is the standard medieval Latin translation for the Slavonic *kniaz*, which is what Iaroslav was called in Rus. This is the same word that a Rusian pilgrim to the Holy Land applied to Baldwin I, whom he described as the *"kniaz* of Jerusalem," and the same word that Rusian authors used in their discussions of rulership: God awards the righteous by appointing a good emperor or *kniaz* to rule their land, while the sinful are subjected to evil and cruel *kniazi* and emperors.[14] The word "archduke" was unknown in Rus and no contemporary from any region applied this title to Iaroslav or to any other Rusian man.

Apparently, Iaroslav becomes "archduke" in the *New Cambridge Medieval History*, because for a modern scholar there can be no king in Kiev: the standard English translation for *kniaz* is "prince," not "king."[15] The passage about the marriage of Iaroslav's daughter is found in the chapter "The Kingdom of the Franks to 1108." It is a common assumption that the *regnum Frankorum* was a kingdom, but the *regnum Russorum* was not. It should be noted that this assumption is shared by scholars of Rus, including Russian and Ukrainian nationalistic historians, who use the untranslated word *kniaz* for Rusian rulers and do not refer to Rus as a "kingdom." Thus, the exclusion of Rus from the club of medieval kingdoms is not a product of bias or snobbery on the part of Western scholars; on the contrary, Western medievalists, when they write about Rus, apparently seek to find equivalents to the expressions normally used by Rus historians. The latter do not represent Rus as a kingdom; one reason for this is a legacy of traditional historiography, which focused on the so-called "period of disintegration." "Disintegration" is the "feudalism" of Rus studies, the dominant lens through which Rusian history was viewed since the early nineteenth century till at least the 1990s, and which is still present in current scholarship. We need, therefore, to discuss it at some length.

Orderly monarchical rule, the story goes, ended in 1054 with the death of Henry I's father-in-law Iaroslav the "Wise." He presided over a "Golden Age," which ended all too soon because of what the nineteenth-century scholars saw as his unfortunate, and irrational, decision to divide the realm between his five sons instead of designating a single heir. The Kievan throne went to the eldest, whom his brothers were supposed to recognize as their overlord. Instead they began to fight him and one another; the next generation continued in the same vein, thus bringing about the "disintegration" of Iaroslav's realm.

In 1097 the six most powerful grandsons of Iaroslav convened at Liubech and decided to establish peace by allocating to each of themselves a territory that had

---

[13] Raffensperger, *The Kingdom of Rus'*; A. V. Nazarenko, *Nemetskie latinoiazychnye istochniki IX–XI vekov: Teksty, perevod, kommentarii* (Moscow: Nauka, 1993), 111, 149–50; Soloviev, "'Reges' et 'Regnum Russiae'."

[14] *Zhite i khozhene Danila Russkyia zemli igumena*, ed. G. M. Prokhorov, in *XII vek*, ed. D. S. Likhachev et al., Biblioteka literatury Drevnei Rusi [hereafter BLDR] 4 (St. Petersburg, Russia: Nauka, 1997), also available as an electronic text at http://lib.pushkinskijdom.ru/Default.aspx?tabid=4934; PSRL 1, 349.

[15] On the history of the use of "duke" as a designator of the supreme ruler of Muscovy and, retroactively, of Rus, see Raffensperger, *The Kingdom of Rus'*, 25–30.

belonged to his father; Kiev was designated to Sviatopolk, whose father was Iaroslav's eldest son. There is no recorded provision for who should inherit the Kievan throne after Sviatopolk.[16] When he died in 1113, there was a popular uprising in Kiev; in the end, the throne passed to Sviatopolk's cousin Vladimir Monomakh (r. 1113–1125), a member of a junior line of Iaroslav's descendants. Thanks to Monomakh, this line rose to prominence and came to be known as the Monomakhovichi.

Monomakh managed both to deflate the social tensions that had led to the uprising, and to establish his authority over other princes; the scope and nature of this authority is debated. At his death, the Kievan throne passed to his eldest son Mstislav the "Great" (1076–1132); the succession was smooth and uncontested.[17] Some scholars, therefore, move the beginning of the "disintegration" to 1132, when the Kievan throne passed (again peacefully) to Mstislav's younger brother, Iaropolk (1082–1139).[18] Then a challenge came from another princely line, the descendants of Monomakhs' cousin Oleg, known as the Olgovichi. They made war on Iaropolk over some disputed landholdings; after Iaropolk's death, an Olgovich wrestled the Kievan throne from the Monomakhovichi line; from that time on, accounts of rivalry between the two clans dominate the pages of Rusian chronicles. There were few undisputed successions in the period between the death of Iaropolk in 1139 and the Mongol conquest in the 1230s.

However, if contested successions had disqualified a country from having kingship, there would have been no monarchies in medieval Europe. In the strongest of them, England, no "succession had been uncontested or without bloodshed" from the tenth century to 1272.[19] It is not disputes over the Kievan throne in and of themselves that gave Rus its reputation of being a "disintegrated" collection of ever-more fragmented lands ruled by an ever increasing number of quarrelling princes. This image of Rus, which dominated historiography till the late twentieth century and is still influential today, is based on the prevailing interpretation of the position of Kiev relative to other centres of power and on the general view of interprincely relations.

According to the "disintegration" narrative, the Rurikids treated the territory under their authority as a family property to be divided among all the legitimate, and sometimes even illegitimate, sons. Since the number of sons, of course, grew exponentially with every generation, and each needed his own dominion, Rus turned into a collection of such dominions. Some of them were quite small, consisting of a wooden fortress and its adjacent countryside, but the man based in the fortress and controlling the surrounding territory was still a *kniaz*, the same word that described Henry I's father-in-law. However, the fact that the sources apply the word *kniaz* to figures who can be

---

16 PSRL 1, 256–57.

17 Franklin and Shepard, *Emergence of Rus*, 340.

18 V. Ia. Petrukhin, "Drevniaia Rus: Narod. Kniazia. Religiia," in *Iz istorii russkoi kultury*, ed. V. Ia. Petrukhin, vol. 1: *Drevniaia Rus* (Moscow: Iazyki russkoi kultury, 2000), 13–402, at 208.

19 Eljas Oksanen, *Flanders and the Anglo-Norman World, 1066–1216* (Cambridge: Cambridge University Press, 2012), 39; Laura Ashe, "The Anomalous King of Conquered England," in *Every Inch a King: Comparative Studies on Kings and Kingship in the Ancient and Medieval Worlds*, ed. Lynette Mitchell and Charles Melville (Leiden: Brill, 2012), 174–94, at 175.

best described as nobles, is not in itself a reason to reject the idea that some, although not all, *kniazi* were kings: the Old Norse *konung*, to which *kniaz* is probably etymologically related, was also used to designate leading men of diverse status. If scholars translate *konung* into modern English as "chief" or "magnate" in some cases, but as "king" in others, why cannot *kniaz* be treated in a similar manner?

The traditional view of the early Kievan princes is that they may have had royal power, but in the end, they proved to be founders of a failed dynasty. On the eve of the Mongol invasion, this "dynasty" had an unknown number of members which, by a conservative estimate, was close to a hundred.[20] Princes did display a sense of a hierarchy: some of them were "juniors" and others "seniors," with an understanding that the former owed obedience to the latter; however, there were no spelled-out rules to determine seniority, no established mechanism to ensure the obedience of the juniors, and, above all, no universally recognized supreme ruler or single centre of power. Until 1169, Kiev, in theory, was supposed to belong to the most senior member of the dynasty; in practice, various contenders fought over it; and the winner anyway controlled no more than a block of lands on the middle Dnieper. Other powerful princes are thought to have been independent of Kiev; they had their own dominions known in scholarly literature as "principalities." Lesser princes were supposed to be subordinate either to the Kievan one or to a "senior" based in a major city other than Kiev, but they changed their allegiances all the time, or else were bidding for full independence. In the course of this never-ending strife, a coalition led by Andrew Bogoliubsky of Suzdalia sacked Kiev in 1169. Suzdalia was located in the northeast, in what is now the heartland of Russia; it included Moscow, then a tiny frontier outpost.[21]

Andrew, although the leader of the victorious coalition, stayed in Suzdalia and did not become the Kievan prince. Instead, he, in the words of the chronicler, "gave" Kiev to his kinsman, who then "gave" it to yet another prince. Suzdalia thus gained supremacy over Kiev. In addition to Suzdalia, a number of competing centres of power emerged in the course of the twelfth century, including the Smolensk principality on the upper Dnieper and Galicia in the south-west, in present-day Western Ukraine and Poland.[22] In the north, there was Novgorod, which was ruled by elected officials and by princes who were invited and dismissed by the citizens' assembly.[23] In other places, the power of

---

20 For the impossibility of establishing the exact number of princes, see O. M. Rapov, *Kniazhaskie vladeniia na Rusi v X—pervoi polovine XIII v.* (Moscow: Izdatelstvo MGU, 1977), 128. See ibid. for lists of the known princes arranged by generations that allow a rough estimation of their numbers.

21 "Bogoliubsky" may mean either "God-loving" or "of Bogoliubovo," which was the name of Andrew's residence. Because of this ambiguity, I leave "Bogoliubsky" untranslated.

22 On these and other major Rusian principalities, see Ostrowski, "Systems of Succession," 30; Franklin and Shepard, *Emergence of Rus*, 323–39.

23 On Novgorod, see Janet Martin, *Medieval Russia, 980–1584*, 2nd ed. (New York: Cambridge University Press, 2007), 112–15; Franklin and Shepard, *Emergence of Rus*, 343–45; Shepard, "Rus," 406; Charles Halperin, "Novgorod and the 'Novgorodian Land,'" *Cahiers du monde russe* 40 (1999): 345–63; P. V. Lukin, *Novgorodskoe veche* (Moscow: Indrik, 2014).

local communities was not institutionalized to the same extent that it was in Novgorod; nonetheless, they played an important role in local politics, supporting some princes and resisting others.

Traditional historiography described the chaotic struggle between all these princes and communities as the essence of the "period of disintegration," which led to the decline of once-powerful Rus and facilitated the Mongol conquest, a narrative best summarized in a humorous poem by the nineteenth-century author Aleksei K. Tolstoy. The poem describes the fatal inability of all Russian rulers to establish public order. Iaroslav the "Wise" almost succeeded in this elusive task, but, "out of love for his children, he divided all the land between them":

> This was a bad idea:
> His sons began to fight
> One pummeling another
> With all his strength and might.

This "pummeling" continued in subsequent generations all the way to the Mongol takeover.[24]

Alternative Interpretations of "Disintegration" and the Question of Kingship

Lamentations of nineteenth-century scholars and their modern followers, presenting "disunity, decline and internecine strife" as the main theme of the twelfth- to early thirteenth-century Rusian history, are hard to reconcile with the overwhelming evidence of growth and prosperity.[25] New lands were brought into cultivation, urban centres grew in size and in number, new settlements emerged, new bishoprics were founded, new cathedrals were built, and international trade thrived throughout the "period of disintegration."[26] A number of scholars, therefore, have rejected the narrative of "decline," and have offered alternative interpretations. Some present Rus essentially as a monarchy (again, not using the word), which was established by the early Kievan princes and then survived, rather than "disintegrated," because there was still a supreme ruler bearing

---

24 A. K. Tolstoy, "Istoriia gosudarstva rossiiskogo ot Gostomysla do Timasheva," in A. K. Tolstoy, *Sobranie sochinenii*, vol. 1, 384–400, at 388. For a conventional narrative on the "disintegration" see, for example, B. A. Rybakov, *Pervye veka russkoi istorii* (Moscow: Nauka, 1964), 145–57. For a review of pre-1990s literature on the "disintegration," see Tolochko, *Kniaz*, 173–75, 220–21n124; Franklin and Shepard, *Emergence of Rus*, 367–69. Post-1990s works reproducing the "disintegration" paradigm include N. F. Kotliar, "K voprosu o prichinakh udelnoi razdroblennosti na Rusi," *Drevniaia Rus: Voprosy Medievistiki* 43 (2011): 5–17; Kotliar, "Nastuplenie udelnoi razdroblennosti na Rusi (kniazia-izgoi)," *Ruthenica* 10 (2011): 69–77; Sverdlov, *Domongolskaia Rus*, 513–14, 659–60; in English see, for example, Hosking, *Russia*, 45–48.

25 Franklin and Shepard, *Emergence of Rus*, 325–38, 340–41, 367.

26 Franklin and Shepard, *Emergence of Rus*, 366–68.

the title of Grand Prince.[27] According to one version of this theory, there were several "grand princes," but the Kievan one still had supremacy over all others until 1169, when this supremacy was "usurped" by Suzdalia.[28] The use of the term "grand prince" in the sources, however, is very irregular, and most historians agree that it was a laudatory epithet, not a title.[29]

Most scholars who refuse to see interprincely relations as meaningless chaotic strife tend to concentrate not on the subject of titles,[30] but on the Rurikids' system of succession. Since its principles are not described in any surviving document, they endeavour to reconstruct this putative system on the basis of chronicle narratives.[31] The sheer number of alternative systems that have been proposed by historians casts doubts on the notion that it is possible to uncover a single "true" one. Moreover, such reconstructions tend to ignore the role of communities in princely succession. Thus, the events of 1113, when the Kievan throne passed not to the son of the deceased prince, Sviatopolk, but to his cousin Vladimir Monomakh, are a cornerstone of theories postulating a complicated "rota" system, supposedly established at the Liubech conference

---

27 *Velikii kniaz*, translated into English alternatively as "Great" or "Grand" Prince; "archduke" (see above) appears to be a particular creative translation of the same term. For a review of the usage of *velikii kniaz* in pre-Mongolian chronicles, see Wladimir Vodoff, "La titulature princièr en Russie du XIe au début du XVIe siècle: Questions de critique des sources," *Jahrbücher für Geschichte Osteuropas* 35 (1987): 1–35, at 20–25. For a review of literature on the term "grand prince," see Dimnik, "The Title 'Grand Prince,'" *Mediaeval Studies* 66 (2004): 253–312, at 253–55; Sverdlov, *Domongolskaia Rus*, 148–52. See also A. A. Gorskii, "Ob evoliutsii titulatury verkhovnogo pravitelia Drevnei Rusi (domongloskii period)," in *Rimsko-Konstantinopolskoe nasledie na Rusi: Ideia vlasti i politicheskaia praktika. IX Mezhdunarodnyi seminar istoricheskikh issledovanii "Ot Rima k Tretemy Rimu," Moskva, 1989*, ed. A. N. Sakharov et al. (Moscow: Rossiiskaia akademiia nauk, Institut Rossiiskoi istorii, 1995), 97–102; Tolochko, *Kniaz*, 128–35.

28 Dimnik, "The Title 'Grand Prince' in Kievan Rus."

29 V. L. Ianin, *Aktovye pechati Drevnei Rusi X–XV vv.*, vol. 1 (Moscow: Nauka, 1970), 20–21; Vodoff, "La titulature des princes russes"; A. V. Nazarenko, *Drevniaia Rus i slaviane* (Moscow: Universitet Dmitriia Pozharskogo, 2009), 53.

30 In addition to "grand/great prince," designators of some princes in the sources include *tsesar* ("emperor", from "Caesar") and *kagan*. *Kagan*, or *chaganus*, was the title of the ruler of Khazaria, a polity that dominated the steppes north of the Caspian Sea and along the Volga in the ninth and tenth centuries. *Kagan* and *tsesar* are discussed in the works listed in the footnote 27; on *kagan*, see also Jonathan Shepard, "Orthodoxy and Northern Peoples: Goods, Gods and Guidelines," in *A Companion to Byzantium*, ed. Liz James (Malden: Wiley-Blackwell, 2010), 171–86.

31 Martin Dimnik, "Succession and Inheritance in Rus' before 1054," *Medieval Studies* 58 (1996): 87–117; Dimnik, *The Dynasty of Chernigov, 1146–1246* (Cambridge: Cambridge University Press, 2003), 8–13; Nancy Shields Kollmann, "Collateral Succession in Kievan Rus'," *Harvard Ukrainian Studies* 14 (1990): 377–88. Among the most sophisticated works written within the tradition of the search for a succession system are A. V. Nazarenko, *Drevniaia Rus i slaviane*, 7–102; Nazarenko, "Poriadok prestolonslediia na Rusi X–XII vv.: nasledstvennye razdely, seniorat i popytki designatsii (tipologicheskie nabliudeniia)," in *Iz istorii russkoi kultury*, vol. 1: *Drevniaia Rus*, 500–19. For a comprehensive review of literature, see Ostrowski, "Systems of Succession," 41–46.

and making Monomakh the legitimate heir to Sviatopolk. However, Monomakh himself was apparently unaware of any rules that would make him the heir to the Kievan throne in 1113: he was invited to Kiev by the citizens, with whom Sviatopolk was clearly very unpopular, and he initially declined the invitation. An uprising then broke out, with the mob attacking Sviatopolk's officials and, unusually, the Jews.[32] Urged by the Kievan elite to come and prevent further violence, Monomakh agreed to become the Kievan prince; as soon as he arrived "all the people were happy and the riot ceased."[33] The sources do not refer to any rules of succession in connection with these events; the decisive factor appears to have been Monomakh's personal popularity. If anything, the eagerness of the chronicler to stress that Monomakh became the Kievan prince unwillingly is hard to reconcile with the idea that he was entitled to this position by hereditary right.

The events of 1113 were not the only occasion of a community being actively involved in princely succession. In the accounts of disputes over the Kievan, and other, thrones, we do see princes and their apologists referring to hereditary rights and dynastic seniority, which shows that there were, indeed, some rules that guided succession. However, these were flexible "rules of play" rather than a fixed "system." The concept of "rules of play" (*Spielregeln*) was, in fact, born as a response to a problem similar to that faced by students of Rusian princely succession, namely, a lack of normative documents.[34] Traditionally, scholars studying periods which did not leave explicit, spelled-out regulations of social and political practices either postulated a reign of chaos and anarchy, or assumed that regulating documents simply did not survive and need to be reconstructed on the basis of available evidence. Gerd Althoff famously showed that, in the absence of a state apparatus, social interaction was guided by implicit, unwritten *Spielregeln*, which were never fully spelled out, but which were rather expressed through behavioural patterns that included both verbal and non-verbal forms of communication.[35]

---

32 The targeting of Sviatopolk's officials is one reason to think that the people were unhappy with his rule; the plundering of the Jews in 1113, the only recorded occasion of violence against them in all pre-Mongolian history of Rus, is usually attributed to some kind of economic grievances of the population involved in the uprising (see Franklin and Shepard, *Emergence of Rus*, 286). The second invitation to Monomakh states that since the Jews are being plundered, it is likely that the mob would next turn to the monasteries "and you will answer to God if the monasteries will be plundered." The fear of the elite Kievans that the monasteries would be the next in line after the Jews suggests that the reasons for attacking the Jews were not religious. The chronicle notes the unusually generous alms that Sviatopolk's widow gave at his death to the poor, which may indicate her awareness of their hostility against her late husband. Finally, the chronicler states that Sviatopolk was mourned by "boyars and by all his men (*druzhina*)," passing over in silence "people" or "Kievans" normally presented as grieving in accounts of princely deaths. PSRL 2, 275–76.

33 PSRL 2, 275–76.

34 "Da es zwischen den Karolingischen Kapitularien und dem Sachsenspiegel so gut wie keine normativen Texte gibt, [...] kamen die Verhältnisse des 10. bis 13. Jahrhunderts gar nicht genauer ins Blickfeld." Gerd Althoff, *Spielregeln der Politik im Mittelalter. Kommunikation in Frieden und Fehde* (Darmstadt: Primus, 1997), 7.

35 Althoff, *Spielregeln der Politik*, 5–7, 12.

These "rules of play for medieval politics" were more flexible and ambiguous than any written norms would be; in the case of Rus, they seem to be a suitable analytic tool to explain the ever-shifting combination of factors that determined princely succession.[36] One such factor was the position of communities, which are often represented in the sources as inviting and rejecting princes. In the case of Kiev, such invitations were usually sent to one of the senior princes, who could plausibly claim a right to the top position in the princely hierarchy. An attempt to choose a prince on the basis of his personal popularity alone proved catastrophic, showing that the leeway allowed by the "rules of play" had its limits. When the Kievans and other communities from the Middle Dnieper region invited Mstislav Iziaslavich, who, according to the dynastic rules of seniority, had no rights to the Kievan throne, most princes put aside their own rivalries and united their forces under the leadership of a senior member of the dynasty for a punitive expedition on Kiev that ended with the notorious sack of the city in 1169.[37]

Among Rus scholars, Simon Franklin and Jonathan Shepard abandoned attempts to reconstruct a fixed system of succession and stressed flexibility of the rules that guided princely politics, and Janet Martin rejected both the notions of "a fully formed, comprehensive system" or the complete absence of a pattern of succession. They thus came close to historians of the early medieval West, who have abandoned "sterile debates about the 'rules' which purportedly determined succession" and have largely agreed that in reality succession was usually influenced by a combination of factors. The title of a work on the Ottonian and Salian kings, whose rights to the throne existed "between birthright and election," may be applied to the Rurikids as well.[38]

Thus, contrary to an underlying assumption that seems to inform much of scholarship on the Rurikids, a fixed system, had it existed in Rus, would not bring it closer to a European "norm."[39] If anything, a fixed system would turn it into an anomaly in early medieval Europe, and into a member of a minority group among high medieval realms. Especially close to Rus was the case of Scandinavia, where a choice of a king from members of an extended royal family "was normally done by leading men, sometimes after a fight [...] Sometimes different assemblies chose different candidates and there were numerous occasions when joint kings were chosen, either by agreement or in rivalry." In twelfth-century Sweden, there were two rival royal clans, Sverker and Erik,

---

36 On the factors that influenced princely succession, see Ostrowski, "Systems of Succession."

37 PSRL 1, 354–55; PSRL 2, 543–45.

38 Franklin and Shepard, *Emergence of Rus*; Martin, *Medieval Russia*, 30. For a review of literature on East Frankish/German succession, see Stefen Patzold, "Königserhebungen zwischen Erbrecht und Wahlrecht? Throngfolge und Rechtmentalität um das Jahr 1000," *Deutsches Archiv für Erforschung des des Mittelalters* 58 (2002): 467–501, at 467–73; for a critique of the search for the "rules" and "legal norms" that allegedly guided succession, see ibid., 473–74. Similarly, recent scholarship on Anglo-Saxon kingship has recognized that "a series of factors were involved [in king-making], which cannot simply be reduced to opposing legal principles," Levi Roach, *Kingship and Consent in Anglo-Saxon England, 871–978* (Cambridge: Cambridge University Press, 2013), 151.

39 Examples of this assumption in works of princely succession in Rus include Nazarenko, *Drevniaia Rus i slaviane*, 48–51; Ostrowski, "Systems of Succession."

just as in Rus there were two clans vying for the Kievan throne, the Olgovichi and the Monomakhovichi.[40]

A trend to stricter rules of succession did exist in some kingdoms as early as the tenth century, but "it was not that anyone formulated a principle of indivisibility [...] or primogeniture"; rather, a practice of bequeathing the realm to the eldest son developed gradually out of a combination of factors, such as dynastic accidents and "the dwindling of royal resources" that precluded carving out "subkingdoms" for younger brothers.[41] The Rurikids, whose dominion sprawled all over the vast East European Plain, had no difficulties carving out territories for junior members of the dynasty and no reason to formulate explicit rules of succession.

Another problematic assumption in Rus scholarship equates an orderly succession system with an efficient government. However, the prevalence of the most orderly of all medieval systems, primogeniture, in tenth- and eleventh-century France, did not translate into a strong royal government, nor did an absence of fixed rules for succession prevent England from being a model of an efficient monarchy. If anything, the strength of English monarchy has been recently *connected* with an absence of fixed rules for who should become the king: "The institution and the idea of English kingship [...] had proved itself to be astonishingly resilient. The person of the king himself was almost an irrelevance; if he governed properly, he could be accommodated within the ideal. If he did not, other men were always available."[42]

If the existence—and even a relative strength and efficiency—of monarchy in a given country is not hinged on a fixed succession system, the question of whether the Rurikids had one, and if yes, what it was, becomes rather irrelevant from a comparative perspective. What is relevant for a discussion of Rus in a European context is whether Rus had kingship. This question is rarely posed explicitly; implicitly, most accounts of Rusian history do treat some princes as monarchs.[43] Simon Franklin and Jonathan Shepard showed that, even though once in a while some princes, most notably Iaroslav, were praised as

---

40 *Contra* Ostrowski, "Systems of Succession," 51. Birgit and Peter Sawyer, *Medieval Scandinavia: From Conversion to Reformation, Circa 800–1500* (Minneapolis: University of Minnesota Press, 1993), 62; Peter Sawyer, "Scandinavia in the Eleventh and Twelfth Centuries," in *The New Cambridge Medieval History*, vol. 4, pt. 2, ed. David Luscombe and Jonathan Riley-Smith (Cambridge: Cambridge University Press, 1999), 297–98; see also Sverre Bagge and Sæbjørg Walaker Nordeide, "The Kingdom of Norway," in *Christianization and the Rise of Christian Monarchy*, ed. Nora Berend (Cambridge: Cambridge University Press, 2007), 121–66, at 147–48.

41 Janet L. Nelson, "Rulers and Government," in *The New Cambridge Medieval History*, vol. 3, ed. Timothy Reuter (Cambridge: Cambridge University Press, 1999), 104.

42 Ashe, "The Anomalous King of Conquered England," 191.

43 For example, the event of Andrew Bogoliubsky of Suzdalia gaining supremacy over the Kievan prince in 1169 is described as a "usurpation" or as a "transfer of the capital city" from Kiev to Vladimir, the centre of Suzdalia (Henrik Birnbaum, *Aspects of the Slavic Middle Ages and Slavic Renaissance Culture* (New York: Peter Lang, 1992), 78, 90, 359; Dimnik, "The Title 'Grand Prince'," 290). Such descriptions imply a single centre of supreme power (a capital city) occupied by a supreme ruler (a monarch). Andrew is as good as called a king when he is said to introduce "the

"autocrats," Rusian written culture as a whole "tended to stress collective action, communal care for the lands, a unity of the extended kin, mutual obligations."[44] Franklin and Shepard, therefore, concentrate on "collective leadership of the princely clan" and horizontal bonds among its members. They refer to princes as "the dynasty," but they use the word interchangeably with "kin" or "clan" and do not discuss the question of whether this dynasty/kin/clan was royal. In a spirit similar to that dominating Western medieval scholarship of the last decades, they prefer to avoid "extraneous vocabulary" and "not to push [...] Rus into any fixed conceptual model derived from elsewhere."[45]

An aversion to extraneous vocabulary and fixed models, shared by Franklin and Shepard with Western medievalists, exists in current scholarship for good reason. However, the unfortunate duty of a historian who seeks to place Rus in a comparative context is to overcome this aversion and to try and describe the Rurikids in extraneous terms. The fact that the number of works devoted to this task can be counted on one person's fingers once again testifies to a deep isolation of Rus studies from wider medieval scholarship. Most of these comparative works juxtapose Rusian princes with monarchs from elsewhere, comparing, for example, the division of power between the sons of Iaroslav "the Wise" and Louis "the Pious," or the Rusian princely court (*Fürstenhoff*) with Western royal (*Königshofes*) and Byzantine imperial courts.[46] How this implicitly acknowledged Rusian kingship relates to either "disintegration" or to the view of all princes ruling collectively as members of a single extended dynasty remains unclear. An examination of Rusian princes from a comparative perspective offers a good opportunity to investigate the reasons for denying the existence of monarchy in Rus, and also to reflect on the concept of kingship in general. Who exactly is the king and how do we know if a country has one?

Kingship: A Problem of Definition

As with other medieval concepts, a modern dictionary is not of much help. The Oxford English Dictionary definition of the king as "the male ruler of an independent state, especially one who inherits the position by right of birth" does not apply to the time when the notion of an "independent state" did not exist. This notion is underpinned by the concept of territorial sovereignty, which derives "from the controversies of the late Middle Ages over the relationship among emperors, popes, and kings in Christendom as a whole."[47]

---

principle of Byzantine absolutism into Russian political life," George Vernadsky, *Kievan Russia* (New Haven: Yale University Press, 1948, reprinted 1972), 220.

44 Shepard, "Rus," 393; Franklin and Shepard, *Emergence of Rus*, 276.

45 Franklin and Shepard, *Emergence of Rus*, 370.

46 Uwe Halbach, *Der russische Fürstenhof vor dem 16. Jahrhundert: Eine vergleichende Untersuchung zur politischen Lexikologie und Verfassungsgeschichte der alten Rus'* (Stuttgart: Steiner, 1985).

47 Lee Manion, "Sovereign Recognition: Contesting Political Claims in the *Alliterative Morte Arthure* and *The Awntyrs off Arthur*," in *Law and Sovereignty in the Middle Ages and the Renaissance*, ed. R. S. Sturges (Turnhout: Brepols, 2011), 69–91, at 72.

In the early and High Middle Ages, it was common for kings to be subordinate to other kings and for kingdoms to be collections of territories with multiple and complicated jurisdictions. The best-known example is, of course, the French possessions of the Anglo-Norman kings, which created power relations of immense complexity, with the English king doing homage to the French king and thus acknowledging his subordination, but, for most of the time before 1214, being more powerful than his French suzerain.

Thus, when the Kievan *kniaz* recognized his subordination to the Suzdalian *kniaz*, this is not in itself a reason to argue that the former was not a king, or that there was no kingship in Rus. If kingship did not disappear from the Carolingian lands as soon as there was more than one kingdom there, it is hard to see why there could not be two, or more, kings in the Rurikids' lands. Even when Andrew Bogoliubsky of Suzdalia is presented as "giving" the Kievan throne to another *kniaz*, this does not necessarily prevent the occupant of that throne from being a king. Before the later Middle Ages, there was nothing unusual about a whole kingdom being "given" to its king by another king. In 952, Berengar of Italy submitted himself to Otto I and "received back Italy to rule through the grace and gift of the king [Otto]," but Italy still remained a kingdom and Berengar its king.[48] Writing in 1120s, William of Malmesbury followed the common practice of describing Scotland as a "kingdom" and its rulers as "kings," and he also stated that they were "appointed" or "promoted to kingdom" by Henry I of England, apparently not seeing any contradiction.[49]

The case of Scotland illustrates problems with another criterion for defining the king; namely, being crowned and anointed. One argument against the existence of kingship in Rus is the absence of coronation and royal regalia in Rusian political practice.[50] The rulers of Scotland, however, had been known as kings for centuries before the first Scottish coronation took place in 1331. Nor was Scotland exceptional in this respect: Swedish kingship had also long predated the practice of coronation, which began in 1210; in Denmark, "a monarchy was already in existence" in the early eighth century, but the first coronation occurred in 1170.[51] Other examples of kingdoms without coronation and anointing include early Anglo-Saxon England and Merovingian Francia. Arguably, these "barbarian" and peripheral polities preserved forms of archaic European kingship, upon which church rites of coronation and anointing were later superimposed; in addition,

---

48 Adalbert, *Continuatio Reginonis*, ed. Friedrich Kurze, MGH: Scriptores rerum Germanicarum in usum scholarum 1 (Hanover: Hahn, 1890), 166, as quoted in Roach, "Submission and Homage," 371.

49 Henry I, "Dunecanum [...] regem Scottorum mortuo patre constituit"; "Edgarum in regnum promovit." William of Malmesbury, *Gesta Regum Anglorum*: The History of the English Kings, ed. R. A B. Mynors, R. M. Thomson, M. Winterbottom (Oxford: Clarendon Press, 1998), vol. 2, 724.

50 Ostrowski, "Systems of Succession," 35. For a review of representations of Rusian princes wearing crowns, which "tend to be exceptions proving the rule," see Jonathan Shepard, "Crowns from the Basileus, Crowns from Heaven," in *Byzantium, New Peoples, New Powers: The Byzantino-Slav Contact Zone*, ed. Miliana Kaĭmakamova, Maciej Salamon, and Małgorzata Smorąg Różyck (Cracow: Towarzystwo Wydawnicze Historia Iagellonica, 2007), 139–59, at 156–57.

51 Michael H. Gelting, "The Kingdom of Denmark," in *Christianization and the Rise of Christian Monarchy*, 73–120, at 75; Sawyer, "Scandinavia," 292, 300.

they could also experience some "cross-fertilization" of the native and Roman imperial rites of rulership, especially in the case of the Merovingians.[52] In these societies, kings came from an extended kin-group (*strips regia*), which had exclusive right to rule because of its special charisma; in the Merovingians, this charisma was famously expressed by their long hair and healing touch. While there is no systematic description of early rites of king-making, comparable to the later *ordines* of coronation and anointing, enthronement and popular acclamation were probably the two key elements.[53]

Representations of princes in Rusian sources strike chords that resonate with this traditional "native" kingship. The Rurikids had a special charisma; when a member of their clan began his rule in Kiev or other prominent centre, the inauguration consisted of him "sitting" or "being seated" on the throne there.[54] On one occasion, the chronicler reports, tantalizingly, that "the people and the Metropolitan" met the incoming Kievan prince and "put him on the throne," without elaborating on the role the metropolitan played in the enthronement. At least one inauguration was planned on Easter, so that "there was a double joy for the people, the resurrection of the Lord and the enthronement of the prince (*kniazhoe sedenie*)."[55] More detailed descriptions of enthronements normally include processions and crowds expressing their joy.[56] Their legitimizing

---

[52] Jonathan Shepard, "Adventus, Arrivistes and Rites of Rulership in Byzantium and France in the Tenth and Eleventh Century," in *Court Ceremonies and Rituals of Power in Byzantium and the Medieval Mediterranean*, ed. Alexander Beihammer, Stavroula Constantinou, and Maria Parani (Leiden: Brill, 2013), 337–71, at 338.

[53] Enthronement was "probably the core of earlier secular king-makings" in Francia (Joseph Canning, *A History of Medieval Political Thought: 300–1450* (New York: Routledge, 2005), 57); in Scotland, the incoming king was seated on the stone throne (Felix James Henry Skene and William Forbes Skene, eds., *Johannis de Fordun, Chronica Gentis Scotorum*, vol. 1 (Edinburgh: Edmonstone and Douglas, 1872), 294, where the chronicler applies the word *cathedra* to the stone, on which the king sat at the inauguration; R. James Goldstein, *The Matter of Scotland: Historical Narrative in Medieval Scotland* (Lincoln: University of Nebraska Press, 1993), 15–17); in Scandinavia, a king or jarl was conducted to the high seat and there assumed full authority (Edward Oswald Gabriel Turville-Petre, *Myth and Religion of the North: The Religion of Ancient Scandinavia* (New York: Holt, Rinehart and Winston, 1964), 259, as quoted in Shepard, "Rus," 395); see also Janet L. Nelson, *Politics and Ritual in Early Medieval Europe* (Oxford: Hambledon, 1986), 264–65. On acclamation, see Canning, *A History of Medieval Political Thought*, 21–22, 67–68.

[54] Princes' special charisma is manifest in a tale about little prince Sviatoslav who was made to ride before the troops after his father's death and throw his spear to begin the battle symbolically. "The spear slipped between his horse's ears and hit the horse's legs because he was a little boy," after which the general commanded the troops, "The prince has started, let us follow the prince!" (PSRL 1, 58). On one occasion, soldiers could not withstand an attack and fled "because there was no *kniaz* there, and not everyone would obey a boyar," that is, a non-princely noble (PSRL 2, 425–26).

[55] PSRL 2, 504; Cf. Roach, *Kingship and Consent*, 74, 166.

[56] Alexandra Vukovich, "The Enthronement Rituals of the Princes of Vladimir-Suzdal in the 12th and 13th centuries," *FORUM University of Edinburgh Postgraduate Journal of Culture and the Arts* 17 (2013) at www.forumjournal.org/article/view/704/978; Tolochko, *Kniaz*, 138–49.

function is evident from the accounts that do *not* refer to subjects joyously welcoming their new prince. Such omissions usually signal problems with the prince's legitimacy.

A particularly telling example is the account of an occasion when Kiev was briefly without a prince while being threatened by the Cumans, a nomadic people from the steppe south of Rus. The Kievans invited the nearest prince, who happened to be Iziaslav Davidovich of Chernigov, to come and protect them. Judging from the urgency of their request and their fear of the Cumans, the Kievans must have been excited to see Iziaslav and his soldiers entering the city; nonetheless, the chronicler mentions neither their joy nor any welcome given to Iziaslav. However, when the lawful prince reached Kiev, ordered Iziaslav to leave, and entered the city, "a multitude of people came to meet him, and he sat on the throne of his forefathers, and all the Rus Land accepted him with joy."[57] The lack of a proper welcome demonstrates that Iziaslav was not the rightful prince of Kiev and stresses the interim character of his brief occupation of the Kievan throne. By the same token, no joy is reported in the account of the arrival to Kiev of Mstislav Iziaslavich in 1167, even though he was invited to take the throne by the Kievans. This omission of joy gives a premonition of Mstislav's overthrow two years later, which occurred because Mstislav's legitimacy as the supreme ruler was not recognized by most of the other princes.[58]

In other words, "a multitude of people" greeting the incoming prince performed a rite—an acclamation of the new ruler or a celebration of the ruler's entrance—as a means to establish his legitimacy.[59] On one occasion, the newly arrived metropolitan is presented as "blessing" the current Kievan prince, who by that time had already occupied the Kievan throne for three years.[60] Some accounts of inaugurations include the prince ceremonially entering the city cathedral and praying publicly, and they also describe not "people," or not just "people," but the metropolitan, bishops, and other church hierarchs meeting the new prince "with Crosses" and placing him on the throne, thus adding a touch of divine sanction.[61]

The role of the ecclesiastics never went beyond such touches; the ideology of sacred Christian kingship, although not completely unknown in Rus, was not systematic or very influential.[62] However, this does not automatically mean that kingship itself did not exist—or we must conclude that it did not exist in Merovingian Francia either. If neither ruling an "independent state," nor holding a fixed ceremony, such as a coronation, defines early, and in some cases high, medieval kingship, what does? According to one

---

57 PSRL 2, 476-78.

58 PSRL 1, 354-55; PSRL 2, 543-45.

59 On the legitimizing function of crowds greeting a ruler's entrance elsewhere, see Shepard, "Adventus, Arrivistes and Rites of Rulership."

60 PSRL 2, 485.

61 PSRL 2, 441, 568, 681. PSRL 1, 306, 423. Cf. the situation in Denmark and Scotland around the year 1000, where there was no regular rites of royal consecration, but "Christian glosses were starting to be superimposed on indigenous rulership." Nelson, "Rulers and Governments," 108.

62 Shepard, "Rus"; Vukovich, "The Enthronement Rituals."

early medieval authority, it was acting like a king; Timothy Reuter, on the basis of his observations of Ottonian kingship, adds that "it would be equally true to say that if you were perceived as a king, then you were one."[63]

It may be thus more productive to define the king by his position in the network of power relations and the social perceptions existing in a given society. This is essentially what scholars of Scandinavia do when they present some *konungar* from their sources as "kings," and others as "chieftains" or "nobles." To see whether the same distinction should be applied to Rusian *kniazi* and whether the most powerful among them were, in fact, "kings" rather than "princes," we need to compare their positions with those of rulers universally recognized as "kings." In the context of the present discussion, which deals with the subject of scholarly terminology and conventions of translation, it appears more appropriate to concentrate on representations of kingship in scholarly literature rather than in primary sources. For now, our task is to see how Western medievalists describe the place of the king in the societies that they study, and then to find out if anyone occupied a similar place in Rus. Medieval kingdoms differed from one another, of course, but there are, nonetheless, some common themes in the historiography of European kingship.

First of all, this is a distinction between a personal kingship, based on "a mixture of the charismatic and the patrimonial," and an administrative one which relied on institutions. In a traditional narrative of European history, "a Weberian transformation" from the former to the latter took place between 1100 and 1350 in most of Latin Europe, with the notable exception of Germany.[64] Like all ideal Weberian types, neither kind of kingship existed in its pure form; most medieval, and even early modern, societies displayed elements of both, and historians often disagree in their evaluations of the character of kingship in a given country and time period. That said, there is a general consensus that England was precocious in creating governmental institutions even before the Norman Conquest and in developing a strong central control over administration of justice in the twelfth century. A similar development took place in the Norman kingdom of Sicily. In contrast with the early development of administrative kingship in England, French kingship of the tenth and eleventh centuries is usually described as "weak"; over the course of the twelfth century the monarchy was increasingly asserting its authority; by the early thirteenth century, there were established institutions of central government.[65]

Germany is traditionally represented as following a "special path (*Sonderweg*)": it remained fragmented and its monarchy weak at a time when other kings were asserting their authority and building governmental institutions. German medieval *Sonderweg* is a subject of debate, with historians pointing to "elements of 'administrative kingship'

---

63 Reuter, *Medieval Polities*, 129, with reference to Isidore of Seville.

64 Reuter, *Medieval Polities*, 388.

65 Riley-Smith and Luscombe, Introduction to *The New Cambridge Medieval History*, vol. 4, 5; John Baldwin, "Crown and Government," *The New Cambridge Medieval History*, vol. 4, 510–29, but see Bisson, *Crisis of the Twelfth Century*, where he argues that kings everywhere, including in England, largely functioned like other lords for most of the twelfth century, and it was only at the end of this century that there were signs of a transition to government as different from lordship.

visible in the Reich," but there appears to be a consensus that, because of the size and diversity of the German empire, a centralized bureaucratic monarchy was neither possible nor desirable there.[66] In this respect, current scholarship, even when it acknowledges differences between Germany and more compact Western European kingdoms, diverges from the classic historiographical tradition, which discussed *Sonderweg* primarily in terms of a failure: German monarchs failed to develop as good institutions as their counterparts elsewhere managed to create, and they also failed to subjugate magnates whose pursuit of selfish interests led to strife, disorder and fragmentation. In contrast with this bleak view, recent historiography tends to see ruling the Empire as a cooperative project of the monarch and magnates; when the cooperation broke down and conflicts erupted, the monarch did not necessarily embody the public good, with magnates being the bad guys. The rulers, who were themselves members of the "aristocratic commonwealth," "also had the capacity to generate disorder."[67]

This approach reflects a change in thinking about relations between monarchs and aristocracy in general, not just in Germany. A lack of a sharp division between royal and aristocratic power brings back the question of definitions: "In a world where kings were dependent on local elites to carry out their will, what can we identify as constituting royal power?"[68] The theme of relations between kingship and aristocracy is of great importance for placing Rusian princes in a European context, and it needs to be discussed in some detail.

State, Kingship, and Lordship

An influential tradition, going back to nineteenth-century legal-constitutional historiography, identified the king with the state. The state, which nationalistic historians imagined as a homeland of a primordial homogenous "people" or "nation," served as the main point of reference and was usually conceived as a centralized monarchy. Correspondingly, magnates were thought of as the rulers' appointees who, at some point, usurped his prerogatives, turned administrative units entrusted to them into their private dominions, and thus initiated the period of "feudal anarchy," which lasted until such a time when the king was able to reimpose his authority, to resume the state-building interrupted by usurping magnates, and to reintegrate his fragmented realm. The king thus stood for centripetal force and public order, while the aristocracy embodied centrifugal tendencies, private interests and general disorder; a struggle between the two was presented as the essence of medieval political history.[69] The "disintegration" of Rus scholarship bears clear marks of affinity to this classic narrative, but is darker than the Western version: it assigns final victory to the forces of chaos destroying the incipient

---

66 Reuter, *Medieval Polities*, 410; Warner, "Reading Ottonian History."
67 Warner, "Reading Ottonian History," 93.
68 Matthew Innes, *State and Society in the Early Middle Ages: The Middle Rhine Valley, 400–1000* (Cambridge: Cambridge University Press, 2006), 4.
69 On this traditional representation of relations between the king and aristocracy and its modern critique, see Timothy Reuter, "The Medieval Nobility in Twentieth-Century Historiography," in *Companion to Historiography*, ed. Michael Bentley (New York: Routledge, 2006), 177–202, at 181–84;

Kievan rulership and facilitating the Mongol conquest, while in the West, apart from Germany with its *Sonderweg*, the forces of good ultimately triumphed when administrative kingship was firmly established in the later Middle Ages. In other words, both narratives are told in hindsight.

Since the later twentieth century, Western medievalists have worked to liberate their field from the practice of writing history back from the present. This practice included not only projecting back to the past our knowledge of later events—such as viewing twelfth-century Rus through a prism of the thirteenth-century Mongol conquest—but also of imposing on the past modern analytical categories, such as public and private. Nineteenth- and earlier twentieth-century historiography associated the king with the "public" and the aristocracy with the "private," but now most scholars think that "public and private power were seldom in opposition in the Middle Ages."[70]

This opposition is now largely abandoned, and so is the teleological view of progress "as a secularized form of Providence" and the modern state as the crown of progress;[71] a rejection of this view resulted in a re-evaluation of relations between monarchy and aristocracy. The transition to an impersonal, institution-based government may still be evaluated positively, of course, but historians no longer see the king from any period or place as promoting this type of goverment and aristocrats as impeding his efforts. Recent research showed that the Carolingians did not make a doomed attempt to create something approximating a modern state, and their king and aristocracy "were not involved in a zero-sum struggle for power, but in a collaborative project better to anchor their collective authority." Correspondingly, aristocratic domination was not "qualitatively different from and opposed to Carolingian royal power." Neither did the two become mutually opposed in the post-Carolingian period, when aristocracy was "a partner with equal rights rather than an opponent to the king."[72]

Interpretations of the positions of the king and aristocracy within early and high medieval society may differ widely, ranging from a largely harmonious view of the ruler governing with the consent of communities and in consultation with his prominent subjects, to the king as one predatory lord among others, all of them jointly oppressing the ordinary people.[73] However, a feature common to most current interpretations is a

---

Innes, *State and Society*, 4–9; Cheyette, "Feudalism," 122–26 and following; Warner, "Reading Ottonian History," 96–97; West, *Reframing the Feudal Revolution*, 5–6.

70 West, *Reframing the Feudal Revolution*, 101; but see Chris Wickham, *Medieval Europe* (New Haven: Yale University Press, 2016), 33.

71 Cheyette, "Feudalism," 22; Davies, "The Medieval State," 281.

72 West, *Reframing the Feudal Revolution*, 100, 101, 104; Warner, "Reading Ottonian History," 93; see also Hans-Werner Goetz, "The Perception of 'Power' and 'State' in the Early Middle Ages: The Case of the Astronomer's 'Life of Louis the Pious'," in *Representations of Power in Medieval Germany: 800–1500*, ed. Björn Weiler and Simon MacLean (Turnhout: Brepols, 2006), 15–36.

73 The first of these views is best represented by Susan Reynolds, *Kingdoms and Communities in Western Europe, 900–1300* (Oxford: Clarendon Press, 1984) and Reynolds, "Government and Community," in *The New Cambridge Medieval History*, vol. 4, 86–111; the second by Bisson, *Crisis of the Twelfth Century*.

lack of opposition between the king and aristocracy, of the kind postulated by traditional constitutional historiography.

Another typical feature of current discussions of the relations between the king and aristocracy is their connection with the debate on feudalism and "feudal revolution." The traditional master narrative of the European Middle Ages postulated that magnates, such as counts and dukes, were originally the king's appointees, entrusted with ruling various territorial units on his behalf. They, however, gradually usurped the regalian rights and came to consider their positions as hereditary, so that territories under their authority became family property. To be able to exercise his authority over the realm, the king sought to become the magnates' feudal lord and to turn the magnates' territories into fiefs held from him. The magnates, in turn, acted as feudal lords of lesser nobles, forming the "feudal pyramid" that ideally included the whole realm.

The classic theory of feudalism thus sought to explain how society functioned during the periods when there was no efficient royal government: in the absence of public institutions, the elite was organized by means of private lord–vassal agreements regulated by "feudal law" and by ethics of personal loyalty. A major point of Reynolds's critique of the "feudal construct" is that there were no such periods during the European Middle Ages: early and high medieval societies were states ruled by effective royal governments, and great men, such as counts, owed service and obedience to the king more as subjects and office-holders to the supreme ruler than as vassals to their lord.[74]

If, for Reynolds, the state existed in the post-Carolingian no less than in the Carolingian period, for other scholars, it was lordship that was "always there." Rees Davies argued that emphasis on state and kingship unjustifiably privileged one source of authority; he proposed "lordship" as an alternative tool of analysis "which respects the continuum of power, rather than necessarily privileging one particular form of power."[75] Davies sees both kingship and lordship as parts of this continuum but for some historians lordship is the only real part, with the state and effective kingship being something of a Carolingian illusion. Scholars, such as Dominique Barthélemy and Steven White, argued that in the early and High Middle Ages, the king's government existed mostly on parchment: the Carolingian royal rhetoric obscured real social and political relations shaped by lordship both before and after the year 1000. These ideas were part of their critique of the "feudal revolution" theory which postulated a breakdown of the Carolingian public order around the turn of the eleventh century. Barthélemy famously argued that what happened around the year 1000 was not the "feudal revolution," but

---

74 Reynolds, *Kingdoms and Communities in Western Europe*; Reynolds, "The Historiography of the Medieval State," *A Companion to Historiography*, ed. Michael Bentley (London: Routledge, 1997), 117–38; Reynolds, *Fiefs and Vassals*, 25–27, 34–35, 111, 138–40, 291, 311, 402–4; Reynolds, "*Fiefs and Vassals* after Twelve Years," in *Feudalism: New Landscapes of Debate*, ed. Sverre Bagge, Michael H. Gelting, and Thomas Lindkvist (Turnhout: Brepols, 2011), 15–26, at 17, 24–25; Reynolds, "There were States in Medieval Europe: A Response to Rees Davies," *Journal of Historical Sociology* 16 (2003): 550–55.
75 Davies, "The Medieval State," 293–96. For a review of literature on the concept of "lordship" and for recent titles using this concept, see West, "Lordship in Ninth-century Francia," 4–9.

"feudal revelation": the sources became more diverse and more detailed, which allowed them to reveal hitherto undocumented aspects of medieval society.[76]

For Thomas Bisson, a foremost proponent of the "feudal revolution," the Carolingian world was not permeated by lordship, which emerged dramatically around the year 1000, but eleventh- and twelfth-century society was. However, his view of post-Carolingian society dominated by lordship is very different from that on which critique of the "feudal revolution" is based. For Barthélemy or White, the prevalence of lordship meant that social relations were negotiated through conflicts and dispute-resolution, and that society was held together by networks of affective relations and regulated by symbolic communication. In other words, this society did not need royal decrees and formal institutions to be able to function quite successfully. For Bisson, it was a story of a crisis, not of success: a wider society suffered from exploitative, arbitrary lordly power not restrained by any central authority.

Within the last decade, medievalists have used "lordship" so much that Charles West recently described the term as "fashionable," and warned that "for all its allure, the concept of lordship has the potential to become tyrannical, too."[77] The "feudal revolution" debate has not been immune to producing "potentially totalizing constructs" of its own,[78] and West's research represents a turn to a more nuanced and varied approach to a range of topics associated with the debate. To clarify the issue of lordship and royal power in Carolingian versus post-Carolingian Francia, he conducted a microhistorical study of the relations between the bishop of Laon, his secular followers, and the king. The study shows that there was, indeed, a more direct and forceful presence of royal power in Laon in the ninth century than in the post-Carolingian period. In the eleventh century, there was no "anarchy," and the king did retain a privileged place; but local affairs were managed by local lords, such as the bishop.[79] Thus, instead of broad-brush images of medieval society either as "always" being effectively ruled by kings, or as "always" being dominated by lordship, or else suddenly undergoing a breakdown of public order and falling into a state of anarchy, we see the workings of royal and lordly power on the ground, as they decide concrete cases, deal with concrete situations; it is through these everyday decisions that a shift in the balance of power from the king to the bishop becomes visible.

Such a shift in Laon can be traced in great detail because of an unusually rich and systematic dossier of documents, providing information that "goes beyond the snapshot— one letter of intercession, or an isolated incident—and instead gives some indication of the nature of relationships in context."[80] In most regions of early and high medieval Europe, it is impossible to perform a similarly detailed investigation of the power dynamics on the ground; nonetheless, recent works by Western medievalists display the

---

76 Barthélemy, *The Serf, the Knight, and the Historian*, 33.
77 West, "Lordship in Ninth-century Francia," 40.
78 Kosto, *Making Agreements*, 13.
79 West, "Lordship in Ninth-century Francia," 31.
80 West, "Lordship in Ninth-century Francia," 19.

same tendency to evaluate the nature of a specific type of authority, be it royal or aristocratic, by analyzing available information about power relations. When they have to rely on "snapshots," as is often the case, they do recognize the fragmentary nature of their evidence and try to avoid unwarranted generalizations.[81] Let us now look at princely power and authority in Rus from a similar perspective.

"Kingdom" or "Aristocratic State"? A Source Problem

Two recent works discuss the question of kingship in Rus with unusual explicitness, and they offer opposing answers: Christian Raffensperger argues that Rus was a "kingdom," on par with other European kingdoms, while Donald Ostrowski describes it as a "headless" or "aristocratic state" with no supreme power and no ruling dynasty. The "dynasty of the Rurikids" was a later invention; "it is more accurate to see princes [...] as an aristocracy who operated in a matrix of fundamentally horizontal power relations." According to Ostrowski, such political organization set Rus apart from other European countries and made it similar to some nomadic polities.[82] Shepard also discusses monarchy in the Rusian context in his essay on the effects of Christianization on Rus. He does not formulate as clear a verdict as Raffensperger and Ostrowski do, but he is closer to the position of the latter. Shepard does write about ties between "Rus princely family" and "other Christian ruling families," with the latter being families of monarchs; and he also refers to "royal power" of princes—after all, his essay is part of an edited volume on "Christianization and the rise of Christian monarchy"—but overall he emphasizes "the prevalence of the sense of a ruling family, as against monarchy" in Rusian culture. "Sense" and "culture" are important here, because Shepard concentrates more on the ideology of rulership than on its practice.[83]

Raffesperger and Ostrowski, on the other hand, are concerned with the practical workings of princely power. The former argues that the main functions of Rusian princes "were the same as for most rulers throughout medieval Europe, and the varying power relations were similar as well." The Kievan prince had supremacy over all other princes—thus being the king—"at least until the second quarter of the twelfth century."[84] It remains unclear, however, whether the state of interprincely relations in later twelfth- and early thirteenth-century Rus supports the notion that kingship still existed there. For this later period, Raffensperger's argumentation is based on Latin sources referring to Rus as *regnum* and to its princes as *reges*; his concrete examples of the Kievan supremacy in any case belong to the time up to 1054.

Ostrowski cites different examples and comes to a different conclusion. He points out that princely conferences of 1097 and 1100 are presented in the *Primary Chronicle*

---

81 One of the best examples of this careful approach is *Problems and Possibilities of Early Medieval Charters*, ed. Jonathan Jarrett and Allan Scott McKinley (Turnhout: Brepols, 2013).

82 Raffensperger, *The Kingdom of Rus'*; Ostrowski, "Systems of Succession," 51.

83 Shepard, "Rus," 392, 396.

84 Raffensperger, *The Kingdom of Rus'*, 43, 45–46

"as attempts to regulate the system by the princes themselves, rather than any vertical imposition of power by the prince of Kiev."[85] In 1100, the leading princes confronted Sviatopolk of Kiev, who had a minor prince Vasilko blinded without due judicial procedure at the instigation of David of Chernigov. According to the *Primary Chronicle*, David slandered Vasilko in front of Sviatopolk and then had him blinded with Sviatolk's consent.[86] It would be hard to expect a "vertical imposition of power by the prince of Kiev"—that is, Sviatopolk—in this particular case, but the character of the 1100 conference does not necessarily preclude a view of Rus as a monarchy. The princes confronting Sviatopolk for blinding one of them without "accusing him before us and proving him guilty" and collectively assigning punishment to the main culprit David may be construed as aristocrats in conflict with the king over the right to be judged by their peers.[87]

In the account of the 1097 conference at Liubech, all the participants, including the Kievan prince, are indeed represented as equals, but we should keep in mind that this account is just that—a representation. The chronicler may have represented the six princes who gathered at Liubech in 1097 as equals because they were, indeed, equals, and the Kievan prince did not have any special status. Or he may have represented the princes as equals because his patron Vladimir Monomakh wanted him to downplay the significance of Sviatopolk, the Kievan prince at the time and Monomakh's rival. Or he may have had any number of other reasons to write the account of the conference the way he did. Why take a representation of Sviatopolk and other princes in the *Primary Chronicle* at face value any more than, say, a representation of the French king and the Rollonid rulers of Normandy by the Rollonid apologist Dudo of Saint-Quentin? In his history of the Normans (late tenth/early eleventh century), Dudo claims that the French king at one point served as a page-boy to the Norman duke. He also relates how William I of Normandy arranged a meeting between the French and the German kings, who were not able to resolve their problems without William's guidance, and how William's men harrowed the place where the German king stayed, bursting into the house and smashing the walls as a punishment for a disrespectful remark about Normans made by one of the Germans.[88] If there is "any vertical imposition of power" in Dudo's history, its source is the Norman duke, not the king. Historians, however, do not deny the existence of a monarchy in West Francia on the basis of Dudo's representations of helpless kings being bossed around by mighty Norman dukes because they see these representations as largely fictional.

Historians of tenth- early eleventh-century Francia have plenty of narrative and diplomatic sources which allow them to put Dudo's Norman propaganda in perspective.

---

85 Ostrowski, "System of Succession," 48.

86 PSRL 1, 257–62.

87 "If you had a charge against him (*ashche ti by vina kakaia byla na n'*), you should have accused (*oblichil by*) him before us and, after having proved him guilty, you could do this [blinding] to him." PSRL 1, 263, 274.

88 Jules Lair, ed., *De moribus et actis primorum Normanniae ducum auctore Dudone Sancti Quintini decano* (Caen: Le Blanc-Hardel, 1865), 194, 196–97.

For historians of Rus, the situation is very different. Before the proliferation of centres of chronicle-writing in the twelfth century, it it hard to reconstruct the actual power relations and to see what model, monarchical or aristocratic, they fit best. For the eleventh century, native written sources are extremely scarce, and where their information cannot be juxtaposed with foreign accounts, we are often left with a unique version of events impossible to refute or corroborate.

Prior to the conversion of Vladimir in 998, there was no writing in Rus, apart from inscriptions found on archaeologically excavated objects.[89] Nor did writing proliferate greatly—or at all—immediately after Vladimir's baptism. Church statutes attributed to Vladimir and Iaroslav "date in their present form from the twelfth century or later still, and the composition dates of the supposed originals are uncertain."[90] A major text undoubtedly originating from the time of Iaroslav is the *Sermon on Law and Grace* (*Slovo o Zakone i Blagodati*) by Metropolitan Hilarion.[91] The *Sermon* celebrates the conversion of Rus; Hilarion describes both Vladimir and his son Iaroslav as "autocrats" ruling over the new Christian realm. However, it is hard to tell how much factual truth there is to these elevated portrayals, and how much should be attributed to the Byzantine tradition of rhetorical eulogy and to the fact that Hilarion, before Iaroslav appointed him to the metropoly, was a priest at Iaroslav's court.[92]

Iaroslav is presented as "the autocrat of the Rus Land" in the *Primary Chronicle* as well. The *Chronicle*, which is the main source for the early history of Rus, survived only in late copies, but it is generally believed to have been compiled in the 1110s, apparently on the basis of diverse extinct sources; according to its colophon, the present text of the *Chronicle* was produced in a monastery that was under the patronage of Vladimir Monomakh.[93] The part of the *Chronicle* covering the time before Iaroslav contains Slavonic translations of tenth-century trade treaties between Rus and Byzantium; apart

---

89 On these objects, see Elena Melnikova, "The Acculturation of Scandinavians in Early Rus' as Reflected by Language and Literacy," in *Vers l'Orient et vers l'Occident: Regards croisés sur les dynamiques et les transferts culturels des Vikings à la Rous ancienne*, ed. Pierre Bauduin and Alexander Musin (Caen: Presses universitaires de Caen, 2014), 363–75.

90 Shepard, "Rus," 389.

91 *"Slovo o zakone i blagodati" Ilariona*, ed. A. M. Moldovan (Kiev: Naukova dumka, 1984). The *Sermon* appears to be composed in the mid-eleventh century; its earliest copy is datable to the second half of the fifteenth century.

92 Franklin, *Sermons and Rhetoric of Kievan Rus'*, xli.

93 On the manuscripts and editions of the *Primary Chronicle*, see Ostrowski, Introduction to PVL, vol. 1, xix–xxvi. For a general information and bibliography on the *Chronicle*, see *Pismennye pamiatniki istorii Drevnei Rusi: letopisi, povesti, khozhdeniia, poucheniia, zhitiia, poslaniia: annotirovannyi katalog-spravochnik*, ed. Ia. N. Shchapov (St. Petersburg: Russko-Baltiiskii informatsionnyi tsentr "BLITS", 2003), 21–23. See also Simon Franklin and Jonathan Shepard, *Emergence of Rus*, 317–19. For an English translation (outdated and to be used with caution), see Samuel Hazzard Cross and Olgerd P. Sherbowitz-Wetzor, *The Russian Primary Chronicle: Laurentian Text* (Cambridge, MA: Mediaeval Academy of America, 1953). A new translation by Horace Lunt is forthcoming.

from these treaties, most material consists of legends, arguably going back to an oral tradition. This makes the early part of the *Chronicle* enjoyable reading and a valuable source for studies of culture and mentality—but much less so for political and social history. Starting with the reign of Iaroslav, the *Chronicle* appears to make use of contemporary annals;[94] however, these annals are short and contradictory. Above all, they are not entirely consistent with the notion of Iaroslav's "sole rule." At any rate, they leave so many holes in the narrative about his reign that it is virtually impossible to determine the nature of his authority beyond the general impression that he, in the words of Franklin and Shepard, "exercised limited rule over a limited area with fairly basic institutions of government."[95]

Most scholars, with a notable exception of Franklin and Shepard, interpret Hilarion's and the chronicler's references to Iaroslav as the "grand prince" and "the autocrat (*samovlastets*) of all Rus"[96] as evidence that, apart from ten years when he shared power with his brother Mstislav, Iaroslav ruled over all the territory known as "Rus" in modern scholarship (except Polotsk which had its own dynasty). However, the annals for 1024–1026 contradict this prevailing view: they represent Chernigov, a major centre in the middle Dnieper region which comprised the "Rus Land," in the most narrow sense, as independent from Kiev. According to these annals, when Iaroslav was in Novgorod, his brother Mstislav, a prince of remote Tmutarokan, attempted to claim the Kievan throne for himself. When "the Kievans did not accept him," and he "went and sat on the throne in Chernigov (*shed sede na stole Chernigove*)," Iaroslav marched on him from Novgorod, and the brothers engaged in battle. Mstislav won and proposed a peace treaty: he would take Chernigov and the territory on the western side of the Dnieper while Iaroslav would keep the other side, including Kiev. This arrangement lasted until Mstislav's death in 1036.[97]

The chronicler does not explain who, if anyone, had occupied the Chernigov throne before the arrival of Mstislav. Later, Iaroslav's son resided in Kiev and "entrusted the throne of Novgorod to his trusted man (*blizoku*) Ostromir."[98] Theoretically, Iaroslav could have done the same with the Chernigov throne. However, if there had been Iaroslav's man in Chernigov, why did he not defend the city and the throne entrusted to him? The chronicle does not mention any resistance when Mstislav "sat on the throne in Chernigov,"

---

94 O. V. Tvorogov, *Drevniaia Rus: Sobytiia i liudi* (St. Petersburg: Nauka, 1994), 15; Petrukhin, "Drevniaia Rus: Narod. Kniazia. Religiia," 184.

95 Franklin and Shepard, *Emergence of Rus*, 244.

96 PSRL 1, 150, 161; *Novgorodskaia pervaia letopis starshego i mladshego izvodov*, ed. A. N. Nasonov, Polnoe sobranie russkikh letopisei, vol. 3 (Moscow: Izdatelstvo Akademii nauk SSSR, 1950; reprinted: Moscow: Iazyki slavianskikh kultur, 2000, with a new introduction by B. M. Kloss), hereafter N1L, 181.

97 PSRL 1, 147–49.

98 L. V. Stoliarova, *Svod zapisei pistsov, khudozhnikov i perepletchkov drevnerusskikh pergamennykh kodeksov XI–XIV vv.* (Moscow: Nauka, 2000), 14. This was before Novgorod acquired its "republican" status.

an expression implying peaceful and lawful accession to power. Did the population there consider Mstislav their rightful prince? This seems all the more probable, given Mstislav's behaviour in respect to Kiev. He left when "the Kievans did not accept him"; nor did he use his military victory over Iaroslav to take the Kievan throne. Apparently, he either did not want to, or could not, seize a princely throne by sheer force, without being "accepted" by the population; he evidently received an "acceptance" in Chernigov, because the men of Chernigov fought for him against Iaroslav.[99] Does this mean that Iaroslav did not have authority over Chernigov? Or that the people of Chernigov rebelled against Iaroslav and defected to his rival? In this latter case, what happened to Iaroslav's men there, if there were any? The brief account does not provide any answers.

The same account leaves the impression that Iaroslav did not have a firm authority over Kiev either: the Kievans "did not accept" Mstislav, but neither did they fight for Iaroslav, and he apparently could not compel them to do so: he confronted Mstislav only after recruiting mercenaries from Scandinavia. After the battle, both princes allegedly rejoiced that their own followers (*druzhina*) did not suffer great casualties and that most fallen soldiers were Scandinavians on Iaroslav's side and the men of Chernigov on Mststislav's. In other words, both princes are represented as warlords, concerned about their followers above all else. Furthermore, even after Mstislav's peace offer, "Iaroslav did not dare to go to Kiev" and he stayed in Novgorod until he managed to "gather many soldiers." There is no information on who these soldiers were and how Iaroslav "gathered" them, but he apparently did not have a regular, institutionalized way to summon an army.[100]

At least, this appears to be the case in the 1020s. In all likelihood, Iaroslav later took some steps to consolidate his rule. His large-scale building programme in Kiev required considerable material resources; his impressive cultural and religious patronage shows him as a ruler concerned about his prestige and the well-being of the realm, not as a warlord who thinks all is well as long as he has his band of followers. After all, neither French and Hungarian kings nor the Byzantine emperor would be willing to establish marriage ties with the family of a mere warlord.[101] They must have had their reasons to perceive Iaroslav as another European monarch, and if they did, modern historians would also do well to think about him as a king. In this respect, Raffensperger's argument is quite convincing. However, modern scholars have to take the word of foreigners that Iaroslav was, indeed, *rex Russorum*: it is virtually impossible to understand how

---

99 Originally, Mstislav's soldiers were drawn from the ethnic groups native to the vicinity of Tmutarakan: he first appeared on the Middle Dnieper "with Khazars and Kasogs." However, in the battle against Iaroslav, Mstislav "put *Sever* in the front, opposite to [Iaroslav's mercenary] Varangians, while he and his men were in the flanks." PSRL 1, 149. This change in the composition of Mstislav's army indicates that he enjoyed support of the Chernigov people. "Sever" was a collective noun signifying the population of the Chernigov land; an individual member of *Sever* was *Severianin*. In Anglophone scholarship, the name of this group is represented as Severians, Severyans or Siverians.

100 PSRL 1, 147–49.

101 Raffensperger, *Reimagining Europe*, 57–90.

Iaroslav's rule was organized and to reconstruct power relations during his reign on the basis of native sources. High-register praise of Iaroslav in the *Sermon of Law and Grace* and in the *Primary Chronicle* does not provide factual information, while the accounts of events that occurred in Iaroslav's time are too brief and disjointed.

The *Chronicle* gets more detailed in the late eleventh and early twelfth century. Some parts of it, such as the dramatic account of Vasilko's blinding, are rich narratives with literary merit, but they exist side by side with laconic records that provide virtually no context. The report about the 1097 Liubech conference is such a record, consisting of just one paragraph. It is unique to the *Primary Chronicle* and thus its representation of princes as equals cannot be checked against any other source.

The situation wherein most information on social and political history comes from just one chronicle compilation changes in the second quarter of the twelfth century. Existing evidence indicates that during the hundred years preceding the Mongol conquest (1230s), centres of written culture proliferated greatly. Unfortunately, historiographical works apparently produced in these centres exist only as parts of later compilations. The notion that multiple extinct chronicles must have been available to the compilers is universally accepted, although textual scholars disagree about proposed reconstructions of the compilations' sources. One indication of the multiplicity of sources used in the compilations is their inconsistent chronological style. An analysis of the dates of eclipses, movable feasts, and occasional references to the day of the week on which a particular holiday fell in a given year, shows a shifting between the two different ways of year numbering used by East Slavonic *literati*. A shift in the chronological style is often accompanied by a shift in the spatial focus of the narrative, so that a group of annals describing events in a particular centre uses one chronological system, while a group of annals concentrating on a different centre uses the other system. The explanation that presents itself is that these annals are taken from two different chronicles.[102]

To complicate matters further, most chronicle compilations survive only in late copies. The earliest existing chronicle manuscript contains the so-called "older" redaction of the *Novgorodian First Chronicle*. The manuscript consists of two parts, which apparently were produced separately and bound together at a later date; the first part is datable to the thirteenth century.[103] Other chronicles are found in massive codices containing collections of various texts. The earliest among them, the *Laurentian Codex*, was, according to its colophon, copied from some "very old books" by a certain monk Laurentius in 1377, in the town of Suzdal. The *Laurentian* starts with the *Primary Chronicle*, thus containing its earliest surviving copy which ends abruptly in mid-sentence in the entry for 1110; its continuation in the *Laurentian Codex* covers the period

---

[102] N. G. Berezhkov, *Khronologiia russkogo letopisaniia* (Moscow: Izdatelstvo Akademii Nauk SSSR, 1963). Strictly speaking, Rusian sources know three chronological styles—two native, and one borrowed from Byzantium—but the Byzantine way to begin the year on September 1 crops up in the chronicles only sporadically. The occasional passages with the Byzantine dating found in the chronicles were probably interpolated from non-annalistic sources.

[103] Nasonov, Introduction to N1L, 5–7.

from for 1111 to 1304 and is usually referred to as the *Suzdalian Chronicle*. In addition, the *Laurentian Codex* contains the works by Vladimir Monomakh: the *Instruction* for Monomakh's sons, a rare example of a mirror for princes in Rusian literature, a letter to another prince with a peace offer, and a prayer probably composed by Monomakh, all of which are interpolated into the *Laurentian* redaction of the *Primary Chronicle*'s entry for 1096.[104]

Another important manuscript is the *Hypatian Codex* datable to the early fifteenth century; there are also several later copies which apparently go back to the *Hypatian*. In the seventeenth century, the *Hypatian Codex* was located in St. Hypatius's monastery in the provincial town of Kostroma in northern Russia, but it is unknown how long it had been there and where it was produced. It is believed to be a copy of a late thirteenth- or early fourteenth-century text probably compiled in the south-western Galician-Volhynian principality.[105] The *Hypatian* begins with the *Primary Chronicle*, and then it seamlessly transitions into a continuation known as the *Kievan Chronicle*, which ends with an elaborate eulogy for Prince Riurik Rostislavich in the entry for 1198/9; the eulogy appears to be produced as a separate text that was interpolated in the chronicle. It is followed by what is known as the *Galician-Volhynian Chronicle* which describes the history of the Galician-Volhynian principality in the thirteenth century and ends at the entry for 1292.[106]

There is no need to go over other codices. The brief overview of the *Laurentian* and the *Hypatian* offered above suffices to show the character of sources available to scholars of Rusian social and political history.[107] Even though such sources need to be used with caution, there is sufficient evidence indicating that accounts of twelfth- and early thirteenth-century events found in late compilations were, indeed, copied from chronicles produced at the time, and not invented by later scribes. One example of such evidence is the account of a rivalry between several aspiring princes of Suzdalia in the 1170s. "Suzdalia" is the conventional name for the north-eastern Rusian principality

---

[104] On the editions and bibliography of the *Laurentian Codex*, see *Pismennye pamiatniki*, 23–26.

[105] PSRL 2; Omeljan Pritsak, ed. *The Old Rus' Kievan and Galician-Volhynian Chronicles: The Ostroz'kyj (Xlebnikov) and Cetvertyns'kyj (Pogodin) Codices*, Harvard Library of Early Ukrainian Literature: Text Series 8 (Cambridge, MA: Harvard University Press, 1990).

[106] Pritsak, Introduction to *The Old Rus' Kievan and Galician-Volhynian Chronicles*; Kloss, Introduction to the reprint of PSRL 2 at www.lrc-lib.ru/rus_letopisi/Ipatius/preface.htm. *Pismennye pamiatniki*, 26–28, see ibid. for bibliography; an important study of the *Galician-Volhynian* that appeared after *Pismennye pamiatniki* is *Galitsko-volynskaia letopis: Tekst, kommentarii, issledovanie*, ed. M. F. Kotliar, V. Iu. Franchuk, and A. G. Plakhonin (St. Petersburg: Aleteia, 2005).

[107] Scholars of the social and political history of Rus have to rely heavily on chronicles that survived in later copies because of the character of the extant authentic pre-Mongol sources. The majority of approximately 300 East Slavonic manuscript books and book fragments from the period before 1300 are liturgical (Franklin, *Writing, Society and Culture*, 23). Authentic contemporary sources related to social and economic history are represented by excavated birchbark letters, but they are too fragmentary to be of much use for subjects discussed in this book.

whose early rulers were based in the town of Suzdal. In the later twelfth century, Suzdal, as the most important centre of the region, was eclipsed by the town of Vladimir.[108] During the 1170s struggle for the princely seat of Suzdalia, the communities of Vladimir and Suzdal supported different contenders. The *Suzdalian Chronicle* gives an emotional account of these events, written from the perspective of the Vladimir townsmen. For the author, the vile men of Suzdal contrive evil against "our town" and fight against the rightful prince supported by the Holy Mother of God herself, to whom the cathedral of Vladimir was dedicated.[109] Laurentius, writing in Suzdal, could hardly refer to Vladimir as "our town" and represent the men of Suzdal as evil; in all likelihood, he, indeed, copied this account from his "old books."

Moreover, very similar narratives, best described as redactions of the same text, are found in codices that are otherwise completely different from the *Laurentian*. Thus, a fifteenth-century collection of diverse texts, ranging from several biblical books to a Slavonic translation of Josephus's *Jewish War*, includes a chronicle compilation, part of which is essentially the same text as the *Suzdalian Chronicle* for the period from 1138/9 to 1214/15, with some editorial touches and a few additions concerning events in the town of Pereiaslavl-Zalessky.[110] The same chronicle, only this time for the period from 1110/11 to 1205/6, is found in yet another fifteenth-century collection of various texts, which survived in two different copies. One copy, known as the *Radziwill Codex*, simply ends at the year 1205/6; in another copy, the chronicle is continued to the entry for 1419, but after the year 1205/6, it diverges from the *Suzdalian* and turns to events in other regions.[111] These collections were apparently produced independently of one another,[112] and the presence of redactions of the same text in all of them is best explained by postulating the existence of an actual chronicle completed in Suzdalia in the early thirteenth century, which received two different continuations, to 1307 in the *Laurentian*, and to 1419 in another codex.

---

108 On the term "Suzdalia," see A. A. Gorskii, "Poniatie 'suzdalskii' v politicheskom leksikone XII–XIV vekov," in *Na poroge tysiachetiletiia. Suzdal v istorii I culture Rossii: k 990-letiiu pervogo upominaniia Suzdalia v drevnerusskikh letopisiakh*, ed. M. E. Rodina (Vladimir: GVSMZ, 2015), 27–32.
109 PSRL 1, 377–78.
110 *Letopisets Pereiaslavlia-Russkogo (Letopisets russkikh tsarei)*, ed. B. A. Rybakov and V. I. Buganov, Polnoe sobranie russkikh letopisei, vol. 41 (Moscow: Arkheograficheskii tsentr, 1995), hereafter PSRL 41; see also O. V. Tvorogov, "Khronograph Arkhivskii," in *Slovar knizhnikov i knizhnosti Drevnei Rusi*, at http://enc-dic.com/rusbooks/Hronograf-arhivski-537.html.
111 *Radzivillovskaia letopis*, ed. B. A. Rybakov, Polnoe sobranie russkikh letopisei, vol. 38 (Moscow and Leningrad: Izdatelstvo Akademii nauk, 1989), hereafter PSRL 38. The text of the *Radzivill Chronicle* can be followed by referring to the variant readings of the *Laurentian* in PSRL 1; there is also a facsimile edition: *Radzivillovskaia letopis. Tekst, issledovaniia, opisanie miniatiur*, ed. M. V. Kukushkina and G. M. Prokhorov, 2 vols. (Moscow: Glagol, 1994–1995).
112 O. Tolochko, "Notes on the *Radziwiłł Codex*," *Studi Slavistici* 10 (2013): 29–42; Kloss, Introduction to PSRL 1, reprint 1997.

This postulation is further confirmed by the fact that most events described in the part of the *Suzdalian* covering the twelfth century are reported in other chronicle compilations as well.[113] The master narrative of the events in twelfth- and early thirteenth-century Rus that emerges from different compilations is the same; it is the details and the authorial points of view that differ. For example, information about an 1195–1197 conflict between the Kievan prince Rurik and Vsevolod the "Big Nest" of Vladimir is found in several chronicles, with the *Novgorodain First* mentioning it in passing, the *Kievan* presenting it from a pro-Rurik standpoint, and the *Suzdalian* supporting Vsevolod.[114] Another example is an armed conflict between the same Vsevolod and some other princes whom he defeated and took prisoner. The *Kievan* and the *Novgorodian First* report that Vsevolod blinded two of these princes before releasing them from captivity.[115] An account of the conflict and the imprisonment of Vsevolod's defeated enemies is found in the *Suzdalian* as well; it also reports that Vladimir townsmen demanded that Vsevolod executed or blinded the prisoners, crying "Why to hold them here?" One redaction has a blank spot after the words, "And Prince Vsevolod, being sad and not able to restrain the people because a multitude of them issued a battle cry [...]" The sentence is unfinished, and after the blank spot a new entry begins. Another redaction similarly refers to the Vladimir mob expressing their hate for the captured princes and yelling, "Why to hold them here?" but then nonsensically states, "And they were released," as if the prisoners' haters wanted to see them free. Apparently, Vsevolod's apologist simply left out the part about the blinding.[116]

This episode exemplifies two features of many Rusian chronicle narratives: partisanship and a rather basic level of literary skills. Most chronicles are essentially apologies of individual princely families and/or particular communities: the *Suzdalian* extols Vsevolod's family and the town of Vladimir that supported this family against rival princes; the *Novgorodian First* expresses the perspective of the Novgorodian regional elite, consisting of ecclesiastics, merchants, and non-princely nobles; while the *Galician-Volhynian* extols the local princely family and vilifies the non-princely elite of Galich for challenging the prince's authority.

The *Hypatian* redaction of the *Kievan Chronicle* presents an unusual, and very interesting, case: it is a panoply of narratives, written on behalf of different princes, often having a dispute or a feud with one another. These narratives are sometimes combined rather crudely, as in the account of the murder of Prince Igor Olgovich in the entry for

---

[113] A nice review of the chronicle information about Suzdalia can be found in E. L. Koniavskaia, "Suzdalskaia zemlia ot Iuriia Dolgorukogo do Aleksandra Nevskogo (po rannim pismennym istochnikam)," in *Na poroge tysiachetiletiia. Suzdal v istorii I culture Rossii*, 33–42.

[114] Berezhkov, *Khronologiia*, 207–8.

[115] PSRL 2, 606; *Moskovskii letopisnyi svod kontsa XV v.*, ed. M. N. Tikhomirov, Polnoe sobranie russkikh letopisei, vol. 25 (Moscow-Leningrad: Izdatelstvo Akademii nauk SSSR, 1949; reprinted: Moscow: Iazyki slavianskikh kultur, 2004, with a new introduction by B. M. Kloss), hereafter PSRL 25, 89; N1L, 35.

[116] PSRL 1, 383–86.

1147. Igor ruled in Kiev briefly before he was overthrown by the supporters of Iziaslav Mstislavich, who became the Kievan prince and had Igor tonsured. Iziaslav was on a campaign, when he found out that Igor's kinsmen, bound to Iziaslav by an oath, planned to kill him treacherously and thus to avenge Igor's overthrow. When this news reached Kiev, an angry mob broke into the monastery where Igor was and lynched him.

These events are reported in all the redactions of the *Kievan* from a pro-Iziaslav standpoint: his brother, left in charge of Kiev in Iziaslav's absence, risks his own life in a failed attempt to save Igor from the mob; Iziaslav laments Igor's death and is told by his men that the ultimate responsibility lay upon Igor's plotting kinsmen. The overall message is that, while no-one deserves to be lynched, Igor was a bad prince who had it coming to him.[117] All these statements are present in the *Hypatian* redaction as well. However, there they are interspersed with statements to the contrary. In the *Hypatian*, Igor is a bad prince in one paragraph and a saintly martyr in the next; Iziaslav, sad and angry at the Kievans upon hearing about the lynching, is absolved from all responsibility for Igor's murder; but soon thereafter he is presented as its instigator and Igor's kinsmen are approvingly quoted as saying, "He killed our brother."[118]

The impression is that the compiler, while working on the entry for 1147, had in front of him two different narratives with opposing messages, and that he copied passages from both almost at random. It does not appear too big a stretch to suppose that one of these narratives was sponsored by Iziaslav and the other by Igor's kinsmen, the Olgovichi of Chernigov. In fact, a number of the annals in the *Hypatian* redaction look very much like excerpts from a Chernigov chronicle, while some others read almost like pages from Iziaslav's biography. These pro-Iziaslav pieces stand out by their literary merit and effective rhetorical strategies, suggesting that they were originally produced by a single author who happened to be a rather sophisticated writer. It is thus likely that the compiler of the *Hypatian* reduction of the *Kievan Chronicle* used a Chernigov chronicle and a pro-Iziaslav literary work.[119]

Not all parts of the *Kievan Chronicle* lend themselves so easily for hypothesizing about their sources. Its accounts of conflicts often include monotonous reports of what all the involved parties did and said without any comments that would express the author's position. A typical passage reads like this:

> In the year 1133. [...] Iaropolk gave Pereiaslavl to Vsevolod Mstislavich [...] Vsevolod's uncle George drove him out of Pereiaslavl. George stayed there

---

117 PSRL 1, 316–18; PSRL 23, 34–35; PSRL 25, 42. In addition, a laconic, one-sentence report of the murder is found in the *Novgorodian Frist* ("In the same year, the Kievans killed Igor Olgovich," N1L, 29).

118 PSRL 2, 352–55, 376.

119 P. P. Tolochko, *Russkie letopisi i letopistsy X–XII vv.* (St. Petersburg: Aleteia, 2003); T. L. Vilkul, "O proiskhozhdenii obshchego teksta Ipatevskoi i Lavrentevskoi letopisi za XII vek (predvaritelnye zametki)," *Palaeoslavica* 13 (2005): 31–37; V. A. Melnichuk, "Letopisanie dvukh vetvei dinastii Olgovichei v sostave Kievskogo svoda XII veka: tekst i kontekst, in *Izvestiia Uralskogo federalnogo universiteta: Gumanitarnye nauki* 105 (2012): 170–79.

for eight days; then Iaropolk made him leave, in accordance with the oath on the Cross, and gave Pereiaslavl to another Mstislavich, Iziaslav [...] In the year 1135, George asked, and received, Pereiaslavl from his brother Iaropolk [...] Because of that, the Olgovochi started a war [...] They presented their request to Iaropolk, "We want what our father held at the time of your father. If you do not give this to us, do not complain about what will happen: you [plural] are to blame, and the blood will be on you [plural]." All this occurred because George drove Vsevolod from Pereiaslavl, and then Viacheslav drove Iziaslav from Pereiaslavl, and they joined the forces with the Olgovichi, and there was a great dispute (*pria*) and a great anger between them. The Olgovichi went [or: left, *idiakhu*], uttering a saying that "you [plural] started ruining us first." [...] Iaropolk made peace with Vsevolod [Olgovich] and gave Pereiaslavl to Andrew.[120]

Such an account leaves the reader wondering whether the compiler combined texts written on behalf of Iarpolk and the Olgovichi, or whether he possibly copied some kind of judicial proceedings or records of negotiations. A reference to the Olgovichi uttering their accusation against Iaropolk and his kin while "going" is particularly tantalizing. Was this their last word when they were leaving failed peace talks? The exact nature of the sources for representations of positions of conflicting princes will probably never be known, but it is evident that many chronicle narratives go back to texts that presented arguments of opposing parties in conflicts. Simon Franklun describes them as "legal documents of a kind [...] designed to justify or condemn, with written evidence, the actions of princes in the present, demonstrate or refute the legitimacy of current claims and campaigns."[121]

Offering alternative accounts of the same events, written from different perspectives and advancing interests of competing princes and communities, twelfth- and early thirteenth-century sources lend themselves to an analysis of power relations better than the meagre eleventh-century ones do, but so far their potential for clarifying the nature of princely authority has not been realized. There is, however, one aspect of twelfth-century sources that is regularly invoked in discussions of the political organization of Rus, and this is the existence of numerous princes based in multiple centres of power.

Rus and Its Princes: Alternative Interpretations

This multitude is, in fact, the main argument against seeing Rus as a monarchy. Ostrowski makes explicit the assumption underpinning the concept of "disintegration" when he writes that Rus was not a monarchy because "princes continued to rule in other towns, whether or not they were in line to rule in Kiev."[122] The proliferation of local centres, each

---

120 PSRL 2, 294–97.
121 Simon Franklin, "Literacy and Documentation in Early Medieval Russia," *Speculum* 60 (1985): 1–38, at 21.
122 Ostrowski, "Systems of Succession," 50–51.

with its own prince, is the cornerstone of both the traditional "disintegration" narrative, and the concept of the Rurikids collective rule which did not need kingship to be successful. Traditional historiography sees multiple centres of princely power as an indication of disunity and decline, while Shepard stresses the positive role that the princely "family concern" played by binding together diverse lands and promoting Christianity along with more sophisticated culture. However, a common denomination of the otherwise opposing views of Rusian political organization is the belief that princes acted "as if the land of Rus' were property to be divided up between all the family's members."[123]

The multitude of centres of princely power is rarely examined in a comparative perspective explicitly; implicitly, it is usually treated as a unique feature of Rus.[124] Ostrowski refers to multiple "local governments" as a reason not to see Rus as a European-style monarchy: since local rulers were princes and since most of them were not eligible to rule in Kiev, they did not comprise the ruling dynasty, but are better thought of as aristocracy. He also notes a virtual absence of references to Rurik from pedigrees of individual princes found in the chronicles, which signals a lack of the Rurikid dynastic consciousness.[125] There is plenty of other evidence showing that princes did not view themselves as members of a single Rurikid dynasty, in addition to that cited by Ostrowski. Probably the most telling in this respect is an account of the talks between the Olgovichi and the Monomakhovichi reported in the *Kievan Chronicle* under 1195. The Monomakhovichi proposed that the right to the Kievan throne should belong to them exclusively, to which the Olgovichi indignantly replied, "We are neither Hungarians nor Poles, but descendants of the same forefather as you." Therefore, they argued, they could legitimately bid for the Kievan throne after the death of its current occupant.[126]

The common ancestor invoked by the Olgovichi was Iaroslav "the Wise," the paternal grandfather of both Vladimir Monomakh and Oleg, the respective founders of the two clans. Oleg and Vladimir, however, were only two among Iaroslav's fifteen grandsons born in Rus. Iaroslav's daughters were married to foreign kings, and their children could not be expected to claim Kiev—but what about the progeny of Iaroslav's thirteen Rus-born grandsons other than Oleg and Vladimir? In the late twelfth century, there was a multitude of princes who were neither Hungarians nor Poles, who descended from the same forefather as the Olgovichi and the Monomakhovichi, but who, nonetheless, never claimed the Kievan throne. The Olgovichi's argument simply ignores them. The dilemma discussed at the talks is whether the Kievan prince can come from one clan only, or from

---

[123] Shepard, "Rus," 393.

[124] A short paper by Alexander Nazarenko is a rare case of an examination of the Rurikids from a comparative perspective. Nazarenko compared "collective lordship of the Rurikids over Rus" to what he saw as the Merovingians' "collective lordship" over Francia: both were ruling clans regarding their countries as a family property. A. V. Nazarenko, "Rodovoi siuzerinetet Rurikovichei nad Rus'iu (X–XI vv.)," in *Drevnie gosudarstva na territorii SSSR, 1985 god*, ed. A. P. Novoseltsev (Moscow: Nauka, 1986), 149–57.

[125] Ostrowski, "Systems of Succession," 31–33.

[126] PSRL 2, 688–89.

either of the two clans; there is no notion of a wider dynasty that would include all the descendants of Iaroslav, let alone all the alleged descendants of Rurik.

Moreover, the talks reported under 1195 were a very rare, if not unique, occasion when the Olgovichi and the Monomakhovichi acknowledged their common ancestry. Normally, they are represented as two different lineages; if family relations between them are mentioned at all, it is relations by marriage, not blood.[127] The notion that these two clans, along with all the other multiple princely lines, formed a single dynasty thus, indeed, may be questioned. After all, medievalists rarely treat all the progeny of a distant common ancestor as a "dynasty." If many ninth- and tenth-century aristocrats originated from junior Carolingian lines, while a number of royal thrones were occupied by representatives of different Carolingian branches,[128] does this mean that the top tier of the Western European elite of the time consisted of a single dynasty? Arguably, this is one way to view it, and this view may, indeed, be implied in the oft-used expression "Carolingian Europe." To treat Rusian princes as members of a single "Rurikid" dynasty is one way to view the top tier of the Rusian elite. This is not the only way, however; alternative approaches to the political organization of Rus may be possible and viable.

The alternative proposed by Ostrowski—his view of Rus as a "headless aristocratic state"—is based on an assumption that Rus could either have the Rurikid dynasty consisting of all princes, or no monarchy at all. After presenting his arguments against the existence of the Rurikid dynasty, he is left with the only option—to consider all princes as members of aristocracy. It remains unclear, however, why we cannot think of some princes as kings and others as aristocrats. Neither ties of kinship between princes, nor the fact that those not eligible to Kiev could "rule in other towns" are sufficient reasons to assign all the princes to a single category, either dynasty, or aristocracy. Royalty and aristocracy were interrelated by blood and marriage everywhere in medieval Europe and thus many regional rulers were kings' kinsmen. If the count of Vermondois during the reign of Charles the Simple was grandson of Bernard of Italy and thus a "distant Carolingian,"[129] does this mean that we should not consider his relations Bernard and Charles as kings, and early medieval Italy and West Francia as monarchies? Nor could aristocrats be related to kings only distantly. Burgundy belonged to the Capet family from 956; its dukes were often kings' brothers or junior sons,[130] but so far nobody has interpreted this as evidence that France was not a monarchy and the Capetians were not a dynasty.

Ostrowski is right in stating that Rusian sources do not know the ruling dynasty of the Rurikids; however, they do know two competing dynasties, the Olgovichi and the

---

[127] For example, PSRL 2, 308, 628, 659.

[128] Bourchard, "The Kingdom of the Franks to 1108," 133–34; Charles Cawley, *Medieval Lands: A Prosopography of Medieval European Noble and Royal Families* at http://fmg.ac/Projects/MedLands/FRANKISH%20NOBILITY.htm.

[129] Christopher Wickham, *The Inheritance of Rome: Illuminating the Dark Ages 400–1000* (New York: Penguin, 2009), 440.

[130] Cawley, *Medieval Lands*, at http://fmg.ac/Projects/MedLands/burgdintro.htm.

Monomakhovichi. As we remember, the founder of the latter, Vladimir Monomakh, became the Kievan prince in 1113, and his line stayed in Kiev until 1139 when the Kievan throne was taken over by the Olgovichi. For the next hundred years the two family groups competed for Kiev, which does not necessarily mean that the winners, when they occupied the Kievan throne, cannot be considered kings. After all, the late Carolingians and the Robertines/Capetians competed for the royal throne of West Francia for about the same length of time, from the accession of the first Robertine king Odo in 888 to the firm establishment of the Capetians with the coronation of Hugh Capet in 987. Unlike in West Francia, the competition for Kiev, of course, ended not with the victory of one dynastic line, but with the Mongol invasion. This does not mean, however, that the period before the invasion could not see a development of a European-style monarchy, as long as we do not subscribe to the teleological view of Rusian history as a process that was somehow predestined to result in the Mongol conquest. Our next task is to examine the relations between the Olgovichi, the Monomakhovichi, other princes, and the broader society in order to see if Rus can be considered a monarchy.

To do so, we need to deal with the question of princes dividing the territory of Rus "as if a family property." It is true that princes who did not rule in Kiev were based in their own centres of power. More significant centres are described in the sources as having "thrones" or "high seats (*stoly*)" and functioning as capitals of principalities. Lesser princes were located in strongholds (*gorody*) and controlled the countryside around the stronghold. The sources use the same word *volost* for all these princely dominions, whether great or small.

Princely Volost: Family Property or Rule by Assent?

The word *volost* (variant *vlast*) signified "domination," "authority," or "power." Thus, Rusian authors, in sync with their contemporaries in other countries, disapprove of a situation when a wife has a *volost/vlast* over her husband—that is, when a man is dominated by his wife or allows her to have power over him.[131] The same word also means "rule," as in the conclusion to an account of the overthrow of the Kievan prince Igor: "And this was the end of Igor's *vlast*" ("Igor's *volost*" in another redaction), that is, apparently, the end of his rule.[132] However, the most widespread usage of *volost* in political narratives is to denote a territory over which a prince exercises his domination, power, and authority.[133] Chronicles often treat Rus as a collection of princely *volosts*, and

---

[131] For example, "Love your wives, but do not give them *vlast* over you," *Instruction* by Vladimir Monomakh, PSRL 1, 246; "He whom his wife *vladeet* is not a man," *Slovo Danila Zatochenika, ezhe napisa svoemu kniaziu, Iaroslavu Volodimerovichiu*, ed. L. V. Sokolova, BLDR 4 at http://lib.pushkinskijdom.ru/Default.aspx?tabid=4942. *Vladeet* (*volodeet*) is the third person singular of the verb *volodeti/vladeti* which describes an act of having a *volost/vlast*.

[132] PSRL 25, 38; PSRL 1, 314.

[133] On the term *volost* in the context of princely politics, see Tolochko, *Kniaz v Drevnei Rusi*, 151–61; Gorskii, "Zemli i volosti," in *Drevniaia Rus: Ocherki politicheskogo i sotsialnogo stroia*, ed. A. A. Gorskii et al. (Moscow: Indrik, 2008), 15–17.

the twelfth-century chronicles in particular "speak of little else but princely disputes" over land and power.[134]

These disputes were indeed often conducted in terms of settling family matters: princes invoked their rights of seniority or the moral obligation of senior family members to treat juniors fairly. The general impression of a princely "family concern" is reinforced by the custom of referring to all princes as "brothers," regardless of how they were related biologically, and by the use of "father" and "son" as terms designating positions in princely hierarchy. On top of this terminology of artificial kinship, we often see the significance of real, biological kinship for getting a good throne or *volost*. When we read that the Kievan prince, an Olgovich, had the power to appoint the prince of Novgorod and was determined to keep it within his clan, but then changed his mind under the influence of his Monomakhovichi-born wife, princely thrones do look like family assets. The *Kievan Chronicle* matter-of-factly reports that a prominent Monomakhovich, Iziaslav Mstislavich, "sent a message to his sister, saying, 'Obtain Novgorod for us by asking my brother-in-law [to give it] to your brother Sviatopolk.' And she did so."[135]

However, for every little story such as this one, reporting cosy dealings between siblings and in-laws, there is another story complicating the view of princes as a property-dividing family concern. The problem with this view is that the "property" played an active, sometimes decisive, part in determining who got what share of it: Rusian sources display "a consistent implication that the prince ruled by assent."[136] An interplay between this implication and the family rules of seniority can be seen from an account of events in the principality of Suzdalia after its prince Andrew Bogoliubsky was killed by his servants in 1174 and died without an heir. In the aftermath of Andrew's murder, several members of the Monomakhovichi clan vied for Suzdalia; brothers Iaropolk and Mstislav Rostislavichi prevailed and took the princely seats in the two main Suzdalian centres, Vladimir and Suzdal. They swore an oath on the Cross to be good rulers and were placed on their respective thrones "with joy." The joy, however, was short-lived. The Rostislavichi confiscated the property of the Vladimir city cathedral, and their officials oppressed the population with arbitrary extortions. The people of Vladimir—at one point the chronicler calls them "lesser people"—found this behaviour unacceptable and invited another prince, Michael Iurievich. They were supported by ordinary members of other Suzdalian communities, while the elite (boyars) sided with the Rostislavichi. In spite of the boyars' political machinations and military skills, Michael and his humble supporters defeated the Rostislavichi, and he became the prince of Suzdalia.[137]

---

134 Simon Franklin, "Literacy and Documentation in Early Medieval Russia," *Speculum* 60 (1985): 1–38; on the charters see at 20, 22–25; on the chronicles, see at 21.

135 "Posla Iziaslav k sestre svoei, reche, 'Isprosi ny u ziate Novgorod Velikyi bratu svoemy Sviatopolku.' Ona zhe tako stvori," PSRL 2, 309.

136 Franklin and Shepard, *Emergence of Rus*, 196. Also see P. V. Lukin, "Veche: Sotsialnyi sostav," in Gorskii et al., *Drevniaia Rus*, 44–60, 81–93 for an analysis of the chronicle accounts about the political significance of local communities and about their interactions with princes.

137 PSRL 1, 374–77; E. L. Koniavskaia, "Letopisnye 'rostovtsy,' 'suzdaltsy' i 'vladimirtsy' vo vremia Iuriia Dolgorukogo i Andreia Bogoliubskogo," *Drevniaia Rus: Voprosy medievistiki* 58 (2014): 37–44

The chronicler presents Michael's victory as God's punishment of the Rostislavichi for breaking their inauguration oath and for trampling upon Michael's dynastic seniority which made him the rightful prince of Suzdalia: "God commanded princes not to transgress their oaths sworn on the Venerable Cross and to honour their seniors (*stareishego brata chestiti*)."[138] The Rostislavichi invoked God's wrath by breaking both commandments, explains the chronicler. What he does not explain is why nobody thought of Michael's seniority and his God-given right to Suzdalia before the people became disappointed with the Rostislavichi. The expression of their disappointment offers an interesting commentary on the concept of a princely *volost*:

> The people of Vladimir started to say, "We have accepted the princes freely and made a sworn agreement with them about everything (*my esmy volnaia kniazia priiali k sobe i krest tselovali na vsem*), but these two behave as if this were not their *volost*, as if they do not plan to stay here as our princes (*iako ne tvoriashchesia sideti u nas*): they plunder not only all the land, but even the churches. Take action, brothers!"[139]

The "action" they took was to support Michael, whose hereditary right to Suzdalia they conveniently remembered as soon as the need for an alternative prince became apparent. An invocation of the hereditary right shows that Suzdalia was, indeed, part of the princes' collective property, and to have a *volost* meant to own a share in the "family concern." On the other hand, Suzdalia was a land belonging to its people, and to have a *volost* meant to be a good ruler to the people. By treating resources of Suzdalia literally as property, the Rostislavichi behaved "as if this were not their *volost*."

This is not the only case when the sources alternate between representations of the *volost* as a hereditary property of the prince and a community ruled by the prince with the consent of the ruled. In addition, the *volost* may also be treated as a grant awarded to the prince by another, higher placed, prince—this latter case will be discussed in Chapter 4. One way to understand these contradictory representations of the *volost* is to think of them as "cultural models," a concept that Stephen White borrowed from cultural anthropology to analyze contradictory representations of the fief in the French epic *Raoul de Cambrai*. The epic, structured as it is around violent disputes over fiefs, knows no "authoritative unambiguous rule about fiefs." Rather, it presupposes the existence of a "malleable and internally contradictory legal culture or discourse that included several different models of what a fief was." Such "presupposed or taken for granted models of the world that are widely shared (although not to the exclusion of other, alternative models) by the members of a society" do not form a coherent system; they function "as resources or tools, to be used when suitable and set aside when not."[140] Apparently,

---

138 PSRL 1, 377.
139 PSRL 1, 375.
140 Stephen D. White, "The Discourse of Inheritance in Twelfth-Century France: Alternative Models of the Fief in *Raoul de Cambrai*," in *Law and Government in Medieval England and Normandy*, ed. George Garnett and John Hudson (New York: Cambridge University Press, 1994), 173–97, at

Michael's hereditary right to Suzdalia was such a tool for the people of Vladimir and their chronicler, and the account of his success in the struggle against the Rostislavichi helps us understand how rights to princely thrones existed "between the birthright and election."

County of Maine, Aquitanian *Castra*: Family Property or Rule by Assent?

The phrase about the birthright and election, as the reader may remember, is borrowed from a study of early medieval kingship, but it does not apply only to royal successions. Before the rise of administrative monarchy with its central control over local governments, we often see medieval sources representing various territorial units as somehow being, at one and the same time, a property of an elite family and a community ruled by assent. Two examples will suffice here. One of them is the account of the events in the late eleventh-century county of Maine from the *Ecclesiastical History* by the Norman historian Orderic Vitalis.

Control over Maine was disputed by the powerful rulers of Anjou and Normandy; in the 1060s, the Normans prevailed, but the *Cenomanni*, that is, the "inhabitants of Maine" of unspecified social status, soon rose against them. They expelled the Normans and sent an invitation to two brothers, marquesses of Liguria, to come and be their counts. The envoys from Maine explained to the brothers that they had hereditary rights to the county because they were related to Herbert the "Wake Dog," who had been the count of Maine before the Norman conquest. The younger brother, Hugh, accepted the invitation, arrived in Maine, and became Count Hugh V. However, the *Cenomanni* soon were disappointed in him. They managed to persuade Hugh that Maine was threatened by the Normans, who wanted to recover their possession of the county, and that it was too dangerous for him to remain there. Hugh decided to return to Italy; therefore, he sold his rights to Maine (*comitatus Cenomannensis*) to the local magnate Helias.

Orderic explains that Helias, and not somebody else, bought the *comitatus Cenomannensis* because his hereditary rights were as good as Hugh's. What Orderic does not explain—showing an affinity with his counterpart from Suzdalia—is why nobody had thought of Helias's rights before the discontent with Hugh became widespread, and why the envoys sent to Liguria had declared that "all the legitimate heirs" of Maine were dead, even though Helias was alive and well.[141] By the same token, the Ligurian brothers had not even known that Maine was their inheritance until they heard about it from the

---

177-78, with reference to Dorothy Holland and Naomi Quinn, "Culture and Cognition," in *Cultural Models in Language and Thought*, ed. Dorothy Holland and Naomi Quinn (Cambridge: Cambridge University Press, 1987), 4, 10.

141 Cf. the words addressed to Hugh and his brother by the envoys inviting them to Maine, "Mortui sunt omnes Cenomannensis principatus legitimi heredes, iamque nullus vobis vicinior est heres" with Helias's argument why Hugh should sell the office to him, "Cognatus tuus sum, domine, suffragioque meo sullimatus es in consulatus honore [that is, the office of the count] [...] me sicut te scias ortum de comitis Herberti progenie [...] consulatus stemma michi dimitte, quod meum debet

Manceau envoys. Through the envoys, the *Cenomanni* declared, firstly, that they were "keeping" or "guarding" the county on behalf of the marquesses of Liguria until such time when the latter would come and claim their inheritance (*hereditatem vestram* [...] *quam nos ultro servamus vobis*); and secondly, that they, the *Cenomanni*, were "having" or "possessing" the same county in peace (*cenomannicam urbem et oppida eius in pace possidemus*).[142]

So, "whose" was Maine after all? If we apply the same logic on which Rus scholars base their representation of Rus as the "collective property" of the Rurikids, we need to conclude that Maine was part of the "collective property" of the Carolingians, to whom the counts of Maine traced their descent. Or is it better thought of as the family property of Herbert the "Wake Dog's" clan? If yes, what were the rules of inheritance that assigned this property to individual members of the clan? Or was it the "possession" of the *Cenomanni*? These questions are impossible to answer, especially if they are formulated in a rigid "either/or" mode. Orderic calls the inhabitants of Maine the count's "subjects (*subiecti*)," but his idea of "subjects" apparently includes a capacity to choose their ruler.[143] On the other hand, is "ruler" the right word? By selling the *comitatus Cenomannensis*—in literal translation, "the county of Maine"—Hugh behaves like an owner of the county, not like its ruler. In short, Orderic's account of affairs in Maine is another illustration of the oft-repeated observation about the impossibility of fitting what we find in medieval sources into our modern categories of public and private, ruler and owner, citizen and subject.

Our second example of aristocratic rights existing "between birthright and election" and defying modern categorization is especially interesting because it comes from an account written from the perspective of a magnate rejected by the population of a territory that he considered his property. In this case, it was not a big territorial unit, such as Suzdalia or Maine, but a *castrum*, that is, a fortress and the countryside around it.[144] In the *Conventum Hugonis* (1020s), the Aquitanian magnate Hugh of Lusignan complains about how he was treated by William V of Aquitaine. Among other things, William did not help Hugh when the latter lost his rightful possession, the *castrum* of Civray. Hugh gives two reasons why Civray was rightly his: this *castrum*—or at any rate, part of it—had been his father's, and also William himself granted Civray to Hugh, presumably confirming

---

esse consanguinitatis jure." Note Helias's claim that he was behind the invitation of Hugh, which is consistent with him being named among the prominent men of Maine who greeted Hugh when the latter first arrived from Italy. Thus, he chose not to put forward his hereditary claims until Hugh was persuaded to get rid of the office of the count. *The Ecclesiastical History of Orderic Vitalis*, vol. 4, ed. Marjorie Chibnall (Oxford: Clarendon Press, 1973), 192, 194, 196.

142 *The Ecclesiastical History of Orderic Vitalis*, vol. 4, 192.

143 *The Ecclesiastical History of Orderic Vitalis*, vol. 4, 198.

144 On a typical *castrum*, see Bernadette Barrière, *Limousin médiéval: Le temps des créations. Occupation du sol, monde laïc, espace cistercien. Recueil d'articles* (Limoges: Presses universitaires de Limoge, 2006), 201; Dominique Barthélemy, "Autour d'un récit de pactes ('Conventum Hugonis'): La seigneurie châtelaine et le féodalisme, en France au XIe siècle," *Settimane di studio / Centro Italiano di studi sull' Alto Medioevo* 47 (2000): 447–96, at 480–83.

the latter's hereditary right.[145] However, neither hereditary right nor the confirmation of this right by the ruler of Aquitaine helped Hugh to become the effective lord of the *castrum* over the objection of the inhabitants (*homines*) of Civray.

"When they saw the oppression which Hugh made to them," the people of Civray, "not being able to bear it," did exactly the same thing as the people of Suzdalia when they were not able to bear the Rostislavichi's oppression. Just as the Suzdalians invited another prince with a hereditary right to their land, the *homines* of Civray "made an agreement with Bernard," another Aquitanian magnate with a hereditary right to Civray, "and handed over (*reddiderunt*) the *castrum* to him."[146] Hugh, therefore, complained to William:

> 'My lord, things are very bad for me, because [Bernard] has now taken away my property (*fiscum*). I beseech you and urge you by the faith which [stipulates that] a lord ought to help his man: let me have either a good *placitum*, or my property [...] or give over to me [Bernard's] hostages [...].' However, the Count did nothing to help, neither arranged an agreement for him (*nec finem non fecit*), nor gave over the hostages to him.[147]

Thus, Hugh describes Civray as his property, but he still does not request that the count of Aquitaine simply go and crush the resistance of the *homines* of Civray and install Hugh as their lord by force. What Hugh wants is some kind of arbitration between himself,

---

145 "castrum vocitatum Sivriacum [...] rectitudo erat Hugoni sicut fuerat patris suo"; "Comes [...] amonuit Ugonem ut fieret homo supradicto Bernardo pro ipsam partem de castro [Civray] qui fuerat patri suo"; "[Hugh] homo fuit Bernardi propter quartem partem de castro supradicto," *Conventum Hugonis*, 543–44. The discussion of Hugh's rights to Civray shifts between the whole *castrum* and its part. It appears that Hugh tried to claim all Civray as his paternal inheritance, but if this had not work, he would have agreed to a part of it. *Rectitudo* may be used here instead of *rectitudine* (just like *Hugoni* is used instead of *Hugonis*), and in this case it signifies "by right." On the other hand, it is possible that the *Conventum* uses *rectitudo* in the sense of "rightful/inherited possession": such an interpretation appears to fit well with the grammatical structure of the sentence about Civray, which would then mean "this castle was Hugh's rightful inheritance," and it also fits with another passage with "rectitudo": William "promisit ut benefaceret ei [Hugh] aut de sua rectitudine aut de alia quę ille placuisset," *Conventum Hugonis*, 547. If we interpret "rectitudo" as "rightful/inherited possession," this statement would mean that William promises to grant Hugh either land that Hugh consider his inheritance or some other land, provided Hugh would find this other land satisfactory.

146 *Conventum Hugonis*, 544–45. *Homines* in this context is probably also closer to the gender-neutral "people" than to "men" because the *Conventum* uses *vir* rather than *homo* when it refers to the "men and women": "coepit viros hac [=ac] mulieris," *Conventum Hugonis*, 546. *Homo*, of course, could signify a "human being," a "person" in general; for example, Hildegard was referred to as *homo* (Theoderic of Echternach, *Vita Sanctae Hildegardis*, in *Jutta and Hildegard: The Biographical Sources*, ed. Anna Silvas (Turnhout: Brepols, 1998), 131).

147 *Conventum Hugonis*, 544–45. *Placitus* could be used in a legal sense meaning a "plea" or "hearing" (Jane Martindale, "The *Conventum*: A Postscript,"14, in Martindale, *Status, Authority and Regional Power*, VIII; Barthélemy, *The Serf, the Knight, and the Historian*, 17); in the *Conventum* this word also is used in the sense of "meeting" or "negotiations" (*Conventum Hugonis*, 546).

Bernard, and the inhabitants of Civray, thus implicitly acknowledging the legitimacy of the latter's actions.

In fact, the inhabitants of the Aquitanian *castra* must have often acted in a similar way. Their regular participation in the distribution of the *castra* among the Aquitanian magnates is evident from a remark made in passing in the *Conventum* about William's agreement with the *homines* of another *castrum*, Thouars.[148] Even more revealing is the fact that the document written from Hugh's standpoint refers to his own *oppressio* of Civray. The *Conventum* presents all Hugh's actions as good and just; the use of *oppressio* in such a context can be explained only if this word did not have any judgmental connotations, but rather was a technical term for the actions of the lord that caused the discontent among the *homines* of his dominion. The existence of such a term suggests that *homines* expressed their discontent on a regular basis.

Oppressio is etymologically close to the East Slavonic *tiagota*, which signified arbitrary and/or excessive demands of the prince; the Suzdalian chronicler used *tiagota* to describe the bad behaviour of officials appointed by the Rostislavichi. The roots of both words have connotations of "weighing down" or "burden." This small linguistic parallel reflects a broader similarity between the accounts of relations between local communities and their *kniaz*, lord, or count. Neither Rusian nor Latin sources, discussing these relations and the distribution of the local centres of power among members of the elite, refer to any central realm-wide authority.

The Kievan Prince and Royal Power: A Hypothesis

Reading the *Conventum* or Orderic's account of the events in Maine, it is easy to forget that Maine and Aquitaine were part of the kingdom of France. The king is largely absent from eleventh-century regional histories and from various sources pertaining to local affairs which were managed by local elites—and yet historians of France tell us not to be "too dismissive" of the kings, even when they had less "temporal power" than many dukes and counts and "had little obvious impact beyond their somewhat migratory court itself." In spite of their "highly limited" authority, these kings "certainly kept alive and viable both the monarchy and the Capetian dynasty" and "thus made possible the great advances in royal power and royal governmental institutions in the twelfth century."[149]

These advances were initially very small. In the first half of the twelfth century, "few chroniclers [...] took note of the French king except when he intruded upon their limited worlds." Not that such "intrusions" happened very often, because the king was chiefly preoccupied with the safety of his own domain. The royal holdings were of "diminutive size," and they were interlaced with "those of local lords who possessed castles that dominated the vicinities. So powerful were these castellans that, for example, it was difficult for the king to travel safely from Paris to Orleans," the two cities on which his domain was centred. A complete "pacification" of the royal domain, so that it was no

---

148 *Conventum Hugonis*, 542–43.

149 Bourchard, "The Kingdom of the Franks to 1108," 121.

longer threatened by powerful castellans, was achieved only in the reign of Louis VII (1137–1180).[150]

Historians of France or Germany note the power of regional rulers and the fact that the monarch himself was a territorial prince, a "dynastically minded magnate," but they insist that he was more than just that. The great duchies and counties of eleventh-century France were "*quasi*-independent," their rulers were "*virtual* kings within their own territories" (emphasis added); the twelfth-century kings in search of means to enhance their power "acted no differently than the contemporary magnates," but, unlike other magnates, "the Capetians were likewise kings, a dignity that offered incalculable advantages."[151] In Rus, however, since the second quarter of the twelfth century at the latest, political power was so dispersed that local principalities were not "quasi-independent," but simply independent from Kiev—or so we are told. European medieval polities may have had weak kings, but it is taken for granted that Rus had none.

"Taken for granted" is the key here, because so far no-one has described concrete manifestations of this fundamental difference between the political organization of Rus and the rest of Europe. The full independence of Rusian principalities and the political power so dispersed as to set Rus apart from European kingdoms are assumptions taken wholesale from nineteenth-century historiography, and they need to be checked against evidence of the sources. A detailed investigation of power relations in twelfth- and early thirteenth-century Rus would require a separate monograph-length study. However, a question of the mere existence or non-existence of royal power in Rus does not require such an investigation. In what follows, we will briefly test a hypothesis that the Kievan prince had power similar in character to the power of medieval personal kingship that existed elsewhere in Europe before the rise of administrative monarchy. It is hard to expect the latter in a polity that did not inherit any Roman infrastructure, that was territorially bigger and more diverse than even the German Empire, and that had ample opportunities to engage in "predatory warfare," an activity which helped the Reich to sustain its "loose structures."[152] Indeed, there is no evidence of a bureaucratic administration of any kind in Rus, although some movement towards "more bureaucratic attitudes" is noticeable from the start of the thirteenth century.[153] In the absence of bureaucracy, the only possible type of monarchy that could exist in Rus would be "a mixture of the charismatic and the patrimonial" typical of personal kingship.

In a personal monarchy, the king ruled directly only his own royal domain, which could well be smaller in size and poorer in resources than the domains of leading

---

[150] Bourchard, "The Kingdom of the Franks to 1108," 511.

[151] Nelson, "Rulers and Government," 114; Reuter, *Medieval Polities*, 410; Bourchard, "The Kingdom of the Franks to 1108," 132; Baldwin, "Crown and Government," 512–13.

[152] Reuter, *Medieval Polities*, 403.

[153] Franklin, "Literacy and Documentation," 35–36; T. V. Gimon, "Drevnerusskie sudebnye dokumenty XIII-XIV vekov," in *Pismo i povsednevnost*, ed. A. O. Chubarian (Moscow: IVI RAN, 2016), 18–48.

magnates of the kingdom. There was thus no central government in the sense that these words acquired later, but, as Janet Nelson remarks in her discussion of tenth-century West Francia, "the notion of 'government' can be variously defined." For one, kings everywhere in medieval Europe, except in Italy, had a special rapport with the church; even when the West Frankish king's military and political power was at its lowest, there was still "a sense of the king's uniqueness, and of his responsibility for the religious well-being of the whole kingdom."[154] The Kievan prince definitely shared this attribute of European kingship: he had special relations with the head of the Rusian church, the metropolitan, whose see was located in Kiev and who had jurisdiction over all Rusian bishops.

Metropolitans were normally sent from Constantinople, except for Hilarion and Clement (Klim Smoliatich) who were appointed by the Kievan prince and consecrated by a synod of local bishops in 1051 and 1147 respectively. The sources are silent about the role of the Constantinople patriarch in the first case; for all we know he might have blessed Hilarion *post factum*. Clement is explicitly reported not to be blessed by the patriarch, and for this reason his appointment was highly controversial with the Rusian ecclesiastical and secular elites.[155] The account of negotiations concerning Clement conducted by the incoming Kievan prince Rostislav Mstislavich in 1159 shows that Kievan princes played a special role in respect to the church, even when they did not try to bypass Constantinople in the matter of the metropolitan appointments. Some context needs to be established here.

The negotiations occurred when Rostislav received an invitation to occupy the Kievan throne after the Monomakhovichi led by Mstislav Iziaslavich fought off the Olgovichi; Mstislav took control of Kiev, but his right to become the prince there was rather dubious according to the dynastic rules of seniority. He, therefore, sent an invitation to the most senior Monomakhovich Rostislav, the prince of Smolensk. Rostislav had good reasons to suspect that Mstislav intended to be the real ruler and to use Rostislav as a figurehead, and he made it clear that he would not put up with this: "I will only go to Kiev on the condition that I have my full free will, so that you [...] walk in my obedience. Thus, I declare to you: I do not want Clement at the metropolitan see, because he [...] was not blessed by the patriarch." Mstislav, in turn, rejected the metropolitan who had Rostislav's backing. After "much dispute" and "angry speeches," the two princes worked out a compromise: "they decided that neither would occupy the metropolitan see, and they made a sworn agreement (*na tom tselovasta khrest*) to bring a new metropolitan from Constantinople."[156] Thus, exercising the actual power of the Kievan prince, as opposed to being one in words only, entailed an ability to ensure that the metropolitan see was occupied by the proper person. Rostislav did not declare his objection to Clement when he was merely the prince of Smolensk; Mstislav apparently showed his true intentions of becoming the *de facto* ruler when he invited Rostislav to Kiev, but did

---

154 Nelson, "Rulers and Government," 120, 112–13.
155 Franklin, *Sermons and Rhetoric*, xxiii, xlv.
156 PSRL 2, 503–4.

not accept his position with regard to the metropolitan. Overall, there is clearly a sense of the Kievan prince's "uniqueness, and of his responsibility for the religious well-being of the whole kingdom," to borrow Nelson's phrase about the French king.

Andrew Bogoliubsky, an ambitious Suzdalian prince, tried unsuccessfully to undermine this uniqueness when he petitioned the patriarch to establish a separate Suzdalian metropolitanate so that the see of Andrew's capital city Vladimir was occupied not by a bishop under the jurisdiction of the Kievan metropolitan, but by a metropolitan in his own right, answerable directly to Constantinople.[157] Andrew's failed campaign for the Suzdalian metropolitanate was part of his programme for putting Vladimir on par with Kiev, and it again shows that the existence of the metropolitan see in Kiev lent a special authority to the Kievan prince.

If we now leave the area of ecclesiastic affairs and look at the strictly temporal powers of personal kingship, one dominant theme of historiographic representations of these powers immediately catches the eye: a basis for royal government was provided by a combination of vertical and horizontal relations between the king and aristocracy. In the tenth century, "effective kings operated in both registers simultaneously," and "did not choose between these as alternatives, either cementing loyalty through horizontal bonds [...] or vertically asserting their own superiority."[158] In subsequent centuries, before government became more formally structured and professionalized in the late Middle Ages, "every ruler had to take counsel with his leading subjects if only because he would need to rely on them to carry out his commands: if his nobles did not agree to go to war and raise forces from their followers a king would have a small army."[159] The king's chief means to ensure that they would agree was to establish his suzerainty over the great magnates of the realm. In 1137, the famous ideologist of the Capetian monarchy Abbot Suger described this suzerainty as a hierarchy with "the king at the apex." However, for most of the twelfth century, such a hierarchy remained as much an ideal as a reality: its "practical effectiveness depended on the king's enforcement," of which he was not always capable, so that "even the royal panegyrist Suger was unable to conceal Capetian weakness when the king confronted great vassals."[160]

Even when the king lacked the institutional means to impose his will on the magnates, his superior status was attested to by the fact that it was he who rallied them against outside enemies. When France was threatened by an invasion from the German Empire in 1124, "magnates as far distant as Burgundy, Brittany and Aquitane, as well as from northern France," joined the king and deterred the attack.[161] Reynolds likewise refers to the participation of German magnates in the king's campaigns to support her thesis about the existence of an efficient royal government:

---

157 Shepard, "Rus," 394; V. Nazarenko, "Nesostoiavshaiasia mitropolia (ob odnom iz tserkovno-politicheskikh proektov Andreia Bogoliubskogo)," in *"Khvalam dostoinyi ...": Andrei Bogoliubskii v russkoi istorii i culture*, ed. M. E. Rodina (Vladimir: GVSMZ, 2013), 12–35.
158 Nelson, "Rulers and Government," 110.
159 Reynolds, "Government and Community," 95, 87.
160 Baldwin, "Crown and Government," 514–15.
161 Baldwin, "Kingdom of the Franks 1," 516.

Germans did not follow their kings to Italy merely for plunder or because each felt a personal obligation to his immediate lord: they surely also felt a duty to obey a royal summons [...] Some ignored their duty and some of them got away with it, but after Henry the Lion, the most powerful noble in Germany, combined absence of service with more open trouble-making, he was punished.[162]

To be sure, the punishment, in the form of confiscation of most of Henry's possessions, was carried out by means of a war against him: Henry was in no way prepared to relinquish peacefully Saxony and other lands that the imperial assembly confiscated from him. Saxony had to be invaded by Barbarossa's army; Henry submitted, and was consequently exiled, only after his allies deserted him and he lost the campaign. Nonetheless, for Reynolds, the ability of the monarch to assemble the German magnates so that they could jointly assign punishment to another magnate testifies to the existence of the "real" government and the community of the realm, internal conflicts and rivalries notwithstanding. What if we apply a similar yardstick to measure the power of the Kievan prince and the strength of the realm-wide community of Rus?

The "Real" Power of the Kievan Prince in the Earlier Twelfth Century: A Brief Assessment

It is well known that Vladimir Monomakh (r. 1113–1125) and his son Mstislav (r. 1125–1132) during their reigns in Kiev had sufficient control over other princes to be able to summon them to campaigns and assemblies and to punish the disobedient. Available evidence about the nature of Monomakh's and Mstislav's authority over regional principalities outside of their personal Kievan domain suggests that it was similar to personal kingship elsewhere: it was exercised through their relations with regional princes. The character of these relations can be glimpsed from an account of an agreement between Monomakh and Gleb of Minsk, which ended a military conflict between them.

Minsk, today the capital city of Belarus, was an important centre in the Polotsk principality, which was ruled by a separate princely branch. Gleb, a member of this branch, was already the prince of Minsk when Monomakh, according to the *Kievan Chronicle* entry for 1117, "gave" Minsk to him. The meaning of "giving" to Gleb what had already been Gleb's own domain is revealed by details of the peace agreement between him and Monomakh:

> Gleb, together with his children and his men, came out of his stronghold and bowed down to Vladimir [Monomakh]. They talked about peace, and Gleb promised to obey Vladimir in all things. After pacifying (*omirev*) Gleb and after instructing (*nakazav*) him about everything, Vladimir gave him Minsk and went back back to Kiev.[163]

Following Reynolds, one may interpret this scene as Gleb becoming Monomakh's "subject and office-holder." Alternatively, Gleb may be submitting himself and his land to Monomakh

---

162 Reynolds, "Government and Community," 106.
163 PSRL 2, 283.

as his lord and receiving Minsk back as a fief. One way or another, Monomakh's "giving" Minsk to Gleb evidently constituted Monomakh's sanctioning of Gleb's position as the prince of Minsk on the condition of Gleb's obedience, the arrangement that was similar to agreements that kings made with their leading magnates.

Monomakh and his immediate successors "gave" various principalities not only to the princes who already ruled there. In the 1110s–1130s, Kievan princes moved regional princes from one territory to another rather freely; however, as time went on, regional princes, like French or German magnates, came to be attached to specific areas and to view their rights to these areas as hereditary. This change is clearly seen in the princely career of Izisalv Mstislavich. In 1127, his father, the Kievan prince Mstislav, "gave" him Kursk, but two years later Iziaslav was transferred from there to the Polotsk principality. In 1132, Mstislav's brother and heir Iaropolk "took Polotsk from" Iziaslav and "gave" him the Pereiaslavl principality instead. After moving Iziaslav from one place to another several more times, Iaropolk "gave" him Vladimir-in-Volhynia, the centre of the Volhynian principality. The next Kievan prince, Vsevolod Olgovich (r. 1139–1146), first planned to send his own appointee to Volhynia, but, according to the chronicler, realized that this would be unrealistic, and eventually he "gave" the same Volhynia to the same Iziaslav who had already ruled there. No source informs us if the "giving" was accompanied by Iziaslav's promise "to obey" Vsevolod "in all things," as Gleb promised to Monomakh, but we do know that Iziaslav took an oath, the content of which is not specified, and that he participated in Vsevolod's campaigns after that.[164] Ever since, the Volhynian principality remained in the hands of Iziaslav and his heirs.

Vsevolod could hardly have been surprised by the failure of his attempts to deprive Iziaslav and other regional princes of what they came to consider their hereditary lands. Before becoming the Kievan prince after Iaropolk's death in 1139, he was the leader of the Olgovichi who "presented their request to Iaropolk, 'We want what our father held at the time of your father'" and started a war when the request was denied. Eventually, "wise" and "prudent" Iaropolk ended the war by "giving the Olgovichi their paternal inheritance, which was what they wanted."[165] Now it was Vsevolod's turn, as the Kievan prince, to "give" other princes *their* inheritances, which they wanted as much as the Olgovichi had wanted theirs.

By the later twelfth century, the Kievan prince could freely grant territories only within his personal domain, and he also had some leeway in sending his appointees to the important principality of Pereiaslavl located on the border with the steppe.[166] Other territories came to be seen as patrimonies of specific princely families. Gerd Althoff, while describing a similar development in the German Empire, calls it "feudalization of offices."[167] German magnates viewed territories under their rule as their hereditary possessions already in the tenth century, and when Otto the Great (r. 936–973) "sought

---

[164] PSRL 1, 296, 301–2; 307–8; 310–13; PSRL 2, 306, 310, 315.
[165] PSRL 2, 300.
[166] PSRL 2, 478–79.
[167] Gerd Althoff, *Family, Friends, and Followers: Political and Social Bonds in Medieval Europe*, trans. Christopher Carroll (New York: Cambridge University Press, 2004), 132.

to restore royal freedom of appointment in the face of claims based on inheritance and blood," he provoked a resistance "from those who did not receive the offices to which, in their opinion, they felt entitled." Otto, a remarkably strong and efficient monarch, refused to sanction publicly the treatment of offices as family property, but he often had to recognize the principle *de facto*, as when he allowed a count to divide among his sons "whatever he possessed as benefices and offices as if they were his patrimony (*quasi heriditatem*)." Eventually, "the royal recognition of dynastic succession" resulted in a development of a stable hierarchy of the ruling elites, "which was no longer subject to the constant changes," as had been the case under the Carolingians.[168] A formation of such a hierarchy in the Empire was part of a rise of a "smaller-scale, more personalised, lordship-based politics" that was occurring across Western Europe. When "larger-scale political systems returned" in the later medieval period, "local lordships did not go away," coinciding and interacting with the royal government.[169] An existence of a stable hierarchy of hereditary regional rulers is thus not an exclusive feature of Rus, and it does not prevent a country from having kingship.

Indeed, such hierarchies were typical of high medieval monarchies, with the partial exception of England, where the king had an unusual degree of control over the distribution of lands and offices. Even there, some earldoms remained in the hands of a single family for such a long time that it is hard not to view them as family property. If the Beaumont family remained the earls of Warwick from 1088 to 1263,[170] does this mean that they enjoyed the continuing favour of all the kings who ruled during this time, or that in practice the earldom was hereditary? Be this as it may in England, on the continent, duchies and counties were often treated as patrimonies of their ruling families in no lesser degree than Rusian principalities were. One example will suffice here.

Among the earliest high medieval texts attributed to a member of lay nobility is a fragment from what appears to be a chronicle of Fulk le Réchin, the count of Anjou (1043–1109).[171] According to the chronicle, Fulk represented the seventh generation of the family who held the honour of Anjou "by God's mercy" (*eumdem honorem tenueram adjuvante divina mesercordia*).[172] The first count did receive this honour from the king of France, but, judging from the chronicle, no king had anything to do with Anjou ever since. The current "wicked" King Philip I (r. 1059–1108), with whom Fulk had conflicts, is briefly contrasted with good Carolingian kings; after that, no other monarch is mentioned at all. The counts of Anjou defend their land from various enemies, conquer other territories, fight between themselves and with their neighbours—all these without any

---

168 Althoff, *Family, Friends, and Followers*, 124–25.

169 Wickham, *Medieval Europe*, 99.

170 Cawley, *Medieval Lands*, at http://fmg.ac/Projects/MedLands/ENGLISH%20NOBILITY%20MEDIEVAL.htm#_Toc388773412.

171 Nicholas L. Paul, "The Chronicle of Fulk le Réchin: A Reassessment," *The Haskins Society Journal: Studies in Medieval History* 18 (2006): 19–35, at 19–25.

172 *Chroniques des comtes d'Anjou et des seigneurs d'Amboise*, ed. Louis Halphen and René Poupardin (Paris: Libraire des Archives nationales et de la Société de l'Ecole des Chartes, 1913), 232.

interference from Paris. Nonetheless, their *honour* is part of a kingdom that the author calls alternatively *regnum Gallie* and *regnum Francie*.[173]

Vladimir Monomakh's control over Rusian principalities was evidently stronger than that of his cousin Philip I over Anjou (or Maine, or Normandy, or Aquitaine). Thus, Monomakh's "giving" of Minsk to Gleb was not a mere formality: two years later, he "took" it "from" Gleb.[174] The chronicler does not explain the reason for this, but the fact of the confiscation of Gleb's domain shows Monomakh's ability to exercise his supreme authority over Minsk; he had similar authority over other remote principalities, such as Volhynia, which he was also able to grant and confiscate at will.[175]

Of course, not all Kievan princes were as powerful as Monomakh, and not all French kings were as weak as Philip I. A detailed account of the evolution of the position of the Kievan prince from a comparative perspective is not a task of this book. Instead of such an account, which, in any case, would have many holes in it because of the fragmentary character of the sources, we will proceed with our brief assessment of the Kievan prince's powers, using again the same yardstick that Reynolds used in her argument about Barbarossa's effective government—the ability to punish a disobedient magnate by confiscating his lands.

Monamakh's son Mstislav clearly had such an ability: after the princes of Polotsk failed to take part in Mstislav's anti-Cuman campaign, he "summoned" them to Kiev, from where they were sent into exile without further ado; Mstislav "appointed his men to their strongholds," thus confiscating the domain of the guilty princes and placing it under his own direct rule.[176] The Polotsk princes suffered the same fate for their absence from Mstislav's campaign as did Henry the Lion for his absence from Barbarossa's Italian campaign—only Mstislav did not have to invade their land in order to carry out the punishment.

The "Real" Power of the Kievan Prince in the Later Twelfth Century: A Brief Assessment

The duty to obey a summons from the Kievan prince on pain of losing one's *volost* still existed in the later twelfth century, although "some ignored their duty and some of them got away with it" probably more often than at the time of Monomakh and Mstislav. The general idea of the regional princes' subordination to the Kievan prince is clearly seen in the accounts of the tumultuous events of the 1150s, when two rivals, Iziaslav Mstislavich and George the "Long Arm," fought for the Kievan throne. George was supported by Vladimir (Volodimerko) of Galich, and when Iziaslav prevailed and became the Kievan prince, he set out to punish Vladimir for his support of George. Iziaslav and his ally Géza II of Hungary went against Vladimir with their troops, defeated him, and then discussed how to proceed. Iziaslav proposed "to put him in custody (*imeve*) and to take his *volost*,"

---

[173] *Chroniques des comtes d'Anjou et des seigneurs d'Amboise*, 237.
[174] PSRL 2, 285.
[175] PSRL 2, 284–85.
[176] PSRL 2, 303–4.

but Géza insisted on leaving Vladimir in his domain on the condition that Vladimir returns everything that he had captured while fighting for George and that he swears an oath "to be together with Iziaslav, always, in all places, and never leave him in good or bad (*ne otluchiti ne v dobre ni v lise*)."[177]

This apparently was not meant literally, since Vladimir was expected to stay in Galich and Iziaslav to return to Kiev; in all likelihood, it was a formulaic pledge of loyalty and obedience. Vladimir made this pledge, but then refused to return the strongholds that he had captured while fighting together with George against Iziaslav; next, he died suddenly under circumstances that, to the contemporaries, indicated a divine punishment of his perjury. His son and heir hastened to contact Iziaslav and to fulfill the oath that his father had sworn and broken. He addressed Iziaslav: "I bow down to you, accept me so that I am what your son Mstislav is to you: just as Mstislav rides at your stirrup at the one side, I, with all my troops, will ride at your stirrup at the other side."[178] There is a clear connection here between showing loyalty and service to the Kievan prince and keeping one's *volost*. This connection is also evident in another episode from the 1150s, when the prince of Chernigov refused to answer the Kievan prince's summons. The Kievan prince then threatened to confiscate Chernigov, but was overthrown before he could carry out the threat.[179]

Volost confiscation is discussed again in an account of a Cuman raid into the Rusian borderland reported under 1177. Roman, a Monomakhovich and the Kievan prince at the time, dispatched four junior Monomakhovichi princes against a Cuman raiding party. One of these princes, David of Smolensk, was late to arrive. When he and his men finally joined the rest of the troops sent by Roman, the Cumans had already taken six border fortresses and were threatening one more.[180] The Rusian troops engaged them, were defeated and fled into the fortress; the Cumans then retreated to the steppe unopposed, carrying booty and prisoners with them. The Olgovichi argued that the Cumans could have been stopped if it were not for David's tardiness, and that David should be punished by the confiscation of his *volost*. Sviatoslav, the senior Olgovich, addressed Roman: "Brother, I do not seek any gain at your expense, but it is our agreement that if one of our men commits [such] an offense, he loses his life, and if it is a prince, he loses his *volost*, and David is guilty."[181] After Roman refused to carry out the confiscation, he lost the Kievan throne to Sviatoslav.[182]

Thus, in the 1170s, the Kievan prince was still expected to summon other princes to fight against external enemies and to confiscate dominions of those who did not perform

---

[177] PSRL 2, 451–53.

[178] PSRL 2, 464–65.

[179] PSRL 2, 499–502.

[180] PSRL 2, 603.

[181] "Brate, ia ne ishchiu pod toboiu nichego zhe no riad nash tak est: ozhe sia kniaz izvinit, to v volost, a muzh u golovu, a Davyd vinovat." PSRL 2, 603–4.

[182] The only account of these events is heavily pro-Monomakhovichi, and it is hard to reconstruct in detail how exactly the Kievan throne passed from Roman to Sviatoslav. PSRL 2, 604; Dimnik, *The Dynasty of Chernigov*, 135–36.

their duty satisfactorily. Moreover, a comparison of mid-eleventh- and late twelfth-century annals suggests that Kievan princes of supposedly "disintegrated" Rus had more institutionalized power in the matters of border defence than the celebrated "autocrat" Iaroslav. In fact, the very same *Primary Chronicle* entry for 1036 that contains the earliest reference to Iaroslav as "autocrat" describes a siege of Kiev by the Pechenegs (Patzinaks), the nomads who dominated the steppe to the south of Rus before the arrival of the Cumans. Iaroslav was able to lift the siege and put the Pechenegs to flight after a day-long fierce battle (*odva odole k vecheru Iaroslav*).[183] In 1036, the enemies could get all the way to Kiev unopposed, but in 1177 Roman dispatched princes under his authority as soon as a raiding party crossed the border. There was no question of the Cumans threatening a major centre, let alone Kiev; nonetheless, the Kievan prince was blamed for his failure to punish this incursion into the borderland and for allowing the Cumans a safe retreat.

Other late twelfth-century annals report that Kievan princes sent troops to patrol the Dnieper ford, which served as the main passageway between the steppe and Rus, and to guard important trading routes in order to prevent the Cumans from "harming (*pakostiti*)" merchants.[184] There is, of course, one famous late twelfth-century case of the Cumans besieging a major city, Pereiaslavl, sacking one significant town, and burning the dwellings located outside the walls of another one.[185] The Cumans did all this damage after they defeated a Rusian expedition led by Igor of Novgorod-Severskii in 1185. Igor was the leader of several insubordinate junior princes who invaded Cuman territory of their own accord and not on the orders of the Kievan prince. Igor's campaign and the subsequent Cuman raid are usually invoked to show the evils brought about by the "disintegration." However, these events are presented in the sources as an extraordinary disaster, not as something that routinely happened in the late twelfth century. Accounts of Igor's campaign and its aftermath—which are exceptionally detailed precisely because the 1185 Cuman raid was so shocking—make it abundantly clear that the junior princes breached the established rules by impinging on the Kievan prince's prerogative to send troops across the border. They acted "in secret" from the Kievan prince Sviatoslav, who was "displeased" by the unauthorized campaign even before he knew about the defeat.[186]

According to the *Suzdalian* chronicler, Igor and his fellow-adventurers claimed that they could attack the Cumans any time they wanted to and saying, "Are we not also princes?" thus implying that they were equal to Sviatoslav and did not need his permission to mount a campaign.[187] Such claims were clearly perceived as outrageous: the

---

[183] PSRL 1, 151.

[184] PSRL 2, 526, 528, 541, 673. On the trade routes and on the fortress near the ford, see Franklin and Shepard, *Emergence of Rus*, 324–28; A. V. Kuza, *Malye goroda Drevnei Rusi* (Moscow: Nauka, 1989), 73.

[185] PSRL 2, 647–48. On the sacked town, see G. Iu. Starodubtsev, "Gochevskii kompleks (letopisnyi Rimov)—gorod XI—XIV vv. na iugo-vostoke Rusi," *Sumska Starovina* 26–27 (2009): 166–71.

[186] Sviatoslav "slysha [...] ozhe shli sut na Polovtsy utaivshesia ego i ne liubo byst emu," PSRL 2, 645.

[187] PSRL 1, 397.

Kievan prince was not just one among others who were "also princes." Rather, the entries for 1185, found in the otherwise differing chronicles, show him at the pinnacle of the pyramid of authority. As soon as Sviatoslav learned that the Cumans defeated Igor and broke into Rus, he summoned (*posla po*) "all the princes, and they came to him and assembled in Kiev."[188] This statement is all the more remarkable for being made by the *Suzdalian* chronicler who generally supported the Monomakhovichi, and who had no motive to exaggerate authority that Sviatoslav, an Olgovich, had over other princes.

To be sure, the same David of Smolensk who had sabotaged the defence effort in 1177 did a similar thing in 1185. The summoned forces arrived in Kiev just in time to learn that the Cumans were besieging Pereiaslavl. Sviatoslav led the troops there to give succour, but the Smolensk contingent refused to go: David's men claimed that they were ready to defend Kiev if need be, but Pereiaslavl was too far away and they had been already exhausted by their long journey from Smolensk. This is the same kind of trouble that medieval kings often had with their magnates before the rise of administrative monarchy: in theory, the king was at the apex of an aristocratic hierarchy, but in practice the magnates' obedience "depended on the king's enforcement." In the age of horse travel and bad roads, the efficiency of the enforcement, in turn, often depended on the distance between the king's and the magnate's base of power.

For Suger, magnates "as far distant as Burgundy, Brittany and Aquitane" joining the king to counter an outside threat testified to the power of the French monarchy. Smolensk was about twice as far from Kiev as the capital cities of these French principalities were from Paris, and it was this faraway location that the men of Smolensk emphasized when they expressed their readiness to defend Kiev, but not other, less important centres. Being located in the forest zone, which was hard for horsemen to penetrate, they were safe from nomadic raids and could not care less about troubles of southern Rus.

It is remarkable, however, that the prince of Smolensk, who had no interest of his own in fighting the Cumans, still answered the anti-Cuman campaign summons issued by the Kievan prince, leaving an impression that something akin to a chain of command did exist in the late twelfth century. This impression is reinforced by the fact that David was careful not to take personal responsibility for staying away from Pereiaslavl, and instead blamed his men, who spontaneously held an assembly (*pochasha veche deiati*) and refused to move on. David probably did not try too hard to make them go on to Pereiaslavl, but the fact still remains that the prince of distant Smolensk, belonging to a different clan than Sviatoslav—David was a Monomakhovich—could not simply refuse to follow Sviatoslav's order, but had to resort to sabotaging it through covert machinations. By the same token, the prince of Pereiaslavl, a Monomakhovich, when threatened by the Cumans, appeals for help to Sviatoslav, thus treating him as the supreme ruler responsible for the defence of the realm.[189] Indeed, when Sviatoslav sailed to Pereiaslavl,

---

[188] PSRL 1, 399.

[189] Vladimir of Pereiaslavl, attacked by the Cumans, "sent to Sviatoslav, to Rurik and to David, saying, 'I have the Cumans here, help me.'" Rurik was the head of the southern Monomakhovichi clan, to which Vladimir belonged, and David was another important Monomakhovich. Nonetheless, Sviatoslav, an Olgovich, is the first on the list of those to whom Vladimir appeals. PSRL 2, 647.

without the obdurate Smolensk contingent but with other troops that he had gathered, the Cumans retreated as soon as they heard that the army of the Kievan prince was coming—a far cry from the situation in 1036, when Iaroslav had to give a pitched battle to the nomads besieging Kiev.

However, the most remarkable aspect of Sviatoslav's position is his lack of personal control over the territory centred on Kiev. This territory was normally under the direct rule of the Kievan prince. As we remember, before the later Middle Ages, a typical medieval king was also a territorial prince who ruled directly only his royal domain, which was his main power base and income source. A region in the Middle Dnieper under the direct rule of the Kievan prince played the role of the royal domain in Rus. In the 1180s, this domain belonged to Rurik, a leading Monomakhovich who had vied with Sviatoslav over the Kievan throne until they reached an agreement: Sviatoslav received "seniority and Kiev," and Rurik the "Rus Land," apparently in the narrow sense of the Middle Dnieper region.[190] The scope of Sviatoslav's authority, his power to summon "all the princes," his responsibility to fight external enemies attacking lands held by other princes of any clan, indicate that "seniority and Kiev" amounted to the position of the supreme ruler. A distinction that the 1180 agreement made between the office of the Kievan prince and the territorial power over the "Rus Land" shows that the two did not coincide, although normally they were in the hands of one and the same person.

The Kievan prince could raise an army by summoning local princes with their troops to fight not only external enemies, but internal rebels as well—although the word is never used by Rus scholars. Franklin and Shepard describe "a major military expedition," which included "a dozen of regional princes," and which was led by the Kievan prince Vsevolod Olgovich in 1144 against the same Vladimir (Volodimerko) of Galich, who later broke his oath to Iziaslav. The ruler of the increasingly rich and powerful Galich principality apparently strove to gain independence from Kiev, but failed to achieve this goal. The 1144 expedition on Galich was caused by Vladimir's objection to Vsevolod appointing his own son to a territory within Vladimir's domain.[191] It was not only Vsevolod's fellow-Olgovichi, but Monomakhovichi as well, who participated in Vsevolod's expedition, which ended with Vladimir "bowing down" to the Kievan prince and paying him a substantial amount of silver. While accepting Vladimir's submission, Vsevolod warned him: "You got away with this transgression, but do not commit any more."[192]

A historian of France writing about a dozen regional magnates led by the king against a local ruler who refused to accept the king's appointee would surely describe this as a subjugation of an aristocratic rebel—and would probably emphasize the number of magnates from faraway regions who answered the king's summons as evidence for the strength of the French monarchy. Historians of Rus, however, have never interpreted Vsevolod's expedition against Vladimir of Galich, or other similar cases, in monarchical

---

[190] PSRL 2, 624.
[191] Franklin and Shepard, *Emergence of Rus*, 329.
[192] "Se chel esi, k tomu ne sogreshai," PSRL 2, 315–16. On Vsevolod's reign, see also A. A. Inokov, "Vsevolod Olgovich—poslednii ob'edinitel domongolskoi Rusi," *Istoricheskoe obozrenie* 12 (2011): 23–57.

terms, because "king" or "rebel" are not part of their conceptual framework. These are notions from the parallel universe of the Western Middle Ages. It is in this parallel universe that scholars investigate the nature of relations between the supreme ruler and regional magnates. Rus historians rarely, if ever, pose the question of what made princes from faraway regions come to Kiev with their troops and fight under the command of Vsevolod or Sviatoslav.

In the case of Vladimir of Galich, we know that there was an oath or a sworn agreement of some sort that bound him to Vsevolod: Vsevolod's expedition to Galich was caused by a formal renunciation of this bond by Vladimir who made a charter with the record of an oath "thrown at" or "cast in front of" Vsevolod, a ritual gesture signifying a break of relations.[193] The charter did not survive, and its contents and date are unknown. What we do know is that a number of princes initially did not recognize Vsevolod as the Kievan prince, and he launched a series of campaigns against his opponents. Since he "sent" Vladimir of Galich on one such campaign, it seems safe to conclude that Vladimir did recognize Vsevolod as the supreme ruler before he became upset with Vsevolod's son.[194]

As a general rule, new Kievan princes are presented as "accepting oaths from," or "establishing the bond of love," or "making sworn agreements" with the leading regional princes, but the chronicles do not provide further details.[195] We do not know how typical or otherwise were the pledges cited above "not to leave" the Kievan prince "in good or bad" and "to ride at his stirrup." They do look like formulae, suggesting that similar pledges were probably given on other occasions, but direct quotations from a regional ruler's oath are found only in the account of Vladimir's perjury and his son's repentance. It is sometimes possible to tease out information about the contents of oaths and agreements from the chronicles, but this is not our task now—nor is the investigation of the complicated relations between Kiev and Suzdalia. In any case, full scope of the Kievan prince's authority and its evolution over time is impossible to reconstruct on the basis of available sources: our information too often consists of fragmentary "snapshots" open to different interpretations. We will conclude our discussion of the monarchy in Rus with two "snapshots" showing the relations between the Kievan prince and regional princes and communities from two different perspectives.

Vsevolod of Kiev and the Community of Novgorod: Two Sources, Two Perspectives

The reader may remember the chronicler treating the appointment of the prince of Novgorod as a matter of a family arrangement between the Kievan prince Vsevolod, his wife, and his brothers-in-law. Let us now look at the matter in more detail. According

---

193 "Roskotorostasia Vsevolod s Volodimerkom [...] i Volodimerko vozverzhe emu gramotu khrestnuiu," PSRL 2, 315.
194 PSRL 2, 304.
195 For example, PSRL 1, 306, 344, 346; PSRL 2, 318, 477, 479–82.

to the *Kievan Chronicle*, the Novgorodians "requested (*isprosisha*)" Vsevolod to appoint to their city his brother Sviatoslav. However, they soon turned against Sviatoslav "because of his wickedness (*pro ego zlobu*)," and requested that he be replaced with Vsevolod's son. Vsevolod granted this request and dispatched his son to Novgorod, but he also arrested several elite Novgorodians and brought them to Kiev. When Vsevolod's son was on his way to Novgorod, however, the Novgorodians changed their mind, informed Vsevolod that they wanted a Monomakhovich, and suggested that he appoint his brother-in-law as their prince. Vsevolod refused, because he did not want to "lose (*perepustiti*) Novgorod to the Monomakhovichi," even to those under his authority.[196] Novgorodians then turned to George the "Long Arm" of Suzdalia, who sent his son to Novgorod. "Vsevolod was angry at that"; consequently, he captured several of George's strongholds, "and whatever George's property he could (*gde chto chuia tovar*)." It was at this point that his Monomakhovichi-born wife convinced Vsevolod to "give" Novgorod to her brother Sviatopolk.[197] In this story, the princes do look like a quarrelling family and Rus like a collection of lands that comprise this family's property.

In the *Novgorodian First Chronicle*, however, the appointment of the prince of Novgorod is a matter not of princely family squabbles, but of the Novgorodians defending their interests vis-à-vis the supreme ruler of the country. That the Novgorodians recognized Vsevolod as such is evident from the way he was presented in their chronicle before and after he became the Kievan prince. Before, he was "Vsevolodko," the diminutive form, which is to "Vsevolod" what "Jimmy" is to "James." However, the main point is not that the Novgorodian chronicler drops the diminutive suffix -*ko* and adopts the respectful "Vsevolod" as soon as the owner of this name secures his position in Kiev. A change in the name form is telling, but more essential is a change in the Novgorodians' behaviour towards Vsevolod and other princes.

From the Novgorodian chronicle, we learn that Vsevolod's brother Sviatoslav had first become the prince of Novgorod when the former was merely "Vsevolodko" of Chernigov. In 1138, Vsevolod and his Olgovichi "brethren" had an armed conflict with the Kievan prince of the time, Iaropolk. After the outbreak of the conflict, the Novgorodians "dismissed (*vygnasha*)" Sviatoslav, but retained and kept in custody his wife and prominent men, "waiting till Iaropolk resolves the issues with Vsevolodko (*zhidushche opravy Iaropolku so Vsevolodkom*)." Apparently, the Novgorodians demonstrated their loyalty to the Kievan prince by treating in this way a close kin of his adversary. Essentially, "Vsevolodko" is presented as a rebel rising against the legitimate ruler. Not wishing to have a rebel's brother as their prince, the Novgorodians offered the position to Iaropolk's brother, George the "Long Arm," who dispatched his son to Novgorod for what would become the first of his two short stints there. At this moment Iaropolk died; soon thereafter, Vsevolod became the new prince of Kiev.

---

[196] PSRL 2, 307-8. At the same time, he "asked" the Novgorodians to give him "their best men," who were then "taken" or "arrested" and brought to Kiev (PSRL 2, 307). Vsevolod was married to Monmakh's granddaughter, the daughter of the late Mstislav the "Great."

[197] PSRL 2, 309.

George "called the Novgorodians to make a campaign against Vsevolodko." They refused; consequently (*togda*), George's son "fled from Novgorod," apparently fearing to stay in the city that was about to recognize the legitimacy of the new Kievan prince whom his father had planned to overthrow. Indeed, the Novgorodians sent envoys to Kiev inviting Vsevolod's brother Sviatoslav back and "swearing an oath," the content of which the chronicler does not describe; the context suggests that the Novgorodians pledged an allegiance to Vsevolod, whom the *Novgorodian First* stops calling "Vsevolodko" from that moment on.[198]

Sviatoslav soon displayed his unspecified "wickedness" and had to leave the city again. Remarkably, even in the heat of conflict with Vsevolod's brother, the Novgorodians showed obedience to Vsevolod himself. When he responded to the movement against Sviatoslav by arresting several prominent citizens and bringing them to Kiev in chains, nobody lifted a finger to resist. The significance of this compliance with Vsevolod's orders becomes clear if we bear in mind that the arrest, made by a man sent from Kiev, occurred in a city known for its strong, politically active, and often violent, community. The Novgorodians routinely expelled, or even arrested, princes; non-princely elite men could be subject to still harsher treatment. Thus, the Novgorodian governor who sided with Sviatoslav was stripped naked, beaten and thrown into a river. After he managed to get out, he was fined and sent into exile.[199] Episodes like this fill the pages of the Novgorodian chronicles; it is thus hard to imagine that Vsevolod's man could come to Novgorod, put prominent citizens in chains and leave with them for Kiev unimpeded, unless Vsevolod was recognized there as the legitimate ruler whose right it was to punish disobedience.[200]

The Novgorodians did confront Vsevolod about his brother and son being unacceptable to them, but they did so within a political framework that presupposed the supreme authority of the Kievan prince. To get a Monomakhovich prince, they requested Sviatopolk, a junior Monomakhovich and Vsevolod's brother-in-law. However, Vsevolod, as we remember, did not want to "lose" Novgorod. He reacted to the request by detaining men from Novgorod who happened to be in Kiev at the moment, in addition to those whom he had arrested before. The stubborn city still did not agree to accept an Olgovich as its prince, and turned to the only Monomakhovich not under Vsevolod's authority, George the "Long Arm." Approaching George appears to be primarily a demonstration intended for Vsevolod: even as George's son took the position of prince of Novgorod, the Novgorodians detained in Kiev kept insisting on their preference for Sviatopolk.

---

198 N1L, 25. "The Novgorodians sent envoys to Kiev, asking Sviatoslav Olgovich [to be sent to them as their prince] and swearing an oath (*zakhodivshe rote*)." Interestingly, at this transitional moment, the chronicler describes the Novgorodians sending their envoys "to Kiev." Probably, he is not sure whether the envoys were dispatched to "Vsevolodko" or to "Vsevolod" and wants to avoid the use of the Kievan prince's personal name.

199 N1L, 26.

200 In addition, to describe the arrest of the prominent men, the chronicler uses the word *pototsisha*, which implied that it was a punishment inflicted by a legitimate power.

The Novgorodian chronicler concludes triumphantly: "The Novgorodian bishop, as well as merchants and envoys, were being forcibly kept [in Kiev] (*ne pushchakhu iz Rusi*), but they still did not want any other prince except Sviatopolk. And he gave them Sviatopolk *i-svoeiu ruku*."[201] This last phrase literally translates "from his own hands" and probably refers to some symbolic gesture that accompanied the act of appointing Sviatopolk to Novgorod. It evidently conveys the idea of Vsevolod's agency: it is not the Novgorodians making a deal with Sviatopolk behind Vsevolod's back, but Vsevolod finally yielding to the Novogorodians' wish.[202] The omission of a personal name is telling: the chronicler assumes that the only "he" who really matters is Vsevolod. In the *Novgorodian First*, we see a drama unfolding between two protagonists, the community of Novgorod and Vsevolod, with other princes cast as background characters.

That George the "Long Arm" and his son were merely pawns in the game between the Novgorodians and the Kievan prince is evident from what happened after Vsevolod agreed to send Sviatopolk to Novgorod. As soon as the Novgorodians heard this news, they arrested George's son and kept him in custody until Sviatopolk's arrival, at which point he was released and sent back to his father. Apparently, the Novgorodians wanted to ensure that he would not try and keep Sviatopolk from becoming their prince. However, the significance of Sviatopolk stemmed not from his personal qualities, but only from his being Vsevolod's appointee: he was "dismissed" from Novgorod after Vsevolod died and his heir in Kiev was overthrown. As soon as Sviatopolk stopped being a representative of the legitimate ruler, the Novgorodians lost their desire to have him as their prince.[203] In other words, Vsevolod, during his tenure in Kiev, was perceived in Novgorod as the ruler of the realm, the Novgorodians as his subjects asserting their interests before the legitimate supreme power, and most other princes as magnates subordinate to Vsevolod.

From this perspective, George the "Long Arm" is not so much Vsevolod's equal, a rival in "interprincely strife," as he is a magnate whose base of power located far away from Kiev allows him to challenge the authority of the supreme ruler. In the *Kievan Chronicle*, Vsevolod's capture of George's strongholds and property may look like an act of "private" vengeance: George's son becomes the prince of rich and important Novgorod, thus frustrating Vsevolod's attempts to secure this position for his own son, and Vsevolod vents his anger by plundering George. However, from the perspective of the *Novgorodian First*, the same event may be better interpreted as a confiscation of a rebel's property by the legitimate ruler. The whole episode seems to fit best in the conceptual framework of "kingship"; Vsevolod looks like a monarch, using his family members as his agents and making political compromises when necessary.

---

[201] N1L, 26. Cf. Berezhkov, *Khronologiia russkogo letopisaniia*, 243.

[202] Rusian sources often use figurative expressions with "hands" while discussing power relations; being "in someone's hands" means to be subordinate to him, as if when a prince had to send his troops on a campaign he did not approve because he was "in the hands" of a senior prince who led the campaign, that is, owed service and obedience to him. See below, chap. 4. If being "in the hands" meant to be under someone's authority, then sending a prince "from one's hands" probably meant sending him as one's agent or appointee.

[203] N1L, 28.

Accounts of foreign relations reinforce the impression of Vsevolod as a monarch. Thus, as soon as his supreme authority was recognized by all major princes, "all the Cuman Land and their leaders (*kniazi*) came for peace talks." The Cumans were close neighbours, well aware of the situation in Rus. For them, political instability spelled an opportunity to raid, while internal order and a strong ruler in Kiev meant the end of raiding and the risk of a Rusian retaliatory expedition into the steppe. By referring to "all the Cuman Land," the chronicler underscores the scale of the peace talks which, on the Rusian side, were conducted by the prince of the borderland Pereiaslavl, the position that always entailed a prominent role in dealings with the Cumans, and by Vsevolod, whom the leaders of the "the Cuman Land" apparently perceived as representing "the Rus Land" as a whole.[204] The chronicle entry about the peace with the Cumans is followed by information about the dynastic marriage between the son of Wladyslaw II of Poland and Vsevolod's daughter; a "Rus contingent" that Vsevolod then sent to Poland, helped Wladyslaw against junior brothers challenging his authority.[205] From these accounts, Vsevolod again emerges as the supreme ruler of Rus, recognized as such by its neighbours.

The two images of Vsevolod in the chronicles are not necessarily mutually exclusive. Just as the German king was a supreme ruler *and* a member of "aristocratic commonwealth," just as the French king "acted no differently than the contemporary magnates," but was still more than simply another magnate, so the Kievan prince was a member of his family, his clan, and of the whole princely network; but he also had a special authority and was not simply one prince among others. The most obvious adjective describing such authority is "royal."

***

Late eleventh- to early thirteenth-century Rus presented a combination of vertical and horizontal power relations typical of medieval realms before the rise of administrative kingship. Horizontal bonds between royalty and aristocracy played an important role in early medieval Europe and were still present in high medieval monarchies. The

---

204 PSRL 2, 308. In the *Kievan Chronicle*, the peace with the Cumans is placed under the same 6648 (1139/40) year as the Vsevolod's agreements with the leading Monomakhovichi. According to the *Suzdalian*, however, the peace was concluded in the next year (*po tom zhe lete*). Berezhkov argues that the idiosyncratic expression *po tom zhe lete*, literally "right after the same year," must have been the original reading that was changed by the compiler of the *Hypatian Codex* to the standard formula "in the same year" (Berezhkov, *Khronologiia russkogo letopisaniia*, 141). Even if this is true, it is all the more remarkable that the chronicler makes a connection between the events of the previous year and the peace: the unusual introductory phrase *po tom zhe lete* frames the talks with the Cumans as a concluding event for the account of the arrangements between Vsevolod and the Monomakhovichi, which, evidently, compelled the Cumans to wish for peace with the now strong Rus.

205 PSRL 2, 308, 312–13. Nora Berend, Przemysław Urbańczyk and Przemysław Wiszewski, *Central Europe in the High Middle Ages: Bohemia, Hungary and Poland, c.900–c.1300* (Cambridge: Cambridge University Press, 2013), 175.

authority of the Kievan prince over regional princes was "a mixture of the charismatic and the patrimonial" familiar to scholars of medieval kingship.

As personal, non-administrative kingship goes, the Kievan variety was not even particularly weak: some twelfth-century kings could envy the number of regional princes answering the summons of Mstislav, Vsevolod, or Sviatoslav. What was, indeed, weak, was not the actual power of the Kievan prince, but its symbolic and ideological underpinnings. However, even in this respect Rus was in good company of monarchies without formal church rites of coronation and anointing, ranging from Merovingian Francia to Scotland.

The most substantial difference between the Kievan prince and European kings found in the sources is the use of the same word *kniaz* to describe the supreme ruler and lesser elite men. However, to use the broad range of the meanings of *kniaz* as a basis for postulating substantial differences in the political and social organization of Rus is to give an outsize privilege to words over concepts and phenomena. This is not to say that differences in Latin and East Slavonic terminology do not have any significance. One possibility is that the words used in Rus and Latin Europe, rather than describing different phenomena, emphasized different aspects of essentially the same phenomenon. A working hypothesis of this book is that Rus had both kings and magnates, much like other European realms, and that *kniazi* described the upper stratum of society comprised of royalty and aristocracy. A corollary hypothesis then is that East Slavonic gave a clearer expression to the continuum between the two, emphasizing similarities between the royal and aristocratic authority.

Western medievalists see the same continuum in their sources, albeit expressed less explicitly. Medieval Latin authors use different words for the king and his magnates, but their texts show that, before the rise of administrative monarchy, both royal and aristocratic authority was based on the grace of God and that monarchs acted "as princes in their own right, not just as kings."[206] Conversely, Kievan princes, as this chapter has tried to show, acted as kings, not just as princes in their own right. Arguably, the purported difference between medieval Europe as a collection of kingdoms and kingless Rus reflects not so much medieval realities as "parallel universes" of different historiographic traditions.

---

206 Reuter, *Medieval Polities*, 401, 410.

Chapter 2

MEDIEVAL TEXTS AND PROFESSIONAL BELIEF SYSTEMS: LATIN, CHURCH SLAVONIC, AND VERNACULAR POLITICAL NARRATIVES

THE PREVIOUS CHAPTER discussed the need for establishing a common ground between the "parallel universes" that are the historiographies of Rus and Latin Europe and some of the many challenges of this task. This chapter will explore the possibilities offered by an engagement with the two historiographic traditions for a better understanding of the interplay between medieval sources and modern interpretative frameworks. If "debates about the relationship between modern interpretations of the Middle Ages and the reality they claim to represent are, implicitly, debates about the protocols we employ when reading medieval texts,"[1] then looking simultaneously at two sets of medieval texts and two different protocols may bring implicit assumptions to light. Making protocols explicit would, in turn, help to reveal circular reasoning which occurs when historians read their sources "in light of protocols that exclude elements outside of their 'professional belief system,'" and then use such readings to reinforce their beliefs.[2] A question of kingship in Rus and Latin Europe is a case in point.

The discussion of relations between the Kievan and regional princes in the previous chapter presents something like a mirror image of recent discussions of relations between the king and aristocracy among Western medievalists. In Rus scholarship, the general assumption is that major princes were equals, and that since the second quarter of the twelfth century at the latest the Kievan prince was just one regional prince among many. The first chapter of this book argued that he was a regional prince—but not just a regional prince, that he was part of a network of interprincely relations—but also occupied a special position above regional princes, that he advanced his family interests—but was also responsible for the safety and well-being of the realm. In short, he was not just a regional prince, but also a ruler; all princes, although closely connected, were not equal.

What differentiates this argument from scholarly representations of the relations between the king and magnates in the medieval West is the position of "but" and "although." Western medievalists argue that the king and magnates, although not equal, were closely connected, that the king was responsible for the safety and well-being of the realm, but that he also advanced his family interests, that he was a supreme ruler, but also a territorial magnate. In short, they argue against the assumption that kings and aristocracy led "a zero-sum struggle for power," that their authority was qualitatively

---

[1] Warner, "Reading Ottonian History," 101.

[2] Warner, "Reading Ottonian History," 101, with reference to Robert M. Stein, "Literary Criticism and the Evidence for History," in *Writing History: Theory and Practice*, ed. Heiko Feldner, Kevin Passmore, and Stefan Berger (London: Hodder Education, 2003), 71.

different, that there was an opposition between public and private power, with the former belonging to the king and the latter to the aristocracy.[3] Western medievalists, until recently, emphasized vertical power relations and the public character of the royal power; Rus scholars, on the other hand, emphasize horizontal power relations and the private character of the Kievan prince's power. This difference is best seen in the way the two historiographic traditions present conflicts between the king and a magnate and between the Kievan and a regional prince respectively: the former is a rebellion, the latter an episode in "interprincely strife."

The "strife" of Anglophone Rus scholars is a translation of *usobitsa*, the word which Russian-speaking historians apply to interprincely conflicts and which may be better translated into English as "private feud." A scholar of Ottonian Germany notes that for the elite of the time "the boundary between a feud over ostensibly private matters and what, to a modern observer, would appear an act of political rebellion was fluid."[4] Modern observers of Rus and Latin Europe locate conflicts reported in their sources on the opposite sides of this fluid boundary. "A relentless struggle for land, high office and status" manifests itself as "aristocratic rebellions" in Germany[5] and as "interprincely strife" in Rus: the "political" versus "private" character of a conflict is in the eye of the beholder. This chapter investigates some reasons for the drastic differences between the beholders' eyes, that is, between the interpretative frameworks of Rus scholars and Western medievalists.

This discussion will be limited to reasons stemming from the nature of medieval sources, not from the preoccupations of the founding fathers of modern historiography. There is, of course, hardly an area of historical research that is not influenced by eighteenth- and nineteenth-century ideologies, with nationalism taking the pride of place among them. In the case of Rus studies, the traditional discourse on the position of the Kievan prince and on interprincely relations was partly shaped by the circumstance of Kiev and Chernigov being located in modern Ukraine and of Suzdalia and Novgorod in Russia.[6] This, and other factors that contributed to the formation of historiographies of Rus and the medieval West, but that are rooted in the modern, not medieval, period will not concern us here. Apart from various ideological lenses used by scholars of Rus and Latin Europe, the differences between the two historiographic traditions are partially explained by the differences in the general character of the sources.

---

[3] West, *Reframing the Feudal Revolution*, 101.

[4] David A. Warner, "Rituals, Kingship and Rebellion in Medieval Germany," *History Compass* 8/10 (2010): 1209–20, at 1211.

[5] Warner, "Rituals, Kingship and Rebellion in Medieval Germany," 1211.

[6] For example, S. M. Soloviev, *Sochinenia*, vol. 2 (Moscow: Golos, 1993-98), 120–22. For a review of Russian nationalistic interpretations of Rusian history, see Dmitro Nalivaiko, *Ochima Zakhodu: Retseptsiia Ukrainy v zakhidnoi Evropi XI–XVIII st.* (Kiev: Osnovy, 1999), 824; Serhii Plokhy, *The Origins of the Slavic Nations: Premodern Identities in Russia, Ukraine, and Belarus* (Cambridge: Cambridge University Press, 2006), 10, 17.

Rusian Chronicles: Elusive Realm, Ubiquitus *Volost*

The previous chapter offered evidence that the power and authority of the Kievan prince were royal in nature and that his position in Rus was not qualitatively different from the position of the medieval king before the rise of administrative monarchy. However, this evidence is based on snippets of information scattered over narratives that often leave an impression that Rus was, indeed, a collection of lands dominated by numerous unruly princes. Accumulated and presented systematically, snippets of evidence found in chronicles suggest that Vsevolod and other Kievan princes discussed in the previous chapter were indeed rulers of the realm. However, reading these chronicles in their entirety helps to understand why most historians are unaccustomed to think about Rus as a political entity on par with other European kingdoms.

The world of medieval Latin authors consists of *regna*. The prominence of *regnum* in medieval sources led Reynolds to argue that the kingdom was seen as "the highest, most honorable, and most perfect of all secular communities," the archetype of a political unit, while the king was the archetype of a ruler.[7] If in practice the king's rule was not always in the best interest of the community, the ideas of good government, and of the public good in general, still existed. They were conveyed by the expression *res publica*, which came into wide use during the "academic explosion of the twelfth century," but had been known to earlier medieval authors as well.[8]

Rusian sources know the type of community which, according to Reynolds, served as a basis for the *regnum*: the unity of the land and the people, when peoples (*gentes*, *nationes*, *populi*) were perceived "in territorial terms" so that they were "assumed to be one" with their lands. This worldview is reflected in the *Primary Chronicle*'s story about Noah's sons, who divided the world among themselves, and gave origin to all existing peoples still inhabiting the regions which were originally allotted to each son.[9] Humanity is divided into peoples (*iazytsi*) and the surface of the Earth into these peoples' lands; land (*zemlia*) with an ethnic modifier signifies a country, such as "Greek Land" for "Greece."[10] However, in East Slavonic literature these lands remain just that—lands, not kingdoms, and the sources do not have any abstract term for the commonwealth.

When Rusian authors expressed ideas that had connotations of the public good, they often referred to the notion of "peace." In this respect, they were similar to their Latin counterparts, for whom *pax* "served as a yardstick for measuring a sociopolitical order" and was associated with good government.[11] Rusian sources also invoked the well-being of the "Rus Land" or of "the Christians," that is, ordinary people, praising princes who maintained internal peace, defended the Rus Land from external enemies, and ensured

---

[7] Reynolds, *Kingdoms and Communities*, 250–51, 258–59; Reynolds, "Fiefs and Vassals after Twelve Years," 54–55.

[8] Reynolds, *Kingdoms and Communities*, 293, 325; Reynolds, *Fiefs and Vassals*, 25.

[9] PSRL 1, 1–6.

[10] Gorskii, "Zemli i volosti."

[11] Jehangir Malegam, *The Sleep of Behemoth: Disputing Peace and Violence in Medieval Europe, 1000–1200* (Ithaca: Cornell University Press, 2013), 6–7.

the safety of "the Christians."[12] In this context, "Rus Land" took a meaning close to the *res publica* of medieval Latin authors; however, on other occasions "Rus Land" was used in such a way that it may be, indeed, difficult to view it as a kingdom.

We have seen the Kievan prince Vsevolod acting as a supreme ruler: punishing those who refused to accept his appointees, summoning regional princes for his campaigns, and maintaining relations with neighbouring rulers. Nonetheless, most historians do not treat him as a king. Actually, neither do the chroniclers—in a sense. They do report events that are consistent with Vsevolod's status as king, but they do not put their accounts in an ideological framework of kingship. Such a framework would presuppose the existence of Reynolds's idealized political entity, a community based on the unity of the people and the land under the king's authority. However, the "Rus Land" of most chronicle narratives has neither clear territorial boundaries nor a clear system of rulership. The only thing that is crystal clear about it is that it includes multiple dominions called *volosts*, which are "held" by various princes—but there is no certainty about how these *volosts* and their "holders" relate to one another and to the larger entity of which they are parts. It is not even clear what is the name of this entity.

The chronicler refers to something that he calls simply "the land" (or "Land"?) in his account of the beginning of Vsevolod's tenure in Kiev, which we need to discuss at some length. Vsevolod was the first Olgovich to become the Kievan prince after the three successive Monomakhovichi, Vladimir Monomakh and his two sons, Mstislav and Iaropolk. After Iaropolk died, presumably childless, in 1138, his brother Viacheslav entered Kiev, but was immediately ousted by Vsevolod and left Kiev without resistance. Vsevolod then sent a peace offer to the leading Monomakhovichi, who may have been expected to oppose the Olgovichi takeover of Kiev. Indeed, they rejected the peace offer and started preparations for a campaign against Vsevolod, but he was too quick for them and attacked first. The chronicler reports—a more appropriate term may be "lists"—all these events impassively, without offering any interpretation or moralizing commentary whatsoever. Vsevolod is neither an usurper nor the rightful heir to the throne; he simply "entered Kiev" and began his rule (*kniazhenie*) there. Correspondingly, the Monomakhovichi are neither plotting a rebellion nor resisting an usurpation: all we are told is that they "did not wish" to have peace with Vsevolod and rather "wished" to attack him; he "did not wait for that" and struck preemptively.[13]

All these actions and "wishes" are presented non-judgmentally; the chronicler drops the tone of objective reporting and expressly condemns a princely behaviour only when Vsevolod goes beyond self-defence and displays an intention "to hold all the land alone." To implement the evil plan of "holding all the land," Vsevolod decided to appoint his brother to the strategic principality of Pereiaslavl, and he ordered its prince, Andrew, a Monomakhvich, to move to Kursk. Andrew valiantly responded:

---

12 For example, PSRL 2, 364, 392.

13 PSRL 1, 306–7; PSRL 2, 302–4. One chronicler adds that Vsevolod supported his message to Viacheslav with a demonstration of force: he started to set fire to the houses outside of the city wall (PSRL 2, 302).

My father was the prince of Pereiaslavl, not of Kursk. It is better for me to die with my men on the land of my father and grandfather than to be a prince of Kursk [...] If, brother, it is not enough of *volost* for you to hold all the Rus Land, and if you want this [Pereiaslavl] *volost*, then the *volost* will be yours after you kill me, but I will not leave my *volost* as long as I live.[14]

Thus, Vsevolod "holds" all the Rus Land, which apparently amounts to having so much power that it is outrageous not to be satisfied with it and to seek more.[15] This "Rus Land" must be something greater than simply a territorial principality of Kiev. Indeed, the chronicler later refers to the "Kievan *volost*" as the personal domain of the Kievan prince, which is evidently smaller than the "Rus Land"; when the latter is used in the sources in the territorial sense, it signifies the area in the Middle Dnieper that includes Kiev, Chernigov and Pereiaslavl.[16] In other words, the Pereislavl principality was somehow Andrew's "*volost*" and also part of the Rus Land "held" by Vsevolod as *his* "*volost*."

In addition, Vsevolod sought to oust the princes from Smolensk and Vladimir-in-Volhynia, located outside on the core Middle Dnieper region, because he "wanted to hold all the land." The chronicler does not explain what this "land" was and how it related to the "Rus Land." What he makes clear is that it included princely *volosts* which Vsevolod tried, but failed, to take from their legitimate "holders." This does not mean, however, that he failed to obtain any authority over these territories: even though he never succeeded in taking Volhynia from its prince Iziaslav, he nonetheless is later reported as "giving" the same Volhynia to the same Iziaslav. Thus, Volhynia, much like Pereiaslavl, was somehow Iziaslav's and Vsevolod's at one and the same time: it was Vsevolod's to give, but he could not give it to anyone except Iziaslav. Still later, it turned out that yes, he could—provided that Iziaslav got another, and better, *volost*. This happened when Andrew of Pereiaslavl died a natural death and Vsevolod "gave" Pereiaslavl to another prince who, with Vsevolod's consent, "gave" it to Iziaslav; Iziaslav moved to Pereiaslavl, and it was only then that Vsevolod could finally "give" Volhynia to his own son.[17] Thus, Vsevolod eventually came to have control over Pereiaslavl, Volhynia, and most other territories that comprised what is known as "Rus" in modern scholarship, but this happened not through a direct takeover. After a series of talks interspersed with demonstrations of force, most regional princes evidently recognized Vsevolod's supreme authority: they "swore oaths," the content of which the chronicler does not report, but from that time

---

14 PSRL 2, 305.

15 For "not enough," the text uses *ne dosyti*, an expression with a very strong negative connotation, implying an outrageous greediness.

16 For the "Kievan volost," see PSRL 2, 310-11, 314. For the usage of the "Rus Land" in the sources and for the territories that constituted the "Rus Land" in the narrow sense, see V. A. Kuchkin, "'Russkaia zemlia' po letopisnym dannym XI—pervoi treti XIII v.," in *Drevneishie gosudarstva Vostochnoi Evropy: Materialy i issledovaniia, 1992–1993 gody*, ed. A. P. Novoseltsev (Moscow: Nauka, 1995), 74–100; I. V. Vediushkina, "'Rus' i 'Russkaia zemlia' v Povesti vremennykh let i letopisnykh statiiakh vtoroi treti XII—pervoi treti XIII v.," in ibid., 101–16.

17 PSRL 2, 304, 310, 313.

on we see them participating in his campaigns and obtaining his consent for transfer of their lands.[18]

Along with these lands, the *volosts* that comprise the rightful dominions of regional princes, we see territories which the Kievan prince could grant according to his own choice.[19] From the chronicle accounts, the distribution of *volosts* emerges as a delicate balancing act: the Kievan prince has to be generous, but also firm: giving away *volosts* on demand signifies weakness. When Vsevolod made other princes swear allegiance to Igor as his heir on the Kievan throne, he admonished them to accept what Igor would give them "out of his own free will (*po vole*)," but not to pressure him in an hour of need (*po nuzhi*). Instead, when Igor encountered a plot to overthrow him and called on the princes who had sworn an oath to him, they "requested many *volosts*" as a precondition for coming to his aid. The chronicler does not tell us if Igor granted the request, probably because it did not really matter: the attitude of the regional princes shows Igor's position as hopelessly weak, and his overthrow appears a logical outcome.

The proper behaviour of a regional prince on a similar occasion is exemplified by the answer that Sviatoslav of Chernigov gave to the Kievan prince when the latter granted Sviatoslav two strongholds, while also informing him about a hostile coalition threatening Kiev. Sviatoslav admitted that he was angry at the Kievan prince for not getting all the territory that Sviatoslav believed was his due, but, he continued, "I never wished you any harm (*likha*). If they are now planning a war against you, God forbid that I seek a *volost* from you."[20] It is not right to put forward demands for a *volost* in the Kievan prince's hour of need and to come to his defence expressly on the condition of getting a specific territory; however, under normal circumstances and not at the time of emergency, Sviatoslav is entitled to receiving grants and to be angry if the granted *volost* does not meet his expectations. Of course, Sviatoslav was not the only prince who got angry when he believed that he did not receive the *volost* he deserved; the chronicles routinely present such anger as a valid reason to start a war. Only once a participant in an interprincely war declared that he had no interest in augmenting his domain. When

---

[18] "Viacheslav, smolviasia so Vsevolodom, da Iziaslavu Pereiaslavl, synovtsu svoemu, a Viacheslav ide v Turov," PSRL 2, 312–13. Vsevolod's supreme control over Pereiaslavl is indicated by the reaction of Vsevolod's brothers to the transfer of Pereiaslavl from Vizcheslav to Iziaslav: they "expressed their displeasure with him (*poroptasha na n'*) that 'he is in league (*liubov imeet*) with the sons of Mstislav, his brothers-in-law and our enemies, and he surrounded himself by them (or: installed them close to himself, *osazhalsia imi okolo*)'." "The sons of Mstislav" in question are Iziaslav and his junior brother Rostislav (see PSRL 2, 311). Rostislav helped Iziaslav in the latter's military endeavours, but otherwise stayed in his patrimonial principality of Smolensk; his rights to it were never disputed by any other prince. The complaint that "Mstislav's sons" are now too close to Vsevolod can only refer to Iziaslav becoming the prince of Pereiaslavl; the verbal construction (*osazhalsia imi okolo*) indicates Vsevolod's agency. If Vsevolod had not controlled Pereiaslavl and if Viacheslav had been free to give it to Iziaslav without Vsevolod's consent, blaming Vsevolod for being "surrounded" by the "sons of Mstislav" would not have made sense.

[19] PSRL 2, 312.

[20] PSRL 2, 498.

the brother of the overthrown Igor advanced against those who kept Igor in custody, he declared, poignantly, "I do not want to obtain a *volost*; I want nothing at all except that you set my brother free."[21] Clearly, a prince fighting in an internal conflict with a goal other than getting a *volost* was a very unusual case. Typically, a barrage of information about who got or lost what *volost* drowns the notion of the community of the realm. All we see are various *volosts*, which are related to one another and to "all the land" in an ambiguous way.

The same ambiguity is present in most pre-Mongol political narratives, although some of them, unlike the accounts of Vsevolod's rule, do discuss the Kievan prince's legitimacy, especially in the context of conflicts over Kiev. A comparison between narratives about princely struggle over the Kievan throne and accounts of internal conflicts in "proper" monarchies not only puts in sharp relief ideologies of legitimate rule that existed in Rusian and Western societies, but it also sheds light on an interplay between medieval texts and realities they purport to represent.

Rusian Chronicles: Conflict and Legitimacy

The question of the Kievan prince's legitimacy became especially urgent in the aftermath of Vsevolod's death in 1146. Vsevolod's designated heir Igor met a strong opposition from the "Kievans," a word that on this occasion apparently referred to the inhabitants of the personal domain of the Kievan prince, not just of the city of Kiev.[22] Evidently, there was discontent among the population who lived under Vsevolod's direct rule: the "Kievans" declared that they "did not want to be as if a hereditary property of the Olgovichi," and accused Vsevolod's and Igor's officials of mistreating them. Igor was overthrown, and a charismatic Monomakhovich, Iziaslav Mstislavich, became the new Kievan prince.[23] The sources favouring Iziaslav present the popular support he enjoyed in Kiev and "all the Rus Land" as the main argument for his legitimacy. Not everyone was convinced, however: Iziaslav's opponents invoked the principle of dynastic seniority.[24] After the outburst of popular hatred against the Olgovichi that culminated in the overthrow of Igor, the only dynasty that could realistically bid for Kiev were the Monomakhovichi, who were thus supposed to assign the Kievan throne to the most senior among them.

There exist various scholarly interpretations of dynastic seniority, which apparently did not always coincide with biological seniority, but they need not concern us here. Whatever methods the people of the time used to calculate the relative positions of dynasty members, they all agreed that the most senior Monomakhovich was Viacheslav.

---

21 PSRL 2, 329.

22 PSRL 2, 321. The assembly of the "Kievans" blamed the officials (*tiun*) of the late prince Vsevolod for "ruining Kiev and Vyshegorod." The latter was a stronghold in the Kievan region, and the assembly either spoke on behalf of the Vyshegorod people or, more likely, included them.

23 PSRL 2, 317–29; Dimnik, *The Dynasty of Chernigov*, 19–22.

24 Yulia Mikhailova and David Prestel, "Cross Kissing: Keeping One's Word in Twelfth-Century Rus," *Slavic Review* 70 (2011): 1–22, at 15.

The problem was that the Kievans kept rejecting him, probably because of his lacklustre record as a military leader. He had never been good on the battlefield and now, at the age of sixty-three and with no sons to lead his troops, he apparently was not fit for the position of Kievan prince, whose responsibilities included providing safety from the steppe nomads. A prince who, during a battle, "stayed away from the troops because of his old age,"[25] could not occupy the Kievan throne no matter what his dynastic legitimacy.

Therefore, George the "Long Arm" of Suzdalia claimed the Kievan throne as the most senior Monomakhovich after the hopelessly inept Viacheslav. Iziaslav refused to give up, citing his own popularity, military prowess, and generosity to other princes.[26] Both had supporters and kept fighting and taking Kiev by turns, until Iziaslav came up with a brilliant plan: he abandoned his proclamations that seniority was irrelevant and conceded Kiev to the true senior Viacheslav. He also offered him "assistance" in exercising the onerous responsibilities of the Kievan prince, thus making Viacheslav a figurehead and himself a *de facto* ruler. This arrangement, known in scholarly literature as a "duumvirate," worked exactly as Iziaslav intended. Seeing the most senior prince on the Kievan throne, many of George's allies left him, and Iziaslav defeated George once and for all.

Thus, dynastic seniority proved an important component of the Kievan prince's legitimacy—so important, in fact, that it was discussed in the terms of rule by God's grace. Iziaslav "honoured God" when he recognized Viacheslav's seniority; Viacheslav referred to his God-given right to Kiev in a speech he made before the final battle between Iziaslav and George, with George being cast as an usurper and Iziaslav as the champion of the legitimate ruler.[27] George was able to achieve his heart's desire and become the Kievan prince only after Viacheslav's natural death in 1154.

George's rule lasted only three years; when he died in 1157, the Olgovichi took Kiev again for a while, but then were defeated by a coalition led by Iziaslav's son, Mstislav, who apparently inherited his father's military brilliance. He also attempted to inherit his father's position of the *de facto* Kievan prince ostensibly "assisting" a legitimate figurehead on the throne. To this end, Mstislav declared that he was fighting off the Olgovichi on behalf of Rostislav who, after George's death, became the most senior Monomakhovich. After defeating the Olgovichi, he indeed invited Rostislav to Kiev, but received a disappointing reply: Rostislav agreed to take the Kievan throne only on the condition that he would be the true ruler and that Mstislav would "walk in his obedience." After "much arguing," Mstislav had to yield: Rostislav enjoyed a broad support of the population and had the right to Kiev according to the rules of seniority. Eventually, Rostislav's right to Kiev was recognized by all major princes who answered his summons and appealed to him for dispute resolutions.[28]

If Rostislav combined all three essential components of the Kievan prince's legitimacy, his successor Mstislav had only one: he was invited to take the throne by the

---

[25] PSRL 25, 53.
[26] Mikhailova and Prestel, "Cross Kissing," 16–18.
[27] PSRL 2, 431.
[28] PSRL 2, 514, 517–18, 521, 525, 528.

Kievans and by other communities from the Middle Dnieper. However, most princes had strained relations with him and did not recognize him as the supreme ruler; in any case, Mstislav's dynastic rights to Kiev were dubious at best. In 1169, a broad coalition of regional princes, who recognized Andrew of Suzdalia as the most senior Monomakhovich, marched on Kiev and overthrew Mstislav. This expedition was organized by Andrew, but he, as we remember, remained in Suzdalia and "gave Kiev" to somebody else who then "gave" it to yet another prince.

It is hard to tell what exactly this "giving" entailed. We do not know whether the recipient of "Kiev" had authority that went beyond his personal domain, the "Kievan *volost*." If he did not, then for the five years between 1169 and Andrew's murder in 1174, the Kievan prince was, indeed, merely one regional prince among others. However, in the last quarter of the twelfth century, Kievan princes undoubtedly behaved like supreme rulers with impressive authority over regions well beyond their personal domain; if they did not have such authority in the immediate aftermath of Mstislav's overthrow, this was no more than a brief interlude. A widespread perception of late twelfth-century Suzdalia emerging as the only centre of real political power in Rus is largely based on the accident of the chronicle of the Suzdalian princes surviving in its entirety, while chronicles of other princely branches were preserved only in disjointed pieces, as parts of larger compilations.[29] These compilations, by their very nature, do not offer a consistent glorification of one princely family, but they do provide an abundance of evidence for the power of the Kievan prince. Nonetheless, twelfth-century conflicts over Kiev are often viewed as "strife" among equals and as a sign of political disintegration that "ruined" Rus.

In fact, the number of these conflicts and the scale of violence and disruption that they brought about may be comparable to wars over royal thrones in contemporary European kingdoms; if anything, the twelfth century in Rus was probably less violent than in England, with its wars between Stephen and Matilda (1139–1153), and the rebellion of Henry the Young King against his father Henry II (1173–1174). However, representations of the contenders' positions and justifications of their claims in the sources nudge historians towards reading English conflicts as "civil wars" in a kingdom, and Rusian ones as "strife" in a "disintegrated" polity.

One reason for such reading of Rusian sources is that they often describe relations between the Kievan prince and regional princes and communities not in terms of the ruler and his subjects, but in terms of emotional bonds, such as love and family sentiment. Iziaslav proposes the idea of "duumvirate" to Viacheslav by proclaiming the latter his "father," to which Viacheslav replies: "You do not have a father and I do not have a son. You are now my son, and you are my brother as well." Soon thereafter, George comes to fight Iziaslav and is unpleasantly surprised to see Viacheslav on the Kievan throne. Being preached about the God-given rights of the most senior Monomakhovich, George agrees that Viacheslav's seniority merits respect, but what are Iziaslav, his brother Rostislav, and their troops doing in Kiev? They should go home and not interfere in matters that concern only Viacheslav and George. Viacheslav's retort to this blurs the difference between

---

29 Dimnik, *The Dynasty of Chernigov*, 1–2.

blood and political kinship by equating George's biological sons with the princes who "proclaimed (*nazval*)" Viacheslav their "father": "You have seven sons, but I do not seek to drive them away from you, and I only have two sons, Iziaslav and Rostislav."[30]

When George finally became the Kievan prince, love and family loomed large in the accounts of his relations with other princes. Rostislav was in Kiev when Viacheslav and Iziaslav died in 1154 within the space of a few weeks, but he did not attempt to secure the newly vacant Kievan throne for himself. He recognized George as the next in line for Kiev and addressed him, "Father, I bow down to you [...] an uncle is like a father to me." George "forgave his anger" at Rostislav for his support of Iziaslav, they "swore an oath on the Cross to be in perfect love," and Rostislav returned to his patrimonial principality of Smolensk. Soon thereafter, he and his men "came to Kiev to his uncle George, and they embraced with great love and great honour and thus remained in joy." Next, Rostislav "made entreaties" about his kinsmen who had also supported Iziaslav against George; George agreed to "accept them in love."[31]

"Love" and "joy" serve as markers of George's legitimacy as he continues to establish the bonds of love with one prince after another and to be joyous in their company; finally, "all the Rus Land" rejoices at his arrival in Kiev. This rite of greeting the legitimate ruler, discussed in the previous chapter, makes a marked contrast with George's previous attempts to take over Kiev, when he may have been "met" or "greeted" by his supporters, but there was no mentioning of joy on anyone's part.[32] By the same token, Viacheslav is never joyous and nobody expresses joy at his sight before he makes an agreement with Iziaslav and becomes part of the "duumvirate." As soon as the combination of Viacheslav's seniority and Iziaslav's popularity made the legitimacy of their position in Kiev irrefutable, they "remained in joy" all the time, and every public appearance of either of them invariably inspired "great joy" in the Kievans who went to fight for them against George "with joy." George's turn to see joyous crowds came only when his legitimacy as the Kievan prince was universally recognized.

However, it was George's successor, Rostislav, whose career exemplified the triumph of legitimacy: in Iziaslav's lifetime, Rostislav "urged him earnestly (*mnogo ponuzhival*)" to honour the rights of Viacheslav; then he stepped down to give way to George and became the Kievan prince only when he was left the most senior Monomakhovich.[33] Consequently, almost every mentioning of Rostislav includes a display of joy, except when he was tearful, sighing, and moaning during Lent.[34] Most other times, Rostislav is joyous, as is everyone around him. It is thus not only crowds in the streets whose joy has political significance; princes' joy also serves as a marker of legitimacy, as long as it is displayed for appropriate reasons, such as being greeted by faithful subjects. In a wrong

---

30 PSRL 2, 430.

31 "Tselovasta mezhi soboiu khrest na vsei liubvi," PSRL 2, 477, 480.

32 PSRL 2, 478.

33 PSRL 2, 422, 504, 520–22.

34 PSRL 2, 530. The only other occasion when Rostislav is represented as sad is the report about his prisoners dying accidentally; a reference to Rostislav's sadness serves to show that this was, indeed, a tragic accident and Rostislav was not responsible for their deaths. PSRL 2, 511.

context, joy taints princely legitimacy, as when the Olgovichi rejoiced at the Cuman victory over the troops of the Kievan prince, a Monamakhovich—or so we are told by the Monomakhovichi's chronicler.[35]

Joy and love are not the only emotions that have political significance. Demonstrative emotional conduct described in the chronicles forms behavioural patterns (*Verhaltensmuster*) and serves as a means of communication.[36] Thus, lesser princes are sad when they experience defeat, dishonour, or a personal loss, but sadness over misfortunes befalling the Rus Land and pity for the suffering population appears to be a monopoly of the legitimate ruler. The Kievan prince organizes an anti-Cuman campaign by exhorting regional princes to have pity for the Christians suffering from nomadic raids; his audience expresses their readiness "to die for the Rus Land and for the Christians and to be among the martyrs."[37] However, when Igor of Novgorod-Severskii leads an unauthorized expedition into the Cuman steppe, he is motivated solely by a desire for personal glory. Far from gaining glory, he is defeated and captured, and the Kievan prince Sviatoslav has to deal with the consequences of Igor's adventurism when the victorious Cumans cross into the Rusian territory. Sviatoslav responds to the raid by sighing deeply, crying, verbalizing his emotions, and summoning regional princes to fight the Cumans—in this order. He does not get to practical military matters before describing how he was angry at Igor and how his anger changed to pity now that Igor was a prisoner.[38] With his authority undermined by Igor's insubordination and the urgent need to ensure the obedience of regional princes, Sviatoslav asserts his position of leadership by expressing his grief, anger, and pity.

Anger and pity serve as markers of legitimacy in the accounts of the Iziaslav-Viacheslav "duumvirate" as well. When Iziaslav entered Kiev for the first time, his chronicler tried to cast him as a legitimate ruler by claiming that he did so out of pity for the Kievans, who did not want Igor as their prince and asked Iziaslav to take care of their city.[39] We already know that this did not work, and Iziaslav eventually had to offer the formal position of the Kievan prince to Viacheslav. Remarkably, it is then, and not earlier, that Viacheslav expresses anger for the first time. The chronicler reports neither anger nor any other emotional reaction of Viacheslav, while describing several occasions when other princes and the Kievans mistreated him and trampled upon his seniority. However, when Iziaslav offers him the throne, Viacheslav "angrily" scolds him for not doing so earlier. For the

---

35 PSRL 2, 603.

36 On the communicative function of emotions in medieval narratives, see Althoff, *Spielregeln der Politik*; Barbara Rosenwein, "Eros and Clio: Emotional Paradigms in Medieval Historiography," in *Mediävistik im 21. Jahrhundert; Staat und Perspektiven der internationalen und interdisziplinären Mittelalterforschung*, ed. Hans-Werner Goetz and Jörg Jarnut (Munich: Fink, 2003), 427–41; *Anger's Past: The Social Uses of an Emotion in the Middle Ages*, ed. Barbara Rosenwein (Ithaca: Cornell University Press, 1998). On emotions in Rusian chronicles, see Yulia Mikhailova, "'He Sighed from His Heart and Began to Gather Soldiers': Emotions in Rusian Political Narratives," forthcoming in *Studia Slavica et Balcanica Petropolitana*.

37 PSRL 2, 538.

38 PSRL 2, 645.

39 PSRL 1, 313.

chronicler, Viacheslav has legitimacy only as part of the "duumvirate," not as an independent Kievan prince. Consequently, Viacheslav gets the "right" to be angry only when he receives Iziaslav's offer. Soon after he accepts it, we hear that on all past occasions, when Viacheslav was driven out of Kiev, he did not defend his right to the throne because he did not want to spill Christian blood.[40] His pity for the Christians shows Viacheslav's mercy, while his anger indicates strength, two key qualities of a legitimate ruler.

For all the high-minded talk of love, pity for innocent lives, righteous anger, and other admirable feelings, the discourse of princely legitimacy never departs far from the subject of *volosts*. Iziaslav appeased Viacheslav's honour and abated his anger by apologizing profusely, and also by offering him "any *volost* you want." After that, they enjoyed mutual "love" as a "father" and a "son" for the rest of their lives. Without a *volost*, however, a prince could not always count on "love" even from his real, biological son. Thus, George's son came over to the side of Iziaslav, his father's rival, because George "wronged him by not giving him a *volost*." Iziaslav remedied the injustice that George had inflicted on the young prince:

> "May God grant that I treat justly all of you, my brethren and kinsmen, and care about you even as I care about my own soul. Now, if your father did not give you a *volost*, I give you this,"—and he gave him Bozhesk, Meshibozhie, Kotelnitsa, and two more strongholds.[41]

These are just a few examples of entangled familial, political, and property relations that dominate the pages of Rusian chronicles, pages filled with countless narratives about princes displaying joy, anger, or sadness, and making agreements with one another and with various communities in pursuit of what they see as their fair share of land and power. This is, of course, not to say that the elites of Latin Europe were not interested in land and power or that conflicts in European kingdoms did not involve an interplay between family and politics. A foremost example of such a conflict is Henry the Young King's rebellion against his father Henry II of England in 1173–1174. However, ideological frameworks employed in the English accounts of this rebellion and in the Rusian chronicles are very different. A scholar of Rus reading English narratives about the reign of Henry II (1154–1189) often has an impression that the two realms existed in different political universes and had nothing in common. Often, but not invariably.

William of Newburgh, Robert of Torigni, Jordan Fantosme: The Realm of England, *Honur*, and *Seigniorie*

Henry II, the founder of the new Plantagenet dynasty on the English throne, is famous for his reforms of law and administration, cultural patronage, and vast territorial additions to the dominions of the Anglo-Norman kings. In spite of all these achievements, Henry's reign saw many upheavals, and his authority and legitimacy as a king was challenged more than once. As the ruler of the vast Angevin dominion, which included England

---

40 PSRL 2, 399, 429–31.
41 PSRL 2, 366–67.

and much of central and northern France, Henry had many internal and external enemies who rallied around his son when he turned against Henry in 1173. The son, Henry's namesake, was formally crowned as the "Young King" to secure an undisputed succession, but he did not exercise any real power. He rebelled against his father after Henry II had given to his other son John some territories previously assigned to Henry the Young King. Detailed accounts of these events are found in the *History* by William of Newburgh and the *Chronicle* by Robert of Torigni.

William of Newburgh tells us that Henry the Younger, at the instigation of "certain persons," wrongly decided that he, and not his father, had the right to be the true king of England, even though his coronation was never meant as a real transfer of power. The persons who stirred up the son against the father used to their advantage Henry the Younger's growing irritation at the fact that his father did not provide him with sufficient means. Henry the Younger fled to his father-in-law Louis VII of France who recognized him as the true king of England, and started together with him a war against Henry II. "Contriving evil from everywhere against his father," Henry the Younger also found allies in Aquitaine, Brittany and Flanders. Some still adhered "faithfully and firmly" to the true king Henry II, but many magnates (*potentes et nobiles*) "began to desert the father for the son," either impelled by hatred or attracted by "emptiest promises."[42] Nothing could be more foolish (*nil stultius*) than their attempts to justify their war against Henry II by putting forward the rights of the son. William cannot emphasize enough that in reality they were fighting either out of hatred or because they saw an occasion to gain something for themselves.[43] Worst of all, Henry the Younger was supported by the "most ferocious" king of the Scots, whose bloodthirsty people, "more savage than wild beasts," ravaged the English province of Northumberland.[44]

William proceeds to describe the course of the war, which ended with the splendid victory of the rightful king. In spite of the great multitude and fierceness of his enemies, Henry II prevailed over them all and "pacified England." Those among his enemies who were not yet defeated in the battlefield were so "terrified and humiliated by his so many illustrious successful deeds" that they asked for peace. The merciful king, after he got back "what was rightfully his (*quod de jure ejus*)," released the captives and restored their "goods and honours (*bona honoresque*)"; however, he destroyed the walls of their castles, "the horns of the proud." He also reconciled with his son. This is how "this more than civil war" ended and the peace of the realm was restored.[45]

Robert of Torigni tells essentially the same story. Henry the Young King was frustrated because his father took away some knights attending him. He "left his father in anger" and went to the king of France. A number of nobles deserted the king and

---

[42] *Historia Rerum Anglicarum Willelmi Parvi, Ordinis Sancti Augustini Canonici Regularis in Coenobio Beatae Mariae de Newburgh in Agro Eboracensi*, ed. Hans Claude Hamilton, vol. 1, English Historical Society Publications Series 15 (London: Sumptibus societatis, 1856) [hereafter William of Newburgh, *Historia*], 164–65.

[43] "Re autem vera proprii vel odii, ut rex Francorum, vel emolumenti, ut comes Flandrensis, negotium porrecta occasione agentes," William of Newburgh, *Historia*, 167.

[44] William of Newburgh, *Historia*, 166, 172, 177.

[45] William of Newburgh, *Historia*, 189, 191–93.

followed the son, as did Queen Eleanor and her sons, Henry the Younger's brothers.[46] Henry the Younger started a war against his father; he was supported by a number of foreign allies and English nobles. One of these nobles acted towards Henry II "unfaithfully," another was motivated by a desire "to disturb the realm of England." The war ended soon after Henry II's troops captured William of Scotland, who had devastated "the northern parts of England." Peace was established, and "the king's three sons humbly submitted themselves to him; the French king and the count of Flanders returned to the king of England the strongholds which they had taken."[47]

William does not explain what exactly the rebels hoped to receive by going over to Henry II's enemies, nor does he discuss the nature of Henry the Younger's "emptiest promises." It is very likely that these were promises of land grants, but the subject of land grants is irrelevant for both William and Robert. Both authors mention landed property for the first time when they describe the peace settlement under which Henry II received what was his and generously returned to the defeated their *bona honoresque*, which he presumably had confiscated. There is no ambiguity in William's and Robert's representation of the realm of England as a clearly defined territory under the rule of a monarch to whom all those living within this territory owe service and loyalty, regardless of any land grants and of any agreements into which they may have entered. To borrow William's phrase, nothing can be more foolish than to try and compare this well-organized monarchy with a polity, the supreme ruler of which is distinguishable from a throng of other princes mainly by the emotions he displays and inspires, a polity dominated by networks of princes who are motivated by "love," kinship, and a desire to preserve and increase territories under their control.

There is, however, another English narrative of the same events of 1173–1174, *Jordan Fantosme's Chronicle*. Fantosme, like William of Newburgh and Robert of Torigni, is on the side of Henry II, the "most honourable" king wronged by his son.[48] In this respect, the position of the three authors is the same. However, unlike William and Robert, Fantosme admits that Henry the Young King, even though he should not have taken arms against his father, had legitimate grievances. The "cruel war" broke out because Henry II, after crowning his son, took from him "some authority (*seignurie*)."[49] Henry the Younger fled to France and initiated hostilities because he found himself in a difficult situation of the *reis de terre senz honur*, that is, a "king of the land without *honur*."[50] *Honur*, just as the medieval Latin *honor*, among its many other meanings, signified a high rank or office, a

---

46 *The Chronicle of Robert of Torigni, Abbot of the Monastery of St. Michael-in-Peril-of-the-Sea*, in *Chronicles of the Reigns of Stephen, Henry II., and Richard I*, vol. 4, ed. Richard Howlett, Rerum Britannicarum Medii Aevi scriptores 82–84 (London: Eyre and Spottiswoode, 1889) [hereafter *Chronicle of Robert of Torigni*], 255–56.

47 *Chronicle of Robert of Torigni*, 259–60, 264–65.

48 *Jordan Fantosme's Chronicle*, ed. and trans. R. C. Johnston (Oxford: Clarendon Press, 1981), 8, 10.

49 *Jordan Fantosme's Chronicle*, 4.

50 R. C. Johnston translates this as "without a realm" (*Jordan Fantosme's Chronicle*, 5), however, normally Fantosme uses *regne*, the standard Anglo-Norman word for "realm."

privilege, or a type of land property also known as a "fief." It is unclear what exactly is the "land" of which Henry the Younger is a king, and how it relates to *honur*, of which he is deprived. Later, Fantosme tells us that the Young King wants to seize revenues from his father's fiefs and to take his father's "land, and fiefs, and inheritance," without explaining the relationships between the three. Thus, instead of the clear-cut realm of England, we see *honur*, inheritance, and fiefs which are related to one another and to "the land" in an ambiguous way; instead of monarchical power over the realm that can belong to one person only, there is *seignurie* which apparently can be divided or shared in some way, as is implied by the expression *auques de seignurie*—some authority.

Moreover, in Fantosme's chronicle, William of Scotland, the great villain of William of Newburgh and Robert of Torigni, sends his troops not to invade "the realm of England," but to recover the territory which, he believes, is rightfully his. At first, he hesitates which side in the conflict he should support. Henry the Young King writes to William "with love," reminds him that they are kinsmen, and that William owes homage and service to him. He also promises William *la seignurie* over Northumberland "that your ancestors had," in exchange for military help against Henry II.[51] William has a difficult dilemma: he has ties of kinship with, and owes homage and service to, both the son and the father, who are now at war; the son gives him the land that belongs to William's *honur* and is "rightfully his (*dreiture*)."[52] William decides to request his inheritance from Henry II and to choose his side in the conflict depending on the old king's response.

Love and family loom large in the exchange between the English and Scottish kings. Henry II "should love greatly" his kinsman William, who will send his troops to fight for Henry II if the English king grants him Northumberland. Henry expresses his surprise (*s'esmerveille*) that William, who in the past "loved him much," now refuses to come to his help unless he gets Northumberland.[53] Addressing William, the envoy says, "You demand [from Henry II] his land as your heritage (*demandez lui sa terre pur vostre heritage*)." Henry, however, will not give William any lands before William shows "love and kinship (*ferrez amur e cusinage*)."[54] It turns out that the "realm of England" includes territories that are at one and the same time Henry II's *terre* and William's *heritage* and that Northumberland is not just an English province, but also the Scottish king's *honur*. Henry II turns down William's request, and William joins Henry the Younger. Then Louis VII of France joins them because he should keep the faith that he pledged to William of Scotland.[55]

---

51 *Jordan Fantosme's Chronicle*, 20.

52 *Jordan Fantosme's Chronicle*, 2, 22. On the relations between William and Henry II and on William's homage to Henry for the English lands that he held, see Seán Duffy, "Henry II and England's Insular Neighbours," in *Henry II: New Interpretations*, ed. Christopher Harper-Bill and Nicholas Vincent (Woodbridge: Boydell, 2007), 129–53, 131–34, 151.

53 *Jordan Fantosme's Chronicle*, 28.

54 *Jordan Fantosme's Chronicle*, 24, 28.

55 Fantosme describes as "reasonable" the advice given to Louis VII by Philip of Flanders, "Tenez al rei d'Escose la fiance afiee," *Jordan Fantosme's Chronicle*, 32. Cf. William of Newburgh, *Historia*, 165.

What William of Newburgh and Robert of Torigni present as "silly" or "foolish (*stultus*)" claims and "emptiest promises" is a matter of much importance for Fantosme. Henry II's enemies are in the wrong, but there is nothing "silly" about their wishes to be true to their agreements or to get the land that they believe is rightly theirs. None of them wages war on Henry II simply out of a desire "to disturb the realm of England"; they defend what they see as their legitimate interests. Fantosme's kings, in addition to being monarchs who rule over their respective subjects, are also lords entering into sworn agreements with one another and with their prominent subjects, agreements based on "love," kinship, and a desire to preserve and increase territories under their control. Fantosme reveals a complicated network of such agreements and alliances, which is completely absent from the writings of William of Newburgh and Robert of Torigni. Even though Fantosme agrees with them that Henry II is the rightful king of England, he uses different means to construct his legitimacy.

William of Newburgh, Robert of Torigni, Jordan Fantosme: Conflict and Legitimacy

William and Robert maintain a clear distinction between the one and only legitimate ruler of England, Henry II, and his enemies, who are either foreign invaders or the unfaithful subjects of the English king, acting out of hatred and sheer malice or out of a desire for personal gain. Henry II is the rightful king, and Northumberland is part of his kingdom, period. Fantosme, however, presents a gallery of royal figures putting forward plausible claims to the same territories. We see the "noble and gracious" Young King deprived of his *honur* and *seignurie* doing the same thing as George the "Long Arm's" son did when he was deprived of a *volost*: he appeals to his father's rival, the "noble king" of France. As for William of Scotland, who seeks to recover his inheritance, Northumberland, "never did a more honourable man govern any realm."[56] What gives Henry II, and not William, the legitimate authority over Northumberland is not the principle of the territorial integrity of the realm of England, but his feelings about the plight of the disputed province.

When Henry heard about the prospect of Northumerland being laid waste by the Scots, " 'By God,—thus the king said,—this will be a great pity.' Then his eyes wept and he sighed deeply."[57] In contrast with Henry's attitude, William approvingly listens to his men's statement, "Northumberland is yours, regardless of who cries or who laughs about it." R. C. Johnston renders this as "whether people like it or not."[58] The Scottish king thinks only about his hereditary rights to the territory that he seeks to obtain; he neither cares about the feelings of the people who live there, nor displays any emotions of his own that would testify to his concern about the well-being of the land and its population.

---

56 *Jordan Fantosme's Chronicle*, 4, 6, 50.
57 *Jordan Fantosme's Chronicle*, 118–20.
58 "Vostre est Northumberland, u quin plure u quin rie," *Jordan Fantosme's Chronicle*, 130–31.

Much like lesser princes in Rusian chronicles, Fantosme's rebels and their foreign allies are sad only when they suffer defeat, dishonour, or a personal loss. The rightful king alone has a monopoly to be sad about the misfortunes of the land, be it Northumberland or all England. Henry II's "heart is sorrowful" because of the sufferings of "his good people" and the devastation of his country.[59] It is this emotional bond, more than anything else, that makes the country and the people "his," and that manifests itself not only through Henry's sighs and tears, but also through public displays of joy. In Fantosme's work, joy is such an important marker of legitimacy that Henry II's enemies rejoice only twice: when they seize a lot of booty, and when William of Scotland makes the decision that will lead to his defeat. Apart from this portrayal of the foolish joy soon to be changed into grief and shame, Fantosme never represents enemies of the rightful king rejoicing, no matter how victorious and how successful they are.[60] Even when "the Young King has accomplished much," he does not display any joy about these accomplishments.[61] It is only Henry II who rejoices over his victories.[62]

However, what makes joy an ultimate signifier of legitimacy is its display not just by the ruler himself, but by the population. One of the rebels, Roger, may be "proclaimed as the lord of all Yorkshire," but there is no information about people of Yorkshire rejoicing when they see their newly proclaimed lord.[63] In contrast with this, we see a detailed description of the joy displayed by the Londoners at the arrival of Henry II from Normandy, and of the splendid welcome they offered him. This scene is part of the narrative that has two major intertwining themes: God's judgment and popular support.

When Henry, on his way from Normandy, is crying and sighing over the plight of Northumberland, the Scots devastate the countryside, desecrate the church of St. Lawrence, murder those who seek shelter in it, and then ride to Alnwick while assuring William that Northumberland is his, regardless of whether the people like it or not.[64] Meanwhile, Henry II reaches England and proceeds to Canterbury, where he resolves the main problem with his legitimacy: Becket's murder in 1170, which, his enemies argued, deprived Henry II of his right to rule.[65] Henry II reconciles with St. Thomas by undergoing a harsh penance, and the restoration of God's grace is evident immediately: Henry does not know this yet, but at exactly the same time that he was in Canterbury, his soldiers defeated the Scots and captured their king in the battle of Alnwick, where God punished the sacrilege committed at St. Lawrence.

Henry receives the news of the victory at Alnwick right after the rejoicing Londoners give him gifts and "honor him greatly."[66] Representations of Henry II in Canterbury and

---

59 *Jordan Fantosme's Chronicle*, 142, 144.
60 *Jordan Fantosme's Chronicle*, 88, 100, 110, 126, 136, 153.
61 *Jordan Fantosme's Chronicle*, 10.
62 *Jordan Fantosme's Chronicle*, 16, 62.
63 *Jordan Fantosme's Chronicle*, 70.
64 *Jordan Fantosme's Chronicle*, 124–30.
65 M. T. Clanchy, *England and Its Rulers: 1066–1307*, 3rd ed. (Malden: Blackwell, 2006), 116.
66 *Jordan Fantosme's Chronicle*, 140–42, 144.

in London show his legitimacy as the one and only true king, but his reception in London is more prominent: a four-line description of Henry's penance is followed by a detailed account of his arrival in London. The Londoners are "joyous at the coming of their lord," they "dress richly" and form a "marvellous procession." "He is indeed a king by right (*cil deit bien estre reis*) who has such people as his subjects."[67] Henry II *deit*, that is, he is entitled or has right, to be king, because Londoners come to meet him in their best clothes. The ultimate justification of the ruler's legitimacy is provided by rejoicing crowds, in London and in Kiev alike. Both Fantosme and the Kievan chronicler apparently believe that the voice of the people is the voice of God, a belief implied in the narrative of Henry II's triumph over William and expressed in Iziaslav's account of how his coalition won Kiev: "God helped us, and all the Rus Land supported us."[68]

This is arguably the most important commonality between the discourses of legitimacy in Fantosme's and Rusian chronicles, but it is not the only one. We have seen the *Realpolitik* attitude of the Rusian authors, who always assume that there is no legitimacy without adequate strength to back it: when regional princes sense a ruler's weakness and refuse to answer his summons unless he meets their demands for land grants, his rule does not last long; an old person, incapable of leading his troops and having no-one to whom he can delegate the task, cannot hold the Kievan throne in spite of his dynastic rights. Fantosme shares these assumptions, and his characters discuss land grants in a language strikingly similar to that of Rusian princes.

The timing of William's request for Northumberland indicates that he perceives Henry II as being weak: William describes Henry's situation as a *busuin*, that is, as a "need" or "emergency," and he wants to use his aid at the king's hour of need as leverage. *Busuin* directly corresponds to East Slavonic *nuzha*, the word meaning "need" or "emergency," which is used to describe a situation when it is not appropriate to request a *volost*. Henry indignantly refuses to grant requests made "because of his *busuin*," and states emphatically that he is not frightened by his enemies' attacks. His is a position of power, and any land grants are out of question before he sees William's "love and kinship," that is, his military aid. Simultaneously with his denial of William's request, Henry tells William's brother David to come to his aid and to receive "such lands and such fiefs as will satisfy all your demands," showing that he does give land to those who serve him, but on his conditions, not theirs.[69] Just like the Kievan prince, the English king has to be generous, but also firm.

Contrary to what one may expect to see in a text about a monarchy with institutions as developed as they were in twelfth-century England, Fantosme also ascribes great importance to the king's martial valour and physical power, the crucial qualities that the old Viacheslav was lacking. Fantosme's Henry II declares, "I have not grown so old that

---

67 *Jordan Fantosme's Chronicle*, 142–44. Cf. Ashe, "The Anomalous King," 187–88.
68 "how God helped us and how all the Rus land supported us (*po nas iala*), and all the Black Caps." PSRL 2, 421. In addition to the support of all the "Rus Land," Iziaslav refers to the support by the Black Caps, the Turkic nomadic *federati* of the Rusian princes.
69 *Jordan Fantosme's Chronicle*, 26–28.

I should lose the land because of my old age (*Ne sui pas si envielli ... ke deive terre perdue, ne pur mes granz hëez*)"; he would not cave in to his son's demands "as long as he can strike with sword or lance." Nothing can be taken by force from a man of Henry II's *vertu*, the word that stands for both physical strength and military power, and that signifies moral virtue as well.[70]

Just as in Rusian chronicles, the moral and material strength of the rightful ruler is communicated through his display of righteous anger. At the news of the rebellion, Henry II behaves in the same way as Sviatoslav does at the news of the Cuman attack brought about by Igor's defeat: first of all, he verbalizes his emotions of grief and anger in front of his barons, and only then does he proceed to give them military orders. Both rulers face challenges to their legitimacy—the insubordination of a junior prince in one case, the rebellion in another; both reassert their position of leadership in similar ways; and both succeed in receiving expressions of loyalty, getting their orders followed and, ultimately, in being victorious. Having seen Henry "saddened and angry" and having heard from him, "I was never so grieved in my life, my body is seized by such rage that I am nearly crazy," his barons are assured that he is the rightful king. They reply, "The land is yours, defend it! Your son is in the wrong to make war on you."[71] In this passage, the essence of relations between the true king, his faithful subjects, and rebels who are in the wrong, is the same as in the works by William of Newburgh and Robert of Torigni, but the dynamics behind the relations is very different.

Overall, the world of William of Newburgh and Robert of Torigni has very little, if anything, in common with Rus. However, the society described by Fantosme has some significant commonalities with the society that emerges from Rusian chronicles. To understand the reasons for similarities between Fantosme's and Rusian chronicles, we need to see what sets Fantosme apart from the two other historiographers, who, moreover, supported Henry II as much as he did.

Monarchical Ideal versus Aristocratic Egalitarianism: Language and Audience

The obvious differences between the works by William of Newburgh and Robert of Torigni and Fantosme's *Chronicle* include the genre, the language, and the intended audience. The former two are Latin histories, and thus belong to the type of literary works written primarily by and for the clergy, especially monks.[72] The genre of Fantosme's work is not easily definable. On the one hand, true to its title, this is a chronicle: an account of contemporary political and military events, to some of which Fantosme claims to be an eye-witness. On the other hand, unusually for a twelfth-century chronicle, it is rhymed and written in the vernacular. Fantosme, who was apparently a learned cleric well versed

---

[70] *Jordan Fantosme's Chronicle*, 8, 12, 18.
[71] *Jordan Fantosme's Chronicle*, 10–12.
[72] Galloway, "Writing History in England," in *The Cambridge History of Medieval English Literature*, ed. David Wallace (Cambridge: Cambridge University Press, 1999), 260.

in Latin, wrote his work in the Anglo-Norman variety of Old French probably because he wanted to reach the widest possible audience; also to counter the pro-Capetian vernacular epic *Couronnement de Louis*, and, most importantly, the vernacular *Life of Thomas Becket*, which contained a thinly veiled comparison of Henry II with Pontius Pilate.[73]

Even though Fantosme's poem does not have any fantastic or legendary elements, its commonalities with epics and romances go beyond the vernacular language and the rhymed form. Laura Ashe showed that Fantosme shared with contemporary insular romances the ideology of kingship "focused upon the reciprocity between king and barons, the people's willing acceptance of a king." The bond between the land, the people, and the king, celebrated by Fantosme, and his tacit assumption that the king rules by assent, are typical of twelfth-century vernacular literature.[74] The main audience of this literature was lay aristocracy. Twelfth-century England produced a number of vernacular historiographical works, but, apart from Fantosme, they were either adaptations of earlier Latin texts, or were devoted to the distant past, or both, or else they described the histories of monastic foundations.[75] Fantosme's *Chronicle*, then, offers a rare opportunity to see contemporary politics from a perspective of the lay elite and not of monastic scholars.

If modern historians employ "protocols" based on their "professional belief systems" while reading medieval texts, medieval historians used their own "protocols" while creating these texts. Timothy Reuter showed that the view of kingship which, until recently, dominated historical scholarship, resulted partly from an intersections of the two "protocols," the modern and the medieval: historians' "tendency to ruler-worship [...] is a product both of our preconceptions and of the *visibility* of rulers in the sources" (emphasis original). The outsize visibility of kings was, in turn, a product of the monastic scholars' professional belief system: "The dependence of historiographers of the High Middle Ages on Cicero and Sallust and Suetonius as well as the patristic and early medieval historical classics" meant that they concentrated on the king and often misled the reader "by using a public and royal (hence 'state-centered') vocabulary for the private and dynastic aspirations of rulers."[76]

This is the vocabulary of William of Newburgh and Robert of Torigni. The attitude of monastic Latin scholars to the task of representing aristocratic politics was neatly captured by the English historian of the previous generation William of Malmesbury in his *Gesta Regum Anglorum*. While describing conflicts that the duke of Normandy, the future "Conqueror," had with "a certain Guy" and with the French king, he mentions some castles that the duke gave to Guy, and then briefly refers to a "broken friendship," a "break of faith (*fidei dissimulatio*)," and to "false accusations" invented to justify the

---

[73] Philip E. Bennett, "La Chronique de Jordan Fantosme: epique et public lettré au XIIe siècle," *Cahiers de civilisation médiévale* 40 (1997): 37–56, at 55–56.

[74] Ashe, "The Anomalous King," 178–79, 186–87.

[75] Peter Damian-Grint, *The New Historians of the Twelfth-Century Renaissance: Inventing Vernacular Authority* (New York: Boydell, 1999), 16–32, 49–67.

[76] Reuter, *Medieval Polities*, 406, 410.

perfidious behaviour.[77] We do not know anything about the content of these accusations, the course of the conflicts, or the conditions on which Guy received the castles: the historian thinks that "it would be long and unnecessary" to relate "what was done by each side, what castles were captured," or to "write down all the disputes that were between them."[78]

Thus, for William of Malmesbury, the degree of detail in his accounts of aristocratic politics is a question of literary style. His goal is to describe the making and breaking of agreements or the outbreaks and settlements of "private" conflicts as briefly and summarily as he can, and to concentrate on the illustrious deeds of the king. When he cannot do so in his *Historia Novella*, commissioned by Earl Robert of Gloucester, who fought on behalf of his half-sister Matilda against King Stephen, he appears uncomfortable dealing with material that does not easily lend itself to patterns borrowed from Sallust and Suetonius. In a valiant effort to achieve the nearly impossible goal of discussing Robert's role in the war between Stephen and Matilda in terms of classical historiography, William describes Robert's men as "supporters of the consul, so to speak (*consulares, ut ita dictum sit*)."[79] Despite the classicizing effort, *Historia Novella* provides more information on the concrete workings of contemporary politics, with all its shifting alliances, aristocratic networks, and struggles to preserve and augment one's landholdings, than does *Gesta Regum Anglorum*. In the latter, much as in the Latin accounts of the 1173–1174 revolt, the nobles supporting the king's rival do so either without any reason at all, or on "slight little pretexts (*levibus occasiunculis*)" of not getting from the king "the lands they wished." What exactly they wished, and why, is beside the point in the narrative where the king, by definition, represents "the side of justice"; if there is any need to discuss his legitimacy, a quotation from Plato about the ruler-philosopher is a more relevant argument than information about who got or lost what land.[80]

In *Historia*, however, one reason for why Robert renounces homage to King Stephen is that the king took away some of his possessions.[81] In terms of literary style *Historia Novella*, with its finely structured narrative and classical references, is as far removed from Rusian chronicles as are all other works by William of Malmesbury; however, if in the *Gesta Regum Anglorum*, both style and content strike a historian of Rus as completely alien, some aspects of *Historia*'s content do bring to mind Rusian narratives of princely politics. Like them, *Historia* represents multiple political players; distribution of lands and offices in *Historia*

---

[77] "Affictis criminibus quibus id merito facere viderentur," William of Malmesbury, *Gesta Regum Anglorum: The History of the English Kings*, ed. and trans. R. A. B. Mynors, R. M. Thomson, and M. Winterbottom (Oxford: Clarendon Press, 1998), vol. 1, 428.

[78] "Longum est et non necessarium si persequar quae hinc inde acta, quae castella capta"; "Longum est et non necessarium referre quantae inter eos contentiones versatae sint," William of Malmesbury, *Gesta Regum Anglorum*, vol. 1, 428, 434.

[79] William of Malmesbury, *Historia Novella: The Contemporary History*, ed. Edmund King, trans. K. R. Potter (Oxford: Clarendon Press, 1998), 84.

[80] William of Malmesbury, *Gesta Regum Anglorum*, vol. 1, 800, 716.

[81] William of Malmesbury, *Historia Novella*, 42.

is an important matter, and not something that comes up only in the context of inventing "slight pretexts" for improper behaviour, just as the distribution of *volosts* is an important matter in the chronicles. In short, while William's learning and literary craftsmanship are always beyond comparison with Rusian chroniclers', his position becomes somewhat reminiscent of theirs as soon as he does not focus on the figure of the ruler and adopts a perspective of an aristocratic participant in a war between two claimants for the throne.

Such a perspective is not often found in works by Latin monastic scholars. Of course, not all their political narratives were devoted to kings. English post-Conquest historiographers, including William of Malmesbury, wrote in detail about the dukes of Normandy before they became English kings; plenty of regional histories, barely mentioning the king, were produced on the continent. However, these histories, for the most part, also focused on one towering figure, the local magnate, often presented in quasi-regal terms and with as much classicizing rhetoric as the author's level of education allowed. In short, accounts of aristocratic politics in local histories are typically filtered through the same screen of Roman, patristic and early medieval historical classics as the king-centred works. The voice of the lay elite appears to find more direct expression in the vernacular literature "produced for the aristocracy, in celebration of their ideals and aspirations."[82]

Political mentality reflected in this literature is surprisingly close to the mentality of Rusian chroniclers. Demonstrative emotional behaviour forms similar patterns and performs similar political functions in the Old French and Rusian narratives.[83] "Nostalgic portraits of ancient kings" in the French vernacular epics indicate that "nobles thought kingship a good thing in the abstract"; however, sympathetic presentation of nobles defending their rights to land from the king in the here and now shows that they "were very wary of making unexamined concessions to actual royal power."[84] *Chansons de geste* often criticize the king from the point of view of "rightfully rebellious barons,"[85] an oxymoron for most Latin historiographers. Rusian chroniclers also portray great and mighty Kievan princes of olde, while displaying wariness of the Kievan princes of their own time, who are often criticized from the point of view of "rightfully rebellious" regional princes. "Autocrat" or "sole ruler" is praise when applied to the princes of the past or when used in a high-register eulogy, indicating that monarchy is a good thing in the abstract; it is a criticism when used in an account of contemporary events. Rusian chroniclers are as obsessed with *volosts* and with relations mediated by land grants as French authors are "with the extent of fiefs, the inheritance of fiefs and the relations of people holding fiefs from one another."[86] The general tenor of Rusian accounts of interprincely relations is

---

82 Ashe, "Anomalous King," 189; William Chester Jordan, *Europe in the High Middle Ages* (New York: Penguin Books, 2004), 15.

83 Mikhailova, "'He Sighed from His Heart'."

84 James R. Simpson, "Feudalism and Kingship," in *The Cambridge Companion to Medieval French Literature*, ed. Simon Gaunt and Sarah Kay (Cambridge: Cambridge University Press, 2008), 197–209, at 202, 208.

85 Ashe, "Anomalous King," 189.

86 Jordan, *Europe in the High Middle Ages*, 15.

based on the ideas of mutual obligations and collective action; they stress horizontal power relations so much and treat princes as equals so often that they engendered the idea of a "disintegrated" Rus, the "headless state" where the Kievan prince did not have any special power.[87] In short, they share "the aristocracy's egalitarian dream," the political ideal represented by "the Round Table, which abolished hierarchies" in the Arthurian romances.[88]

Ashe argues that the marginal role these romances assigned to the king explains their absence from twelfth-century England, with its long history of strong kingship. In contrast with the continental tradition, insular romances celebrate a just and strong monarch; however, they also "tacitly place in the hands of barons the right to judge, and accept or reject, the king." Consequently, in romances, not the king's person, but England itself, is the focus of loyalty and identity. All these features are present in Fanosme's *Chronicle*, in which the literary form and political ideology of English vernacular fiction are applied to real-life contemporary politics.[89] The king has a prominent place in this ideology, but not the key place: "the key value is the sanctity of the English land."[90]

La Terre, *Zemlia*, and *Regnum*

If we now return to Reynolds's kingdom, "the highest, most honourable, and most perfect of all secular communities," for which the unity of the land and people forms a basis and which is absent from the Rusian sources, we have to conclude that it is equally absent from Fantosme. To be sure, he uses the word *regne*, realm, interchangeably, or along with, *terre* and *honur*, but it does not have connotations that Reynolds ascribes to the medieval concept of kingdom. Just like the Rus Land, or simply "the land (*zemlia*)," and not the political unit ruled by the monarch, is the main reference point for Rusian authors, so is the English land, or simply "the land (*la terre*)" for Fantosme. It is not the archetypal ruler, the king's presiding over a territory, that sanctifies it, by turning a mere "land" into the archetypal political unit, a "kingdom." For Fantosme and Rusian authors, it is the other way around. Fantosme's king himself derives power from his connection with the land.[91] In Rus, the Kievan prince, or the aspiring Kievan prince supported by the chronicler, also has a special connection with the land: as we have seen, he alone laments its misfortunes, organizes its defence from external enemies, and inspires love and joy in its population, while his challengers only pursue their own interests. Fantosme shows how the clash between the interests of many powerful players brings suffering to the land of England, just as the Rusian chroniclers show how the clash between the interests of many princes brings suffering to the Rus Land and to "the Christians."

---

87 See chap. 1.
88 Michel Bur, "The Seigneuries," in *The New Cambridge Medieval History*, vol. 4, 548.
89 Ashe, "Anomalous King," 183, 186, 188–89.
90 Laura Ashe, *Fiction and History in England, 1066–1200* (New York: Cambridge University Press, 2007), 104, 107.
91 Ashe, *Fiction and History in England*, 104, 107.

However, if Rusian chroniclers share Fantosme's attitude to the sanctity of the land as the key value, they do not necessarily connect it with the figure of the legitimate supreme ruler. Another key value of the Rusian sources is closer to the continental vernacular literature with its dream of aristocratic egalitarianism: the good of the Rus Land is more often connected with the ideas of cooperation, reciprocity, and mutual love between all princes. The political programme prevalent in the chronicles is expressed in "Iaroslav's Testament," the speech of Iaroslav the "Wise" to his sons that he allegedly made on his deathbed. In this speech, Iaroslav does bequeath the Kievan throne to his oldest son; however, the emphasis is not on this heir's special status, but on power sharing. Other sons receive their allocated dominions; Iaroslav's admonishes them to live in brotherly love, "not to transgress your brother's boundaries" and to obey the eldest brother "as you obey me; may he be instead of me for you." The eldest heir is to see that no prince "commits wrongdoing (*obideti*) against his brother," and to help "the one who is being wronged." If you fail to live in love and peace with each other and to obey the eldest brother, Iaroslav warns, "you will ruin the land that your forefathers obtained by their great labour."[92]

The main points of the "Testament" provide recurring themes for subsequent accounts of princely politics. Good princes of the present defending the Rus Land in battles inherited the "sweat" and "labour" of their heroic forefathers. The leading princes hold a peace conference because external enemies rejoice at their strife and tear the land apart. The princes resolve their disagreements about the allocation of *volosts* in order to stop "ruining the Rus Land" by internecine conflicts. They declare, "Let us be united in one heart and take good care of the Rus Land." When a conflict is about to erupt again, the Kievans convince the princes to start negotiations and not to "ruin the land that your forefathers, fighting for the Rus Land, obtained by their great labour and courage." A good regional prince sacrifices his legitimate interests "for the sake of peace in the Rus Land," when he does not seek to obtain his rightful inheritance that the Kievan prince gave to someone else.[93]

This ideology centred on the land and on the ancestors who won it with their sweat and labour looks very different from the ideas of good government based on the *regnum* as described by Reynolds. However, it does not always look that different from the ideas associated with the *regnum* in the sources. According to Reynolds, Flanders and Normandy were occasionally called *regna* because they were "particularly well-governed areas" with rulers so powerful that they were perceived to be "like kings"; such usage of *regnum*, Reynolds argues, indicates the connection between the notion of *regnum* and the idea of a good and strong government.[94] However, on an occasion when Dudo explicitly and forcefully describes Normandy as suffering from the lack of a good ruler, he still calls it a *regnum*. Norman and Breton "counts and princes" ask Rollo to transfer power to his son William and to make him their "duke, count, and patrician." Rollo can no longer

---

92 PSRL 1, 161.
93 PSRL 1, 256, 264.
94 Reynolds, *Kingdoms and Communities*, 260, 278.

take good care of Normandy because of his old age: "For that reason, foreign peoples already afflict us and tear away all that is ours. There are division and strife (*duellum*) among us, and the concord that should exist in a *regnum* is not established and therefore *publica res* is destroyed and wasted."[95]

This *regnum*, with concord as its ideal state and internal strife as its main curse, is no different from the "land" of Rusian sources, especially since the Normans also obtained it "by the labour of battles and sweat of fighting," a formula that may go back to the shared Scandinavian roots of the Rusian and Norman dynasties.[96] It is, indeed, difficult to see how the use of *regnum* in the magnates' speech signifies the alleged perception of Normandy as an "especially well-governed area." It is equally hard to imagine that Dudo, in one and the same passage, would pay so little attention to the terminology of rulership as to represent "counts" as subjects of another "count" (who is also a "duke" and a "patrician"), but that he would simultaneously split hairs about what region "deserves" to be called *regnum*. Dudo's use of *regnum* may be better explained if we suggest that in his mind it was not connected with any specific type of governance, good or bad, royal, ducal, or comital, but that he simply used this word to designate a "land" in the sense of any relatively large and coherent territorial unit. Indeed, Reynolds herself refers to an occasion when the Latin *regnum* was translated into the vernacular as *la terre*.[97]

If a medieval translator could understand the *regnum* simply as the "land," then the Latin authors who called Normandy or Flanders *regnum* probably did so because they had in mind the vernacular *terre*. In other words, just like *fevum* or *vassalus* used in a medieval text do not necessarily indicate the existence of "feudalism," so *regnum* does not necessarily indicate the existence of the monarchical ideology. Conversely, Fantosme displays such ideology without hinging it on the notion of *regne*, the vernacular correspondent of *regnum*. For him, the restoration of royal authority challenged by domestic rebels and foreign invaders is the way to end to the sufferings of the land; for Dudo, the same goal is achieved by a capable, vigorous duke; and for the Rusian chronicler, this is obtained by cooperation among the princes. However, for all of them, the starting point and key value is not royal power, but the well-being of the land, be it *regnum*, *terre*, or *zemlia*. Arguably, the authors who did present the king as the archetypical good ruler and the kingdom as the highest form of a secular community superimposed these ideas on the pre-existing ideology that was centred on the land.

Language and Ideology: East Slavonic versus Church Slavonic

Picking up all the diverse strands of our discussion, we see one underlying theme: differences in the political narratives produced in Rus and Latin Europe may reflect primarily

---

95 *De moribus et actis primorum Normanniae ducum*, 181.

96 "trado regnum, labore certaminum sudoreque praeliorum adeptum," Lair, *De moribus et actis primorum Normanniae ducum*, 182; but see Petrukhin, "Drevniaia Rus Narod. Kniazia. Religiia," 182 on the "sweat" of a good ruler as a Byzantine trope.

97 Reynolds, *Kingdoms and Communities*, 271.

differences in the character of their written cultures. Possibly, there is so much information about internal conflicts between members of the elite in the Rusian chronicles not because Rus had more such conflicts than other European polities, but because the chroniclers paid more attention to them. The Kievan prince may look less powerful than a contemporary European king not because this actually was the case, but because Rusian authors were less interested in representing the power of the supreme ruler than their Western counterparts were. In other words, Rusian and Western authors used different "protocols" while writing their accounts of contemporary politics and presented their material through different ideological lenses.

The most obvious difference is the role of the classical heritage. Rusian chroniclers did not display any dependence on Cicero, Sallust, and Suetonius, typical of medieval Latin historiographers; indeed, there is no evidence that they knew who Cicero, Sallust, or Suetonius were. Most Rusian *literati* did not have direct access to the Mediterranean cultural heritage available to their Western and Balkan counterparts in Latin and in Greek respectively; the knowledge of the classical, patristic, and early medieval literature in Rus appears to be limited to a relatively small corpus of Church Slavonic translations.

Church Slavonic was the language of religion and learning created for the purpose of translating from the Greek, and based on the language of the South Slavs; how it related to the spoken language of the East Slavs, the core population of Rus, is a matter of debate. Church Slavonic and East Slavonic have been described as two different languages, two dialects of one language, and two registers of one language, "bookish" and "practical."[98] In any case, most Rusian political narratives are in East Slavonic, with occasional inclusions of what Simon Franklin describes as interaction and "mutual contamination" of the two registers.[99]

Remarkably, the more Church Slavonic "contamination" a source contains, the closer it comes to representing Rus as an orderly monarchy. On the one hand, as a language of Scripture, Church Slavonic brought with it connotations of Old Testament historical narratives with their sacred kingship. On the other hand, the same classical tradition that shaped the writings of the Western monks brought up on Cicero, Sallust and Suetonius reached Rusian educated elite indirectly, via Church Slavonic literature which reflected the Byzantine imperial ideology, which, in turn, reflected the Roman imperial ideology. Even as a reflection of a reflection, twice removed from its original sources, this ideology was still capable of giving a flavour of a well-organized monarchy to a representation of

---

98 Franklin, *Writing, Society and Culture*, 87. See also Dean S. Worth, "Was There a 'Literary Language' in Kievan Rus'?," *The Russian Review* 34 (1975): 1–9; Worth, "([Church] Slavonic) Writing in Kievan Rus'," in *Christianity and the Eastern Slavs*, ed. Boris Gasparov and Olga Raevsky-Hughes (Berkeley: University of California Press, 1993), 141–53; B. A. Uspenskii, *Iazykovaia situatsia Kievskoi Rusi i ee znachenie dlia istorii russkogo literaturnogo iazyka* (Moscow: Nauka, 1983), 9–54. For more titles on the relation between Church Slavonic and the vernacular of Rus, see Franklin, *Writing, Society and Culture*, 85–88.

99 Franklin, *Writing, Society and Culture*, 88.

a medieval polity, regardless of how monarchical and how well organized the polity was in reality.

In a handful of texts discussing political organization, written entirely in Church Slavonic, Rus looks like a "normal" European kingdom, especially in the most sophisticated Rusian literary work, the *Sermon on Law and Grace* by Metropolitan Hilarion. Francis Thomson, who vehemently denies that there was any knowledge of Greek in Rus, makes a possible exception for Hilarion. Thomson sees him as the only Rusian author who may have read Greek works in the original.[100] The *Sermon*, composed in the mid-eleventh century, celebrates the conversion of Rus; it includes an elaborate encomium to Vladimir that makes a case for his sanctity and Vladimir's son, the current Kievan prince Iaroslav, is presented as the autocrat of Rus ruling by God's grace.

In fact, a contrast between the majestic figure of the Kievan prince in the *Sermon* and multiple squabbling princes in most post-Iaroslav sources is a cornerstone of the traditional "disintegration, strife and decline" narrative of the Rusian history. An alternative interpretation offered by Franklin and Shepard is similar to Barthélemy's "feudal revelation": "cracked facades" of the borrowed Byzantine imperial ideology covered the reality of Iaroslav's "limited rule over a limited area with fairly basic institutions of government." In the aftermath of the conversion, the elite "based its images of authority and authenticity on a sense of direct *translatio* from Byzantium." During this "age of primary borrowing," "the presentation was neater than the substance." Since the early twelfth century, with the Rusian culture "going native," the presentation began to match the substance better.[101]

To be sure, on the few occasions when Rusian twelfth-century political organization is presented through the lens of Byzantine imperial ideology, it looks as "neat" as the eleventh-century "Golden Age" painted by Hilarion: the one and only ruler reigns over the entire realm. In a Church Slavonic eulogy, inspired by the *Sermon on Law and Grace*, the late twelfth-century Kievan prince Rurik Rostislavich, accompanied by his "God-favored children," thinking "the emperor's thought," and belonging to the long line of the "autocrats holding the throne of Kiev," appears no less majestic than Hilarion's Iaroslav.[102] However, in contrast with Hilarion's time, such representations comprise a tiny minority of the available sources—not because the number of Byzantine-style, Church Slavonic texts declined, but because the number of East Slavonic texts, which displayed no interest in the imperial ideology, increased exponentially.

When these two types of texts discuss the same events and personalities, the contrast cannot be greater. A case in point is the image of one and the same prince, Vladimir Monomakh, in his East Slavonic autobiographical *Instruction* and in a Church Slavonic Lenten homily addressed to him by the Greek metropolitan of Kiev Nicephorus I. Both

---

100 Francis Thomson, "'Made in Russia.' A Survey of the Translations Allegedly Made in Kievan Russia," in *Millenium Russiae Christianae: Tausend Jahre Christliches Russland*, ed. Gerhard Birkfellner (Cologne: Bőhlau, 1993), 295–354, at 307.
101 Franklin and Shepard, *Emergence of Rus*, 244, 313, 315.
102 PSRL 2, 708–9.

are essentially "mirrors for princes" which discuss the duties of a ruler using Monomakh as an example. However, Nicephorus's elaborate discussion of the principles of Christian government, his portrayal of a stately ruler, "active by proxy and authority rather than in person," can be no more different from Monomakh's text, which is "barely concerned at all with the abstractions of rule" and which presents the author as a hands-on heroic warlord. Franklin and Shepard have shown that these differences are "rhetorical as much as factual": Nicephorus's "well-cultivated courtly imagery" is informed by "his own Byzantine presuppositions about rulership," while Monomakh's "rhetoric of self-presentation matches the political culture of his dynasty."[103] Shepard neatly captures the character of this culture when he describes it as "essentially 'home-brewed'."[104] The "brew" did include ingredients from Scriptural, patristic, Byzantine, and other sources, but they were selected and arranged with the goal of advancing the indigenous political agenda.

"Brotherly Love" and the Cult of St. Boris and Gleb

The monarchical ideology of Western medieval authors was inspired not only by classical historiography, but also by the Old Testament kings. Unlike works by Sallust and Suetonius, the Old Testament was, of course, known to Rusian chroniclers who occasionally did employ its concept of sacred kingship. When they did, the result was similar to that of their Western counterparts: the reader was left with the impression of an orderly monarchical rule. The best example is probably the *Suzdalian* chronicle, which presented Vsevolod of Suzdalia (r. 1176–1212) as the uncontested supreme ruler of Rus. During the same time when the panegyrist of Rurik of Kiev used imperial imagery to praise the "autocracy" of the Kievan princes, Vsevolod's chronicler employed Old Testament imagery to perform a similar task in respect to the Suzdalian princes. In the *Suzdalian* chronicle, we read that Vsevolod "sent" his oldest son Constantine to be the prince of Novgorod because it was the oldest city in Rus. When Constantine arrived in "his city" Novgorod, the people

> put him on the throne, and bowed down, and kissed him with honor, as the prophet says, "Your representative, God, forever and ever, you love justice and hate lawlessness, because of that your God has anointed you" (Hebrews 1:9) [...] As the prophet says, "God, may you give judgment to the king (*tsesarevi*) and rectitude to the son of the king (*synovi tsesarevi*) to judge your people justly" (Isaiah 32:1).[105]

The chronicler passes in silence all the complicated developments in relations between the leading princes and the Novgorodian community that normally would lead to the appointment of the prince of Novgorod. From other sources, we know that Vsevolod,

---

103 Franklin and Shepard, *Emergence of Rus*, 313–15.
104 Shepard, "Crowns from the Basileus," 156.
105 PSRL 1, 422–23.

while being a powerful ruler, was not an anointed king governing all Rusian lands, and that he could not simply "send" his son to Novgorod.

These other sources consist mostly of chronicle narratives, the tenor of which is very different from that of the passage about Constantine. For the most part, Rusian authors discussing contemporary politics and turning to Scriptural authority invoked not sacred kingship, but brotherly love. In the context of interprincely relations, the two favourite Scriptural quotations were, "Behold, how good and how pleasant it is for brethren to dwell together in unity" (Ps. 133:1), and, "If anyone says, 'I love God,' and hates his brother, he is a liar" (John 4:20). Since all princes were "brethren" and addressed one another as "brother," these quotations were used to condemn internal conflicts and to promote the ideal of collective action, cooperation, and power sharing among the princes.[106]

Chroniclers emphasize respect for the property rights of all "brethren" and non-violation of sworn agreements between princes as ways to achieve this ideal. Franklin showed that this agenda of Rusian *literati* explains much about their selection of the Byzantine material available to them in Slavonic translations, in particular, the prominent place that chroniclers gave to non-canonical stories describing sworn agreements about the division of land between brothers, ranging from the sons of Noah to those of Jacob.[107] These apocryphal stories, stressing God's punishment for violators of agreements who tried to take over their brothers' rightful dominions, promoted the same political ideas as Scriptural quotations praising brotherly love.

A crucial role in the formation of this ideology of "brotherly love" was played by the cult of princely brothers Boris and Gleb, who were murdered in the course of a fratricidal struggle for the Kievan throne after the death of Vladimir in 1015. Vladimir himself had been brought to power by his victory in a bloody struggle that followed the death of his father, Sviatoslav. Indeed, such struggles may be expected in the absence of primogeniture or other clear rules for succession. It was the death and subsequent veneration of Boris and Gleb that put an end to fratricidal forms of rivalry between heirs.

According to texts associated with this cult, Boris was well-placed to ascend the Kievan throne after Vladimir, but he refused to do so out of respect for the rights of his half-brother, Vladimir's eldest son Sviatopolk. In the *Primary Chronicle*, Boris says in response to his men urging him to fight off Sviatopolk and to become the Kievan prince, "I will not raise my hand against my older brother. As my father is dead now, he will be in place of a father for me."[108] This is the first instance of the use of the formula "in place of a father" that figures prominently in the discourse of interprincely relations. Boris's peaceful intentions did not save him from Sviatopolk who sent assassins to murder first him and then their younger brother Gleb. Some chronicle accounts also contain information about the murder of one more brother, Sviatoslav, who, however,

---

[106] PSRL 1, 252–53, PSRL 2, 328–29, 393. On Psalmic quotations in the *Primary Chronicle*, see Donald Ostrowski, "Identifying Psalmic Quotations in the PVL," PVL, 217–50.

[107] Simon Franklin, "Some Apocryphal Sources of Kievan Rus Historiography," *Oxford Slavonic Papers* 15 (1982): 3–27.

[108] PSRL 1, 132.

was not venerated.[109] The sources concentrate on Boris and Gleb, and describe how they died martyrs' deaths, praying and not making any attempts to resist. The *Primary Chronicle* contrasts their brotherly love with the "Cain-like" behaviour of Sviatopolk, who thinks, "I will kill all my brothers and will obtain the sole rule over Rus (*priimu vlast Ruskuiu edin*)."[110] Sviatopolk's rule lasted for four years: in 1019, yet another brother, Iaroslav, the future "Wise," defeated him and became the prince of Kiev; Sviatopolk died in exile.[111]

The chronology of the texts about Boris and Gleb is murky, but their cult clearly emerged during the reign of Iaroslav, who not only actively promoted it, but also, together with his brother Mstislav, pioneered the type of interprincely relations that came to be sanctified by the cult. In contrast with previous conflicts between princes, which ended with the victory of one participant and the flight and/or death of the defeated side, Iaroslav and Mstislav, as we remember, "divided the Rus Land along the Dnieper," and the oldest brother Iaroslav received the more prestigious part containing Kiev, even though he lost battle to Mstislav. After working out this agreement of power sharing, "they began to live in peace and brotherly love. Strife and tumult ceased, and there was a great tranquility in the land."[112]

From that time on, even though the "peace, brotherly love, and great tranquility" often remained an ideal rather than a reality, princes did not assassinate each other. The succession of the Kievan and other thrones was rarely completely smooth, but it was never again accompanied by a fratricidal bloodbath comparable to those following the death of Sviatoslav and Vladimir. The only case of a political assassination after the murder of Boris and Gleb in 1015 occurred 200 years later, in 1217, when two princes of Riazan, "thinking like Sviatopolk," treacherously killed at a feast six other princes who had lands in the Riazan principality. The murderers did not achieve their goal of establishing uncontested domination of the region, and were eventually driven out of Riazan.[113] This case is clearly anomalous. The notoriety of Sviatopolk the "Cain-like," whose grave, according to the *Primary Chronicle*, emitted a terrible stench "even until the present day,"[114] apparently compelled the princes to abstain from following in his footsteps and killing their rivals.

---

[109] N. I. Miliutenko, *Sviatye kniazia-mucheniki Boris i Gleb* (St. Petersburg: Izdatelstvo Olega Abyshko, 2006), 99–100.

[110] PSRL 1, 139.

[111] PSRL 1, 141–45. On the cult of Boris and Gleb, see Miliutenko, *Sviatye kniazia-mucheniki*; Gail Lenhoff, *The Martyred Princes Boris and Gleb: A Sociocultural Study of the Cult and the Texts*, UCLA Slavic Studies Series 19 (Columbus, OH: Slavica Publishers, 1989); *The Hagiography of Kievan Rus'*, ed. Paul Hollingsworth, Harvard Library of Early Ukrainian Literature, Translation Series (Cambridge, MA: Harvard University Press, 1992), 3–32, 97–134; Monica White, *Military Saints in Byzantium and Rus, 900–1200* (Cambridge: Cambridge University Press, 2013), 132–66.

[112] PSRL 1, 149.

[113] PSRL 1, 440, 444.

[114] PSRL 1, 145.

Thus, largely thanks to the cult of Boris and Gleb, a murder of a prince, if not in battle, effectively became taboo. Boris and Gleb came to be seen as patrons of all the Rusian princes and as special heavenly protectors of the country.[115] From heaven, Rus was watched over by two princely brothers; on earth, it was dominated by princes often represented in the sources not as individuals, but as groups of two and more kinsmen who often, although not always, were siblings. Family groups prevail over individual portraits in extant representations of princes in the visual arts,[116] and they figure prominently in Rusian political narratives, a feature that may also be connected with the cult of Boris and Gleb.

One example of a princely group is found in the account of the relations between four brothers Rostislavichi and Andrew Bogoliubsky of Suzdalia during the period when Andrew, in the aftermath of the taking of Kiev in 1169, had power to appoint the Kievan prince. At one point, he "gave Kiev" to the Rostislavichi, but then tried to take it back. Some chronicle accounts treat the Rostislavichi as a collective body, creating the impression that Kiev belongs not to a specific person, but to the Rostislavichi as a whole. When Andrew tries to revoke this grant, he also deals with all the Rostislavichi.[117] The previous chapter discussed occasions when two princes ruled in Kiev jointly, and also the case of two brothers, namesakes of the Rostislavichi mentioned above (the sons of another Rostislav), being princes of Suzdalia. Even the hideous Riazan murderers were brothers. In the chronicle narrative about them, they formulate their goal in oxymoronic terms: to kill other Riazan princes "so that the two of us may obtain the sole rule [over Riazan]."[118] Thus, even the "sole rule" could be shared among two partners.

This prominence of princely groups and pairs in Rusian sources may owe to the fact that the patrons of all princes were venerated as a pair, while their cult, in turn, was profoundly influenced by the Byzantine cult of military saints, as Monica White recently has shown. Remarkably, the Byzantine military saints were venerated collectively as "a unified phalanx of imperial patrons," and were often depicted in art not individually, but in groups and pairs.[119] Thus, contrary to a once popular view, the cult of Boris and Gleb was not a product of entirely indigenous, uniquely Rusian developments. In addition to being influenced by the Byzantine religious culture, it was also connected with other early medieval cults of ruler-martyrs.[120] However, Byzantine and other borrowings were once again put at the service of the "home-brewed" political ideology.

---

115 White, *Military Saints in Byzantium and Rus,* 203, 212, 224.
116 Shepard, "Rus," 395–96.
117 See chap. 4.
118 PSRL 1, 440.
119 White, *Military Saints*, 112, 137.
120 Norman W. Ingham, "The Sovereign as Martyr, East and West," *The Slavic and East European Journal* 17 (1973): 1–17; Ingham, "Genre Characteristic of the Kievan Lives of Princes in Slavic and European Perspective," in *American Contributions to the Ninth International Congress of Slavists*, ed. P. Debreczeny (Kiev, September 1983), vol. 2: *Literature, Poetics, History* (Columbus: Slavica, 1983), 223–38; Ingham, "The Martyred Princes and the Question of Slavic Cultural Continuity in the Early

"Brotherly Love," Aristocratic Ideology, and Horizontal Power Relations

This ideology was essentially aristocratic, which helps to explain the peculiar character of most twelfth-century representations of the Kievan princes, such as the accounts of Vsevolod's reign discussed above. The chronicler reports facts that show Vsevolod as a supreme ruler of considerable power, but he does not celebrate this power the way his Western counterparts celebrate kingship. Nor is he Vsevolod's opponent and a supporter of another claimant to the throne. He does recognize Vsevolod's legitimacy as the supreme ruler; it is just that the subject of supreme rulership incites neither a theoretical interest nor an emotional response from him.

What does excite the chronicler is the subject of the regional princes' rights, such as the admiration he expresses for Andrew, who would rather die than obey Vsevolod's order and move from Pereiaslavl to Kursk. This passage shows the significance of the cult of Boris and Gleb for twelfth-century political ideology: if Andrew has to die defending his land, he says, "this would not be anything new for our kin. The same thing occurred before: did not Sviatopolk kill Boris and Gleb?"[121] Sviatopolk's murder of Boris and Gleb was, of course, not exactly "the same thing" as Vsevolod's intention to appoint his own brother to Pereiaslavl and to give Andrew another territory as a compensation. Apparently, the cult of the junior brothers murdered by the Kievan prince came to provide an ideological framework for the defence of the rights of lesser princes against any actions of the Kievan prince that they perceived as illegitimate.

The dynamics between the Kievan and other princes reported by Rusian authors is similar to that between the king and magnates in Western royal histories, or between the duke or count and nobles in regional histories; what differs is the authorial position, which is monarchical in Western narratives, and aristocratic in Rusian ones. Western regional historians do marginalize kings, but, in the famous words of one of them, they present their local ruler as "more a king than a duke."[122] These regional quasi-monarchs are portrayed as supreme rulers of their territories, distributing lands and offices as they see fit and rightfully crushing the resistance of rebellious nobles, behaving just as kings do in royal histories.

Whether a high medieval Latin historian chooses a realm-wide or a regional perspective, he depicts a legitimate supreme ruler and his subjects who may be either good and loyal, or bad and rebellious. Alternatively, it may be an account of a struggle for the throne, with one side cast as the rightful one and the other as supporting a "tyrant" or "usurper." Neither of these perspectives gives a place for a positive representation of resistance to the legitimate ruler's orders that we see in the account of Andrew's valiant

---

Middle Ages," in *Medieval Russian Culture*, ed. Henrik Birnbaum and Micahel Flier, vol. 1, California Slavic Studies 12 (Berkeley: University of California Press, 1984), 31–53.

[121] PSRL 2, 305.

[122] According to Adémar, William of Aquitaine "was thought to be more a king than a duke (*potius rex quam esse dux putabatur*)." *Ademari Cabannensis Chronicon*, 161–62.

response to Vsevolod. In the West, a "rightfully rebellious" character is easier to find in a vernacular epic than in a history or chronicle. Indeed, the confrontation between Andrew and Vsevolod looks like a scene from *Raoul de Cambrai* or some other French "epic of revolt" expressing an aristocratic worldview.

Another feature of Rusian political narratives that strikes a chord with the aristocratic culture is related to princely groups mentioned above. These groups provide further evidence for the prominence of the horizontal power relations and the collectivist character of Rusian political culture. These features have traditionally been viewed as setting Rus apart from European kingdoms, where the elite was organized by means of vertical power relations between individuals, the lord and his man or the king and his magnate. However, starting in the 1990s, the exclusive role of vertical interpersonal bonds in the West has been put into question, along with so many other aspects of the medieval socio-political organization.

First, Gerd Althoff showed the importance of kin-groups and other collective relationships in the German Empire before the twelfth century, arguing that hierarchical relations between lord and man cannot be properly understood if they are isolated from the context of "cooperative" bonds between equals.[123] A particularly prominent role was played by the sibling bond. Indeed, in a recent study by Jonathan Lyon, the political significance of "princely brothers and sisters" in the German Empire looks similar to that of their Rusian counterparts.[124] Hélène Débax recently examined the traditional view that joint lordship, when two or more partners of equal status dominated the same locality, was only typical of the Occitan-speaking southern France and remained "marginal and alien" to the social organization defined by feudo-vassalic relations (*la féodalité*) that existed in other European regions. Débax produces evidence of shared lordship in northern France, Italy, and the German Empire, arguing that the phenomenon was widespread in medieval Europe, but the sources from Languedoc reveal it particularly well.[125] The bulk of Débax's material consists of the charter evidence for a *castrum* divided, or held jointly, by a group of lords of equal status, who are often sibling coheirs. *Castrum* is usually translated as its modern cognate "castle," but *castra* described by Débax, with their fields, pastures, vineyards, and markets, are better thought of as districts centred on the "castle" proper, that is, a fortified settlement. Such a district is similar to a small Rusian *volost*, consisting of a walled settlement (*gorod*) and the adjacent countryside.

Rusian sources reveal little about these small units; most of their information is about major principalities analogous to duchies or counties. A direct comparison of the princely groups we see in Rus with Débax's "co-lords (*coseigneurs*)" is thus impossible; however, the general idea of *la coseigneurie* as "a domination shared or exercised jointly

---

[123] Althoff, *Family, Friends, and Followers*, 102.

[124] Jonathan R. Lyon, *Princely Brothers and Sisters: The Sibling Bond in German Politics, 1100–1250* (Ithaca: Cornell University Press, 2013).

[125] Hélène Débax, *La seigneurie collective: Pairs, pariers, paratge, les coseigneurs du XIe au XIIe siècle* (Rennes: Presses Universitaires de Rennes, 2012), 22, 13.

at a given level of the ladder of power" is clearly present in Rusian sources.[126] Overall, Débax shows the significance of horizontal power relations for the social organization of the elite, and she combats the traditional view that they were a distinct characteristic of southern France, while the vertical relations prevailed in the areas that Bloch once described as the "feudal zone of Europe." Débax argues that both types of relations were present in various regions of the medieval West, and she connects the visibility of shared lordship in the Occitan sources with the notion of the *paratge*, the key value of the aristocratic culture of Languedoc.

The *paratge*, sung by troubadours and symbolizing the moral superiority of the Occitan culture over the Albigensian crusaders who destroyed it, is literally translated as "peerage," but it stands for "all the aristocratic values," such as loyalty, bravery, and generousity, designating the nobility of birth and character. Débax suggests that the *paratge* and *pariers* (coheirs) have more in common than a lexical similarity, both being connected with the practice of co-lordship. A more traditional interpretation of the socio-political aspect of the *paratge* sees it as an expression of the spirit of equality that set Languedoc apart from the hierarchical North.[127] In other words, earlier scholarship viewed the *paratge* as a manifestation of the differences between the social organization of Languedoc and northern France, while Débax argues that these differences were not real, and that the *paratge* referred to a phenomenon that was present across the north-south divide but which received better expression in the Occitan culture. At the most abstract level, the *paratge* in socio-political context is somewhat kindred to the Rusian "brotherly love": an aristocratic ideal sanctifying power sharing.

If this ideal, so prominent in Rusian narratives of interprincely relations, received a better expression in the vernacular cultures of the medieval West, then Rusian chronicles may be most productively compared with vernacular accounts of contemporary politics written from an aristocratic standpoint. The problem is that in high medieval Western Europe such accounts are virtually non-existent. *Jordan Fantosme's Chronicle* is written in the vernacular and it describes contemporary politics, but the author incorporates elements of the aristocratic worldview only in order to win over his aritstocratic audience and to make his defence of the king's cause more persuasive. Fantosme's text, as we have seen, still has more parallels with Rusian chronicles than do works by his Latin-writing counterparts, but cannot be compared directly to the bulk of Rusian sources which are written from the viewpoint of the regional princes.

High medieval Western vernacular literature giving full expression to the aristocratic worldview consists mostly of poetry and fiction; in addition, there are records of sworn agreements between members of aristocracy from Languedoc written in Occitan. Rusian chronicles mention charters containing sworn agreements between princes, but not a single such charter survived. There can be no direct comparison between the Occitan oaths and Rusian chronicle narratives because of the different nature of these sources. The nature of Western vernacular poetic narratives is also different from the chronicles

---

126 Débax, *La seigneurie collective*, 21.
127 Débax, *La seigneurie collective*, 9–10, 11.

reporting current events. Above all, the vernacular literature of the West is a product of a much more sophisticated culture than Rusian, so that a juxtaposition of the fine troubadour poetry with the uncouth reports of quarrelling princes, implicit in a comparison between the *paratge* and "brotherly love," may look almost sacrilegious.

Fortunately, there is an eleventh-century text from Aquitaine that is analogous to Rusian narratives of interprincely relations in everything from the uncouth style to the subject matter to the authorial position. This is the celebrated *Conventum Hugonis* (1020s).

Rusian Chronicles and the *Conventum Hugonis*

The *Conventum* is the account of a dispute between the Aquitanian magnate Hugh of Lusignan and William V of Aquitaine, who is represented in the text as Hugh's *dominus* and *senior*, that is, lord. According to the *Conventum*, written from Hugh's perspective, he was a bad lord. The *Conventum* is a series of episodes showing Hugh as a good and faithful man fulfilling all his obligations to William, who broke his promises to reward Hugh's faithful service, did not grant Hugh lands that Hugh considers rightly his, and mistreated him in other ways. Therefore, Hugh finally *defidavit* William, that is, defied him, or formally broke their relations of lord and man. It appears that the main goal of the *Conventum* is to justify Hugh, and to place responsibility for the broken agreement on William.

"Appears" is a key word here, because the goal is never stated. The text does not have any introduction, does not provide any context, and hardly explains anything at all. It begins abruptly, in *medias res*: "A certain official named Aimery took a *castrum* called Civray from Bernard his lord and this *castrum* was Hugh's right as it had been his father's." Then it goes on and on in a similar manner. For example:

> Afterwards the count became much more sad and angry (*contristavit se*) with Aimery about the *castrum* called Chizé, which Aimery had seized, and the count and Hugh stood together in the dispute with Aimery. The count besieged the *castrum* called Malval because of the offense which Aimery had committed against him and took it.
>
> [...]
>
> Hugh went to the fortress at Gencay and burned it down and captured men and women and carried off everything. Coming to the count he said to him: "My lord, give me permission to rebuild the *castrum* which I have burnt." And the count said to him: "You are Fulk's man. How can you build the *castrum*?"[128]

Western medievalists describe the *Conventum* as a one-of-a-kind text. Jane Martindale expresses a common opinion when she calls its form of composition "unparalleled," while Dominique Barthélemy, apparently at a loss for words to convey its uniqueness,

---

[128] *Conventum Hugonis*, 542, 544, 546.

exclaims, "Quel document, pourtant!"[129] However, to a scholar of East Slavonic chronicles the *Conventum* looks comfortably familiar, especially when it comes to its form of composition. There is no transition between episodes; the narration consists of short sentences and follows the same style: X had a certain *castrum* ... X came to Y and said ... Y answered ... X was angry and burned Y's *castrum* ... X and Y made peace ... X and Y broke their peace .... Change *castrum* to *volost*, and this will become a faithful description of the majority of East Slavonic political narratives.

Similarities are not limited to form and style, but extend to the content and perspective as well. The *Conventum* is often contrasted with the Latin chronicle by Adémar of Chabannes written within the same time period and containing the famous portrayal of the same William. According to Adémar, William, perceived by people "to be more a king than a duke," "subjected all Aquitaine to his power (*imperium*) so that nobody dared to raise a hand against him"; "the Aquitanian magnates (*promores*) who attempted to rebel against this duke were all either subdued or destroyed."[130] In contrast with this royal-like figure ruling over his Aquitanian subjects and crushing the rebels, William of the *Conventum* operates through a network of agreements binding him to various individual magnates of Aquitania and of neighbouring territories. The *Conventum* does not differentiate the latter from the former in their relations to the "Duke of the Aquitanians" (who is "the count" in the *Conventum*). William's agreements with Hugh and with various other Aquitanians are treated in exactly the same manner as his agreements with Sancho VI of Gascony and with Fulk Nerra of Anjou.[131]

Indeed, in the *Conventum*, William appears to have no more *imperium* over the Aquitanians than he has over the Gascon or Angevin count. Thus, when a certain Aimery seizes a *castrum*, this is not a question of the "duke of the Aquitanians" enforcing the law and dispatching someone under his power to return the seized property and to punish the transgressor. Rather, William becomes "sad and angry (*contristavit se*)"[132] with Aimery, just as any Rusian prince would be with someone who had seized his *volost*. In his anger and sadness, William starts a *contentionem* with Aimery, that is, a dispute or hostility. In this *contentio* against Aimery, "Hugh and William stood together," and Hugh "helped [William] as best he could" when William was besieging one of Aimery's *castra*. With Hugh's help, he successfully captured this *castrum*, and the *Conventum* explains that William did so "because of the offense (*pro malifacto* [sic]) which Aimery had committed against him."[133] *Malefactum*, which signifies "offence"

---

[129] Dominique Barthélemy, "Autour d'un récit de pactes", 447–96, 452–53; Martindale, *Status, Authority, and Regional Power*, VIIb, 531.

[130] *Ademari Cabannensis Chronicon*, 161–63. On Adémar's representation of William, see B. S. Bachrach, " 'Potius Rex quam Esse Dux putabatur': Some Observations Concerning Adémar of Chabannes' Panegyric on Duke William the Great," *The Haskins Society Journal* 1 (1989): 11–21.

[131] *Conventum Hugonis*, 545, 546.

[132] Martindale treats *contristavit* as an example of "the blurring of 'anger' and 'sorrow' " typical of the language used in the eleventh-century Poitevin texts. Martindale, *Status, Authority, and Regional Power*, VIIb, 550–51n20.

[133] *Conventum Hugonis*, 544.

in medieval Latin,[134] plays in the *Conventum* the same role as *obida* (offence, wrong, dishonour) plays in the Rusian chronicles. Seizing or damaging one's land constitutes an "offence"; he who has suffered it should avenge himself by seizing or damaging the offender's land in turn.

In this respect, there is no difference between Willliam and the prominent Aquitanians over whom he supposedly has *imperium*: William captures Aimery's property to avenge the *malifactum* committed by Aimery, just as Geoffrey the viscount burns Hugh's land and mutilates his men to avenge the *malifactum* committed by Hugh.[135] It does not make any difference to Geoffrey that Hugh was committing the *malifactum* against him on William's orders: for Geoffrey and Hugh, as they are represented in the *Conventum*, William is not a ruler who sends his subordinate to punish a rebel, but just another player in the local aristocratic politics. The very notion of "rebellion" is alien to the *Conventum*. Correspondingly, when Hugh helps William against Aimery, he does not see himself as punishing a rebel on the ruler's orders, but rather as doing service to a lord with whom he is bound by an agreement. This agreement apparently stipulates mutual obligations: after Aimery was defeated by the joint forces of William and Hugh, "the count promised him [Hugh], as a lord should rightfully promise to his man (*sicut debit Senior promittere suo homini rationem*), not to make any agreement or alliance (*finem vel societatem*) without Hugh." Then he broke this promise and made a *finis* with Aimery "without consulting Hugh."[136] From the point of view reflected in the *Conventum*, by doing so, William did not exercise his *imperium* over Hugh and Aimery as their duke, but rather acted towards Hugh as a bad lord.

Hugh's highest duty that emerges from the *Conventum* is not being a good subject to the ruler of Aquitaine, but preserving and defending his hereditary lands. Serving William as his *homo* is a means to this end: in return for his loyalty and support, Hugh expects from William grants of lands that belonged to Hugh's deceased kinsmen and assistance in defending his possessions if necessary. These expectations were frustrated: when Geoffrey burned Hugh's land, "the Count in no way helped Hugh [...] Hugh has lost his land and still does not have it (*adhuc suam terram Ugo perditur*); and because of the Count, he lost other land which he had held in peace." Nor did William ensure that Hugh received other territories to which he had hereditary rights. Therefore, Hugh and his men came to the conclusion that "the count was treating him badly," and Hugh made preparations to defend a disputed *castrum* "against all men," presumably including William. Fearing to lose Hugh, William promised to grant him some other lands that Hugh considered his right; when he broke this promise, Hugh broke off his faith with him. From the standpoint of the *Conventum*, he had no other choice. The William of the *Conventum* apparently shares this opinion. Instead of "subduing or destroying" his rebellious magnate, as Adémar's William does, he works out a compromise: he gives Hugh one

---

134 J. F. Niermeyer, *Mediae Latinitatis Lexicon Minus* (Leiden: Brill, 1976), 630.
135 *Conventum Hugonis*, 543.
136 *Conventum Hugonis*, 544.

of the requested *castra* in exchange for Hugh renouncing his claims to other lands; Hugh then swears fidelity to William and his son.[137]

The *Conventum* is based on the same ideas about relations between a magnate and a ruler that guide the behaviour of the regional princes in respect to the Kievan prince in most chronicle narratives. Andrew of Pereiaslavl submits to the authority of the Kievan prince after he is assured that he would continue to hold his land in peace. So do other princes when Vsevolod "gives" them the lands they already have, that is, presumably, after he guarantees that the lands will remain theirs.[138] When a regional prince does not have such a guarantee and faces the threat of being deprived of his rightful dominion, his natural course of action is to oppose the Kievan prince, using force if need be.

This is what Sviatoslav of Chernigov and his son Oleg did when "evil men" falsely told them that the Kievan prince Rostislav planned to imprison Oleg and to give Chernigov to someone else—or, at any rate, the chronicler states that this information was false. According to the chronicler, Rostislav had no such plans, but Sviatoslav and Oleg believed the slander and joined a claimant for the Kievan throne who tried, unsuccessfully, to overthrow Rostislav. Their men argued that Rostislav's behaviour gave Sviatoslav and Oleg the right to consider themselves not to be bound by the oath they had sworn to him (*est prav* [...] *v khrestnom tselovan'i*). In addition, Sviatoslav's men said, "You, Prince, have already ruined your *volost* by supporting Rostislav, and he gives you very little help anyway (*on ti vsiako lenivo pomogaet*)." The security of the *volost* was the councillors' central argument, while the alleged threat of the son's imprisonment played a secondary role. The chronicler concludes in a tone of regret: "This is how Sviatoslav was compelled to break his love with Rostislav (*nuzheiu povedesia ot Rostislavli liubvi*)" and to go over to his enemies.[139]

The wording echoes the *Conventum*, where relations between Hugh and William before the break-off are also described as "love." This is just one of many lexical parallels between the *Conventum* and East Slavonic political narratives. The statement that Hugh, by supporting William, *perditur* his land, corresponds to the words of Sviatoslav's men "ruined your *volost*" almost verbatim: *perdo* means "to destroy, ruin" as well as "to lose." *Finis* in the meaning of "agreement" corresponds to the East Slavonic *dokonchanie*, which literally means "finishing" and is also used to signify "agreement." East Slavonic expressions that look almost like calques from the language of the *Conventum* are so

---

137 *Conventum Hugonis*, 544, 546, 548.

138 Vsevolod gave up his plans to deprive the Monomakhovichi of their lands, and "gave them what they asked" (PSRL 2, 306). After that, we see them in the same lands where they were before, but Vsevolod exercises supreme authority over these lands. For example, we know that Vsevolod obtained supreme control over Iziaslav's Vladimir-in-Volhynia, because he gave it to his own son when Iziaslav moved from there to more prestigious Pereialsavl (PSRL 2, 312–13). Andrew of Pereiaslavl did not bequeath it to a heir of his choice; the next prince of Pereiaslavl was chosen by Vsevolod. It is unlikely that Andrew did designate the heir of Pereiaslavl, but that the chronicler simply omitted this information: the chronicler pays much attention to Andrew, and he describes a heavenly portent that allegedly accompanied his burial (PSRL 2, 309).

139 PSRL 2, 513–14.

numerous that they would require a separate study. Arguably, similarities in the language reflect similarities in the authors' worldviews.

Thus, the chronicler presents Rostislav as the rightful Kievan prince, but he does not blame Sviatoslav for joining the forces of Rostislav's enemies. If anyone is to blame, it is the "evil men" who spread misinformation about Rostislav's intentions. Sviatoslav had no choice: he could not be expected to remain loyal to the ruler who, he believed, was going to take away his rightful land. Apparently, this is how Rostislav himself viewed the matter: we read that after he prevailed over the hostile coalition that Sviatoslav supported, Sviatoslav "swore an oath on the Cross to Rostislav," presumably pledging allegiance to him; after that, he remained in his Chernigov.[140] Sviatoslav's behaviour is justified by references to his men's opinion, who all considered it Sviatoslav's unfortunate duty to turn against the Kievan prince; much like Hugh's men, who appear in the narrative for the first time when his relations with William reach the lowest point, urged him to stand up to William.[141] The role of the councillors is another similarity between the two narratives.

Arguably, the same features of the *Conventum* that set it apart from other political narratives produced in Latin Europe make it close to Rusian accounts of interprincely relations. According to its editors and translators, the *Conventum* "ought perhaps to have been written in the vernacular," or probably even was written in the vernacular, since its idiosyncratic form of Latin may have been a spoken language in eleventh-century Aquitaine.[142] Another idiosyncratic feature of the *Conventum* is its perspective. In accordance with the tendency of vernacular texts to express the position of aristocracy, the *Conventum*, in the words of one of its most prominent scholars, is part of "discourse in terms of which nobles [...] legitimated their own conduct [...] as they represented, evaluated, and tried to control political relations between lords and *fideles*."[143] By the same

---

[140] PSRL 2, 520.

[141] "Visum fuit Ugoni et ad suos ut male tractaret ei comes," trans. Martindale as "It seemed to Hugh and his men that the Count was treating him badly." It is, of course, quite likely that by *et ad suos* the author of the *Conventum* actually meant *et suis*. On the other hand, there is another possibility: *ad suos* may have been grammatically correct and then it would mean "according to his men." In this case, *visum fuit Ugoni et ad suos* might indicate not simply that Hugh and his men were of one opinion about William, but that Hugh was actually influenced by his men. In any case, it is remarkable that Hugh's *sui* appear in the narrative at the moment when Hugh is prepared to defend a disputed *castrum* "against all men (*contra omnes*)," presumably including William. *Conventum Hugonis*, 546.

[142] Hyams, Introduction to the *Agreement between Count William V of Aquitaine and Hugh IV of Lusignan*. Martindale thinks that, in connection with the *Conventum*, "it is necessary to make some allowance for the possibility that spoken Latin survived in some form—even into the eleventh century," and she notes that "the 'errors' with which the text is studded have many affinities with the 'late' or 'vulgar Latin'," Martindale, *Status, Authority and Regional Power*, VIII, 4, 24; for a review of literature on the language of the *Conventum*, see ibid., VIII, 3–4.

[143] Stephen White, "A Crisis of Fidelity in c. 1000?," in *Building Legitimacy: Political Discourses and Forms of Legitimacy in Medieval Societies*, ed. Isabel Alfonso, Hugh Kennedy, and Julio Escalona (Boston: Brill, 2004), 46.

token, most chronicle narratives represent discourses in terms of which lesser princes legitimize their own conduct. The two discourses appear to be remarkably similar.

**

The historiographical fate of the *Conventum* is inextricably linked to the changes in medievalists' "professional belief system." At the turn of the twentieth century, it was used to show that the area where it was produced was a state of its own, virtually independent from royal control. After this view became outmoded, the *Conventum* was by and large forgotten, and was only of interest to regional historians, mostly as a source on Poitevin topography. Barthélemy noted the paradox of François-Louis Ganshof, the author of the classic work on feudalism, using extensively legal notices from the Loire valley, but ignoring "the most original and most rich of them," the *Conventum*.[144] Apparently, this messy narrative, a string of disjointed passages about who said what and who burned what *castrum*, did not fit the neat "feudal system" of Ganshof's studies.

It was when the neatness of this system was called into question that the *Conventum* was resurrected from oblivion and became medievalists' "new favourite." Some have argued that this change in historiographical perspective resulted in undue neglect of other sources that are perceived as contradicting the *Conventum* and supporting the outmoded view of feudalism.[145] Being only human, historians cannot produce an overarching synthesis based on a perfectly balanced, impartial use of all evidence available to them. What evidence makes it into the historiographic mainstream and what remains marginalized depends on many factors, including the general character of the corpus of sources. This chapter argues that a comparative analysis of the socio-political organizations in Rus and in the high medieval West based on the numerically prevalent type of narrative sources from the two regions means comparing apples to oranges.

A comparison has to be based on narratives, because too few diplomatic sources from Rus survived. However, most high medieval political narratives reflect the realities of their society through the lens of their authors' Latin scholarship, a facility which did not exist in Rus. This is not to say that East Slavonic texts, which comprise a majority of Rusian sources, provide a direct, unmediated view of reality—no text does. However, Rusian chroniclers, in selecting and arranging their materials, were evidently guided by principles different from those employed by authors of Latin chronicles and histories. These texts show the differences between the two written cultures, but when it comes to comparing the two societies, it is not always possible to know whether we deal with different forms of social organization or with different modes of representation. A juxtaposition of the East Slavonic chronicle narratives with *Jordan Fantosme's Chronicle* and the *Conventum* suggests that the difference in the modes of representation may have

---

[144] Barthélemy, "Autour d'un récit de pactes," 452–53.
[145] Dirk Heirbaut, "Not European Feudalism, But Flemish Feudalism: A New Reading of Galbert of Bruges's Data on Feudalism in the Context of Early Twelfth-Century Flanders," in *Galbert of Bruges and the Historiography of Medieval Flanders*, ed. Jeff Rider and Alan V. Murray (Washington, DC: Catholic University of America Press, 2009), 58.

played a role in the formation of the view of Rus's "special path." One aspect of this "special path," that of horizontal power relations between partners of equal status jointly dominating a locality, is similar to an aspect of another society with an alleged "special path," that of southern France. Débax's argument about this form of social organization of the elite being widespread in Europe, but more visible in the Occitan sources, supports the suggestion about the significance of the vernacular versus the "learned" language raised by an analysis of *Jordan Fantosme's Chronicle* and the *Conventum*.

One feature that distinguishes the *Conventum*, the Rusian chronicle passages which bear most resemblance to it, and *Jordan Fantosme's Chronicle*, is their connection with oral political discourse. This connection goes beyond the vernacular or semi-vernacular language of these texts. Fantosme's work was apparently intended for singing or reading aloud.[146] The *Conventum* must have been "a succession of complaints voiced, and for the most part literally voiced, by Hugh."[147] The speeches reported in the Rusian chronicles are, in all probability, close to the speeches actually delivered on behalf of princes; by the same token, when the chronicler reports what a prince's men "said to him," it is likely that he partially represents their actual words. Thus, the three elements that make the title of Martindale's essay on the *Conventum*—dispute, settlement, and orality—are all present in Fantosme and in the Rusian chronicles as well.[148]

The oral political discourse that can be glimpsed from the Western vernacular sources is closer to the Rusian chronicles than is the discourse of medieval Latin historiography. Similarities between the vernacular sources reflecting the aristocratic worldview and narratives of interprincely relations suggest that the majority of Rusian princes, instead of being viewed as members of an anomalously big and ultimately failed ruling dynasty, may be compared to Western aristocracy. Such a comparison is the task of the next chapter.

---

146 Bennett, "La Chronique de Jordan Fantosme," 37–56.
147 Martindale, *Status, Authority, and Regional Power*, 8, 4.
148 Martindale, "Dispute, Settlement and Orality."

Chapter 3

ELITE DOMINATION IN RUS AND LATIN EUROPE: PRINCELY POWER AND BANAL LORDSHIP

THE ORIGINS OF princely domination in Rus are described in what is probably the most famous, and most commented on, passage from the *Primary Chronicle*. It tells us that in the mid-ninth century "the Varangians from across the sea" collected something called *dan* from the Slavic and Finnic population, in what is now northern Russia, until the people refused to give them *dan* and drove them away.

> And they started to govern themselves, and there was no justice among them, and one kin made a war against the other. There was strife among them, and they started to make war on one another. And they said to one another, "Let us seek a prince who would govern us and would judge us justly." And they went across the sea to the Varangians [...] and said, "Our land is vast and abundant, but there is no order in it. Come and be our princes and govern us."

Three brothers with their kin volunteered to go, and the oldest brother, Rurik, founded the dynasty that later established itself in Kiev.[1]

This brief paragraph has been analyzed, interpreted in all possible and impossible ways, and hotly debated by historians and by ideologists of all sorts since the mid-eighteenth century. However, the debates have been concerned almost exclusively with only one aspect of the passage: the ethnicity of Rurik and the role that the Scandinavians, called "Varangians" in East Slavonic, played in the formation of Rus. Contrary to overwhelming evidence for the prominence of Scandinavians in early Rus, there are still people in Russia and Ukraine—including some scholars—who feel that the idea of "foreigners" from overseas dominating the Slavs somehow offends their sensibilities, and who seek to construe Rurik and his Varangians as Slavic.[2] Needless to say, Rurik, who is not mentioned in any other source, probably never existed in the first place, and even if he did, his invitation, as it is presented in the chronicle, can only be legendary. The

---

[1] PSRL 1, 19–20.

[2] Literature on the Scandinavians in early Rus is vast. For a general review of scholarship on this topic, see V. Ia Petrukhin, "Legenda of prizvanii variagov i Baltiiskii region," *Drevniaia Rus: Voprosy medievistiki* 32 (2008): 41–46. An important recent work is Pierre Bauduin and Alexander Musin, eds., *Vers l'Orient et vers l'Occident: Regards croisés sur les dynamiques et les transferts culturels des Vikings à la Rous ancienne* (Caen: Presses universitaires de Caen, 2014). Scholars denying the importance of the Scandinavians for the early Russian history are known as "anti-Normannists." The latest, to my knowledge, "anti-Normannist" work seeking to present the Varangians of the Rusian sources as Slavs and not Scandinavians is A. N. Sakharov et al., *Izgnanie normannov is russkoi istorii* (Moscow: Russkaia panorama, 2010). The book of the leading anti-Normannist Apollon Kuzmin first published in 2004 was reprinted in 2012: A. G. Kuzmin, *Kreshchenie Kievskoi Rusi* (Moscow: Algoritm, 2012).

story, although included in the entry for 862, must have been composed much later. Most likely, it reflects the ideas about princes that existed at the time of the compilation of the *Primary Chronicle* in the early twelfth century.

It is these ideas, and not the ethnicity of the legendary protagonists, that are of great interest in the context of this chapter, which discusses modes of elite domination in Rus and in the high medieval West. The first chapter argued that relations between the Kievan and regional princes were of the same type as those that existed between the king and magnates before the rise of administrative monarchy, and the second chapter presented evidence for similarities between the aristocratic worldview and the worldview reflected in the narratives of princely politics. Of course, on the most abstract level, the social positions of princes and aristocracy were similar: both were a military elite dominating a predominantly agricultural society. However, such domination could take very diverse forms. The task of this chapter is to compare the concrete forms it took in Rus and in the high medieval West.

There is a small number of studies that implicitly compare Rusian princes to Western nobility by describing some interprincely relations as "feudal" or "based on vassalic principles."[3] However, the authors of these studies do not explain what they understand as "vassalic principles," apparently assuming that Western feudalism is a coherent system as described in traditional textbooks and that its principles are self-evident. The same assumption is shared by their critics, who point to evidence from Rusian sources that does not fit the definition of feudal society as it was presented in the classic works of the earlier twentieth century, apparently unaware that neither does plenty of evidence from the medieval West.[4] The deep chasm between the scholarship of Rus and of the medieval West is most evident in the striking lack of response on the part of Rus scholars to the broad reconsideration of the paradigms of medieval history that has so profoundly changed Western medieval studies in the last two decades. This change has affected Russian scholars who study the medieval West,[5] but not those studying Rus. To my knowledge, the single exception to the indifference of Rus scholars to the debate on feudalism was a response to the Russian translation of Reynolds's *Fiefs and Vassals* by Anton Gorskii. He noted the potential for a comparative analysis of the social organization of Rus created by the reconsideration of the classic theory of feudalism, but so far this potential has not been realized.[6]

---

[3] Tolochko, *Kniaz*, 178. Pashuto, "Cherty politicheskogo stroia Drevnei Rusi."

[4] For literature on "feudalism" in the context of Rusian/Russian history, see P. S. Stefanovich, "'Feodalism' na Rusi: istoriia voprosa," *Prepodavanie istorii v shkole* 6 (2011), 24–29; for a critique of the treatment of "feudalims" in the works by historians of Rus, see Yulia Mikhailova, "O nekotorykh napravleniiakh v sovremmennoi medievistike i ikh znachimosti dlia izucheniia Drevnei Rusi," *Srednevekovia Rus* 12, ed. Anton Gorskii (Moscow: Indrik, 2016), 63–94.

[5] See, for example, I. V. Dubrovskii et al., *Konstruirivanie sotsialnogo. Evropa. V–XVI vv.* (Moscow: Editorial URSS, 2001); Galkova et al., *Feodalizm: poniatie i realii*.

[6] Anton Gorskii, "O 'feodalizme': 'russkom' i ne tolko," *Srednie veka* 69 (2008): 9–26; Gorskii, *Russkoe Srednevekov'e* (Moscow: Astrel, 2009); Gorskii, "'Russkii' feodalizm v svete feodalizma 'zapadnogo,'" in I. G. Galkova et al., *Feodalizm: poniatie i realii*, 190–92.

Such an analysis immediately faces the same stumbling block that was discussed in Chapter 1 in connection with the "parallel universes" of different historiographic traditions: there is no established correspondence between Latin and East Slavonic social and political terms, which scholars either leave untranslated or translate by using modern cognates, such as "fief" for *fevum*. Russian-speaking historians of Rus, in particular, almost never translate their source quotations and use an extensive vocabulary consisting of terms transplanted from medieval texts. *Dan* is one such term. It figures prominently in discussions of princely power and authority in the sources and in accounts of interprincely relations, but scholars of Rus hardly ever discuss its meaning. It is, therefore, hard to tell whether Russian and Ukrainian historians writing about *dan* use it as an untranslated East Slavonic word, or translate it to its modern cognate, which is spelled exactly the same and means "tribute."

Dan—Tribute, Taxation, or Neither?

The story about the invitation of the Varangians is not the only Rusian text that identifies paying *dan* with being subject to a prince. Thus, according to another passage from the *Primary Chronicle*, Khazarian elders predicted that one day the Khazars would pay *dan* to Rus, and "this came to be [...] for the Rusian princes have a dominion over Khazars even until the present day."[7]

Dan is traditionally translated into English as "tribute." Franklin, in what appears to be the only existing scholarly discussion of this term, notes that "tribute" is the "archaic and perhaps primary" meaning of *dan*, but that, in the course of time, the word came to signify different things.[8] In the passage about the Khazars, rendering *dan* as "tribute" appears quite appropriate, and so it does in the stories about early princes, such as Igor, whose failed attempt to extort too much *dan* from the Derevlians, one of the East Slavic groups, is described in the *Primary Chronicle*. His followers pointed out to Igor that they were "naked" compared to men of another leader, who boasted fine clothes and weapons, and they proposed a remedy: "Go with us, prince, to collect *dan*, so that both you and we may profit." Igor agreed and went with his men to the Derevlian land where "they demanded more and more *dan*, and made violence" until the desperate Derevlians killed Igor and his followers.[9]

Rusian texts continue to use the word *dan* for payments received by the princes from the population throughout the pre-Mongolian period. Nonetheless, it appears that for the eleventh and twelfth centuries, *dan* can be translated legitimately as "tribute" only when it describes furs collected from the tribal huntsmen of the northern forests, but not when applied to payments received from the core population of Rusian principalities—even

---

[7] PSRL 1, 17. Khazaria was a polity that dominated the steppes north of the Caspian Sea and along the Volga in the ninth and tenth centuries.

[8] Simon Franklin, "On Meanings, Function and Paradigms of Law in Early Rus'," *Russian History/Histoire Russe* 34 (2007): 63–81, at 79–80.

[9] PSRL 1, 54–55, under 945.

though the word is the same.[10] In this respect, *dan* is not different from many—if not all—medieval terms, the meanings of which changed both over time and from place to place. It is well known that Latin texts use the same words, *duces* and *comites*, for members of early war-bands and for the rulers of territorial units in the high and late medieval realms. However, historians translate these terms differently: as "leaders" and "followers" in the former case, and as "dukes" and "counts" or "earls" in the latter. To apply the same terms to the twelfth-century princes and to Igor appears to be wrong for the same reason that it would be wrong to describe the rulers of Normandy in the same terms as the early Viking raiders.

Unlike Igor, who goes to the land of the Derevlians to plunder them, later princes are represented as collecting *dan* only from their own *volosts*. The implication of the sources that princes rule by assent is inconsistent with rendering this *dan* as "tribute," that is, a coerced payment imposed by an external power.[11] Accounts of late eleventh-early thirteenth-century events clearly differentiate between the legitimate *dan* and arbitrary extortions. In cases when eleventh- and twelfth-century princes did behave as conquerors extorting payment by force, the sources use the word *tiagota* (hardship, oppression), not *dan*. For example, during the chaotic period in the aftermath of the 1169 taking of Kiev by the Suzdalia-led coalition, one of the short-term occupants of the Kievan throne accused the Kievans of not preventing the capture of his wife and son by his political rival. "In his anger, he contrived an oppression for the Kievans," demanding from them the sum necessary for ransoming his family, and he "imposed payments on [*poproda*] all Kiev, on the abbots, and priests, and monks, and nuns, and on the Latins and on the merchants conducting long-distance trade (*goste*)."[12] To stress the arbitrary and oppressive character of the payments that the angry prince imposed on the Kievans, the chronicler lists the categories of people who appear to be normally exempted from *dan*, such as clergy and foreigners ("Latins").[13]

Another angry prince, Vladimir of Galich, frustrated by his participation in a failed military expedition, left the camp of his allies near Kiev and marched back to Galich together with his men. He made an ultimatum to the inhabitants of Michesk, the first town that he encountered on his way:

> "Give me as much silver as I want or else I will sack your town." They did not have as much silver as he wanted from them, and they took silver [jewellery] from their ears and necks, melted it, and gave it to Vladimir. Vladimir, having taken the silver, went on. And he took silver in the same manner from all the places on his way until he reached his own land.[14]

---

10 On these furs, their collection and the trade in them, see Janet Martin, *Treasure of the Land of Darkness: The Fur Trade and its Significance for Medieval Russia* (New York: Cambridge University Press, 2004).

11 Franklin and Shepard, *Emergence of Rus*, 196.

12 PSRL 2, 579.

13 For a discussion of the term "Latins" in this passage, see Lukin, "Veche," 125.

14 PSRL 2, 417.

The chronicler assumes that a prince does not use force to extort arbitrary payments from the people in his *volost*, as is evident from the fact that Vladimir stopped demanding silver by threat as soon as he reached his land. Silver paid by those who had the misfortune to live along the route that Vladimir took to Galich can be described as "tribute," but the chronicler makes it clear that this was not a regular *dan*. Vladimir of Galich simply robbed the people on his way, but a prince receiving regular payments from his *volost* performed essential social functions in exchange for these revenues. Just how essential a prince was for a *volost* can be seen from the chronicler's hint that only the intercession of the Mother of God made it possible for the city of Vladimir to last seven weeks without a prince.[15]

In the first chapter, we have seen that princes raised and led military forces. This military function was important, but most sources give even more importance to the administration of justice, normally presented as the prince's main duty. In the legend about the first Rusian princes quoted at the beginning of this chapter, providing justice is the *raison d'etre* of princely power. The verbs *kniazhiti* ("to be a prince"), *volodeti* ("to dominate, rule, govern"), and *suditi* ("to act as a judge, to administer justice, to hold a court") are used interchangeably: the people need somebody who would "govern and judge" them; therefore, they tell the Varangians, "Come and be our princes and govern us."[16] In this context, "to be princes" is synonymous with "to judge."

A very different kind of text, an epistle by the Kievan metropolitan Nicephorus to Vladimir Monomakh, expresses the same understanding of princely power: in order to be saved, the prince needs, first and foremost, to be good at providing justice for his people (*khraniai sudbu*).[17] Monomakh himself includes administration of justice among his routine occupations, when he describes his habit of beginning all his everyday activities with a prayer: "I praise God before I sit down to have a council with my men, or to dispense justice to the people, or before I go hunting."[18] Abbot Polycarp, of the Kievan Caves monastery, presented justice as the main princely duty in his conversation with Prince Rostislav Mstislavich, reported in the *Kievan Chronicle* under 1167. Rostislav wanted to become a monk, but Polycarp talked him out of it. A prince could not abandon his worldly responsibilities, argued Polycarp, because God appointed princes "to uphold justice (*pravdu deiati*) in this world, to judge justly, and to keep their oaths on the Cross."[19]

Franklin proposed "taxation" as a better translation for *dan* in his discussion of the foundational charter for the Smolensk bishopric issued by the same Rostislav.[20] The

---

15 PSRL 1, 377.

16 PSRL 1, 19–20.

17 *Poslanie Nikyfora mitropolita kievskago k velikomu kniaziu Volodimeru cynu Vsevolozhiu, syna Iaroslavlia*, in *Chista molitva tvoia: pouchenie i poslaniia drevnerusskim kniaziam Kievskogo mitropolita Nikifora*, ed. G. S. Barankova (Moscow: Ikhtios, 2005), 114–15.

18 PSRL 1, 247.

19 "vam Bog tako velel byti: pravdu deiati na sem svete, v pravdu sud suditi i v khrestnom tselovanii vy stoiati," PSRL 2, 530.

20 Daniel H. Kaiser, *The Growth of the Law in Medieval Russia* (Princeton: Princeton University Press, 1980), 58, 215; Franklin, "On Meanings, Function and Paradigms of Law," 78.

charter includes a list of settlements under Rostislav's authority with annual payments collected there, and it allocates a tithe on them to the bishop, such as, "In Toropichi, a *dan* of four hundred grivnas [is collected annually], and the bishop is to take from that forty grivnas."[21] Franklin argues that Rostislav's charter reflects "straightforward community taxation" rather than "tribute," because the payments in the Smolensk list "had become institutionalized as part of the system of government."[22]

While it is true that rendering *dan* of the Smolensk charter as "tribute" is problematic, "taxation" may also be problematic, because it is too statist and ignores the property aspect of princely *volosts* discussed in Chapter 1. If we view the *dan* of the Smolensk charter as taxation, and the Smolensk region as an administrative unit ruled by Rostislav, should not all the *dan* go to the prince and his administrators? Instead, the charter states that the bishop is to take a tithe on "all the *dan*, great and small, whether it is the prince's, or the princess's, or belongs to whomever else."[23] We will return to "whomever else" later; for now it suffices to note that the division of the *dan* into "prince's" and "princess's" makes it look more like an income received from personal property than taxation.

This aspect of *dan* is even more evident in the account about the conflict between Rostislav's sons (the Rostislavichi) and Andrew Bogoliubsky of Suzdalia. As mentioned above, Andrew, when he had power over Kiev, granted it to the Rostislavichi. He then accused them of not fulfilling the obligations that they owed to him, and decided to revoke his grant. He told the Rostislavichi to vacate Kiev and the strongholds in the Kievan region, and added, "You have your Smolensk, go ahead and divide it among yourselves."[24] This passage contrasts the Kievan region controlled by Andrew with Smolensk, the Rostislavichi's inheritance. The mocking proposition to divide this inheritance apparently is intended to remind the Rostilavichi that the income from Smolensk is not sufficient for three princes and to underscore their dependence on Andrew, who has the power to grant good *volosts*. In other words, for Andrew, the region described in the Smolensk charter is the property of late Rostislav that now passed to his sons.

The chroniclers imply that *volosts* are princes' properties when they equate having a *volost* with receiving revenue from those living within its borders. The idea that a *volost* is its prince's main source of income underpins a complaint about the unfair treatment

---

21 "Ustavnaiai i zhalovannaia gramota smolenskogo kniazia Rostislava Mstislavicha tserkvi Bogoroditsy i episkopu," in *Drevnerusskie kniazheskie ustavy XI—XV vv*, ed. Ia. N. Shchapov (Moscow: Nauka, 1975), 141-42. For an English translation of the charter, see Daniel H. Kaiser, ed. and trans., *The Laws of' Rus' - Tenth to Fifteenth Centuries* (Salt Lake City: Charles Schlacks Jr., 1992), 51-53. Grivna was a unit of value related to a silver standard. On Rusian money, see V. L. Ianin, *Denezhno-vesovye sistemy russkogo srednevekovia: Domongolskii period* (Moscow: Nauka, 1956); Thomas Noonan, "The Monetary History of Kiev in the Pre-Mongolian Period," *Harvard Ukrainian Studies* 11 (1987): 383-443.

22 Franklin, "On Meanings, Function and Paradigms of Law," 80.

23 "A chto sia narechet oblasti Smolenskoe, ili mala ili velika dan, liubo kniazha, liubo kniaginina, ili chia si khotia, praviti desiatinu sviatei Bogoroditse," "Ustavnaiai i zhalovannaia gramota smolenskogo kniazia," 143.

24 PSRL 2, 569-70.

to which the head of the Olgovichi clan submitted a junior prince Sviatoslav. The senior Olgovich, Iziaslav Davidivich of Chernigov, became the Kievan prince and granted to Sviatoslav some territories in the Chernigov principality. Sviatoslav, however, believed that the Kievan prince unjustly retained better parts for himself and gave others to his own nephew. All that was left to Sviatoslav were "Chernigov with seven empty districts (*gorody*) [...] they are populated by *psareve*, and the Cumans devastated them all, while he and his nephew hold all the rest of the Chernigov Land."[25] The districts apparently were not literally empty: they were populated by some kind of people whom Sviatoslav called *psareve*. This reference to *psareve*, which is the plural form of *psar*, a word related to *pes* (dog), is unique for the twelfth century; in later documents *psar* signifies a lord's man who works in a kennel and takes care of the hunting dogs.[26] It is difficult to imagine seven districts so full of kennels that all their inhabitants would be busy caring for dogs. Probably, Sviatoslav uses *psareve* as a derogatory epithet to express his frustration about the population of his *volost*.[27] Whoever the *psareve* were in this passage, they must have been some kind of people who did not provide Sviatoslav with adequate income: this appears to be the only sense in which a territory populated by *psareve* could be described as "empty."

The senior Olgovich, who granted the "empty districts" to Sviatoslav, did not stay in Kiev for long. He was overthrown by the Monomakhovichi coalition and eventually found himself in the small *volost* of Vyr. He tried to win Kiev back and rejected exhortations to make peace with the new Kievan prince. He argued that other princes, after the peace is made, "will go back to their *volosts*," but he did not have anywhere to go: "I cannot die from hunger in Vyr, I prefer to die here [fighting]."[28] We can be sure that he was not literally starving; this was just his way of expressing the idea that the resources of Vyr, a small stronghold with adjacent countryside in the Chernigov principality, were not sufficient for a prince of his rank.

A Special Kind of Property

The importance of *volosts* as sources of income is manifested by the fact that they had monetary value. At least, this was the case at the turn of the twelfth century, when the Kievan prince Rurik granted a *volost* to Prince Roman, but then a complicated situation arose,

---

25 PSRL 25, 65. In a different redaction of the *Kievan Chronicle* in the *Hypatian Codex*, the same passage reads, "they are populated by *psareve* and Cumans," PSRL 2, 500. The Cumans were the nomads who lived in the steppe to the south of Rus; no sources other than this passage contain any information about the Cumans living in Rus. Therefore, I assume that the reading from PSRL 25 is more correct. The districts "populated by Cumans" in the *Hypatian* probably resulted from a mistake of the scribe who accidentally skipped the word "devastated." In this passage, *gorody* apparently states as a metonymy for districts centred on the seven strongholds.

26 *Slovar Russkogo iazyka XI—XVII vv.*, ed. G. A. Bogatova et al., vol. 21 (Moscow: Nauka, 1995), 36.

27 A derogatory connotation of the word *pes* is evident from the Rusian law postulating that, under some circumstances, a burglar caught red-handed may be killed on the spot without a trial, "as if he were a dog (*vo psa mesto*)." "Russkaia pravda. Prostrannaia redaktsia," in *Zakonodatelstvo Drevnei Rusi*, ed. V. L. Ianin (Moscow: Iuridicheskaia literatura, 1984), 66.

28 PSRL 2, 517.

which will be discussed in the next chapter, and Rurik had to ask Roman to give this *volost* back. Roman agreed to return the *volost* on the conditions that he expressed thus: "Give me another *volost* instead of this one, or give me its worth in money (*kunami dasi za nee vo chto budet byla*)."[29]

It is most probable that *volosts* had monetary "prices" already in the early twelfth century. The *Primary Chronicle* entry for 1110 describes the conference of the leading princes convened in order to punish the crime of one of them, David, who had another prince blinded. They decided to confiscate David's *volost* and to give him a smaller *volost* and 400 grivnas.[30] The smaller *volost* and money must have been a partial compensation for the confiscated *volost*, because the chronicle presents the decision of the conference as a rather lenient punishment, but still a punishment, which would not have been the case if David had received full compensation. The 400 grivnas appear to cover part of the difference between the value of the confiscated *volost* and the smaller one granted to David by the conference. If this is true, then the princes were able to calculate the monetary value of the two *volosts*. A basis for such a calculation can be seen in the list of payments collected from various localities in the Smolensk principality in the charter issued only two decades after David's lenient punishment.

Being a property with monetary value is a characteristic that the Rusian *volost* shares with territorial units discussed in high medieval accounts of aristocratic politics. Aquitanian magnates were able to calculate the worth of their *castra* in money. Thus, when Hugh's enemy burnt and plundered one of his *castra*, this was "such a great evil to Hugh and his men that Hugh would not accept [even] fifty thousand solidi," presumably if this sum would have been offered as compensation.[31] William V of Aquitaine "*reddidit*" another *castrum* and received money for it.[32] It is hard to say what exactly "*reddidit*" means here, but it seems clear enough that William in one way or another exchanged a *castrum* for a sum of money.[33] A complicated series of agreements and counter-agreements concerning yet another *castrum* included, at one point, William's proposal to Hugh to "buy it from Count Fulk with your and my money."[34]

---

29 PSRL 2, 685 (under 1195).

30 PSRL 1, 274.

31 "Bernardus et sui operati sunt malum Ugoni et viris suis quantum nec accipere potest per quinquaginta mil. solid." *Conventum Hugonis*, 545.

32 "Reddidit Comes Gentiaco [the castle of Gençay] [...] pecuniamque accepit et terram dominicam." *Conventum Hugonis*, 547. I do not understand what the "demesne" is that William received while "giving away" the castle, and I was not able to find any discussion of this passage in scholarly literature.

33 It is apparent from the context that it could not mean "returned," which is, of course, the primary meaning of *reddo*. One translation renders it as "surrendered" and another as "disposed of" (*Agreement between Count William V of Aquitaine and Hugh IV of Lusignan*; Martindale, *Status, Authority and Regional Power*, VIIb, 547). *Redditus* indeed meant "surrender," and also "gift"in medieval Latin. Niermeyer, *Mediae Latinitatis Lexicon Minus*, 895.

34 "si ego valeo acaptare [the castle] cum comite Fulconi de pretio meo et de tuo," *Conventum Hugonis*, 546.

Castrum of the *Conventum* has been rendered in English as "fortress"[35]; however, the context suggests that it may be better understood in the broader sense of a territorial unit that included both the stronghold and the surrounding rural area.[36] This was the predominant meaning of *castrum* in the documents produced in the neighbouring region of Languedoc, where the word stood for "a unity of the fortification and the land which depended on it." A typical grant of a *castrum* included "lands, vineyards, forests, waters, pastures," the authority over the "men and women who depend on the *castrum*," and all the payments generated by the ownership of the land and by the rights of jurisdiction over the population ("taxes, qu'elles soient de nature foncière ou banale").[37] In all likelihood, it was these payments that provided the basis for calculating the monetary value of the *castrum*.

If *castra* of the *Conventum* are similar to small *volosts* consisting of a fortress and its vicinities, counties resemble larger *volosts*, those centred on a city and including multiple strongholds. A *comitatus*—the word that stood for "county," "count's rule," or "office of the count"—could have a monetary value as well, as is evident from the account about the count of Maine selling his rights to the county for 10,000 shillings (*pro comitatu Cenomannensi decem milia solidorum [...] recepit*).[38]

In all these cases, Rusian *volosts*, Aquitanian *castra*, and the Manseaux *comitatus* are treated as property: princes, lords, and counts, respectively, estimate their monetary value, buy and sell them, and apparently view them as sources of income. Does this mean that territorial units under the control of Rusian princes and Western lords and counts were their land property and that payments they received from the population—*dan*, in the Rusian case—can be viewed as rent? There are several problems with such an interpretation. For one thing, the sources differentiate territorial units controlled by Rusian princes and Western magnates from their personal estates. A prince or count owned estates that were located in his *volost* or county, but did not coincide with it. Conversely, he could own land property in somebody else's *volost* or county, while other people owned estates located within the territorial unit under his control.

---

35 *Agreement between Count William V of Aquitaine and Hugh IV of Lusignan*, passim; Martindale, *Status, Authority and Regional Power*, VIIb, passim.

36 In narrative sources, *castrum* often stood not just for the stronghold, but for the whole district centred on the stronghold, a district which more legalistically minded authors called *castellaria* or *vicaria castri*: "since the revenues of the lordship were collected at, and its unity expressed by, the administrative center, it was natural to refer to the lands and *caput* collectively as 'the castle,'" Charles L. H. Coulson, *Castles in Medieval Society: Fortresses in England, France, and Ireland in the Central Middle Ages* (Oxford: Oxford University Press, 2003), 54. The *Conventum* uses *castrum* interchangeably with *terra*. Thus, when an enemy burned Hugh's *castrum*, this meant that Hugh "lost his land" ("Ioszfredus [...] incendit castro Mosolio, cepit caballarios Ugoni [...] et satis alio facto. Comes vero nihil iuvavit Ugoni [...], sed adhuc suam terram Ugo perditur"), *Conventum Hugonis*, 543. See also above, p. 000.

37 Hélène Débax, *La féodalité languedocienne XIe-XIIe siècles: serments, sommages et fiefs dans le Languedoc des Trencavel* (Toulouse: Presses universitaires du Mirail, 2003), 163.

38 *The Ecclesiastical History of Orderic Vitalis*, vol. 4, 198.

A distinction between a prince's *volost* and his personal estate can be clearly seen in a description of the spoils of victory in an interprincely war that followed the overthrow of the Kievan prince Igor in 1146. The account of the war is highly reliable: it is found in all redactions of the *Kievan Chronicle* and is also confirmed archaeologically.[39] Some context needs to be established here. As mentioned above, Igor was the designated heir of the Kievan prince Vsevolod. When Vsevolod died and Igor moved to Kiev, he gave his *volost*, centred on Novgorod-Severskii, to his younger brother Sviatoslav. Sviatoslav began to "hold" Novgorod-Severskii in addition to the *volost* of Putivl that he had had previously. Soon, Igor was overthrown and imprisoned, and Iziaslav Mstislavich became the Kievan prince in his stead. Iziaslav and his allies decided that Igor's former *volost* of Novgorod-Severskii should now be theirs, but Sviatoslav was allowed to hold in peace his original *volost* of Putivl on the condition that he would not seek to liberate Igor. It was on this occasion that Sviatoslav declared that he did not care about any *volost* and that his only desire was to see his brother free.[40] He started a war against Iziaslav, was defeated, and fled; thus all the territory under Sviatoslav's control passed into the hands of Iziaslav, who granted it to the two brothers Davidovichi.

Izislav's wording of the grant, reported in two redactions of the *Kievan Chronicle*, is very interesting. He addresses the Davidovichi: "All Sviatoslav's *volost* will be yours, but whatever in the *volost* belongs to [the imprisoned] Igor, whether serfs (*cheliadi*) or property (*tovara*), will be mine; and we will divide Sviatoslav's serfs and property."[41] Thus, the *volost* as a whole is "Sviatoslav's"; however, within it, there is some Sviatoslav's property distinct from the rest of the *volost*. This differentiation is observed consistently. Later, Iziaslav reminds the Davidovichi how much good he did for them:

> I gave Sviatoslav's and Igor's *volosts* to you, I drove Sviatoslav away together with you; this is I who found a *volost* for you and gave you Novgorod[-Severskii]

---

39 PSRL 23, 32–33; PSRL 25, 38–39. Interpretations of the precise relations between archaeological findings and the information found in the chronicle vary, but it is clear enough that the area where the fighting took place according to the chronicle, indeed, suffered from a war conducted in the mid-twelfth century. V. P. Kovalenko and R. S. Orlov, "Raboty Novgorod-Severskoi ekspeditsii," in *Archeologicheskie otkrytiia 1979 goda*, ed. B. A. Rybakov (Moscow: Nauka, 1980), 281–83; Liudmila Iasnovska, "Davnioruski starozhitnosti Novgorod-Siverskogo Podesennia," *Siverianskyi litopys: vseukrainskyi naukovyi zhurnal* 11 (2005): 9–26, at 20.

40 PSRL 2, 329.

41 PSRL 2, 337; cf. PSRL 25, 38. There is no consensus on the meaning of the word *cheliad*, which appears to refer to lower-class people of various status (see M. N. Tikhomirov, *Krestianskie i gorodskie vosstaniia na Rusi* (Moscow: Nauka, 1955), 14, 26; L. V. Cherepnin, "Rus: Spornye voprosy istorii feodalnoi zemelnoi sobstvennosti v IX–XV vv," in *Puti razvitiia feodalisma*, ed. A. P. Novoseltsev et al. (Moscow: Nauka, 1972), 174; I. Ia. Froianov, *Rabstvo i dannichestvo u vostochnykh slavian: VI–X vv* (St. Petersburg, Russia: Izdatelstvo Sankt-Peterburgskogo Universiteta, 1996), 104–24.) I translated *cheliad* as "serfs" here because they are apparently treated as property, while the standard word for "slave" is *kholop*, although the meaning of *cheliad* as "slaves" in this passage cannot be ruled out.

and Putivl. [Remember,] we took Sviatoslav's livelihood and divided his property (*imenie*) between ourselves, while I took Igor's property.[42]

Here again we see Sviatoslav's *volost* and Sviatoslav "property" as two different things: the former goes to the Davidovichi, the latter is divided among all the members of Iziaslav's coalition. Moreover, the same Sviatoslav's *volost* also contains property that is *not* Sviatoslav's, but Igor's.

We get a glimpse of this property in the description of Iziaslav's and his allies' pillaging. First, they sacked "Igor's little village where he had a well-arranged mansion" stocked with large quantities of food supplies, wine, mead, iron and copper. After plundering all these, the victors set fire to the mansion, the church, and the barn "where there were nine hundred grain stacks." The plundering, in which the victorious coalition engaged, appears to have been selective. Thus, the townspeople offered to surrender to Iziaslav if he would swear an oath to them, presumably promising not to sack their town. Iziaslav swore an oath and kept it: "He kissed the Cross [as was the way to seal oaths]; and he dismissed their governor (*posadnik*), and appointed his man as their new governor"—and this was all, as far as the people of Putivl were concerned. Their persons and property did not suffer any violence. The same, however, cannot be said about Sviatoslav's property: upon entering Putivl, Iziaslav and his allies divided among themselves what the chronicler calls Sviatoslav's "residence" or "compound (*dvor*)". The description of the spoils suggests that this was something like a castle or a palace complex: it had 700 serfs and "so many things that one could hardly move them," including "five hundred Birka barrels of mead and eighty jugs of wine." The compound included a church that the victors also treated as Sviatoslav's property. After listing all the plundered church objects, such as books, incensories, and priestly garments, the chronicler concludes, "They did not leave anything that had belonged to the prince [Sviatoslav], but they divided all that was his."[43]

There is thus a clear differentiation of Putivl as a place controlled by Sviatoslav from the property that he owns in Putivl. The property is pillaged and divided; the control over the town and the region around it passes from Sviatoslav to Iziaslav and then to the Davidovichi. Apparently, this transfer of control was what Iziaslav meant when he said, "Sviatoslav's *volost* will be yours," the act that he later described as "giving" Putivl to the Davidovichi.

From this account, *volost* emerges not as a land owned by the prince, but as a unit over which he has some rights other than those of a landowner. The chronicler does not explain what those rights are, because he evidently expects his readers to know them. The prince controlling the *volost* owns some property located on the territory

---

42 PSRL 2, 346–47; PSRL 25, 41. The chronicler shifts between the singular and the plural form of *volost*: the region centred on Novgorod-Severskii and Putivl was held now by one, now by two princes. When united under the power of one prince, it was one *volost*; when there were two different princes, the area became two *volosts*.

43 PSRL 2, 333–34. The word that I translated as "Birka barrel" is *berkovskii* (variant: *berkovets*), literally meaning "of Birka"; it is a measure of weight equal to 160kg.

of this unit, as do other princes. And not just princes: now and then, the sources mention ecclesiastical and lay non-princely property, such as "village" or "livelihood," located within this or that *volost*.[44] Especially interesting is a reference to "boyars' villages" in an account of another princely war, found in the *Suzdalian Chronicle*. As the reader might remember, this chronicle describes the triumph of the rightful prince, Vsevolod the "Big Nest," supported by the good townsmen of Vladimir, over the greedy Rostislavichi supported by evil boyars. After a victorious battle, in which Vsevolod's forces killed some of these boyars and captured others, they "took the boyars' villages"; while returning to the city of Vladimir in triumph, the victors were "bringing the prisoners with them and driving along the horses and cattle" plundered from the villages.[45]

This account is not as detailed as the one about the sacking of Sviatoslav's property in Putivl. It is impossible to tell with certainty if the plundering described by the *Suzdalian* chronicler was also selective, but this appears to be the case: just as Iziaslav's coalition did not damage Putivl outside of Sviatoslav's compound, Vsevolod's men probably did not sack the Suzdalian countryside indiscriminately and targeted only the property of the Rostislavichi's supporters. At the very least, this passage clearly indicates the existence of non-princely land property on the territory that was the Suzdalian princes' *volost*.

Actually, this is what should be expected, since all the territory of Rus was controlled by princes, and thus it all was comprised of princely *volosts*—but at the same time, princes were not the only landowners. A small *volost* of a lesser prince might consist of just his personal domain, but a larger *volost* included the prince's lands and also estates belonging to other landowners. Therefore, when such a *volost* was transferred from one prince to another, it was not a transfer of land property, but rather a transfer of the princely rights, of a specific form of control over the *volost*'s territory, which was not the same as land ownership.

In the context of such transfers, the meaning of *volost* is close to the meaning of *comitatus* in Orderic's account about the payment of 10,000 shillings *pro comitatu Cenomannensi*.[46] In the late eleventh century, when Hugh V sold the *comitatus* of Maine to Helias, the territory of the county of Maine included the count's personal estates, as well as estates belonging to other landowners, ecclesiastical lands, and multiple castellanies—areas around castles controlled by the lords of these castles.[47] The sale of the *comitatus Cenomannensis* apparently did not affect the rights of the lay and

---

44 P. S. Stefanovich, *Boiare, otroki, druzhiny: Voenno-politicheskaia elita Rusi v X–XI vv.* (Moscow: Indrik, 2012), 455–59. I am grateful to Peter Stefanovich for allowing me to consult with the manuscript of this work before it was published. Stefanovich, "Boiarstvo i tserkov v domongolskoi Rusi," *Voprosy istorii* 7 (2002): 41–59.

45 PSRL 1, 382; PSRL 41, 107.

46 See chap. 2.

47 Richard E. Barton, *Lordship in the County of Maine, c.890–1160* (Woodbridge: Boydell, 2004), 66–72, 112–13, 126.

ecclesiastical landowners who held estates in Maine.[48] Therefore, what Hugh V sold was not the county of Maine in the sense of a territorial unit, but rather the rights of a count.

Judicial Rights, Banal Lordship, and "Feudal Revolution"

Charles West argued that a sale of a county became possible for the first time in the late 1000s because of a social change that occurred during the eleventh century. This was a time of transition from the early to the high medieval social organization, sometimes referred to as the "feudal revolution." It was marked by a gradual differentiation between the ownership of land and the exercise of domination, "meaning that both could be more readily treated as elements of transferable property." West used evidence from the area between Marne and Moselle, but the process that he described was not limited to this area. He analyzed eleventh-century charters that discussed domination of a locality "as if it were itself something that was owned: reified 'political' power."[49]

West refers to the sale of the county of Porcien in the 1090s, the same decade when the sale of the *comitatus Cenomannensis* took place, to illustrate his point that "lordships were increasingly able to be transferred en bloc, or, conversely, formally split," because aristocratic domination was newly defined as a "thing" differentiated from landowning. Domination was converted into "exchangeable units" and became an object of property. Social power "was now a thing in itself."[50] Evidently, it was this "thing" that Hugh V sold to Helias: reified comital political power consisting of domination over the county of Maine. Such domination over a locality "permitted extractions of various sorts to be made" from those living in the locality.

These extractions were not derived from the ownership of land, because the rights to make them could be transferred with, or without, the transfer of land. One set of charters from the mid-twelfth century describes the rights to make such extractions from a certain village near Rheims as having *vicecomitatus* at this village. The *vicecomitatus*—but not the village itself—was owned by the monastery of St-Thierry. The same distinction is shown by other texts "recording the transfer of similar rights, but not the land over which they were exercised."[51] Apparently, such a *vicecomitatus* is of the same nature as the *comitatus Cenomannensis* in Orderic's account of the bargain struck by Hugh V and Helias: both were "exchangeable units" of aristocratic domination, not a land, but a set of rights over the people living on the land.

---

48 Thus, in 1090, the *Cenomanni* "rebelled against the Normans, ejected their castellans (*custodibus*) from the strongholds and installed (*constituerunt*) a new prince [Hugh] for themselves," *The Ecclesiastical History of Orderic Vitalis*, vol. 4, 192. However, when Orderic describes the transfer of the *comitatus Cenomannensis* from Hugh to Helias, he does not mention any ejection of castellans.
49 West, *Reframing the Feudal Revolution*, 186.
50 West, *Reframing the Feudal Revolution*, 230, 185–87, 196.
51 West, *Reframing the Feudal Revolution*, 185.

According to West, these rights were first and foremost judicial. He detected a group of new, more or less synonymous, terms that "spring into the charters and other sources" from the mid-eleventh century and that designated "rights pertaining to justice and jurisdiction, that could be, and were, distinguished from ownership of land." *Vicecomitatus* was one of them. Other words included *consuetudo*, *justicia*, and, most prominently, *bannum*. The Germanic root *ban* borrowed into Latin expressed the idea of giving command, and in the region studied by West it was synonymous with *justicia*. *Comitatus* could also be used synonymously with *justicia* to mean a set of judicial rights.[52] For Orderic Vitalis, these rights were an integral aspect of the *comitatus Cenomannensis*: as a result of his purchase of the *comitatus*, Helias "provided justice to his subjects (*subiectis aequitatem seruauit*)."[53] In fact, most of the county of Maine at that time was controlled by castellans who exercised rights of jurisdiction over their lordships and who were largely independent of the count. Apart from his personal estates, the count controlled only the city of La Manse.[54] Probably, by the "subjects" to whom Helias "provided justice," Orderic meant the townsmen of La Manse, or maybe he, writing a few decades after the events, was not well familiar with the actual balance of power in Maine in the 1090s. What is important for us here is not how accurately Orderic represented the actual position of Helias, but the connection that evidently existed in Orderic's mind between having *comitatus* and exercising justice.

A more specific term used in Maine to designate "the power of judgment and the imposition of fines and penalties" was *vicaria*, while *bannum*, unlike in the region studied by West, "constituted a lord's broader power to command, especially in organizing military force."[55] Apparently, there were regional variations in terminology which described various aspects of aristocratic domination. The essential point is that, regardless of which words were used in which regions, there existed terms that signified judicial and administrative rights over a certain territorial unit which were not equivalent to ownership of this unit as a land property. The person who had these rights was entitled to impose judicial fees, fines, and penalties on the population living on the territory under his *bannum*.

West argues that these rights were at the core of banal lordship, the English translation of *seigneurie banale* first introduced by Georges Duby in his classic study of the Mâcon region in Burgundy.[56] According to Duby, the emergence of *seigneurie banale* marked the change that occurred around the year 1000 and that "concerned the distribution of the power of command. This power, called in some areas the ban, lost its public character at that moment; individual lords appropriated it and used it to impose

---

52 West, *Reframing the Feudal Revolution*, 184–85, 230.
53 *The Ecclesiastical History of Orderic Vitalis*, vol. 4, 198.
54 Barton, *Lordship in the County of Maine*, 126.
55 Barton, *Lordship in the County of Maine*, 134.
56 "Comme elle repose sur le droit de commander, d'édicter des règlements et de punir les contrevenants, c'est-à-dire sur le droit de ban, nous proposons d'appeler seigneurie banale," Duby, *La société aux XIe et XIIe siècles dans la région mâconnaise*, 174.

exactions for themselves in connection with their castellanies."[57] In a nutshell, this is a formulation of what later became known as the "feudal revolution" theory. In Chapter 1 we saw a critique of this theory, postulating that the power relations typical of banal lordship had already existed under the Carolingians, and that the new practices of charter writing brought about the "feudal revelation" which made these relations more explicit.

West proposed a convincing interpretation of the Carolingian sources that sidesteps the opposition between state and lordship, royal and aristocratic authority—the opposition underpinning both the classic "feudal revolution" theory and the revisionist "feudal revelation" approach. He presented relations between the Carolingian king and aristocracy as "a collaborative project better to anchor their collective authority." Eventually this project was such a success, and the dominance of aristocrats indeed became anchored so securely, that it no longer needed "to be underpinned by royal authority." The king still retained a special position, but he became less necessary for the workings of local affairs, which led to "the gradual winding-down of Carolingian kingship."[58] This newly secure local aristocratic domination is, essentially, banal lordship, which thus does represent a new regime established in the course of the "feudal revolution." However, it did not originate from lords' usurpation of regalian rights, but from a successful reorganization of the social order achieved by the joint efforts of royalty and aristocracy.

The rest of this chapter examines a hypothesis that *volost* signified a territory over which its prince had a set of rights similar to those that characterized aristocratic domination established in the course of the "feudal revolution." Under this hypothesis, Iziaslav first conquered from Sviatoslav and then granted to the Davidovichi essentially the same "thing" that Charles West found in his Lotharingian charters: reified political power consisting of domination over the areas centred on Putivl and Novgorod-Severskii. It is a transfer of this "thing" that the chronicler describes as giving Sviatoslav's *volost* to the Davidovichi, as opposed to pillaging Sviatoslav's land property.

The prince's political domination is likewise differentiated from his land property in the Smolensk charter: Rostislav allocates a tithe on the *dan* paid "throughout of what is known as the Smolensk region (*chto sia narechet oblasti Smolenskoe*)" to the bishop, and he also gives some land to the cathedral church from his personal estates (*uezd kniazh*) located within the Smolensk principality.[59]

Rusian Princes: Justice and *Dan*

Dan is one key element of princely domination that emerges from Rusian sources; another is administration of justice. We have seen the connection between the two in

---

57 Georges Duby, *The Chivalrous Society*, trans. Cynthia Postan (Los Angeles: University of California Press, 1977), 168.

58 West, *Reframing the Feudal Revolution*, 101, 136. For a similar development in Italy, see Chris Wickham, "The 'Feudal Revolution' and the Origins of Italian City Communes," *Transactions of the Royal Historical Society* 24 (2014): 29–55.

59 "Ustavnaiaia i zhalovannaia gramota smolenskogo kniazia," 143–44.

the legend about the origins of princely authority: "there was no justice" as soon as *dan* payments stopped; the Varangians were invited to be princes when the people realized that paying *dan* was worthwhile because it would bring justice back. In accounts of contemporary events, *dan* is often found in the plural, *dani*, implying that it consisted of different kinds of payments. Indeed, *dani* described in the Smolensk and Novgorod charters include custom duties, as well as payments on markets, taverns, fishing rights, and more.[60] The most frequently mentioned payments owed to the prince are *vira* and *prodazha*, typically used together and in the plural: *viry i prodazhi*. *Vira* originally meant wergild, but later it came to signify a penalty paid to the prince; *prodazha* eventually came to represent a judicial sanction, but in the twelfth century it probably had a broader meaning and could signify various exactions made by the prince.[61] The sources consistently name judicial revenues among, or along with, such exactions and imply that they were an important source of income for princes. For example, the bad advisers of the Rostislavichi in Suzdalia "taught them to grab more and more (*uchakhut na mnogoe imanie*)"; therefore, the princes' governors (*posadniki*) "greatly oppressed people with *prodazhi* and judicial penalties (*prodazhami i virami*)."[62] The chronicler thus assumes that if a prince seeks to enrich himself, he would make his officials impose excessive judicial penalties on the population. He takes it for granted that princes have judicial powers and receive revenues generated by these powers; he only objects to abuse of justice resulting in unfair and excessive extractions.[63]

As long as judicial penalties were fair and appropriate, they were seen as an integral part of princely rule, as is evident from the *Primary Chronicle* story which relates how Vladimir, soon after his conversion to Christianity, experimented with replacing judicial fines with other forms of punishment. However, his councillors were concerned that this new policy made it difficult to meet military expenses:

---

60 "Ustavnaiaia i zhalovannaia gramota smolenskogo kniazia," 142–43; "Ustavnaia gramota novgorodskogo kniazia Sviatoslava Olgovicha tserkvi Sv. Sofii v Novgorode," in *Drevnerusskie kniazheskie ustavy*, 148.

61 Kaiser, *The Growth of the Law*, 65–82; Martin, *Medieval Russia, 980–1584*, 79–81; Ianin, *Zakonodatelstvo Drevnei Rusi*, 62.

62 PSRL 1, 374.

63 An interesting reference to this kind of abuse is found in one account of the overthrow of Igor Olgovich. All redactions of the *Kievan Chronicle* report that the "Kievans" accused the officials of the late prince Vsevolod of "ruining" them and that the assembly made Igor swear that he would try them personally when possible (*ashche komu nas budet obida, da ty pravi*), PSRL 2, 321–22. One version of the story continues that the assembly also demanded that Igor, when delegating justice to his officials, must ensure that they "would only collect the established fees and fines and would not impose any arbitrary payments." Igor did not keep this promise, and was overthrown. "'A chto byli tivuni brata nashego Ratsha i Tudor, a tem ne byti, a koim budet byti, ino im imati k sudu urokom, a v svoiu voliu im liudei ne prodovati.' Igor zhe tako obechshiasia. I iako zhe obeschavsia […] i ne pocha po tomu chiniti, iako zhe liudi khotiakhu." PSRL 25, 37. Unfortunately, it is unclear how much this statement reflects the realities of the twelfth century; since this passage is only found in one redaction of the chronicle, it is impossible to know whether it was part of the original report or was added later.

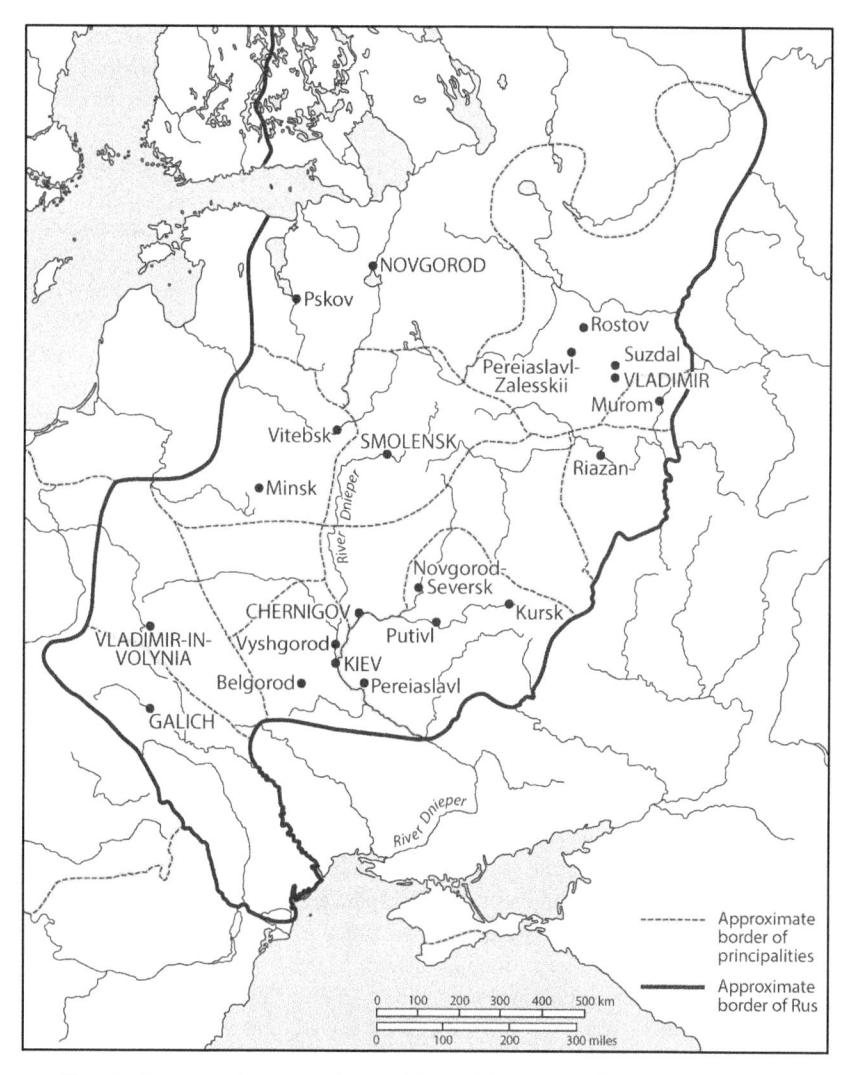

Map 1. An approximate territory of Rus, with Novgorod's dependent lands, in the twelfth century.

And the bishops and elders said, "Much warfare is going on, and if a fine (*vira*) is collected, it can be spent on horses and weapons." And Vladimir said, "Let it be so." And [henceforth]Vladimir followed the custom of his father and grandfather.[64]

---

[64] PSRL 1, 126–27; see also Shepard, "Rus'," 403.

Judicial revenues are represented here not only as a fundamental aspect of princely power, but also as one of the very few continuities between the pagan and Christian periods. According to the Rusian narratives, Vladimir's conversion reformed him personally and also created "a new people" who abandoned their old pagan ways.[65] However, this radical change did not affect what the chronicler believes to be the time-honoured practice of filling the prince's treasury with judicial fines.

In reality, this practice did not yet exist at the time of Vladimir's grandfather and thus was not as ancient as the chronicler thought it was. As an account of tenth-century events, the story is, most likely, apocryphal; present in all redactions of the *Primary Chronicle*, it must have been composed no later than the first quarter of the twelfth century.[66] Its author evidently believed in the central importance of revenues generated by the prince's supreme right to administer justice for the functioning of the military elite. The church statute written on behalf of Vladimir also presents judicial revenues as the most important component of the princely income, but its usefulness as a source for the princely judicial powers in the pre-Mongol period is undermined by the statute's uncertain dating. Its earliest copy is from the fourteenth century; in spite of its internal attribution to Vladimir, it appears unlikely that the original was produced before the twelfth century; the statute's provisions thus may reflect realities of the twelfth, thirteenth, or early fourteenth centuries.[67] Equally uncertain is the dating of the so-called "Iaroslav's Church Statute"—that is, a document internally attributed to Iaroslav the "Wise," but most likely composed after Iaroslav's lifetime.[68]

There exist three other princely statutes discussing judicial revenues which also survived in late copies, but these copies are believed to be faithful representations of twelfth- and thirteenth-century originals. One of them is a Novgorodian document "generally attributed to the thirteenth century, and its sources perhaps to the reign [in Novgorod—Yu. M.] of Prince Vsevolod Mstislavich (1135–1137)."[69] This document is not of much use in the context of the present discussion: the relations between the prince and the community in thirteenth-century Novgorod were not necessarily typical of other regions of Rus; in addition, the existing text was probably compiled in the late thirteenth century, which is outside of the chronological scope of this book.[70] Another Novgorodian statute is much more relevant: it is believed to be actually drawn by the prince to whom it is internally attributed, Sviatoslav Olgovich; its internal dating to 6645 *anno mundi*, that

---

65 Francis Butler, *Enlightener of Rus': The Image of Vladimir Sviatoslavich across the Centuries* (Bloomington: Slavica, 2002), 52.

66 Kaiser, *The Growth of the Law*, 75–76; PVL, 995–97.

67 "Ustav kniazia Vladimira o desiatinakh, sudakh i liudiakh tserkovnykh," in *Drevnerusskie kniazheskie ustavy*, 12–84; Kaiser, *The Growth of the Law*, 50–54; Shepard, "Rus," 389.

68 "Ustav kniazia Iaroslava o tserkovnykh sudakh," in *Drevnerusskie kniazheskie ustavy*, 85–139; Kaiser, *The Growth of the Law*, 54–57.

69 Kaiser, *The Growth of the Law*, 58.

70 Shchapov, *Drevnerusskie kniazheskie ustavy*, 153–57; V. L. Ianin, *Novgorodskie posadniki*, 89–93.

is, 1136/7 AD appears highly plausible.[71] This is a short document that establishes the fixed sum for the tithe to be received by the Novgorodian bishop; the issuer decrees that if one tenth of the actual princely income falls short of this sum, it is to be supplemented from the prince's treasury. This statute lists judicial fines (*viry*) among the most important categories of princely income; Daniel Kaiser believes that figures found in the document "supply a rough estimate […] of the prince's expectations from traditional fees extracted for criminal offenses."[72]

The most detailed description of the sources of princely income is found in the foundational charter of the Smolensk bishopric. Its single sixteenth-century copy was found in a Swedish archive, along with copies of three more related documents from Smolensk; there is a general consensus that its original was drawn in the second third of the twelfth century, most likely in 1136/7, and that it was issued by Rostislav Mstislavich of Smolensk.[73] This charter also represents judicial revenues as a key source of princely income: Rostislav grants the bishop half of the fines from some crimes, as well as jurisdiction over certain types of crimes and over certain groups of people; the remaining judicial penalties collected in the Smolensk principality are excluded from tithing.[74] Thus, the documents issued by the prince of Novgorod and the prince of Smolensk in the 1130s support the implication of the twelfth-century narrative sources about the importance of revenues generated by princely judicial powers.

The picture that emerges from Rusian sources is in line with observations of historians of comparative law concerning interactions between a "horizontal" legal system, "where conflict resolution is essentially a matter for the parties directly involved—offender and victim" and a "vertical" power structure which imposes itself on a traditional "horizontal" society.[75] Rusian legal codes and other sources, such as birchbark letters discussing conflict resolution, show a largely "horizontal" system, where "most acts of violence, theft and disputes were settled on the spot by the individuals concerned or by their kin or community, without reference to the procedures laid down in writing by the prince or enforced by his agents."[76] An absence of such references in itself does not preclude the involvement of princes or other authorities in the administration of justice in accordance with the customary law. Thus, in a high medieval seigniorial or manorial court, "complex questions might be referred to 'wise men,' who had a particular understanding of the norms in question." According to a medieval account of a case tried at the court of the bishop of Bath in 1121, "those who were older and more learned in the law

---

71 Shchapov, *Drevnerusskie kniazheskie ustavy*, 147–48; Kaiser, *The Growth of the Law*, 58; Ianin, *Zakonodatelstvo Drevnei Rusi*, 224.

72 Kaiser, *The Growth of the Law*, 59.

73 Shchapov, *Drevnerusskie kniazheskie ustavy*, 140–46; Kaiser, *The Growth of the Law*, 58; Franklin, "On Meanings, Function and Paradigms of Law," 78.

74 Shchapov, *Drevnerusskie kniazheskie ustavy*, 141, 144.

75 Kaiser, *The Growth of the Law*, 11–12.

76 Shepard, "Rus," 404; cf. *The Growth of the Law*, 15; Franklin, "On Meanings, Function and Paradigms of Law," 72–77.

left the crowd and weighed [...] all the arguments they had heard and settled the case."[77] When Vladimir Monomakh, in his *Instruction*, presents himself as "dispensing justice to the people," or when he encourages his sons to "provide justice to a widow and an orphan personally" and not to "allow a strong man to ruin" the poor, it is easy to imagine a scene that is similar to the court held by the bishop of Bath: a crowd of locals and the ruler as mediator ensuring that the norms of the customary law are applied correctly, in accordance with the judgment of the respected community elders. Such a procedure would include the prince, but it does not require any specific written provisions.

Unfortunately, Monomakh never provides any details of what his "dispensation of justice" looked like; all we can conclude from his *Instruction* is that it was a routine occupation, listed on par with holding a council and hunting. Indeed, twelfth-century sources other than the *Instruction* show an increasing interference of princes in judicial matters.[78] Such an interference, even in its beginning stages, had rich income-generating potential.

Since paying compensation to the victim plays a prominent role in a traditional horizontal legal system, "litigation may prove profitable" for representatives of a vertical power structure who manage to turn part of the compensation into a judicial fine payable to themselves. Kaiser cites African cases of a certain number of cattle redeeming a homicide; originally, all cattle went to the victim's kin, but later a percentage of it became a legal fine.[79] Thus, for litigation to be profitable, there is no need for a sophisticated professional legal system, which clearly did not exist in Rus. Nor is there a need for a state monopoly on justice. In Rus, as in other medieval societies, many crimes were dealt with and many conflicts were resolved by the community itself. Nonetheless, the prince's interference in the judicial matters, however small it may be by later standards, made his income from what Kaiser translates as "bloodwites and fines" "already sizable enough in the twelfth century"; a legal code, the earliest copy of which is from the thirteenth century and which is "linked by internal evidence to the eleventh and twelfth centuries," shows "the trend towards subordinating the interests of the victim to the profit of the increasingly long arm of the prince."[80]

Concrete workings of the Rusian legal system—or systems, because they probably varied in different communities—do not need to concern us here. What is relevant for the subject of this chapter is the fact that princes received judicial income, and that the sources consistently represent "bloodwites and fines" as an important means to fill the prince's treasury. This suggests that princely domination in Rus was analogous to aristocratic domination in the West: to be the prince of a certain territory means to have judicial and administrative rights over this territory, rights that permit the prince to make "extractions of

---

77 Michael Lobban, "Sociology, History, and the 'Internal' Study of Law," in *Law, Society and Community: Socio-Legal Essays in Honour of Roger Cotterrel*, ed. Richard Nobles, David Schiff (New York: Routledge, 2016), 48.
78 Kaiser, *The Growth of the Law*, 79–80.
79 Kaiser, *The Growth of the Law*, 12, 193.
80 Kaiser, *The Growth of the Law*, 74, 18, 82.

various kinds," which Rusian sources describe as *dan*.[81] The prince could choose to donate parts of these extractions to someone else, but the supreme right to *dan* belonged to him. The only regular recipient of *dan* other than princes was the city of Novgorod with its special "republican" status.

If *dan* signifies extractions derived not from landownership, but from jurisdiction in the broad sense of the word as "the power or right of exercising authority," then it is not surprising that land in twelfth-century Rus could be transferred with or without *dan*, just as land in the region studied by Charles West could be, since the mid-eleventh century, transferred with or without *bannum*. Thus, a list of the donations that Andrew Bogoliubsky gave to the cathedral church in Vladimir includes settlements "with *dan*."[82] Such wording implies that Andrew could choose to donate the settlements, but at the same time to continue collecting *dan* from them. The right to *dan* is again differentiated from the ownership of settlements in the account of the events following Andrew's death, when his successors took away "settlements and *dani* (plural of *dan*)" donated by Andrew.[83]

Conversely, *dan* could be transferred without transfer of land. Thus, Rostislav of Smolensk allocated a tithe to the bishop not only from the *dan* that was collected in the Smolensk region, but also from the Suzdalian *dan* that Rostislav hoped to receive from George the "Long Arm": "If George returns *dan* from Suzdalia (*Suzhdali zalesskaia dan*), [the cathedral of] the Holy Mother of God is to receive a tithe on whatever will be the amount of this *dan*."[84] It is not entirely clear what is meant by George "returning" some *dan* from his own principality to the prince of Smolensk, and why Rostislav expected George to do so.[85] However, these details of princely politics are beside the point here. What is important to us is that Rostislav expects to receive *dan*, but not the territory from which it is collected.

"Castles" and "Towns": The Power of Language

In addition to the judicial power and collection of *dan*, the two terms that set princes apart from the rest of the secular elite are *volost* and *gorod*. Both princes and non-princely nobles owned land, but only princes had *volosts*. Every *volost* was structured around one, or more, fortified sites, called *gorod* (variant *grad*), traditionally translated as "town." *Gorod* and *volost* are often used interchangeably; the name of the *gorod* may serve as a metonymy for the *volost* centred on it. For example, in the account of an interprincely

---

81 Cf. West, *Reframing the Feudal Revolution*, 185–86.
82 PSRL 1, 348.
83 PSRL 1, 375.
84 "Ustavnaiaia i zhalovannaia gramota smolenskogo kniazia," 143.
85 For commentaries on the passage about the Suzdalian *dan*, see Ianin, *Zakonodatelstvo Drevnei Rusi*, 215; A. N. Nasonov, *"Russkaia zemlia" i obrazovanie territorii drevnerusskogo gosudarstva: Istoriko-geograficheskoe issledovanie* (Moscow: Nauka, 1951), 50; L. V. Alekseev, *Smolenskaia zemlia v IX–XIIIvv: Ocherki istorii Smolenshchiny i Vostochnoi Belorussii* (Moscow: Nauka, 1980), 197–99; V. A. Kuchkin, *Formirovanie gosudarstvennoi territorii severo-vostochnoi Rusi v X–XIV vv* (Moscow: Nauka, 1984), 74–76.

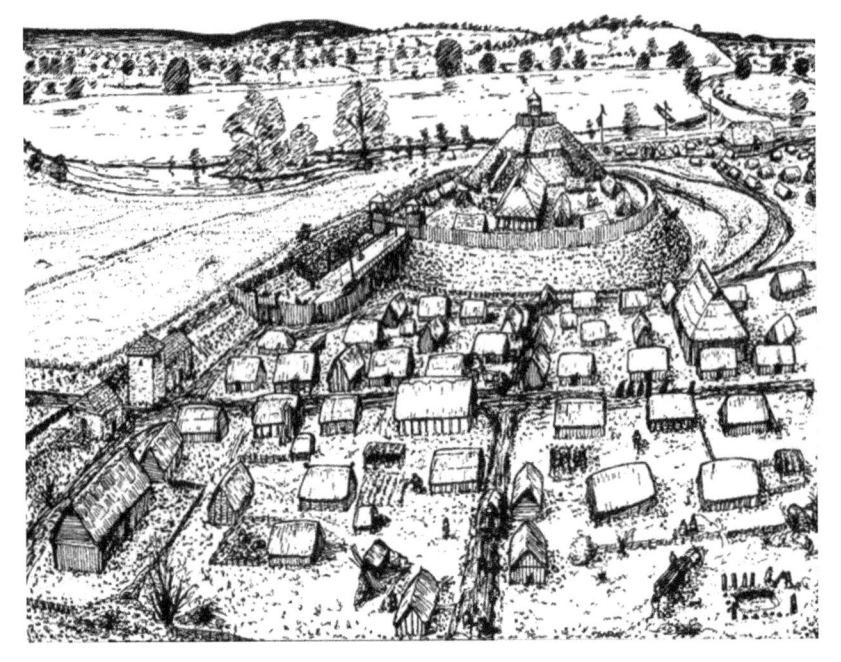

Figure 5. A "castle" in twelfth-century England.
Reconstruction of the early Norman castle at Gloucester in the early twelfth century.[86]

war discussed above, "Putivl" sometimes is used for the town of Putivl, and sometimes it stands for all the *volost* that Iziaslav and the Davidovichi conquered from Sviatoslav.

In the case of Putivl, which, in addition to the central fortified area, had substantial suburbs, the translation of *gorod* as "town" is quite appropriate.[87] However, the same word *gorod* is used in the sources for small enclosures that can be better described as fortresses. One of many examples is an account about the Kievan prince granting a regional prince the *gorod* of Dorogychin, the act that the chronicler also describes as giving the regional prince a *volost*.[88] Archaeological excavations show that Dorogychin had a central area of 100 x 60 metres enclosed by timber walls; the adjacent settlement outside of the walls was 300 x 100 metres.[89] In other words, this was a wooden fortress.

---

86 Timothy Darvill, "Excavations on the Site of the Early Norman Castle at Gloucester, 1983–84," *Medieval Archaeology* 32 (1988), 47.

87 The English translation of the title found on the book's title page is "The Annalistic City of Sneporod and Its Neighbourhood 10th–13th Centuries." "City" in this case is an erroneous translation of the modern Russian *gorod*. A more correct English translation of the title would be "Sneporod of the Chronicles and its Vicinity in the 10th–13th centuries."

88 Kuza, *Malye goroda*, 81.

89 An account of the conflict between Vsevolod and four lesser princes found in the *Kievan Chronicle* entry for 1142 reports the princes' dissatisfaction with the land grant that they received from Vsevolod. The princes referred to Vsevolod's grant as *volost*, and when the conflict was

Figure 6. A "small town" in twelfth-century Rus.
Reconstruction by G. V. Borisevich of the town of Sneporod in the Pereiaslavl principality. Yury Morgunov, *Letopisnyi gorod Sneporod i ego okruga, X-XIII veka* (St. Petersburg: Institut Archeologii Rossiiskoi Akademii Nauk, 2012).[90]

The primary meaning of *gorod* was "defensive walls, fortifications," which gave origin to the secondary meaning of a "walled-in settlement" of any size and character. Since medieval towns normally had defensive walls, *gorod* indeed signified "town," among other things.[91] That "town" was not the *gorod*'s only, or even primary, meaning is a very well-known fact reiterated again and again by scholars of Rusian urban development and of Rusian fortifications, who keep reminding their readers that not every *gorod* mentioned in the sources was a "true" town, since the word stood for any fortified enclosure.[92] Many Rusian excavation sites have been described by archaeologists as "a fortified countryside residence," a "castle-like type of settlement," or simply as a "castle."[93] This, however, has little, if any, effect on scholars of social and political history

---

resolved, the chronicler concludes that Vsevolod *uladivsia o volost*, that is, reached an agreement about *volost*. The chronicler describes Vsevolod's grant by giving the names of the four *gorody* that the four princes received from him. Apparently, each prince received one *gorod*, presumably with the surrounding countryside. PSRL 2, 310–12.

90 Kuza, *Malye goroda*, 93. Kuza describes the excavated earthen ramparts; on earthen ramparts as an indication of the existence of timber walls, see Iu. Iu. *Morgunov, Drevo-zamlianye ukrepleniia iuzhnoi Rusi X-XIII vekov* (Moscow: Nauka, 2009), 4, 20–21.

91 R. I. Avanesov et al., *Slovar drevnerusskogo iazyka (XI–XIV vv.)*, vol. 3 (Moscow: Russkii iazyk, 1990), 2167.

92 For example, Morgunov, *Drevo-zamlianye ukrepleniia*, 18; Kuza, *Malye goroda Drevnei Rusi*, 27, 43.

93 For example, Kuza, *Malye goroda Drevnei Rusi*, 25; T. N. Nikolskaia, *Zemlia viatichei: K istorii naseleniia basseina verkhnei i srednei Oki v IX–XIII vv.* (Moscow: Nauka, 1981), 72–75, 92–96; V. V. Sedov, *Selskie poseleniia tsentralnykh raionov Smolenskoi zemli (VIII–XV vv.)*, Materialy i issledovaniia po arkheologii SSSR series 92 (Moscow: Izdatelstvo Akademii Nauk SSSR, 1960), 123–24; Sedov, "Nekotorye voprosy geografii Smolenskoi zemli (po materialam ekspeditsii 1960 g.)," *Kratkie soobshcheniia Instituta arkheologii* 90 (1962): 12–23, at 20.

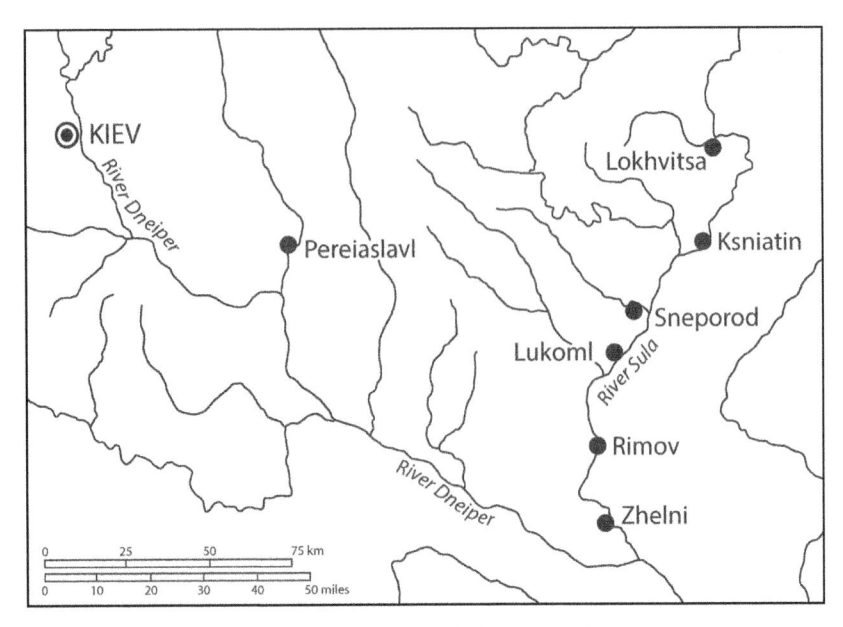

Map 2. Fortifications on the border with the steppe.

of Rus who habitually refer to any *gorod*—indeed, to any settlement mentioned in the sources and not explicitly called a "village"—as a "town." Correspondingly, the general works on Russian and Ukrainian history continue to name the absence of castles as one feature that differentiated Rus from the West.

This persistent misconception shows the powerful effect that an interaction between a modern and a medieval language can have on our perception of the past, and it illustrates once again the complexities inherent in the translation of historical terms. Or, in the case of *gorod*, it is rather a lack of translation that is at the root of the confusion. The common treatment of *gorod* in Russian-language historical works can be best described as a transplantation of the untranslated medieval term into a modern context, a transplantation that alters the medieval word's meaning. As the reader must have already guessed, in modern Russian, the word indeed signifies "town" (or "city"). To anyone knowing Russian, whether a native or non-native speaker, *gorod* looks so familiar, so simple and straightforward, that it is virtually impossible to think about it as a historical term in need of special translation. Thus, the automatic reflex of a Russian speaker who sees the word *gorod* has proved to have a stronger effect on historians than the combined evidence of linguistics and archaeology.

Moreover, Russian archaeologists seem to fall under the same spell of the modern meaning of *gorod* not only in their use of euphemisms for "castle," but also in their research of what is known in Russian archaeology as "a problem of small towns." The archaeologists working on this problem seek first to establish criteria for what constitutes an urban settlement—a town or a city, both of which are described by the same Russian word *gorod*—and then to find out which excavated settlements meet these criteria. Research on "small towns" has produced a number of fine works of scholarship containing highly valuable studies of individual fortified settlements, but the question of how to classify these settlements into urban and non-urban remains unresolved.[94]

"Small towns" pose a problem because the urban status of big towns, or cities, is self-evident. However, there are no universally accepted characteristics that allow to differentiate between a "small town," a "fortress," and a "castle." All of them were fortified, and all of them performed not just military, but economic and administrative functions as well. According to one proposition, a "castle," as opposed to "town," is characterized by "underdeveloped" craft production and a "stronger" connection with agriculture.[95] It seems to be a rather hopeless task to find objective criteria that would allow us to measure how "strong" craft or agriculture was in any given place, all the more so because tools for specialized craft production apparently used by highly professional artisans have been found on sites that otherwise look like "rural estates (*usadby*)."[96] Other proposed characteristics of an "urban settlement" are equally problematic, and it is hardly surprising that archaeologists have never agreed on how to distinguish "small towns" from the general mass of Rusian walled settlements.

English- and French-speaking scholars fall under the spell of modern language no less than their Russian counterparts. An Anglo- and Francophone analogue of the Russian "problem of small towns" is a quest for a "true" castle. Since *castrum* and other words traditionally translated into English as "castle" and into French as *château* signify any walled settlement, castle scholars have proposed various criteria that would allow them to distinguish "true castles," that is, fortified lordly residences.[97] Just like Russian researchers of "small towns," scholars working in the area of castle studies, or castellology, have produced numerous fine studies of fortified enclosures, but no unambiguous criteria for the "true castle."[98] Their task appears even more elusive than the search for Rusian "small towns": towns did exist in Rus, and in other medieval societies, but there was hardly any place in medieval Europe that served exclusively as a "fortified private residence." According to Charles Coulson, the distinction between public

---

94 The most important work on "small towns" is Kuza, *Malye goroda Drevnei Rusi*. The present state of scholarship is best expressed by the title of an essay by Vladimir Koval, "Small Towns: An Undefinable Concept." See this essay for a review of literature on the archaeology of "small towns" and for the latest state of research, V. Iu. Koval, "Malye goroda: neulovimaia kategoriia," forthcoming. I am grateful to Vladimir Koval for allowing me to consult the manuscript of this work before it was published.

95 Sedov, *Selskie poseleniia*, 123–24.

96 Nikolskaia, *Zemlia Viatichei*, 94–96.

97 For example, Reginald Allen Brown, *English Castles* (Woodbridge: Boydell, 1976), 2–3, 16–18, 44–46.

98 Among the most important English works on castles are David King, *Castellarium Anglicanum* (Millwood: Kraus International, 1983); Brown, *English Castles*. For a review of works seeking to define "castle" and to differentiate it from other types of fortified settlements, see Coulson, *Castles in Medieval Society*, 33–41.

and private fortifications and the monopolization of the word "castle" for the latter "is a matter not of medieval development [...] but of modern historiography" that has projected back into the Middle Ages the concepts of the later period when "defense of the nation became a governmental monopoly."[99] This modern development resulted in what Abigail Wheatley describes as "the unhelpfully narrow definition of the castle in common currency."[100] All medieval castles were, to a greater or lesser degree, centres of administration, craft production, and commerce—that is, in addition to their military role, they performed functions that in the modern period are associated with towns.[101] The wide overlap between medieval terms for "private fortifications and fortified communal and urban enclosures" reflects the lack of a clear distinction between them in medieval life.[102]

It is true that Latin has an extensive vocabulary to describe walled settlements, in contrast with East Slavonic, where *gorod* is the only term. However, for the most part, different words inherited from antiquity, such as *castrum*, *oppidum*, or *civitas*, did not correspond to different types of medieval settlements, but were used indiscriminately: the same word described places of vastly different size and character, while different words were applied to one and the same settlement, which could be called, for example, now *castrum*, now *civitas*.[103] Probably the closest modern

---

99 Coulson, *Castles in Medieval Society*, 30–31.

100 Abigail Wheatley, *The Idea of the Castle in Medieval England* (Woodbridge: York Medieval Press, 2004), 51.

101 Peter Ettel, "Frankish and Slavic Fortifications in Germany from the Seventh to the Eleventh Centuries," in *Landscapes of Defence in Early Medieval Europe*, ed. John Baker, Stuart Brookes, and Andrew Reynolds (Turnhout: Brepols, 2013), 261–84, at 272–74, 279–80; Coulson, *Castles in Medieval Society*, 182; O. H. Creighton, *Castles and Landscapes* (New York: Continuum, 2002), 1, 223.

102 Wheatley, *The Idea of the Castle*, 44.

103 "In France fortresses of every possible kind were 'castles,' be they entire ancient towns, newer ecclesiastical precincts, great territorial *capita*, and lesser castellated mansions, descending on scale down to ephemeral earthworks and campaign-forts (some British 'castles' of 1066–c. 1110 fall into this category)"; in England, "nearly all the forms, from the Gallo-Roman cathedral city of the fifth century to the gun-forts, built to the order of Henry VIII [...] were known to contemporaries as *castra* or *castella*," Coulson, *Castles in Medieval Society*, 2, 30; Orderic Vitalis "uses *castellum* and *castrum* interchangeably with several other Latin words, such as *municipium*, *praesidum* and *oppidum*, to describe a range of defenses from fortified towns to military defenses and fortified houses. This usage is echoed in other documents of the time," Wheatley, *The Idea of the Castle*, 26; "Die Burgen der Slawen wurden in der lateinischen Überlieferung des Früh- und Hochmittelalters mit den Begriffen *civitas*, *urbs*, *castrum* oder *castellum* bezeichnet," Sébastien Rossignol, "Die Burgen der Slawen in der lateinischen Überlieferung des 9. bis 11. Jahrhunderts," in *Siedlungsstrukturen und Burgen im westslawischen Raum. Beiträge der Sektion zur slawischen Frühgeschichte der 17. Jahrestagung des Mittel- und Ostdeutschen Verbandes für Altertumsforschung in Halle an der Saale, 19. bis 21. März 2007*, ed. Felix Biermann, Thomas Kersting, and Anne Klammt (Langenweissbach, Germany: Beier and Beran, 2009), 31–38, at 31. According to Rossignol, the difference in the meanings of *castrum/castellum* and *civitas* existed in the heartland of the German Empire, but was lost on the periphery, ibid., 32. In Poitou, *castra* were "places of importance, such as a town or a

equivalent of these medieval terms is the German *Burg*.[104] Symptomatically, there is no parallel to the search for the "small town" or "true castle" in German scholarship. The wide range of the meanings of *Burg* seems to encourage German scholars not to privilege one meaning of a medieval term over all others, and then to try and separate settlements that conform to this one meaning. The situation when English and French scholars of fortified enclosures concentrate on the features associated in the modern mind with "castle," while Russian scholars concentrate on those associated with "town," stems from modern language, not from any real difference in the objects of their research.

In reality, Rusian, English, and French walled-in settlements other than big cities had the same general structure. Contrary to the "anachronistic expectation of a castle as a tower-like building of masonry," most castles before the late twelfth century, and many of them later, consisted of a wooden fortress situated on a raised earthwork and/or on a natural hill, cliff, or promontory. A fortress could also include a tower, known as a donjon or keep, made of timber, stone, or a combination of the two. In addition to the dwellings within the walls, there was usually some kind of settlement adjacent to the fortress.[105] This is exactly how a typical Rusian *gorod* looked as well.[106] In addition, like *gorod*, Latin terms could stand not just for the walled settlement, but for all the area centred on it. *Civitas* referred both to an administrative or ecclesiastical district and to the capital of such a district, and only an analysis of the context can reveal which meaning is used in any particular case.[107] A *castrum* was normally the centre (*caput*) of a district sometimes called *vicaria castri*, *castellania*, or *castellaria*, but it was used synonymously with *castellaria* and stood not just for the chief place, but for the whole district as well. In the words of Coulson, "since the revenues of the lordship were collected at, and its unity expressed by, the administrative center, it was natural to refer to the lands and *caput* collectively as 'the castle.'"[108] The same can be said about the relations between *gorod* and *volost*.

---

monastery, surrounded by walls of some sort. [...] The chroniclers did not confine themselves to the term *castrum* to describe these walled enclosures—they used *castellum*, *oppidum*, and *munitio* almost as freely [...]. Hence in any particular case it is impossible to be certain what sort of a fortress the terms *castrum* or *castellum* designated," Sidney Painter, "Castellans of the Plain of Poitou in the Eleventh and Twelfth Centuries," *Speculum* 31 (1956): 243–57, at 247–48. See also J. F. Verbruggen, "Note sur le sens des mots castrum, castellum, et quelques autres expressions qui désignent des fortifications," *Revue belge de Philologie et et d'Histoire* 28 (1950): 147–55.

104 Coulson, *Castles in Medieval Society*, 4; Ettel, "Frankish and Slavic Fortifications," 261n1.
105 Barrière, *Limousin médiéval*, 188–206; Coulson, *Castles in Medieval Society*, 18, 52, 66–70.
106 Morgunov, *Drevo-zemlianye ukrepleniia*, 17–25, 146–51; Kuza, "Ukreplennye poseleniia," 39–41.
107 Niermeyer, *Mediae Latinitatis Lexicon Minus*, 183–84; Sébastien Rossignol, "*Civitas* in Early Medieval Central Europe—Stronghold or District?" *Medieval History Journal* 14 (2011): 71–99.
108 Coulson, *Castles in Medieval Society*, 21, 49–63, 54; Barthélemy, "Autour d'un récit de pactes," 480–83.

Gorod and the Dawn of Princely Power in Rus

A spatial organization of their power is thus another feature that Rusian princes share with high medieval lords based in castles. Princes are the only members of the Christian lay elite in Rus who are represented as "having," "holding," or "sitting in" a *gorod*. As may be expected, control over *gorody* is connected to receiving *dan*. Thus, *gorody* and *dan* go hand in hand in a story from the *Primary Chronicle* describing how one of the early princes, Oleg, established his power in what would later become Rus: "Oleg began to build *gorody*, and he made [various ethnic groups] pay him *dan*."[109] This passage describes the events that allegedly had occurred about two centuries before the *Primary Chronicle* was compiled. It is hard to say how accurately or otherwise it represents Oleg's activities; however, for the purpose of the present discussion, it is more important to note that the chronicler apparently sees a connection between building *gorody* and imposing *dan* on the population. It appears that the best translation for *gorody* in this passage is "castles": the chronicler evidently had in mind not urban centres, but strongholds built in order to impose Oleg's domination.[110]

Just as building strongholds was necessary for imposing *dan* on a previously independent population, control over existing strongholds was crucial for collecting *dan* from the surrounding area. The *Primary Chronicle* thus describes the success of one participant in an interprincely conflict: "He conquered all the regions of Murom and Rostov and appointed his governors (*posadniki*) to the strongholds (*gorody*) there and began to collect *dan*."[111] Here again princely domination over a territory is identified with receiving *dan* from the population of this territory, and princely control over the strongholds is represented as a means to ensure payment of *dan*.

---

109 "Oleg nacha gorody staviti i ustavi dani Slovenom, Krivichem i Meri," PSRL 1, 24.

110 Another example of a connection between *gorody*—which, in this case, again clearly stands for "castles"—and *dan* is present in the mid-thirteenth-century account of the subjection of the Jatvingians (Yotvingians, Jatvians), a Baltic ethnic group living on the territory of present-day Lithuania, Belarus, and Poland, to Prince Daniel Romanovich of Galich. After Daniel's victorious campaign against them, the defeated Jatvingians "gave him *dan* and promised to be subservient to him and to build *gorody* [on Daniel's orders] in their land (*Iatviazi* [...] *dan dasha i obeshchevakhusia rabote byti emu i gorody rubiti v zemle svoeī*)," PSRL 2, 835. These events, reported in the *Galician-Volhynian Chronicle* under 1257, probably took place in 1254 or 1255 (Mikhailo Hrushevskyi, *Khronologiia podii Galitsko-Volynskogo litopisu* (Lviv: Zapiski Naukovogo tovaristva imeni Shevchenka, 1901), 38). This is after the Mongol invasion and, therefore, strictly speaking, out of the chronological scope of this book. However, although Prince Daniel formally submitted himself to Batu in 1245, his principality remained *de facto* independent until 1259 or 1260, when it was subjugated by the Mongol general Burundai. Even after this date, it retained significant autonomy. The *Galician-Volhynian Chronicle* shows a great degree of continuity throughout the thirteenth century, and the assumption of the chronicler about the vital role of *gorody* for subjugating the newly conquered population arguably reflects the attitude that existed in pre-Mongol Rus.

111 PSRL 1, 237.

The rise of castles has traditionally been seen as an important part of the "feudal revolution"; archaeological data showing the growing number of castles supports evidence of the written sources about the emergence of new patterns of elite domination in the eleventh century.[112] There appears to be a similar connection between written and archaeological evidence for the emergence of princely power in Rus, although all reconstructions of the early history of Rusian princes are inevitably much more tenuous than are the theories of Western medievalists: the rise of princely power in Rus occurred during a period for which native written sources are virtually non-existent. The earliest reliable contemporary sources go back to the late eleventh and early twelfth centuries, and they present a system of princely domination that is already there: we see multiple princes in their *volosts*, collecting *dan*, judging, governing, protecting, and exploiting the population under their authority, dividing and combining their *volosts* in various ways, conquering *volosts* from and granting them to one another—but there is little information on how or when all of this came to be. The available information is not enough to produce a comprehensive account of princes' rise to power, but it may be used for hypothesizing about the time period when this rise began.

P. S. Stefanovich performed an exhaustive analysis of the tenth-century treaties between Rus and Byzantium in conjunction with the Byzantine account about a visit of the Rusian leaders to Constantinople.[113] He has demonstrated that the organization of the Rusian elite as it emerges from these tenth-century documents is quite different from the representation of the social organization in eleventh-century sources. In the latter, princes are sharply differentiated from non-princely elite (boyars). In contrast, in the tenth-century documents, princes and boyars, described with the same Greek word *archontes*, are of equal standing, with only the Kievan prince having a slightly higher status than the rest of the elite. Stefanovich argues that princes and boyars "parted ways" during the reign of Vladimir I (d. 1015), who succeeded in turning legitimate power into the monopoly of princes.[114] He also noted that this period saw a curious phenomenon known among Russian archaeologists as "double centres (*parnye tsentry*)," or "transfer of towns."

Archaeological data show a significant growth in the number of fortified sites from the eleventh century on, as well as a noticeable change in the configuration of their network that occurred at the turn of the same century. Namely, around the year 1000, a number of settlements, which had thrived in the ninth and tenth centuries, declined; at the same time new centres emerged, some in such close proximity to the older ones that archaeologists describe them as "double" or "transferred" towns consisting of the older abandoned settlement and a newer one founded nearby. Those newer centres continued to exist throughout the pre-Mongol period. The number of fortified settlements was growing exponentially all the way up to the Mongol invasion in the 1230s; this growth especially accelerated in the second half of the twelfth century. However, no matter how many new settlements appeared in the later eleventh, twelfth, and early thirteenth

---

112 West, *Reframing the Feudal Revolution*, 144.
113 Stefanovich, *Boiare, otroki, druzhiny*, 337–440.
114 Stefanovich, *Boiare, otroki, druzhiny*, 415, 428, 441.

centuries, this growth did not result in the abandonment and decline of existing centres, as had happened around the year 1000.[115]

A growth in the number of fortified enclosures indicates increasing control by the elite over the territories where these enclosures were built. On the other hand, a shift in the location of some prominent centres that occurred at the turn of the eleventh century suggests a change in the organization of this emerging territorial lordship. If princes emerged as a distinct social stratum which monopolized the control of strongholds and the exercise of legitimate power during the time of Vladimir, this means that a reorganization of the Rusian elite occurred in the late tenth–early eleventh century, precisely the period in which archaeologists describe the phenomenon of the "double" or "transferred" centres. Stefanovich, therefore, suggests that the two phenomena—the reorganization of the location of the strongholds and the rise of the princes, which apparently took place at the same time—are connected.[116]

This suggestion is hard to prove with certainty, but all evidence indicates that some kind of change did take place in the organization of the elite in Rus at the turn of the eleventh century. Interpretations of this change will probably never leave the realm of the hypothetical, but as hypotheses go, Stefanovich's reconstruction appears rather convincing.

"Banal Lordship" Hypothesis: Limitations of Rusian Sources

The parallel between princely domination in Rus and elite domination in the high medieval West proposed in this chapter also belongs to the realm of the hypothetical. It is for the reader to judge how convincing the hypothesis that Rusian princes were similar to lords exercising the power of *ban* is. A constellation of the characteristics that Rusian sources attribute to princes is reminiscent of high medieval lords of the castles, but the nature of the sources, which are either fragmentary, or compilatory, or both, makes it impossible to reconstruct the workings of princely power in the same detail as much better documented social relations in the regions of Latin Europe where banal lordship was shown to exist.

As the reader already knows, birchbark documents are among the only surviving original written sources, apart from liturgical books. However, they survived not as a collection of letters and they were found not in an archive or library; instead, they are random strips of birchbark, sometimes as little as a few square centimetres, found by archaeologists in the streets and households of Novgorod, where the anaerobic environment is uniquely beneficial for the preservation of organic materials; a handful of birchbark fragments with writing on them was found elsewhere. A modern analogue

---

[115] V. Ia. Petrukhin and T. A. Pushkina, "K predystorii Drevnerusskogo goroda," *Istoriia SSSR* 4 (1979): 100–112; E. N. Nosov, "Novgorodskoe gorodishche v svete problemy stanovlenia gorodskikh tsentrov Povolkhovia," in *Gorodishche pod Novgorodom i poseleniia Severnogo Priilmenia: Novye materialy i issledovaniia*, ed. E. N. Nosov, V. M. Goriunova, and A. B. Plokhov (St. Petersburg: Dmitrii Bulanin, 2005), 19–22.

[116] Stefanovich, *Boiare, otroki, druzhiny*, 442–43.

would be a collection of paper pieces picked up from sidewalks or found in the trash. Some birchbark fragments do mention princes administering justice or officials collecting payments from the population, but a lack of context makes interpreting them a very difficult task.[117] For example, one fragment, beginning in the middle of a word, asks the addressee for the names of those who "did not give" or "did not pay" something. The author plans to send to these non-paying people an official (*iabetnike*), and he also instructs the addressee to collect something from "newly arrived people (*prikhozhono*)" so that each pay their proper share (*kako razrubile*).[118] A reference to the *iabetnike* makes the publishers think that the payments discussed in the fragment were taxes. Other fragments refer to *vira*, which, as we remember, signified a judicial payment, to *pochestie*, which described one kind of payment owed to the prince in the Smolensk charter, and to *poliudie* mentioned in the chronicles as something collected by princes.[119] In the context of the present discussion, the main value of these tiny fragments, each consisting of less than a full sentence, is the fact that authentic twelfth-century documents know the terms found in the sources that survived in late copies, which adds to the latter's credibility.

There are also several letters of substantial length that refer to princely judiciary. In one of them, dated to the 1160s–1190s, the author threatens to bring the addressee to the joint court of the prince and the bishop if the latter does not pay 12 grivnas that he owes to the author because of a girl; if the addressee does not pay voluntarily and go to court, he is bound to lose more than 12 grivnas.[120] Several alternative reconstructions of the situation with the girl that led to the payment obligation have been proposed.[121]

---

117 For example, Gr. St. R.12, in *Novgorodskie gramoty na bereste: iz raskopok 1962–1976 gg.*, ed. A. V. Artsikhovskii, V. L. Ianin, and A. A. Zalizniak, Novgorodskie gramoty na bereste 7 (Moscow: Nauka, 1978) [hereafter NGB 7], 152–53; Gr. 550, in *Novgorodskie gramoty na bereste: iz raskopok 1977–1983 gg.*, ed. V. L. Ianin and A. A. Zalizniak, Novgorodskie gramoty na bereste 8 (Moscow: Nauka, 1986) [hereafter NGB 8], 23–24; Gr. 664, in *Novgorodskie gramoty na bereste: iz raskopok 1984–1989 gg.*, ed. V. L. Ianin and A. A. Zalizniak, Novgorodskie gramoty na bereste 9 (Moscow: Nauka, 1993) [hereafter NGB 9], 54.

118 Gr. St. R.12.

119 Gr. 115, in *Novgorodskie gramoty na bereste: iz raskopok 1953–1954 gg.*, ed. A. V. Artsikhovskii, Novgorodskie gramoty na bereste 3 (Moscow: Nauka, 1958) [hereafter NGB 3], 48; Gr. St. R.17, in NGB 9, 105–6; Gr. 226, in *Novgorodskie gramoty na bereste: iz raskopok 1956–1957 gg.*, ed. A. V. Artsikhovskii, V. I Borkovskii, Novgorodskie gramoty na bereste 5 (Moscow: Nauka, 1963) [hereafter NGB 5], 49. On *poliudie*, see P. S. Stefanovich, "Poliudie po letopisnym dannym 1154–1200 g.," *Drevniaia Rus: Voprosy medievistiki* 62 (2015): 97–103.

120 Gr. 155, in *Novgorodskie gramoty na bereste: iz raskopok 1955 g.*, ed. A. V. Artsikhovskii and V. I Borkovskii, Novgorodskie gramoty na bereste 4 (Moscow: Nauka, 1958) [hereafter NGB 4], 34–36.

121 B. B. Kafengauz, "Zametki o novgorodskikh berestianykh gramotakh," *Istoriia SSSR* 1 (1960): 168–74; L. V. Cherepnin, *Novgorodskie berestianye gramoty kak istoricheskii istochnik* (Moscow: Nauka, 1969), 69; V. L. Ianin, *Ia poslal tebe berestu* (Moscow: Izdatelstvo MGU, 1975), 163–64; A. A. Zalianiak, *Drevnenovgorodskii dialekt* (Moscow: Nauka, 1995), 318.

In a letter dated to the 1160s–1170s, the author informs the two addressees that he either did not receive a court hearing, or lost it (*ia tiazhe ne dobyle*), and that his wife paid to Prince David 20 grivnas which the addressees had promised to the prince.[122] The prince is almost certainly David of Smolensk, one of the sons of the Rostislav who issued the much-discussed charter. The relations between the author and the addressees and the significance of the 20-grivna payment have received different interpretations.[123] In addition to birchbark documents, a prince's ruling of a court case is mentioned in an inscription carved on a wall of the church of St. Panteleimon in Galich, most likely during the princely tenure of Mstislav Mstislavich Udatnyi, who ruled in Galich in 1217–1227. Its idiosyncratic language and ambiguous syntax makes the inscription open to alternative interpretations, but the most widely accepted reading is:

> During the reign of Prince Mstislav when Ignatius held office, Liakh was sued for not paying the debt of the two carpenters, but was not found guilty. He paid what he was supposed to pay [*vykladennoe dal*]. The witnesses are [list of names]. The prince ruled to dismiss the case [*sudil ne iskati nikomu zhe*], and whoever does not obey [...].[124]

The inscription and birchbark letters show that the existence of the prince's judicial rights and revenues in the twelfth and early thirteenth century was not an invention of later scribes, but do not tell us much more.

Thus, the information about concrete cases that comes from authentic documents is extremely fragmentary, while the information about the princely rights and prerogatives in the chronicles is too generic. It is princes in general, as a social stratum, who are represented as having a monopoly on revenues generated by judicial and administrative rights and on control of strongholds. When it comes to concrete princes and their dominions, information is scant; in addition, what little information we have concerns big principalities, not smaller units comparable to the *castra* of Latin sources. The chronicles present princes seeking, defending, and conquering strongholds, but they are mostly silent on what a prince does in his stronghold when he is not busy fighting for it. The general logic of the chronicle narratives creates the impression that for a prince to "have" a stronghold means to collect *dan* and to govern the area around it, but such activities are assumed, not documented.

One reason to make this assumption is a consistent differentiation between princes and non-princely members of the elite in their relation to *gorod*. The difference between

---

[122] Gr. 603, NGB 8, 66–67.

[123] V. L. Ianin and A. A. Zalizniak, *Novgorodskie gramoty na bereste: iz raskopok 1990–1996. Paleografiia berestianykh gramot i ikh vnestratigraficheskoe datirovanie* (Moscow: Nauka, 2000), 115; *Pismennye pamiatniki*, 273.

[124] A. A. Gippius, "Galitskie akty XIII v. iz tserkvi sv. Panteleimona," in *Pismennost Galitsko-Volynskogo kniazhestva: Istoriko-filologicheskie issledovania*, ed. Jitka Komendová (Olomouc: Univerzita Palakeho v Olomouci, 2016), 49–64, at 52–53; Gimon, "Drevnerusskie sudebnye dokumenty," 25–26. "Liakh," which is East Slavonic for "Pole," may be either a personal or an ethnic name.

them is the same as the distinction that the Western sources make when they write about "X's stronghold" versus "X's man/men in the stronghold." For example, the *Conventum Hugonis* describes various *castra* as "Hugh's," or as belonging to Hugh's father, uncle, or other relatives.[125] Conversely, some men are described as being "of" a *castrum*, such as "Joscelin of the *castrum* of Parthenay."[126] Clearly, this is another way of saying that Parthenay belongs to Joscelin. On the other hand, when a certain Peter "unjustly" held a *castrum* that had belonged to Hugh's uncle, Hugh went and "threw Peter's men" out of there.[127] Apparently, Peter was not physically present in the *castrum*, but rather he had entrusted it to his men. There is a clear difference between the "holder" of the *castrum* and the men who guard the *castrum* on his behalf. Similarly, in connection with another disputed *castrum*, the *Conventum* mentions "a man who guards the tower." Hugh seeks to control this man in order to be able to control the *castrum*.[128] Hugh, Joscelin, and Peter of the *Conventum* were lords of the castles, and the Aquitanian sources in general, not just the *Conventum*, differentiated between such lords and men who took care of the castles on the lords' order.[129]

A similar differentiation existed in the neighbouring Anjou, where the most powerful castellans who held their castles and the surrounding territory by hereditary right were called *domini*, or lords, the appellation that distinguished them from the commanders appointed by the count to guard castles that were under his direct control. The *domini* "formed a rank of nobility second only to the count and were the bedrock of Angevin military and political organization."[130] In other regions, the words used to describe the person in charge of a castle did not necessarily indicate whether he was an independent lord or an appointed custodian.[131] However, this does not mean that the distinction between the two did not exist, or it would have been impossible for anyone to claim more than one castle. Magnates, such as Hugh of Lusignan, could only be physically present in one *castrum* at a time; somebody must have looked after their other *castra* in their absence.

By the same token, a prince who controlled more than one *gorod* resided in the most important one. As for other strongholds under his power, he could either appoint his men to look after them or send his adult sons or younger brothers there, or else he could "give" them to lesser princes who were not immediate family members. In the first of these cases, the prince's appointee was called *posadnik* (plural *posadniki*),

---

125 *Conventum Hugonis*, 543, 546, 547.

126 "de castro Parteniaco Ioselinus," *Conventum Hugonis*, 542.

127 *Conventum Hugonis*, 547.

128 "Ait Ugo [to William], 'Da mihi illum qui custodit turrem [...] ut si Aimericus habuerit castrum sine meo consilio [...] ille homo reddat mihi turrem,'" *Conventum Hugonis*, 546.

129 Painter, "Castellans of the Plain of Poitou," 249.

130 W. Scott Jesse, *Robert the Burgundian and the Counts of Anjou, ca. 1025–1098* (Washington, DC: Catholic University of America Press, 2000), 2.

131 Dominique Barthélemy, "Note sur le titre seigneurial, en France, au XIè siècle," *Archivum Latinitatis Medii Aevi* (54) 1996: 131–58.

a term that, in line with the convention to translate *gorod* as "town," is often rendered as "governor." The Western analogue of *posadnik*, a lord's man in charge of a castle, is usually described in scholarly literature as a "guardian" or "custodian." However, if we keep in mind that a castle was the administrative centre of the territory around it, the person in charge of the castle can be also viewed as a "governor." Regardless of how we translate *posadnik*, the important point is that no *gorod* or *volost* is ever described as "his." Rather, the *posadnik* himself is always "his" in respect to some prince, such as "Iaropolk's *posadniki*" or "Mstislav's *posadnik*."[132] The chronicles report how one prince drove the *posadnik* of another prince from a disputed *gorod* and installed his own *posadnik* there, or how the *posadniki* of a defeated prince vacated *gorody* entrusted to them and fled before the advancing winner, and similar episodes, always showing the *posadnik* as his prince's agent with no independent political role.[133]

On the other hand, even a territorial unit that a lesser prince held "from" somebody is still described as "his." If a prince "sat in" or "held" a certain *gorod*, no matter on what conditions, this is "his" *gorod* and the *volost* centred on this *gorod* is "his" *volost*. The difference between a prince and a *posadnik* in their relations to the *gorod* is quite evident from the chronicle entry describing what Vsevolod the "Big Nest" of Suzdalia did with his five newly acquired *gorody*: he "gave Torchesk to his son-in-law Rostislav Rurikovich, and he sent *posadniki* to the other [four] *gorody*."[134] In other words, he gave one *gorod* to another prince and kept the remaining four for himself. Since Vsevolod had a residence in the city of Vladimir, the capital of his Suzdalian principality, he had to appoint his men to be guardians (or "custodians," or "governors") of the strongholds where he was not physically present. The grant of Torchesk creates layers of authority: Torchesk is described as both Vsevolod's and Rostislav's. We will discuss such arrangements in the next chapter; for now, it is important to note that there was no layering of authority over the places where Vsevolod sent *posadniki*: these four *gorods* were simply Vsevolod's.[135]

The Smolensk charter shows the *posadniks* and *tiuns* collecting *dan* and administering justice: a list of crimes, the jurisdiction over which the prince grants to the bishop, is concluded with the injunction that "neither prince, nor *posadnik*, nor *tiun*, nor whoever else, great or small" may try the cases and collect judicial fines that belong to the bishop. The distribution of revenues from the jurisdiction over one type of crime, abduction of a girl, is described as, "whatever the prince takes, is to be divided in half with the

---

132 PSRL 2, 291, 519.
133 For example, PSRL 2, 333, 342, 523, 685.
134 PSRL 2, 685.
135 In fact, the situation with Torchesk is somewhat more complicated, since Vsevolod had received Torchesk and the other four *gorody* from yet another prince Rurik. This is discussed at length below, in Chapter 4, but for the present discussion of the *posadniki*, we can ignore the role of Rurik and concentrate on the actions of Vsevolod in respect to the five *gorody*.

bishop, or whatever the *posadnik* takes from a trial of this crime (*chto vozmet svoi tiazhi*), is to be divided in half with the bishop."[136] A consistent representation of the *posadnik* and *tiun* as prince's men implies that they tried cases and collected judicial revenues on the prince's or princess's orders. As we remember, the charter describes *dan* collected in the Smolensk region as "prince's, or princess's, or whoever else's." Married women in Rus could own property; we know about a princess who received a *gorod* as a wedding gift.[137]

Evidently, a princess, most likely the wife of the Smolensk prince, owned judicial and administrative rights over some territories in the Smolensk principality. "Whoever else" receiving *dan* in the Smolensk region were probably other members of the princely family, or lesser princes to whom the prince of Smolensk would "give" a *gorod*, as major princes are often represented to do. It is most unfortunate that we can only assume that he made such grants, because the Smolensk chronicle, whose existence is attested to by several surviving fragments, is lost.[138]

In regions discussed in the extant chronicles, we see lesser princes "holding," "having," and "receiving" or "being granted (*nadeliti, nadelenie*)" individual strongholds on a regular basis. Such grants often appear to be the regional ruler's sanctioning of the prince's hereditary right. Just as the *Conventum* represents the count granting to Hugh the *castra* that belonged to his father or other kinsmen, or criticizes the count when he does not do so, the Rusian chroniclers assume that the rulers of big principalities are supposed to "give" strongholds to the lesser princes who have hereditary rights to them.[139] Such strongholds, together with the rural areas around them, comprised the lesser princes' *volosts* located within large principalities which, in turn, were *volosts* of the major regional princes. While there is no direct documentation of a lesser prince collecting *dan* and having judicial and administrative rights over the population of his *volost*, it appears that a grant of a *volost* without such rights would have been meaningless. If a lesser prince "has" a stronghold, but the *dan* from the area centred on his stronghold goes not to him, but to someone else, what makes the stronghold "his"? What would have been the difference between such a prince and a *posadnik*? Most importantly, what would then constitute a *volost*'s worth in money, if, as we have seen, a *volost* was different from the prince's personal land property?

Finally, a complaint of Sviatoslav of Chernigov about his "empty" *volost*, discussed earlier in this chapter, shows that the *dan* from areas centred on strongholds of the Chernigov principality went not to the Chernigov prince, but to whoever "held" the

---

136 "Ustavnaiaia i zhalovannaia gramota smolenskogo kniazia," 144.
137 PSRL 2, 658.
138 Shchapov, *Pismennye pamiatniki*, 46.
139 PSRL 2, 296, 384, 444, 496; A. K. Zaitsev, *Chernigovskoe kniazhestvo X–XIII vv* (Moscow: Kvadriga, 2009), 66–69.

particular stronghold. This is the only possible explanation of Sviatoslav's statement that he made a great sacrifice (*koliko na sia postupakh*) when he agreed "to take Chernigov with seven empty *gorody*." As we remember, the senior Olgovich and the former prince of Chernigov moved on to become the Kievan prince and left the Chernigov principality to Sviatoslav. Sviatoslav, however, was "angry" that the new Kievan prince did not make him a "proper grant of the Chernigov *volost* (*Chernigovskoi volosti ne ispravil*)." The "improper" character of the grant consisted of the Kievan prince retaining parts of the Chernigov principality for himself and giving others to his own nephew. Consequently, the two of them "held" most of the Chernigov land, while Sviatoslav was left with the position of the Chernigov prince and seven strongholds that did not provide him with an adequate income.

Apparently, being the Chernigov prince did not entitle Sviatoslav to the *dan* from all the territory of the Chernigov principality; the *dan* from the areas centred on individual strongholds was collected by "holders" of these strongholds. Interestingly, Sviatoslav still found the position of the Chernigov prince valuable: he was outraged by the threat of the Kievan prince to move him from Chernigov to a lesser centre, Novgorod-Severskii, in violation of his oath on the Cross, which, according to Sviatoslav, was "not to deprive me of Chernigov under any circumstances." This outrage is expressed in the same speech, where Sviatoslav complains that Chernigov "with seven empty *gorody*" does not bring him any substantial material benefits.[140] Apparently, the position of the Chernigov prince had sufficient non-material advantages that made Sviatoslav want to keep it. Chernigov was the main city of a major principality, and if Sviatoslav's authority was similar to that of the Smolensk prince, he probably valued the political prestige connected with being the ruler of the Chernigov land. From the Smolensk charter, the prince of the main city, Smolensk, emerges as the effective ruler of the principality. We have seen that he had the authority to decree the tithing on all the *dan* and to grant the bishop the jurisdiction over certain criminal cases throughout all the Smolensk land; he also established the size of *dan* to be collected in all parts of his principality, even though not all of this *dan* went to his treasury. Apparently, to have this political authority amounted to having the Chernigov or Smolensk *volost*. The same word, however, was applied to the territorial units within big principalities. We have seen that *volost*, like virtually all medieval terms, has a wide range of meanings, and since this word is so central to the accounts of princely politics, we need to look at its semantic field from a comparative perspective.

Volost, *Honor*, and *Poesté*

As a word that signifies the prince's rule, his authority over a certain territory, and also the territory itself, *volost* is similar to the medieval Latin *honor*, a term which "encompasses the holding of land with the personal standing derived from its

---

[140] PSRL 2, 498–500.

holding" and that can mean both a "land unit" and "power or authority."[141] Old French, in addition to the vernacularized forms of *honor*, such as *honur, oner, enor*, etc., also has a term, *poesté*, which means both "power/authority" and "domain, realm." However, unlike *honor*, *poesté* signifies not only legitimate power, such as a lord's power over his domain, but also "raw" physical power, power as "strength" or "might," which is especially evident when, in the plural form *poestez*, the same word takes a meaning of "army." Dictionaries do not include "strength" or "might" among the meanings of *volost/vlast*; however, it is used in this sense on at least one occasion. In a story about a noble youth who wanted to join a monastery against his father's will, the abbot addresses the aspiring monk: "What if your father arrives with a great *vlast* (*s mnogoiu vlastiiu*) and forcibly takes you from here?" The father did as the abbot expected: "Having taken many servants (*otroky*) with him," he broke into the monastery and led his son away by force.[142] In this passage, *vlast* does not refer to authority or legitimate power. On the contrary, the father first complained to the prince, asking him to retrieve his son from the monastery; only after the prince refused to grant this request, the father decided to take the matter into his own hands and to use *vlast*, which here clearly stands for crude physical strength derived from the great number of presumably armed servants.

Thus, both vernaculars, East Slavonic and Old French, have words that combine the meanings of "physical strength," "domain," and "power/authority." The two latter, but not the former, are present among the meanings of the Latin *honor*. The vernacular *poesté* and *volost/vlast* appear to reflect the idea that holding one's domain requires adequate strength, displaying the "Realpolitik" attitude that we have encountered in the narratives about the old and weak Viacheslav not being suited to be the Kievan prince, and in Henry II's proclamations of his physical strength and military might in Jordan Fantosme. A rich, and often hard-to-translate, narrative effect is created by an interplay between the different meanings of *volost*, *honor*, *poesté* and other words which describe the objects of all the disputes, negotiations and agreements that fill the pages of medieval chronicles and histories.

One example is the speech of Andrew of Pereiaslavl during his stand-off with the Kievan prince Vsevolod, much discussed above. As we remember, Andrew was ready to die defending his hereditary right to the *volost* of Pereiaslavl, and he compared Vsevolod, who planned to move him to Kursk, with Sviatopolk the "Cain-like": "The same thing occurred before: did not Sviatopolk kill Boris and Gleb for the sake of *volost*?" In fact, Sviatopolk killed Boris and Gleb because he wanted to get rid of his brothers in order to be the sole ruler

---

141 Ashe, *Fiction and History*, 98; "l'ambivalence qui s'attache à tout le vocabulaire chevaleresque et vassalique: l'*honor* est à la fois un fief et un pouvoir," Dominique Barthélemy, *La société dans le comté de Vendôme: de l'an mil au XIVe siècle* (Paris: Fayard, 1993), 557.

142 Nestor, *Zhitie prepodobnaago ottsa nashego Feodosiia*, ed. O. V. Tvorogov, in *XI–XII veka*, Biblioteka literatury Drevnei Rusi, ed. S. D. Likhachev et al., vol. 1 (St. Petersburg: Nauka, 1997) [hereafter BLDR 1], also available as an electronic text at http://lib.pushkinskijdom.ru/Default.aspx?tabid=4872#_ednref26.

of all Rus.[143] Thus, to say that Sviatopolk committed his crime "for the sake of *volost*" is possible only if *volost* is understood as "power" or "rule." In contrast with that, the *volost* that is the subject of the conflict between Andrew and Vsevolod is a specific territory. The rhetorical strategy of Andrew's speech is based on the polysemy of *volost*—and even if the speech purposely manipulates different meanings of the word, this manipulation would have been impossible if there had been a clear distinction between *volost* as a territory and *volost* as power.

The size of a *volost*'s territory and the scope of the power derived from its holding varied greatly. We have seen *volosts*, such as Dorogychin, consisting of a walled-in place of a few hundred square metres and the countryside around it. At the same time, when the Rusian chronicler reports that, after the death of Casimir of Poland, Casimir's brother Mieszko "sought to deprive Casimir's sons of their *volost*," *volost* means supreme power over Poland, since Mieszko tried to depose his nephew Leszek as Duke of Poland.[144] Rusian accounts of the Fourth Crusade report that the Franks installed Baldwin of Flanders "as their own Latin emperor" and "divided all the *vlast* among themselves [...] And this is how the empire of God favored Constantine and the Greek Land perished [...] and it now belongs to the Franks."[145] In this passage, *vlast*, which is a variant spelling of *volost*, stands for power over the Byzantine Empire.

We have seen Jordan Fantosme using *honur* in a similar sense—as power over a kingdom—when he explains that Henry the Young King rebelled against his father because he found himself in a situation of a king *senz honur*, which R. C. Johnston translates "without a realm."[146] Likewise, in a thirteenth-century Anglo-Norman poem, *honur* refers to the realm of biblical King David: "David held these two *honurs* [Judea and Israel], by means of which he was a king and a sovereign prince."[147] However, more often, *honor* describes not a realm, but its part, the dominion of a local lord or ruler, ranging from a big principality, such as Anjou, the *honor* of Fulk le Réchin, all the way to a *castrum*.[148] Arguably, what all these vastly different *honores* have in common is the "political" or "public" flavour of the power that the holder/owner/ruler had over his *honor*'s territory, from royal authority over the realm, to the judicial and administrative rights of the lord of the castle. It is tempting to think that this was also the common

---

143 PSRL 1, 139.

144 PSRL 2, 686.

145 N1L, 145.

146 *Jordan Fantosme's Chronicle*, 4–5.

147 "Ces dous honurs David tint en sa main / Dunt il fut reis e prince soverain," in *Poème anglo-normand sur l'Ancien Testament*, ed. Pierre Nobel, Nouvelle bibliothèque du Moyen Âge 37 (Paris: H. Champion, 1996), 490.

148 *Chroniques des comtes d'Anjou et des seigneurs d'Amboise*, 232, 237; In the *Conventum Hugonis*, the *castrum* of Parthenay is referred to as *honor*; in response to Hugh's claims that he should receive several *castra*, William says, "I will not give you those *honores* that you ask from me," thus using *honor* as a synonym for *castrum*. Then he agrees to give Hugh the *honor* of Hugh's late uncle: "kastrum [sic], turrem, and omnem istam honorem," *Conventum*, 542, 547–48.

denominator of all the different usages of *volost/vlast*: what the Byzantine emperor, the Kievan prince, the duke of Poland, and the prince of Dorogychin had in common was the "political" character of their power, which, at the level of Dorogychin, would be similar to banal lordship.

***

The goal of this chapter was to apply to Rusian material Charles West's idea of the judicial and administrative rights over a location as a special form of property differentiated from land ownership.

Princely rights over his *volost* do emerge from the sources as a form of property that is different from owning land within the same *volost*. It is then logical to suggest that princely domination was of the same nature as banal lordship, that the prince exercised the judicial and governmental—what historians used to call "regalian"— rights that were similar to the high medieval *ban*, and that *dan* constituted the extractions that the French historians describe as *taxes banales*, as opposed to *taxes foncières*. To be sure, the prince's jurisdiction was superimposed on communities that managed many of their own affairs in accordance with traditional norms and customary law. However, the present discussion is concerned not with the question, fascinating though it is, of the princely authority versus community self-rule, but with the question of the rights of princes versus the rights of non-princely nobles. In this respect, the information from the Rusian sources is rather unambiguous: whatever external administrative and judicial authority was imposed upon communities, these rights belonged to princes.

The East Slavonic *kniazi*, the term that we translate as "princes," would then signify the social stratum comprised of territorial lords with judicial and administrative rights, distinct from noble landowners without such rights. Representations of *dan* in Rusian sources, its connection with princes' right and duty to exercise justice, as well as the semantic field of *volost*, point in that direction, but our information is too scant to come to any definitive conclusion. With diplomatic sources largely lost and narrative sources surviving in fragments, as parts of later compilations, the nature of the relations between the prince and his *volost* may be reconstructed only hypothetically.

There is no conclusive evidence for Rusian princes being analogous to banal lords, but the spatial organization of princely domination is probably the strongest argument in support of such an analogy: just like high medieval Latin Europe, Rus was dotted by strongholds that were, at one and the same time, military fortifications and administrative and economic centres of the countryside around them. Areas dominated by these strongholds, conventionally described as "castles" in the West and as "towns" in Rus, were the basic territorial units of high medieval polities. The bulk of Rusian narrative sources are accounts of disputes between princes over rights to such units. Interprincely relations, unlike relations between princes and lesser nobles or between princes and the population, are a relatively well-documented aspect of the Rusian socio-political organization. The subject of the next chapter is a comparative analysis of agreements that individual princes and/or small princely groups, akin to Hélène Débax's co-lords, concluded with one another.

Chapter 4

INTERPRINCELY AGREEMENTS AND A QUESTION OF FEUDO-VASSALIC RELATIONS

THIS CHAPTER COMPARES personal ties of political friendship, service, loyalty, and obedience that existed between princes in Rus and between members of lay elite in Latin Europe. A discussion of such ties inevitably leads to the subject of "feudalism." A personal bond known as the "feudal contract" is at the core of the narrow definition of feudalism as a legal system based on the lord's grant of fief in exchange for the vassal's service and obedience. A broader, more widely used model, going back to Mark Bloch's classical work, does not reduce feudalism to the feudo-vassalic bond, but includes this bond among the defining features of "feudal society," along with a subject peasantry, the fragmentation of public authority, and the dominance of the warrior aristocratic class. Within this latter class, there was a "widespread use of service tenement (i.e. the fief)" and ties of obedience and protection that assumed the distinctive form of vassalage, and, "in the midst of all this, the survival of other forms of association, family and State."[1]

As is well known, the concept of feudalism has been subject to much critique, which has become particularly vigorous since the 1990s. According to its most radical critic, Susan Reynolds, the union of fief and vassalage that is at the heart of the "feudal contract" never was sufficiently formal, systematic, and widespread to justify the traditional view of it as central to the medieval social order; to the extent that feudo-vassalic relations existed at all, they were a creation of late medieval jurists. Some aspects of Reynolds's thesis have been broadly accepted. Most historians agree that earlier scholarship mistakenly saw feudo-vassalic relations in the early Carolingian period. This mistake appears to be the ultimate manifestation of the "confusion of words, concepts, and phenomena" that, according to Reynolds, is at the core of the problem with "feudalism": as soon as historians encounter in their sources words, such as *vassus* or *beneficium* (thought to be synonymous with *feodum*), they assume the existence of the textbook fiefs and vassals. Studies of these and other terms describing power and property relations have demonstrated that words, with what look from a modern perspective like "feudal" connotations, had, in fact, a wide variety of meanings; and that there is, indeed, no evidence that the early medieval *beneficium* was the type of property traditionally described in scholarly literature as "fief."[2]

At the same time, few historians heeded the call to abandon the concept of feudo-vassalic relations altogether. Most see these relations as an important aspect of twelfth-century social organization, and date their origins to the same, or to the previous, eleventh century. On the other hand, few, if any, scholars still think of feudo-vassalic

---

[1] Bloch, *Feudal Society*, 446.

[2] Paul Fouracre, "The Use of the Term Beneficium in Frankish sources: A Society Based on Favours?," in *The Languages of Gift in the Early Middle Ages*, ed. Wendy Davies (Cambridge: Cambridge University Press, 2010), 62–88.

relations as an ubiquitous, uniform institution, dominating the medieval social order so much that it turned "other forms of association" into no more than survivals from the past of little significance for "feudal society." Much attention has been directed to other kinds of interpersonal ties since Gerd Althoff's pioneering work on "kinship, friendship, and loyalty" was published in 1990.[3]

Scholarship of the 1990s and early 2000s brought to light diverse forms of interpersonal bonds, emphasizing their fluidity, the ambiguity of medieval terms that described them, and difficulties in fitting these bonds into legalistic categories typical of earlier discourse on feudalism. Many of these studies noted that relations more or less corresponding to the definition of "feudo-vassalic" existed alongside other bonds, but their authors were not interested in the question of how feudo-vassalic relations developed, or what their significance was for the evolution of the social order.[4] More recent evaluations of the place of feudo-vassalic relations vis-à-vis other social bonds present something of a reaction against what historians of the new generation apparently see as the hypercriticism of the 1990s.

This recent turn is probably best exemplified by the 2012 article on Ottonian Germany by Levi Roach. The article analyzes tenth-century narratives that include descriptions of the ritual of homage, and it rejects their traditional feudo-vassalic interpretation=, showing that homage, in this case, did not create "a putative 'feudal contract'," a conclusion in line with Reynolds's thesis. However, Roach challenges another aspect of her thesis. Reynolds postulates that there was no connection between early medieval social bonds and feudo-vassalic relations, which she, of course, sees as an invention of academic lawyers, not as a product of an organic development. In contrast, Roach does see in his early medieval material "important developments towards something approximating" the feudal system "of textbook lore." This system "comes more fully into view" by the second half of the twelfth century.[5]

Charles West also views the high medieval social organization as, to borrow Roach's phrase, "something approximating" the classic feudal system. He presents the development of feudo-vassalic relations as an important part of the gradual change that took place over the course of the eleventh century. It was closely connected with another aspect of this change, the differentiation between ownership of land and ownership of jurisdiction over the population living there, which we discussed in the previous chapter. West argues against the view, prevalent among critics of the "feudal revolution" theory,

---

[3] Althoff, *Family, Friends, and Followers*.

[4] This attitude is probably best represented by most essays in *Feudalism*, especially Gerd Althoff, "Establishing Bonds: Fiefs, Homage, and Other Means to Create Trust," 101–14, and also by Elizabeth Brown's review of this volume, Elizabeth A. R. Brown, Review of *Feudalism: New Landscapes of Debate*, edited by Sverre Bagge, Michael H. Gelting, and Thomas Lindkvist, *The Medieval Review* 6 (2012) at https://scholarworks.iu.edu/dspace/bitstream/handle/2022/14548/12.06.10.html?sequence=1. Another example is Claudia Garnier, *Amicus amicis, inimicus inimicis: Politische Freundschaft und fürstliche Netzwerke im 13. Jahrhundert*, Monographien zur Geschichte des Mittelalters series 46 (Stuttgart: Anton Hiersemann, 2000).

[5] Roach, "Submission and Homage," 355, 378.

that feudo-vassalic relations and lordship of the high medieval type already existed in Carolingian society. He insists on distinguishing the early medieval informal personal ties of loyalty and reciprocity between high-status men and their followers, from the later, much more clearly defined, feudo-vassalic relations.[6]

To summarize, traditional scholarship imposed modernizing legal clarity on diverse types of interpersonal relations between members of the early and high medieval elite and interpreted all "honourable" personal bonds in feudo-vassalic terms. The 1990s–early 2000s critics of "feudalism" showed that early and high medieval Europe knew, to use what appears to be one of Reynolds's favourite expressions, "a whole range of" ties between members of the elite. The strand of criticism directed against the "tyranny of the feudal construct" argued that feudo-vassalic relations neither existed in the Carolingian period, nor grew out of something that did exist before the advent of academic lawyers. Another strand, the one directed against the notion of the "feudal revolution," defined feudo-vassalic relations rather loosely, identifying them with most forms of unequal agreements among the elite and, therefore, postulating their existence both before and after the putative "revolution." Current scholarship sees both interpretations as "flattening historical change," and it returns to a stricter definition of feudo-vassalic relations, differentiating them from general oaths and ties of fidelity, "the kinds of bonds which Gerd Althoff has taught us so much to appreciate."[7] In respect to the feudo-vassalic bond, these less formal interpersonal agreements are treated as something like a primordial soup, parts of which, over the course of the eleventh and/or twelfth centuries, gradually coalesced into more formalized relations, not identical, but similar to "the feudal system of textbook lore."

Oaths in Rus: Terminology and Sources

The "primordial soup" of sworn agreements is clearly seen in Rusian sources. Their general stance on oaths is exemplified by a statement that God commanded princes, in order to be saved, to fulfill two main obligations: to uphold justice and to keep oaths.[8] "Cross-kissing (*krestotselovanie*)", which signifies an oath on the Cross, is one of the most common words describing relations among the princes and among members of the upper social strata in general. To "transgress one's Cross-kissing" means to break an oath on the Cross. Such a perjurer is called *krestoprestupnik*, "a Cross-transgressor." "To kiss the Cross to somebody on something" is to make a sworn promise; for two or more parties to kiss the Cross "between themselves" or "to each other/to one another" is to make a sworn agreement; "to lead" or "to bring (*voditi*)" someone to the Cross is to receive a sworn promise from this person.

Chronicles mention one or another of these actions on almost every page, but apparently just as often pass them in silence, judging from numerous reports of princes

---

[6] West, "Lordship in Ninth-Century Francia."
[7] West, *Reframing the Feudal Revolution*, 208; Roach, "Submission and Homage," 378.
[8] PSRL 1, 377; PSRL 2, 530.

accusing one another of not having kept their oaths, with the oath itself never having been mentioned before. A typical passage from an account of a dispute reads, "You kissed the Cross to us, promising to observe the treaty concluded with [Prince] Roman (*na Romanovom riadu*). If you are now bringing back old disagreements that we had at the time of Rostislav, you are breaking the treaty."[9] This passage is found in the *Kievan Chronicle*, but neither this chronicle, nor any other source, contains any information whatsoever about the treaty concluded with Roman and the attendant oaths. This and similar cases may be explained by the compilatory nature of our sources. As noted above, all Rusian chronicles are unwieldy combinations of pieces apparently taken from diverse narratives; it is possible that the original source used by the compiler described the treaty made with Roman, but this description, for one reason or another, did not make it into the text we have now. The fourteenth-century scribe Laurentius who made the earliest surviving copy of a compilation that includes various pre-Mongol texts famously complained that his exempla consisted of books so old and decrepit (*vetshany*) that he was not always able to make sense of them.[10]

However, not all omissions are caused by the loss of original sources. For example, the unbroken account of an episode in an interprincely war, apparently copied from the original intact, relates how one prince, Gleb, besieged by Iziaslav Mstislavich in the fortress of Gorodok, "became frightened (*uboiavsia*), came out of Gorodok and bowed down to Iziaslav, and made peace (*umirisia*) with him." However, after Iziaslav left, Gleb returned to his original alliance with Iziaslav's enemies, explaining to them, "I was forced to kiss the Cross to Iziaslav against my will (*po nevoli esm khrest tseloval*), because he besieged me, and there was no help from you."[11] If not for this explanation, we would have never known that Gleb's bowing down and making peace included kissing the Cross.

It seems very likely that princes concluding peace normally made oaths on the Cross and that chroniclers simply do not mention this routine unless they have a special reason to do so. For example, in the same oft-invoked account of a conflict between Vsevolod and Andrew over Pereiaslavl, Andrew defeated Vsevolod's troops sent to remove him from Pereiaslavl by force. He pursued them all the way to the border of the Pereiaslavl principality, but at that point he stopped his men and did not allow them to go beyond the border. After that, he made peace with Vsevolod. This probably would have been all we knew, if it were not for an unusual circumstance that the chronicler describes thus: "Vsevolod and Andrew made peace. And Andrew kissed the Cross, but Vsevolod did not kiss the Cross yet, and a fire accidentally started in Pereiaslavl on that night. Vsevolod, however, [...] did not send his men there." In the morning, he took care to point out to Andrew that he was not yet formally bound by an oath when the fire presented him with a "God-given (*mi bykh Bog dal*)" opportunity to reverse his defeat, and to achieve his original goal of seizing Pereiaslavl. After making this speech, Vsevolod

---

9 PSRL 2, 670.
10 PSRL 1, 488.
11 PSRL 2, 360.

"kissed the Cross to Andrew."[12] The chronicler apparently expects the reader to know that a peace between two princes involve their "kissing the Cross to" each other.

In this particular case, the chronicler judged details of the peace-making process worth telling, because they represented a key episode in establishing Vsevolod's legitimacy as the new Kievan prince. In not pursuing Vsevolod's troops beyond the border, Andrew showed that he would not use his position as the prince of the strategically located Pereiaslavl against Vsevolod, which must have been what Vsevolod feared when he wanted to take Pereiaslavl from Andrew and to give it to his own brother. Not attacking Pereiaslavl during the night fire appears to be Vsevolod's symmetrical answer to Andrew stopping his men at the border: Vsevolod shows that as long as Andrew does not threaten his position in Kiev, he does not seek to remove him from Pereiaslavl. When the process of oath-taking did not reveal such rich layers of meaning, chroniclers saw no reason to mention it explicitly.

The fire that gave Vsevolod a chance to show his magnanimity also gives us a chance to get the idea that an oath on the Cross must have been an elaborate ceremony, if Andrew took it on one day, and Vsevolod on the next. The details of this ceremony are not recorded anywhere, although one accusation of a perjury begins, "You kissed the Cross to us, and your lips did not yet get dry."[13] Was the Cross sprinkled with something, such as holy water? Was kissing the Cross somehow imagined as producing the same effect as kissing a person on the lips? More likely, the oath was accompanied by a kiss between the parties making the sworn agreement. Accounts of peace and other agreements often include a kiss, even when the parties are not equal.

Chronicles mention written documents called *krestnaia gramota*, in literal translation, "charter of the Cross." None of these charters survive. The context indicates that they must have been records of the oaths sworn on the Cross.[14] All mentions of "charters of the Cross" refer to them as physical objects to be used in rituals of breaking an agreement, declaring a war, or else demanding explanations for a perceived breach of an oath. Treating charters as instruments of symbolic communication, rather than simply as text records, was a typical high medieval attitude. Thus, in twelfth-century Languedoc, a written record of an oath was burned publicly to signify the annulment of the oath. Even for societies with such highly advanced written culture and administration as twelfth-century England and Flanders, a physical copy of a treaty "was not simply a text, but an object encapsulating the Anglo-Flemish relationship on a symbolic, totemic level."[15]

A "charter of the Cross" appears for the first time in the *Kievan Chronicle* entry for 1144. The chronicler, in his usual laconic manner, informs us that "Vsevolod had a conflict (*roskotorastasia*) with Vladimir [...] and Vladimir threw (*vozverzhe*) the charter of the

---

[12] PSRL 2, 305–6.
[13] PSRL 2, 536.
[14] PSRL 1, 412–13; PSRL 2, 314–15, 346–47, 461–62, 670, 686, 693. See also Franklin, "Literacy and Documentation," 23–24.
[15] Débax, *La féodalité languedocienne*, 324; Oksanen, *Flanders and the Anglo-Norman World*, 72.

Cross to Vsevolod. Vsevolod with his brethren then marched on Vladimir." In Vladimir's case, "throwing" the charter must have signified a renunciation of his oath to Vsevolod, which Vladimir presumably justified by arguing that Vsevolod broke whatever promise he had made to Vladimir. We do not know when the oath recorded in the charter, which Vladimir "threw," had been sworn, but this probably happened before 1140, because in the entry for 1140 Vsevolod "sends" Vladimir on a campaign.[16] In all likelihood, Vladimir, along with other major princes, swore an oath to Vsevolod when the latter ascended the Kievan throne in 1139.

In fact, all mentions of "charters of the Cross" involve either a Kievan or a Suzdalian prince; during the time periods when the charters are mentioned, these princes were effective monarchs. It thus looks like these were records of a ceremony which established relations between the ruler and his most prominent subjects, as was typical for personal monarchy elsewhere. Our best guess, then, is that the "charters of the Cross" we see in the chronicles reflect something similar to individual friendship treaties that early medieval kings, such as Henry I the "Fowler," made with the leading magnates of their realms.[17] New Kievan princes are often said to "accept" other princes "into love," which from some more detailed accounts emerges as a ritual involving an oath on the Cross.

In Chapter 2, we saw George the "Long Arm" establishing "love" with other princes when his right to the Kievan throne was universally recognized, in contrast with earlier occasions when he briefly seized Kiev, but was not generally considered the rightful Kievan prince. When he did become the legitimate supreme ruler, his former opponents submitted themselves to him and were "accepted into love"; however, the most active among them, Mstislav, did not dare to leave his stronghold, fearing that George would seize (*imet*) him. George did not insist that Mstislav arrive personally; in a literal translation, he "sent to Mstislav with Cross-kissing, and accepted him into love."[18] It would be interesting to know what the "sending" consisted of, but there is no information on that; the information we can glean from this account is that "acceptance into love" included kissing the Cross.

Oaths on the Cross were in no way limited to cases involving the Kievan and Suzdalian princes. Accounts of interactions between lesser princes, and between princes and communities, often include oaths on the Cross, but they do not mention "charters of the Cross," whether because such oaths were not recorded, or because the sources are patchy, and a handful of references to the "thrown" charters in the chronicles is not representative. There is no doubt, however, that lesser princes did conclude sworn agreements: they "kiss the Cross to" one another all the time. We also see "people" "kissing the Cross to" various princes; in some cases, princes made inaugural oaths on the Cross, but it is unclear whether such cases were typical outside of Novgorod, where

---

[16] PSRL 2, 314–15, 304. The *Kievan Chronicle* contains chronological mistakes; however, these two entries appear to be chronologically correct: by all evidence, the entry for 1140 describes the events of 1139–1140, and the entry for 1144 those of 1144–1145. See Berezhkov, *Khronologiia*, 146.
[17] Althoff, *Family, Friends, and Followers*, 82.
[18] PSRL 2, 480–81.

it was an established practice. In other places, a prince "kissing the Cross to the people" may have been an exception rather than the rule.[19]

"Love" and "Friendship"

Likewise, "love" was not limited to the ties that bound the Kievan prince with his most prominent subjects. Lesser princes, as well as "people," that is, in all likelihood, elite men acting on behalf of their communities, often entered into relations described in the sources as "love (*liuby, liubov*)". This word stood for personal affection and erotic love as well, but in the chronicles, it took the same range of meanings as "love" of Western political narratives that signified loyalty, peace, agreement and alliance.[20] Its meanings thus overlapped with those of *amicitia*, political friendship. The latter has been an object of numerous studies, which often treat political love and friendship as a single category. The two words indeed are often used together in the sources, as in, for example, "[being] linked by ties of sworn friendship, we do not wish to break the bonds of our concord and love," or "we will be allied by a strong bond of love and friendship."[21]

There may be a difference between the usages of "love" and "friendship" in political contexts, but it is related not to the contents of the agreements that these words describe, but to the character of the sources where the usages occur. It appears that "love" is the primary word choice in texts written in the vernacular or connected with an oral tradition, while the learned Latin authors prefer "friendship." To prove or disprove this suggestion, more research is needed, but a general impression is that twelfth-century vernacular literature uses mostly "love," and occasionally "love and friendship," while the Latin historiographers of the same period use "friendship," and occasionally "friendship and love." Indeed, the works on medieval political friendship have shown that the term which signified it, *amicitia*, is rooted in classical tradition. According to Althoff, it is hard to tell "how much the medieval bond of *amicitia* owed to its ancient predecessor, because the medieval bond had similarities with the Germanic *amicitia*, too."[22] However, he does not explain what Germanic term signified this bond, because he discusses all alliances of love and friendship summarily, concentrating on their contents and not on the terminology. The essence of the relations described in the sources as

---

19 PSRL 1, 373; PSRL 2, 320–22, 494–95, 526.

20 On meanings of political "love" in Western narratives, see Débax, *La féodalité languedocienne*, 126; George Fenwick Jones, *The Ethos of the Song of Roland* (Baltimore: Johns Hopkins Press, 1963), 40; Fredric Cheyette and Howell Chickering, "Love, Anger, and Peace: Social Practice and Poetic Play in the Ending of Yvain," *Speculum* 80 (2005): 75–117, at 84. On Rusian political "love," see Mikhailova, "'He Sighed from His Heart and Began to Gather Soldiers'."

21 "Ego et Arnulfus, conjuratae amicitiae intricati copula, nolumus concordiae et dilectionis [...] nostra [...] scindere," *De moribus et actis primorum Normanniae ducum*, 204; "firmo dilectionis et amicitie [sic] vinculo confederavimus," an unpublished manuscript of the agreement between the two bishops, Philip von Heinsberg of Cologne and Ulrich of Halberstadt, as quoted in Claudia Garnier, *Amicus amicis*, 18; cf. "ki de vus departirunt amur ne druerie," *Jordan Fantosme's Chronicle*, 2.

22 Althoff, *Family, Friends, and Followers*, 68.

amicitia may well "not demonstrably owe any more to one tradition than the other,"[23] but the word has profoundly classical connotations. It is likely that the medieval learned authors applied this term to the relations which in oral discourse were known as "love."

Indeed, Rusian chroniclers, blissfully unaware of Sappho or Catullus, did not see any problems with statements such as that two princes "made a great love with each other (*stvorista liubov' mezhi soboiu veliku*)."[24] Similarly, the *Chanson de la Croisade* could describe the king's men as his "lovers,"[25] and the author of the *Conventum Hugonis*, who, to put it mildly, was not very well versed in classical Latin, could write that Hugh did not marry a certain girl "because of his love for the count (*propter eius amorem*)."[26] This means that the count wanted to prevent an alliance between Hugh and the girl's father; therefore, he commanded Hugh to take back his promise to marry the girl. Hugh obeyed, even though this deprived him of a chance to obtain a politically useful connection through marriage. The author and the audience of the *Conventum* apparently never thought that Hugh could love the count in any other sense than in showing him the obedience due to a lord. By the same token, the poet and the audience of the *Chanson de la Croisade* understood the king's "lovers" as his faithful companions. However, for authors more familiar with the classical tradition, such statements may have looked awkward. Therefore, they either used Latin terms signifying spiritual love, such as *caritas* and *dilectio*, or, more often, described as *amicitia* that which was probably called "love" in the vernacular.

In accordance with the general tendency of Rusian chronicles to be closer to the Western vernacular, rather than to Latin, sources, they prefer "love" by far, but occasionally use "friendship" as well. To be precise, the abstract nouns signifying friendship—*druzhba* and *priiatelstvo*—are found very rarely, if ever, in political narratives, but once in a while the chroniclers use "friend" and "to be friends" in political contexts. Political "love" and "friendship" in Rus are very similar to the bonds described in works on Western *amicitia*: pragmatic agreements, based on the principle of *do-ut-des*, and encompassing both "horizontal" relations between equals and "vertical" hierarchical agreements.[27] When the sources describe the creation of the bond of political "love," they normally refer to oaths on the Cross; the expressions, such as "they kissed the Cross to be in love," are very common.

Networks of sworn agreements played an important role in princely politics. Ties created by oaths on the Cross had a strong element of mutuality and reciprocity, and they

---

23 Althoff, *Family, Friends, and Followers*, 68.
24 PSRL 2, 403.
25 William of Tudela, *Chanson de la croisade*, 1:70, as quoted in Fredric L. Cheyette, review of *La féodalité languedocienne aux XI–XII siécles: serments, sommages et fiefs dans le Languedoc des Trencavel* by Hélène Débax, *The Medieval Review* 12 (2004) at https://scholarworks.iu.edu/dspace/bitstream/handle/2022/5661/04.12.14.html?sequence=1.
26 *Conventum Hugonis*, 542.
27 Garnier, *Amicus amicis*, 5. On political friendship in Rus, see M. L. Lavrenchenko, "'Priiateli' russkikh kniazei (po tekstam letopisei za XII vek)," *Slavianovedenie* 2 (2015): 96–108.

were generally similar to "processes and techniques with which people in the Middle Ages sought to engender the obligation to help and support," brought to light by Althoff.[28] These were the ties that, in combination with royal power, dominated the organization of the elite in early medieval Europe and that continued to be an important aspect of high medieval social organization. The rest of this chapter will be devoted to the question of whether Rus had the type of relations that marked the transition from the early to high medieval period, that is, whether some ties between members of the Rusian elite can be described as feudo-vassalic.

Feudo-vassalic Relations in Current Scholarship

Feudo-vassalic relations are at the core of the classic "narrow" or "legal" definition of feudalism formulated by François-Louis Ganshof:

> A body of institutions creating and regulating the obligations of obedience and service—mainly military service—on the part of a free man (the vassal) towards another free man (the lord), and the obligation of protection and maintenance on the part of the lord with regard to his vassal. The obligation of maintenance had usually as one of its effects the grant by the lord to his vassal of a unit of real property known as a fief.[29]

This "union of fief and vassalage" constituted the feudo-vassalic bond. The bond of vassalage was created by the ritual of homage, in which the man to become vassal put his hands between the hands of the lord and swore an oath of fealty. The lord then invested the vassal in his fief by handing over a symbolic object, such as a sword or spear. By performing these acts, the parties entered into a "feudal contract" that defined their mutual obligations. A failure of either party in their obligations ended the contract, and the property returned to the lord.[30]

The modern critics of the classic teaching on feudalism pointed out that homage was a flexible rite used to signify various types of relations. It is often mentioned with no connection to receiving a land property grant, and in contexts where it is not likely that such a grant was made. Conversely, many records of grants that look much like fiefs of the classic feudal theory do not include the triad of homage, oath of fealty, and investiture. Neither does the fief, as used in the sources, always conform to its textbook definition. Stephen White showed that multiple and mutually contradicting understandings of the notion of fief could co-exist within the same text. His analysis of the French vernacular epic, *Raoul of Cambrai*, demonstrates that this poem, structured as it is around

---

[28] Gerd Althoff, "Establishing Bonds: Fiefs, Homage, and Other Means to Create Trust," in Bagge, Gelting and Lindkvist, *Feudalism*, 101–14, at 101. On sworn agreements in Rus, see P. S. Stefanovich, "Krestotselovanie i otnoshenie k nemu tserkvi v Drevnei Rusi," in *Srednevekovoaia Rus* 5, ed. A. A. Gorskii (Moscow: Indrik, 2004), 87–113; Mikhailova and Prestel, "Cross Kissing."

[29] Ganshof, *Feudalism*, xvi.

[30] Ganshof, *Feudalism*, 70–81.

violent disputes over fiefs, knows no "authoritative unambiguous rule about fiefs" and no "coherent system of real property law." Rather, it presupposes the existence of a "malleable and internally contradictory legal culture or discourse that included several different models of what a fief was."[31]

By the same token, the basic meaning of "vassal" was simply "man," and in the literary texts it typically signified not any kind of legal status, but "brave and noble man," while "vassalage" stood for "manly" qualities, such as loyalty and bravery.[32] Finally, the "oath of fealty" is a scholarly construct, not the term used in the sources other than those written by academic lawyers. Magnus Ryan has shown that not only is there no consensus among modern scholars about what constitutes an oath of fealty, but that "medieval rulers, lawyers, and polemicists reached no consensus either." From his analysis, medieval theoretical works on fealty emerge as "professional legal reactions to a notoriously slippery concept."[33]

The flaw of earlier scholarship was that any reference to homage or another word associated with the classic model of feudalism "was taken *pars pro toto*."[34] This was the main reason for Reynolds and her cohort to deny the existence of feudo-vassalic relations altogether. Newer works, however, argue that the past overgeneralization is not a reason to think that the relations between lord and man described by the classic theory, minus modernizing overlegalistic strictures, were an artificial construct, not a genuine part of the social organization of the high medieval elite.

Thus, Charles West argues that high medieval lordship was qualitatively different from earlier cases when Carolingian magnates gave their followers benefices consisting of land property. During the earlier period, a connection between land and service was, at best, generally acknowledged, but not spelled out. The service was not a true obligation, because it allowed "the degree of negotiability" that later became unthinkable, such as when a follower of the bishop of Laon "simply refused to the bishop's face" to perform his appointed task and did not suffer any consequences. On a few occasions when the bishop did revoke his grants, the reasons he provided created a picture "of a total breakdown of trust, rather than a simple breach of any particular rule." One bishop's man was stripped of his benefice after he had failed to come and see the bishop for a number of years, and had committed other transgressions, too.[35]

West does not give contrasting examples from his Laon sources of the eleventh century, when relations between the bishop and his men "seem to have been increasingly formalized."[36] However, it is not difficult to think of cases supporting West's point. In

---

31 White, "The Discourse of Inheritance in Twelfth-Century France," 177.

32 Theo Venckeleer, "Faut-il traduire VASSAL par vassal?" in *Mélanges de linguistique, de littérature et de philologie médiévales, offert à J. R. Smeets*, ed. Q. I. M. Mok et al. (Leiden: Université de Leiden, 1982), 303–16.

33 Magnus Ryan, "The Oath of Fealty and the Lawyers," in *Political Thought and the Realities of Power in the Middle Ages*, ed. Joseph Canning and Otto Gerhard Oexle, Veröffentlichungen des Max-Planck-Instituts für Geschichte, 147 (Göttingen: Vandenhoeck and Ruprecht, 1998), 211–12.

34 Roach, "Submission and Homage," 366.

35 West, "Lordship in Ninth-Century Francia," 16–18.

36 West, "Lordship in Ninth-Century Francia," 29.

the *Conventum Hugonis* from the 1020s, Hugh of Lusignan complains that his *senior* and *dominus* William summoned him to attend an assembly (*placitum*), when Hugh was in the middle of a conflict with a certain Bernard. Hugh tried to argue that it was risky for him to leave his land when Bernard was uttering threats (*minat ut mihi faciat mala*), but William still forced Hugh to accompany him (*ad vim et sine voluntatem eius duxit eum secum*). While Hugh and William were "lingering" at the assembly, Bernard besieged Hugh's wife and did "much evil" to Hugh and his men.[37] To ignore his lord's summons even once, let alone for a few years, as the Laon bishop's man did in the ninth century, evidently was not an option for Hugh.

A change in relations between lord and man was accompanied by new developments in symbolic communication. West connects an appearance of homage in the sources with "an increase in formality and sharper definitions of social relations." This does not mean that the person who performed homage always entered into vassalic service and received a fief. In West's argumentation, it was not the kind of "a direct connection between fiefs and homage," in respect to which Reynolds's critique "is fully justified." The significance of homage lies in the fact that this was "a ceremony instituting a specially binding relationship between aristocrats of different rank, in a way which went beyond a mere oath." The emergence of such a ceremony indicated "a sharper conceptual grasp of 'lordship' and its implications, a clearer way of articulating the degree and form of honourable dependence." It was thus part of the same social development that gave rise to feudo-vassalic relations, not necessarily a part of the relations themselves—although in the second half of the twelfth century homage indeed became more firmly associated with receiving a fief.[38]

It appears, however, that homage was not as prominent in vernacular literature as if was in Latin. The *Song of Roland* does not use the word, although it does mention joining hands once, as part of Marsile's false promise to submit himself to Charlemagne. There is nothing about homage done by Roland or other characters who serve the king faithfully; the formulaic expression for being, or becoming, one's man is "*par amur et par feid* (through love and loyalty)."[39] The *Conventum Hugonis* describes relations between Hugh and William as "love," and also as "faith," "fidelity," and "friendship," but never mentions homage, although Hugh is called William's *homo* and at one point he "defied (*defidavit*)" William, an action traditionally interpreted as a formal renunciation of homage.[40] In the case of the *Conventum*, this may be because of its time period, the early eleventh century, which was before the heyday of homage. It is interesting to see the attitude of Jordan Fantosme, a vernacular author from the late twelfth century.

---

37 *Conventum Hugonis*, 545.

38 West, *Reframing the Feudal Revolution*, 206, 209–10, 212.

39 Klaus van Eickels, "'Homagium' and 'Amiticia': Rituals of Peace and their Significance in the Anglo-French Negotiations of the Twelfth Century," *Francia* 24 (1997): 133–40, at 137; Jones, *The Ethos of the Song of Roland*, 43–44.

40 Hugh acted "propter eius [William's] amorem fidelitatemque," suffered losses "per fidelitatem tuam[William's]," "misit se Ugo in credenda et in amicitia comiti seniori suo, et fecisset pro eius amore [...]," *Conventum Hugonis*, 542, 543, 546.

Fantosme refers to the homage that William of Scotland performed to both the father and son, Henry II and Henry the Young King, who are now at war with each other, and he presents it as a difficult dilemma for William. When the son promises him Northumberland, he decides to request the same territory from the father and to renounce his homage if it is not granted. On the other hand, the messages that both kings send to William requiring his service contain plenty of references to love and kinship, but not a single one to William's homage. The Young King begins with the same expression that Rusian princes use when inviting somebody to join forces with them: "King Henry the Young sends to you with love (*vus mande par amur*)."[41] He then reminds William that, firstly, they are kinsmen, and, secondly, he is William's *seignur*. Love and kinship thus come before lordship.

Likewise, when the old king expresses his indignation at William for refusing to come to his aid unless he gets Northumberland, he mentions neither William's homage, nor his own status as William's lord. He describes what William owes to him as *amur e cusinage*, that is, again, love and kinship. He expresses the idea that William should continue his service as before, and not put forward requests for more grants, by contrasting William's improper request with his correct behaviour in the past, when the Scottish king "loved him greatly without showing any [intentions of doing] harm to him (*plus amot senz mustrer nul damage*)."[42] This may have been a reference to William's oath: high medieval French oaths that a man swore to his lord typically included the promise not to do any harm to the lord,[43] and Norman England, of course, had close cultural and po litical ties with France. *Damage* appears to be the vernacular equivalent of the Latin *dampnum* (damage, harm); as we know from the famous letter by Fulbert of Chartres, the first obligation of "he who swears fidelity" is not to do any harm to the lord.[44] Henry II's castigation of William thus appears to use the language of vassalic obligations; an absence of reference to William's homage suggests that, for Fantosme and his audience, homage did not have primary importance in the context of relations between lord and man.

This impression is confirmed by the striking absence of any reference to the homage that barons of Brittany owed to Henry II. Fantosme expresses his indignation at those rising against Henry II, and then has Henry make a speech about the justice of his cause.

---

41 *Jordan Fantosme's Chronicle*, 20–22. The main meaning of *par* is, of course, "through" or "by," but it can also mean "with." Cf. expressions, such as, "envoys from Sviatoslav arrived to him with love" (PSRL 2, 513), that is, with an invitation to join Sviatoslav's rebellion against the Kievan prince.

42 Johnston translates this as "loved him most dearly without offering him any hurt," *Jordan Fantosme's Chronicle*, 28–29.

43 Stephen White, "Stratégie rhétorique dans la *Conventio* de Hugues de Lusignan," in *Histoire et société: mélanges offerts à Georges Duby*, ed. Georges Duby (Aix-en-Provence: Publications de l'Université de Provence, 1992), 147–57, at 148, 152; White, "A Crisis of Fidelity in c. 1000?," 27–49, at 43; Débax, *La féodalité languedocienne*, 101.

44 "Ne sit in dampnum domino de corpore suo [...] ne sit ei in dampnum de secreto suo uel de municionibus [...] ne sit ei in dampnum de sua iustitia," *The Letters and Poems of Fulbert of Chartres*, ed. F. Behrends (Oxford: Clarendon Press, 1976), 90–92.

Henry explains why his enemies, a prominent Breton baron Ralph de Fougères among them, are in the wrong. This seems the perfect occasion to refer to the well-attested fact that barons of Brittany performed homage to the English king.[45] Instead, Henry says that they *sunt en mes poestez*, which Johnston translates as "are feudally subject to me." Given what is known about the status of Brittany from other sources, it is fair to say that its barons were, indeed, "feudally subject" to Henry II, but Fantosme's Henry does not use any "feudal" language. In a literal translation, he says that they are "in my power," or "under my control," or possibly "within my dominions." He then continues, "But Ralph de Fougères is in revolt against me."[46] Thus, the best way to convince Fantosme's audience that a baron of Brittany was acting treacherously in turning against Henry II was not to refer to his homage or fealty, but to Henry's *poestez* over him.

Unlike the differences between Latin and vernacular texts discussed earlier in this book, less attention to homage by the vernacular authors cannot be explained by the role of classical tradition. Homage, of course, was a distinctly medieval phenomenon and not a notion borrowed from Roman historiography; there was no word for it in classical Latin. Fantosme's talk about generic love, kinship, and *poestez*, instead of obligations of homage, probably reflects the general tendency of vernacular authors to display less conceptual clarity than their Latin counterparts. If homage indicated "a sharper conceptual grasp of 'lordship' and its implications," this may have been the very reason why Latin authors would be more interested in it. It is probably not a coincidence that Stephen White made his argument about a "malleable and internally contradictory" understanding of the fief on the basis of vernacular poems, while Charles West's Latin, predominantly diplomatic, sources supported his view that "the term fief was called upon" to describe the emergence of a new "distinctive kind of property."[47]

Rusian chronicles, as the reader already knows, are not texts in which one may expect to find much conceptual clarity and precision—in this respect, they are the ultimate example of vernacular literature. It is still possible, though, that some chronicle accounts do provide enough specific detail about personal bonds to justify viewing these bonds as feudo-vassalic. In the previous chapters, we encountered multiple occasions of one prince "giving to," or "taking from" another prince various territorial units, from a principality to a fortress. Our next task is to see whether there was a connection between "giving" a territory and an obligation to provide service to the giver; and if yes, how strictly defined was this connection, and under what circumstances did the giver revoke his grant. We will also see if Rus knew a ritual that created a specially binding, unequal, but honourable relationship.

---

45 J. A. Everard, *Brittany and the Angevins: Province and Empire 1158–1203* (Cambridge: Cambridge University Press, 2000), 44.

46 *Jordan Fantosme's Chronicle*, 12.

47 White, "The Discourse of Inheritance in Twelfth-century France"; White, "Giving Fiefs and Honor: Largess, Avarice, and the Problem of 'Feudalism' in Alexander's Testament," in *The Medieval French Alexander*, ed. Sara Sturm-Maddox and Donald Maddox (New York: State University of New York Press, 2002); West, *Reframing the Feudal Revolution*, 206.

Senior, Father, and Lord: Terminology of Hierarchical Relations in Rus

As always, we have to begin with the question of terminology. One East Slavonic word, *stareishii* (elder, senior), directly corresponds to the Latin *senior*, which gave origin to "seignior." It was often used in the same way as *senior* was used in the Carolingian period: a general word of respect applied to different figures.[48] However, the same word *stareishii*, and the abstract noun derived from it, *stareishinstvo* (seniority), also had the technical meaning of a special status that, by the second half of the twelfth century, was formally conferred on a prince. An account of a struggle for the Kievan throne reports that one prince was "seeking seniority among the Olgovichi for himself (*ishcha sobe stareshinstva v Olgovichakh*), but they did not concede Kiev to him." He then went over to the opposite side, and they "put seniority on" him and "gave him Kiev."[49] This seniority clearly is not a general word of respect.

"Putting seniority on" and "taking it off" a prince, as well as "pronouncing" a prince as a senior, often comes up in the context of a struggle for Kiev, but does not have an exclusive connection with the Kievan throne. Seniority appears to be a position of the leader of a princely group, typically, a kin-group, such as a clan or its branch. It thus created a hierarchical ladder, when the senior of a particular family branch was under the power of the senior of the whole clan. In the earlier period, political and biological seniority were closely connected, although it was not always simply a question of age. However, over the course of the twelfth century, political seniority became less and less connected with the biological position of the prince within the extended family. The prince who unsuccessfully sought "seniority among the Olgovichi" was not even an Olgovich himself, but a Monomakhovich. Even though they refused to make him their senior, his request apparently was not perceived as outlandish, indicating that in the 1170s, political seniority did not necessarily have a biological component.

Some information about this formal seniority can be gleaned from the 1195 account of a dispute between the senior of all the Monomakhovichi clan, Vsevolod the "Big Nest" of Suzdalia, and the Kievan prince Rurik, the senior of the southern, Dnieper-based branch of the Monomakhovichi. The story merits to be told at some length, because it offers valuable insights into several aspects of interprincely relations, and we will have to return to it more than once.

It all began when Vsevolod accused Rurik of not fulfilling his obligations to Vsevolod as the senior of all the Monomakhovichi. Rurik's violation was that, upon becoming the Kievan prince, he distributed the *volosts* under his authority and did not grant any territory to Vsevolod, but "gave away everything to other, junior, princes." Vsevolod then demanded the land that Rurik had given to prince Roman and had sworn an oath not to give it to anyone else. Rurik consulted the metropolitan, who gave him the following opinion:

---

[48] Reynolds, *Fiefs and Vassals*, 36; West, "Lordship in Ninth-Century Francia," 33.
[49] PSRL 2, 576–77.

If you made a mistake (*v oblazne*) of giving a *volost* to a junior before the senior and kissed the Cross to him, I absolve you from your oath and take it upon myself. Listen to me and take the *volost* from [Roman] and give it to the senior; as for Roman, give him another *volost* as a compensation.[50]

For now, we will stop at this point and will follow further developments between Rurik, Roman, and Vsevolod later. The reaction of the metropolitan makes it clear that Vsevolod's seniority is a formal status that gives him specific rights. However, it is equally clear that this is not the status of seignior in the "feudal" sense: there is no reference to any service owed to Vsevolod, and Rurik's obligations to him are not derived from a contractual agreement between the two, but from a collective decision made by all the Monomakhovichi. Vsevolod begins his message to Rurik with, "You [plural] have pronounced me the senior of our Monomakhovichi clan. However, now you [singular] have sat on the Kievan throne" and did not give Vsevolod his due.[51]

If for Rurik and his southern Monamakhovichi "brethren" Vsevolod was "senior," in respect to some other princes he was "father and lord." "Father (*otets*)" is the most common word in the context of hierarchical relations. In its most general sense, it signifies the obligation of obedience. When junior Monomakhovichi princes conquered the Kievan throne from the Olgovichi and invited the senior of their clan, Rostislav, to be the Kievan prince, Rostislav warned them against entertaining hopes that he would be their puppet: "I will go to Kiev on the condition that I have my full free will, so that you truly (*v pravdu*) have me as your father and be obedient."[52] Similarly, the people of Polotsk swore an oath on the Cross to their new prince "that they will have him as their father and will walk in obedience to him."[53] To represent the ruler as the "father" of his subjects was, of course, common to many regions and time periods.

Along with this generic usage, on some occasions, "father" took a more specific meaning. In the second half of the twelfth century, in the context of interprincely agreements, it was being increasingly paired with "lord (*gospodin*)," as in the report of Vladimir of Galich submitting himself to Vsevolod the "Big Nest." Vladimir found himself battling a number of Rusian and Hungarian rivals who sought to control the rich and strategically located Galich principality. Therefore, in 1190, Vladimir found two powerful protectors. One of them was no less a personage than Frederic Barbarossa, to whom Vladimir promised to pay 2,000 grivnas annually.[54] The other one was Vsevolod, whom Vladimir "entreated" to be his "father and lord" and to secure Galich for him. His promise to Vsevolod was: "I will be God's and yours with all [the land of] Galich,

---

50 PSRL 2, 683–84.

51 PSRL 2, 683–84.

52 PSRL 2, 503.

53 "Prislashasia polotchane [...] s liuboviu, iako imeti ottsem sobe i khoditi v poslushani ego, i na tom tselovasha khrest," PSRL 2, 445–46.

54 PSRL 2, 666.

and I will always be in your will." Vsevolod accepted Vladimir's proposal and made "all the princes" and the king of Hungary swear on the Cross (*vodi ia ko krestu*) not to seek Galich.[55] Apparently, it was this agreement between Vsevolod and Vladimir that compelled the southern Monomakhovichi to recognize Vsevolod as the senior of all the clan. They were now sandwiched between Vsevolod's Suzdalia on the east, and Galich, controlled by Vsevolod, on the west. Probably, this is what Rurik meant when he said, "It is impossible for us to be without Vsevolod, and we have put seniority on him." This sounds almost like, "We could not help putting seniority on him."[56]

It seems likely that Vladimir's promise to Vsevolod "to be in his will with all Galich" signified military service and was similar to the promise that his father Iaroslav gave on the occasion discussed in Chapter 1 when he submitted himself to Iziaslav Mstislavich in 1152. In the entry for 1152, Iaroslav addresses Iziaslav as "father" ("lord" is not mentioned), "bows down" to him and, as the reader may remember, pledges to be "in Iziaslav's will" and to "ride at Iziaslav's stirrup" together with all the Galich forces.[57]

"Bowing down," "riding at one's side," and "being in one's will" are formulaic expressions that repeatedly crop up in descriptions of a lesser prince "pronouncing" a more powerful and/or senior prince as his "father," or "father and lord," and being "accepted" as his "son." These descriptions do not always explicitly refer to the "son's" service and the "father's" granting of land, but a connection between the "father—son" relations, service, and grants of *volosts* is present often enough. One example concerns another political "son" of Iziaslav Mstislavich, Rostislav. Rostislav, who was a biological son of George the "Long Arm," "had a conflict with his father, because he did not give Rostislav a *volost* in Suzdalia." Therefore, he came to Iziaslav, "bowed down to him," complained about being wronged by his father, and declared, "I have come, putting my trust in God and you [...] I want to fight for the Rus Land and to ride at your side." The "Rus Land" here is the dominion of Iziaslav as the Kievan prince, in contrast with Suzdalia, which was not part of the "Rus Land" in the narrow sense. Iziaslav responded to this declaration by giving to Rostislav five strongholds. After that, he "took Rostislav to a conference (*snem*)," where Iziaslav and his allies discussed their plans for a military campaign; next he "ordered" Rostislav to stay in one of the newly granted strongholds on the border with the steppe and "guard the Rus Land," that is, to defend the part of the border controlled by the stronghold from nomadic incursions. There seems to be a clear enough connection between Rostislav's service and the grant of five strongholds.[58]

Soon, Iziaslav was told that Rostislav had come to him as George the "Long Arm's" agent to stir up Iziaslav's subjects behind his back. Having heard these accusations, Iziaslav "summoned" Rostislav; he arrived, and Iziaslav, who at that time was in a camp, ordered him to go to a separate tent. Then, Iziaslav's men came to Rostislav and delivered a speech on Iziaslav's behalf, describing Rostislav's entry into Iziaslav's service and his

---

[55] PSRL 2, 667.

[56] PSRL 2, 685–86. There is no evidence that the southern Monomakhovichi were in any way subordinate to Vsevolod before the 1190s.

[57] PSRL 2, 465.

[58] PSRL 2, 366–68.

alleged transgression. The speech again shows a connection between the grant of *volost* and service: "I gave you a *volost*—even your [real] father did not give you what I gave to you, and I also ordered you to guard the Rus Land. This is what I told you, 'I am going [on a campaign], and you guard the Rus Land.'" The repetition appears to stress how well established Rostislav was in Iziaslav's service, in order to make his treachery all the more dishonourable. Rostislav denied the accusation and asked for a hearing where he would have an opportunity to face his accusers and to prove them wrong. Iziaslav denied this request and told Rostislav to go back to his father without any further arguing.[59]

Iziaslav as a "father" has thus a considerable and rather clearly defined power over his political "son," but in this case, Rostislav's situation of being a young prince without any *volost* of his own may have made it easier for Iziaslav to exercise his authority over Rostislav. Indeed, the denial of a proper hearing appears atypical, if not abusive. Relations between the brothers Rostislavichi and Andrew Bogoliubsky of Suzdalia, present a more complicated dynamics between a "father" and "sons," revealing mutuality of obligations, a distinction between granted and patrimonial possessions, and the "sons'" defence of their rights. The complicated history of their relations is reported in the *Kievan* and *Suzdalian* chronicles from contrasting perspectives.

In this case, the "father's" grant consisted of nothing less than Kiev, which the coalition organized by Andrew and led by his son took in 1169. Andrew did not go to rule in Kiev, as victorious princes had done before, but remained in Suzdalia. His son also returned to Suzdalia after he had "put (*posadi*)" his uncle Gleb, Andrew's younger brother, on the Kievan throne. Between 1169 and Andrew's death in 1174, Kiev stopped being the residence of the supreme ruler of the realm and became another *volost*, very valuable and prestigious to be sure, but still a *volost* to be granted by the Suzdalian prince. In 1171 Gleb died, and Andrew "gave" Kiev to Roman Rostislavich, because, as he pointed to the Rostislavichi, "You have pronounced me a father; therefore, I wish you well and give Kiev to your brother."[60] We do not know when they made the "pronouncement," but there is an indication that, when they did, they swore an oath on the Cross to Andrew; it is very likely that Andrew also swore an oath to them. This is evident from the account of their falling out: the Rostislavichi explicitly refer to their own oath on the Cross, and they hint that Andrew violated his oath to them.

According to a pro-Rostislavichi chronicler, Andrew "began to make accusations (*viny pokladyvati*)" against them. First, he demanded that they hand over to him several prominent Kievans who, he claimed, caused the death (*umorili*) of his brother Gleb. The Rostislavichi considered this unjustified and refused to do so. "And Andrew said to Roman, 'You and your brothers do not walk in my will; so, you go from Kiev, and David from Vyshegorod, and Mstislav from Belgorod. You have your Smolensk, go ahead and divide it among yourselves.' "[61]

---

59 PSRL 2, 372–73.

60 PSRL 2, 567.

61 PSRL 2, 569–70. For a chronological commentary on the *Kievan* entries for 1173–1174, see Berezhkov, *Khronologiia russkogo letopisaniia*, 189–91.

Vyshegorod and Belgorod were two strongholds in the Kievan region. Apparently, the "Kiev" of Roman's grant was not just the city, but also the area around it, and Roman granted parts of the territory that he had received from Andrew to his brothers. Alternatively, Kiev and its region may have been Andrew's grant to all the Rostislavichi as a collective body: the narrative oscillates between presenting Andrew as dealing with individual brothers and with the Rostislavichi as a whole. In any case, after the Kievans whom Andrew considered guilty were not handed over to him, he revoked his grant and ordered the Rostislavichi to leave Kiev. They obeyed, and Andrew gave Kiev to his brother Michael, who, in turn, gave it to the next brother, Vsevolod (the future Big Nest), and to their nephew Iaropolk.

In the meantime, the Rostislavichi appealed to Andrew, arguing that they did not deserve to be deprived of their grant and hinting that they were considering resistance to Andrew's unjust treatment of them, as can be seen from their message:

> This is indeed so, brother (*tako, brate*), we have pronounced you our father rightfully, and we have kissed the Cross to you, and we are faithful to our oath on the Cross, wishing you well. But now, behold, you deprived our brother Roman of Kiev, and you are driving us out of the Rus Land [in the narrow sense] without any offense on our part (*bez nashee viny*). May we all rely on God and on the power of the Cross (*za vsemi Bog i sila krest'naia*)![62]

The opening of the message indicates that the Rostislavichi express their agreement with some statement previously made by Andrew, but not reported by the chronicler. In all likelihood, Andrew reminded them that they had sworn an oath on the Cross to "wish him well" and to regard him as their "father." The Rostislavichi agree that they, indeed, did all these things, and they also insist that they remain true to their sworn obligations to Andrew. It also appears that they, in turn, accuse Andrew of breaking his oath to them. Such an accusation is implied by the Rostislavichi's reference to the "power of the Cross," which was widely believed to avenge perjurers.

Andrew gave no answer to this message. Therefore, the Rostislavichi, with the exception of the oldest brother Roman, "placing their trust in God and in the power of the Venerable Cross," made a surprise attack on Vsevolod and Iaropolk in Kiev. Roman presumably chose to comply with Andrew's orders and stayed in his patrimonial Smolensk. Since the Rostislavichi belonged to the princely line generally favoured by the Kievans, it is very likely that they were helped by the population. The chronicler does not report any siege or battle. The Rostislavichi simply "went to Kiev," "seized (*iasha*)" Vsevolod, Iaropolk, and their men (who were soon released), and "gave Kiev" to Rurik Rostislavich. When Andrew heard about these new developments, he "burned with anger" and ordered his sword-bearer:

> Go to the Rostislavichi and tell them, "You do not walk in my will. You, Rurik, go to your inheritance (*otchinu*) Smolensk, to your brother." Tell David, "And you

---

[62] PSRL 2, 570.

go to Berlad, I forbid you to be in the Rus Land." And say to Mstislav, "You are at the root of it all, I forbid you to be in the Rus Land."[63]

The Rostislavichi's reply to that was:

> Until now, we had you as a father by love. But if you have sent us such speeches, not as if to a prince, but as if to your subject and a commoner (*podruchniku i prostu cheloveku*), you do what you have contrived, and may God's will prevail in all things (*a Bog za vsem*)![64]

With this official break of relations on both sides, Andrew sent to Kiev an army that included the forces of many princes subordinate to him. While listing the names of these princes, the chronicler makes an interesting remark: Andrew "commanded" Roman (*kazal biashet*), the only Rostislavich who remained faithful to him, to send his son with armed men to join Andrew's army, "and thus Roman, against his will (*nuzheiu*), had to send his son and men of Smolensk to fight against his own brothers, for Roman was then in Andrew's hands."[65] Biological kinship here is clearly superseded by artificial kinship created by a sworn agreement. Roman and Andrew were cousins once removed, and if Roman supported such a distant relative against much closer kin, it is hard to see any other reason than Roman's faithfulness to the oath that he took when "pronouncing" Andrew his "father." A Western medievalist encountering a reference to an aristocrat who has no choice but to send military aid to someone, because he is in this person's hands, would surely interpret this as evidence of vassalic status. Relations between Andrew and Roman do not display the negotiability that Charles West found in his ninth-century Laon documents. In contrast with the bishop's man, who could simply refuse to perform the task that the bishop had given him, Andrew's "son" could not even refuse to send his troops against his own brothers.

"Fathers" and "Sons" in a Comparative Perspective

It appears that Andrew was prepared to reward Roman's loyalty by renewing the grant of Kiev. Unfortunately, at this point the chronicle account, hitherto flowing smoothly, becomes fragmented and tangled. The available information indicates that Andrew's forces were defeated, but soon thereafter, he and the Rostislavichi somehow repaired their relations, judging from the fact that the Rostoslavichi "asked" Andrew to make Roman Rostislavich the prince of Kiev, which seems to indicate that they again considered Andrew their "father." Andrew gave a friendly reply, telling them to "wait for a while" because he needed time to discuss the matter with his "brethren" in the Dnieper region.

---

63 PSRL 2, 572–73. Berlad was a region at the coast of the Azov Sea and in the lower Dnieper and Danube, which, as far as it is known, was under no-one's political authority. In Rusian sources, it is presented as a land of vagabonds and outcasts of all sorts.
64 PSRL 2, 573.
65 PSRL 2, 574.

"Brethren" in such a context described members of one's kin-group, and the fact that the Rostislavichi—who were also based on the Dnieper—apparently were not among Andrew's "brethren" shows once again that their relations were not "dynastic," that is, based on biological kinship. These relations ended abruptly: Andrew died before he had a chance to contact his "brethren"; what exactly happened during the time that elapsed between the defeat of Andrew's forces and his death remains murky.[66]

This is the problem with much Rusian material: a source hints at rich possibilities and leads to interesting suggestions, but its incomplete character stands in the way of reaching a conclusion. Before moving to a few exceptionally detailed narratives that, arguably, provide firmer ground for a discussion of "father"-"son" relations as feudo-vassalic, we will look at what can be gleaned from incomplete accounts, such as the story about Andrew and the Rostislavichi. The tenor of the account found in the *Kievan Chronicle* resonates with the *Conventum Hugonis*: both texts are written from the perspective of a subordinate party in contractual hierarchical relations, and they both share the idea that "a limited feud was an appropriate sanction for a fidelis to use against a lord who had violated his obligations to his man."[67] In the Rusian case, we need to change a fidelis to a "son" and a lord to a "father"; but otherwise there are clear similarities between the Rostislavishi's behaviour towards Andrew and Hugh's use of "a limited feud" in his dispute with William.

A contrast between the pro-Rostislavichi narrative of the *Kievan Chronicle* and the pro-Andrew account of the same events in the *Suzdalian* is also similar to the oft-invoked contrast between the *Conventum* and the representation of relations between William and Aquitanian magnates in the chronicle written by William's admirer, Adémar. Instead of the complicated relations based on the idea of mutual obligations emerging from the *Conventum*, Adémar's William holds *imperium* over his Aquitanian subjects and crushes those of them who dare to move against him.[68] Andrew's chronicler had to admit that his prince stopped short of crushing the disobedient Rostislavichi, but otherwise Andrew's power, as presented in the *Suzdalian*, can rival the *imperium*. The *Suzdalian* entry for 1173 informs the reader that Andrew "sent his son" on a campaign, and that he also "sent Roman Rostislavich to Kiev to be a prince there."[69] The chronicler simply assumes that Andrew has as much power over Roman Rostislavich as he has over his own son, without any reference to a prior sworn agreement between them. According to the entry for the next year, "the Rostislavichi did not submit (*nepokorshimsia*) to Prince Andrew and did not walk in his will," the ultimate manifestation of which was their capture of Andrew's brother and nephew in Kiev. Andrew, therefore, sent an army to punish them, but the troops "returned without achieving a success (*ne uspev nichto zhe*)."[70] Apart from the reference to "walking in Andrew's will," the two accounts cannot be more different.

---

66 PSRL 2, 577–80.
67 White, "A Crisis of Fidelity in c. 1000?," 46.
68 "qui comiti eidem rebellare conabantur, Aquitanici promores, omnes vel edomiti vel prostrati sunt," *Ademari Cabannensis Chronicon*, 163.
69 PSRL 1, 364.
70 PSRL 1, 364–65.

As we have seen, the Rostislavichi agreed that they had "to walk in Andrew's will," but in their view, they did keep this obligation. They did not consider their refusal to turn in the Kievans, in whose guilt they apparently did not believe, as a violation that merited Andrew's treatment of them. It is important to note, though, that they did recognize Andrew's right to revoke his grant in case of a *vina* on their part, the word meaning both "guilt, offense, transgression" and "reason." As we remember, the Rostislavichi argued that Andrew was in the wrong when he deprived them of Kiev, Vyshegorod, and Belgorod without a *vina*; the way they framed their argument suggests that they accused Andrew of breaking his oath to them by behaving in this way.

It appears that they had a point and that Andrew's punishment of them may have been, indeed, too harsh. A "father" always had the option to revoke not all, but part of, the granted territories. This is how Sviatoslav Olgovich of Novgorod-Severskii punished a prince who went over to the opposite side in a war over Kiev between Iziaslav and George the "Long Arm." Sviatoslav supported George, but one prince subordinate to Sviatoslav went over to Iziaslav. After Iziaslav died and George became the Kievan prince, the defector asked for mercy, and received it: Sviatoslav "gave him three strongholds (*gorody*), but took from him Snovsk, Korachev, and Vorotinesk, because he had defected from Sviatoslav." In this case, the transgression was admittedly greater than what the Rostislavichi were guilty of, but the transgressor still either kept three strongholds, or received them in lieu of the confiscated *volost*.[71]

The *Kievan* chronicler states that, in sending an army against the Rostislavichi, "Prince Andrew, who otherwise was so wise and so valiant in all his deeds, ruined his reason by immoderation (*nevozderzhaniem*)."[72] For the Rostislavichi and their chronicler, Andrew's truly unacceptable act was his second message to them. In his first message, Andrew differentiates between the Kievan land, over which his 1169 victory gave him overlordship, and the Rostislavichi's Smolensk, which was their own domain inherited from their father Rostislav. The Rostislavichi recognize in principle Andrew's right to deprive them of the Kievan land: they leave it on his order, send him a message arguing that the order was not justified, and return to Kiev without his permission, only because they did not receive an answer from him. While doing all this, they still consider themselves Andrew's "sons" and describe their relations as "love." They declare a formal break of their relations by telling Andrew, "Until now, we had you as a father by love"—that is, we stop having you as a father from now on—only when he threatens to to deprive them of *their own* land, land that they held not from him, but by right of inheritance. According to Andrew, only one Rostislavich could go to Smolensk, while the two others had no right "to be in the Rus Land," which in this context apparently included Smolensk and whatever other *volosts* the Rostislavichi might have had. From the Rostislavichi perspective,

---

71 PSRL 2, 477, 479; Zaitsev, *Chernigovskoe kniazhestvo*, 67–68. The transgressor is not called Sviatoslav's "son," but he is clearly subordinate to Sviatoslav. "Giving" a *volost* often consisted of a permission to continue holding the same *volost* as before; the status of the three strongholds before Sviatoslav "gave" them is unknown.

72 PSRL 2, 572–74.

by his attempt to confiscate the *volosts* which he did not grant, Andrew overstepped the boundaries of what a "father" could rightfully do to punish his "sons."[73]

The distinction between Kiev and Smolensk made in Andrew's first message, and Andrew's threat to drive the two Rostislavichi from the Rus Land in his second message is reminiscent of Henry II's plans to punish rebellious Ralph de Fougères in *Jordan Fantosme's Chronicle*:

> I will do as I wish (literally: will do my will, *ferai mes volentez*) regarding Ralph de Fougères. I will leave him all free within his own domain (*dedenz ses poestez*) by such an agreement that he becomes my faithful man (*afiez*). If he rises against me again […] he will hold neither fief, nor his inherited land in Brittany (*ne fieus ne heritez*).[74]

After his first transgression, Ralph will be free "in his own domain," which presumably means that Henry II will take from Ralph whatever he had granted to him, but he will not touch Ralph's own land on the condition that he becomes faithful to Henry again. Apparently, this was the arrangement between Andrew and the oldest Rostislavich, Roman: Andrew confiscates Kiev, but he does not touch Roman's own domain on the condition that Roman remains "in Andrew's hands," as the chronicler puts it. Henry threatens that if Ralph rises against him again, then Henry will confiscate Ralph's own land and will drive him out of Brittany. This is exactly what Andrew attempted to do to the two Rostislavichi. Interestingly, Henry's position here is milder than Andrew's: Ralph is fighting on the side of his enemies, but Henry still plans to take only his fiefs, not Ralph's own domain, which he will confiscate only if Ralph breaks faith with him for a second time. Andrew, on the other hand, takes away the granted *volost* because of a slight infraction and tries to confiscate the inherited domain the first time the Rostislavichi resort to "a limited feud." In the end, as we know, Henry II did not drive anyone out of Brittany or out of any other part of his dominion: he reconciled with the rebels, and returned to them their *bona* and *honores*, just as Andrew in the end reconciled with the Rostislavichi.

Apart from parallels between concrete episodes of Western aristocratic and Rusian princely politics, Rusian chroniclers' manner of expression often brings to mind the language of the *Conventum* and vernacular political narratives. One example is political "love" as discussed above. We saw that one of its meanings is the loyalty that a man owes to his lord; when the Anglo-Norman author Wace pairs it with "wishing well," he comes very close to the formula that Rusian chroniclers use for "father"–"son" relations. According to Wace, a man cannot serve two lords, because it is impossible to "love them equally" and not to "wish for one better than for the other."[75] "Wishing well" may be interpreted as a positive recasting of the negative injunction "not to do harm," typical of oaths that men swore to their lords.

---

73 PSRL 2, 572–73.

74 *Jordan Fantosme's Chronicle*, 18.

75 "Dous seignors bien ne servireit / ne egalment nes ameret […] que a l'un mielz ne volsist," *Le Roman de Rou de Wace*, ed. A. J. Holden, vol. 2 (Paris: Éditions A. and J. Picard, 1973), 287.

In fact, there may be at least one Rusian parallel to this negative injunction as well. In an exchange, mentioned above, between Sviatoslav of Chernigov and the Kievan prince, Sviatoslav expresses his readiness to fight against the Kievan prince's enemies despite being angry at him because of the unsatisfactory grant that he gave to Sviatoslav. Sviatoslav, unhappy as he is about his bad *volost*, will still come to the Kievan prince's defence, because, he says, "I never wished you any harm (*likha*)." Later, Sviatoslav refers to the oath that the Kievan prince swore to Sviatoslav, when he ascended to the throne, granted Chernigov to Sviatoslav, and promised not to take it back; it is hard to imagine that the oath was unilateral and that Sviatoslav on that occasion did not, on his part, swear an oath to the new Kievan prince. Sviatoslav's words about "not wishing harm" are not explicitly presented as a quotation from his oath, but, given the context, it is likely that this was the case.[76]

If this is true and if Sviatoslav, indeed, referred to his sworn obligation, this would mean that his oath included an expression close to the injunction "not to do harm," which is often found in Latin oaths of fidelity and which Fulbert of Chartres discusses in his letter on the proper relations between lord and man.[77] However, in most cases, Western parallels to exchanges between Rusian princes are easier to find in a vernacular epic or in a text written by somebody like the author of the *Conventum Hugonis*, not by a fine Latin scholar, such as Fulbert. One such parallel is the idiosyncratic phrase that the *Conventum* uses to express the idea of Hugh's loyalty to William: *misit Ugo in Deo et in illo* (William). The primary meaning of *misit* as "sent" would be, of course, nonsensical in this context; one of the meanings of *mittere* in medieval Latin was "to decree," which makes it somewhat similar to a hard-to-translate expression that George the "Long Arm's" son Rostislav used when he submitted himself to Iziaslav: "I *narek* God and you," with *narek* meaning "called," "proclaimed," or "pronounced." The translators of the *Conventum* conveyed the general idea of both Rostislav's and Hugh's statements when they rendered *misit Ugo in Deo et in illo* as "Hugh placed his trust in God and William."[78]

Another difficult expression from the *Conventum* refers to Hugh's claim that he was in the right when he defied William. Before doing so, Hugh went to William's court and *misit eum in ratione de sua rectitudine*.[79] *Ratio*, among other things, signifies "legal cause," "claim," and also "righteousness"; the main meaning of *rectitudo* is "justice," but it can also mean "righteousness" and "right."[80] It is hardly possible to translate with certainty the description of what Hugh did at William's court before defying him. The two English translations of the *Conventum* have it as "put his case before him [William] about his [Hugh's] right."[81] Whatever the exact meaning, the phrase *ratione de sua rectitudine*

---

76 PSRL 2, 498, 500.

77 *The Letters and Poems of Fulbert of Chartres*, 90–92.

78 *Conventum Hugonis*, 544.

79 *Conventum Hugonis*, 547.

80 Niermeyer, *Mediae Latinitatis Lexicon Minus*, 883–84, 892. On *ratio*, see also Martindale, *Status, Authority, and Regional Power*, VIIb, 551n22.

81 *Agreement between Count William V of Aquitaine and Hugh IV of Lusignan*; Martindale, *Status, Authority, and Regional Power*, VIIb, 547a.

undoubtedly has strong connotations of self-justification, of Hugh demonstrating that he is in the right in regards to his agreement with William.

This phrase seems close to the East Slavonic expressions, which are also difficult to translate, *prav v krestnom tselovanii* and *opravlivatisia v krestnom tselovanii/v krestnoe tselovanie*. The first of these expressions literally means "right in one's Cross-kissing," and the second means "to make oneself right" or "to justify oneself in Cross-kissing." These expressions are used constantly in accounts of disputes involving sworn agreements. A prince who leaves an agreement because of the other party's perjury is "right in his Cross-kissing"; when he presents evidence that an oath to him was, indeed, perjured, he "justifies himself in his Cross-kissing." Conversely, a prince accused of not keeping his promises "justifies himself in his Cross-kissing" by proving the accusation wrong.[82]

Such accusations often use the term *vina*, which we have encountered in the exchange between Andrew and the Rostislavichi. This is another key word in the discourse on sworn obligations: the main point of princes "justifying themselves in their Cross-kissing" is to show that the *vina* for the rupture of an agreement lays with the other side. A good prince turns down a proposal to join an alliance against a person with whom he is bound by an oath: "I kissed the Cross to him, and I cannot turn against him (*na n' vstati*) without a *vina*."[83] When two princes "began to look for a *vina* between themselves," this apparently means that they started to accuse each other, to look for an excuse to break their sworn agreement, and each wanted to blame the breaking on the other party. Their search for *vina* succeeded, because soon thereafter one of them "threw the charter of the Cross" at the other, they formally broke their relations and started a war.[84]

Fantosme's Earl Duncan wants to prevent a similar development between his king, William of Scotland, and Henry II. In his speech at William's council, he refers to *achaisun*, the word that has exactly the same range of meanings as *vina*: "reason," "pretext," and "excuse," on the one hand, and "accusation," on the other hand.[85] William seeks the opinion of his men when he receives a proposal from Henry the Young King to go over to his side and to be rewarded with Northumberland, which he considers his rightful possession. The council decides that William should first request Northumberland from the old king. Earl Duncan gives good advice: request "what is rightly yours (*voz*

---

[82] Mikhailova and Prestel, "Cross Kissing," 19–21.

[83] PSRL 2, 489.

[84] "Pochasta na sia iskati viny," PSRL 2, 314–15. The two princes were Vladimir (Volodimerko) of Galich and the Kievan prince Vsevolod. The account of their conflict may have been a combination of two sources. It contains a short report, where Vladimir and Vsevolod look like equals: "In the same year, Vsevolod quarreled with Vladimir, because Vsevolod's son became the prince of [the city of] Vladimir[-in-Volhynia], and Vladimir threw the charter of the Cross in front of Vsevolod, and Vsevolod with his brethren then mounted a campaign against him." The report is followed by a detailed narrative, the first sentence of which repeats the information already given in the previous line of the chronicle: "In the same year, the Olgovichi mounted a campaign against Vladimir." The list of participants includes not only Olgovichi, but also some Monomakhovichi, and the narrative represents Vsevolod as a supreme ruler subduing a rebel.

[85] *Anglo-Norman Dictionary*, at www.anglo-norman.net/gate/.

dreitures)" from Henry II in a nice manner, by way of *bele parole*, and not by threats, so that your relations may not be broken, and so that you still may continue serving him as his liegeman (*liges hum*). Act reasonably, and do not seek *achaisun* to do any *ultrage*.[86] This apparently comes down to advice not to seek a reason to break the agreement with Henry, not to seek grounds for doing anything wrong, insulting, or excessive, which would break relations between the two kings—in other words, not to do what the two princes did when they were "looking for a *vina*."

In the same episode, William uses a related word, *achaisunment*: it would not be right to take up arms against the old king before requesting William's inheritance (*eritement*) from him. If Henry II refuses, then William can renounce his homage to him without *achaisunment*.[87] The dictionary meaning of this word is "legal action," but the English king obviously cannot take any legal action against the attack that the Scottish king is contemplating. Johnston translates *senz achaisunment* as "without contestation."[88] The context makes it clear that William describes a situation in which his renunciation of homage and his attack on Henry II would be justified by Henry's wrongful treatment of him. *Achaisunment*, with its meaning of a legal action and the root conveying the idea of "blame" and "reason," encapsulates in one word what a Rusian prince is doing when he "justifies himself in his Cross-kissing" by laying the blame for the broken agreement with the other side.

The vernacular *achaisun* or *achaisunment* probably lurks behind William of Malmesbury's cryptic comment about a Norman aristocrat who acted perfidiously towards William of Normandy and became estranged from him by means of "invented accusations, by which it would seem that he did this rightly (*affictis criminibus quibus id merito facere viderentur abalienavit se a comite*)."[89] If William of Malmesbury had been as interested in details of aristocratic politics as Jordan Fantosme and Rusian chroniclers were, we probably would have read about the estranged aristocrat acting in a way similar to a Rusian prince justifying himself in his Cross-kissing, or Fantosme's William of Scotland seeking a way to renounce his homage without *achaisunment*.

The Scottish king's concern about his homage adds another layer to a comparison between Fantosme and Rusian chronicles. Even though homage does not have as great an importance in Fantosme's work as it has in some other late twelfth-century sources, it is still present there. Until now, we have talked about sworn agreements, but Fantosme's

---

86 "Li vielz reis est rednable, si li faites raisun / De faire nul ultrage ne querez achaisun," *Jordan Fantosme's Chronicle*, 22. The dictionary meanings of *ultrage* are: insult; excess; presumption; sin, transgression. Johnston translates "De faire nul ultrage ne querez achaisun" as "seek no occasion to give him [Henry II] grounds for offense," *Jordan Fantosme's Chronicle*, 23. However, it seems that the original does not include a specific reference to "him" or to Henry II in connection with *ultrage* which should not be done. This is Johnston's interpretation of what Earl Duncan means, but in the original it remains ambiguous what is the *ultrage* and who should not be doing it.
87 "Rende lui sun humage senz achaisunement," *Jordan Fantosme's Chronicle*, 20–22.
88 *Jordan Fantosme's Chronicle*, 23.
89 William of Malmesbury, *Gesta Regum Anglorum*, vol. 1, 428.

characters were bound not only by oaths, but also by a special ritual. Homage did not always create a feudo-vassalic bond; it signified honourable submission of various kinds, such as recognition of a new ruler by his prominent subjects, or a peace agreement that showed the seniority of one party.[90] Conversely, homage is not necessarily mentioned in the sources every time they describe agreements that are feudo-vassalic in content.[91] Nonetheless, it is often connected with an entry into vassalic service, and the growing importance of homage in the twelfth century went hand in hand with the growing importance of feudo-vassalic relations. Our next task is to find out whether Rusian sources know "a ceremony instituting especially binding relationship between aristocrats of different rank, in a way which went beyond a mere oath."[92]

"Bowing Down": A Rusian Ritual for Creating a Hierarchical Relationship

Admittedly, we see a reference to such a ceremony in a plea by a prince pursued by Iziaslav Mstislavich during a war for Kiev between Iziaslav and George the "Long Arm." George's son, Gleb, found himself in a fortress, cut off from his men and supplies; he wanted to surrender on the condition that he receive safe conduct, and he sent to Iziaslav a message:

> You are as much a father to me as George is. I bow down to you. I do not interfere into your dispute with my father (*s moim ottsem sam vedaesh*), but allow me to go to my father. Swear an oath on the icon of the Holy Mother of God that you will not seize me, but will allow me to go to my father, and I will come to you personally (*sam*) and bow down to you.[93]

Gleb evidently believes that an oath followed by his bowing down to Iziaslav in person is more binding than a mere oath. He does not dare to go to his father right after Iziaslav swears not to seize him, but he wants to perform a ritual of submission in order to have a better guarantee of safety.

The significance of this ritual is clearly seen from the way the chronicler describes Vsevolod's campaign against Vladimir of Galich, who "threw the charter of the Cross" in front of Vsevolod. A large army then marched on Vladimir with the goal of "compelling (*nudiashche*) him to come and bow down to Vsevolod."[94] This goal was achieved when Vladimir lost a battle and asked for peace: "Vsevolod made a peace with him, and

---

90 Paul Hyams, "Homage and Feudalism: A Judicious Separation," in *Die Gegenwart des Feudalismus/ Présence du féodalisme et présent de la féodalité/The Presence of Feudalism*, ed. Natalie Fyrde, Pierre Monnet, and Otto-Gerhard Oexle, Veröffentlichungen des Max-Planck-Instituts für Geschichte 173 (Göttingen: Vandenhoeck and Ruprecht, 2002), 13–49, at 26–34.
91 Débax, *La féodalité languedocienne*, 212.
92 West, *Reframing the Feudal Revolution*, 209–10.
93 PSRL 2, 395.
94 Cf. a refusal to do homage as the cause of war, West, *Reframing the Feudal Revolution*, 208.

Vladimir arrived and bowed down to him." It was on this occasion that Vsevolod said, "You got away with this transgression, but do not commit any more." He also kissed Vladimir and "returned to him Ushitsa and Mikulin."[95] These were two strongholds in the Galich principality; apparently, Vsevolod's army had captured them during the campaign. Thus, Vladimir assumes a posture of submission before Vsevolod; after that, they exchange a kiss, and Vsevolod transfers strongholds to Vladimir. Soon thereafter, Vladimir goes on Vsevolod's campaign.[96] It is difficult not to see similarities with homage, which was often followed by the senior party attempting to "minimize humiliation" and introduce elements of equality. These actions most often took the form of a kiss and/or an honourable reception, such as a banquet.[97]

The latter is present in our first example of bowing down. After Iziaslav accepted Gleb's submission, he invited Gleb to a banquet and then had him escorted to the border of Iziaslav's dominion. The whole episode is similar to what Western medievalists traditionally called *hommage de pais*. In this case, Gleb apparently called Iziaslav "father" in the generic sense of a respected seniority figure; he did not receive from him any territories, and he clearly did not promise him service and loyalty, because this would have meant going over to his side in the war that Iziaslav waged against Gleb's biological father George. Gleb probably wanted to make sure that his "bowing down" was not understood in this sense, when he said that Iziaslav was "as much a father" to him as George.

These episodes represent two common situations of "bowing down": making peace while recognizing the seniority of the other party, and receiving a *volost* from a senior prince, typically a real or "pronounced" father. Entry into service of the *volost* giver is sometimes mentioned in connection with this latter case. Thus, when George's son Rostislav went over to Iziaslav, whether sincerely or play-acting on George's orders, he "arrived to Iziaslav in Kiev, and, having bowed down to him," expressed his desire to fight for the Rus Land and to ride at Iziaslav's side, while also mentioning that he did not have any *volost*.[98] As we remember, Iziaslav granted him five strongholds which he took back when Rostislav was accused of treachery.

On another occasion, a *volost* was granted as a reward for past service. Rostislav of Smolensk, who replaced his brother Iziaslav in the Kievan "duumvirate" after Iziaslav's death, rewarded prince Sviatoslav for guarding Kiev during the interim period between the death of Iziaslav and the arrival of Rostislav. When Rostislav arrived in Kiev to take the place of his late brother, he "bowed down" to Viacheslav, and promised "to have you as a father and lord and to be in your will." In this anomalous case, the promise was a formality, which gave Rostislav the opportunity to rule on behalf of the old and inept Viacheslav. As soon as Rostislav became the *de facto* Kievan prince, he addressed Sviatoslav: "'I give you Turov and Pinesk, because you arrived to my father Viacheslav

---

95   PSRL 2, 315–16.
96   PSRL 2, 318.
97   Eickels, "'Homagium' and 'Amiticia,'" 136–37; Hyams, "Homage and Feudalism," 18.
98   PSRL 2, 366–67.

and protected my *volosts* for me. For this, I grant (*nadeliaiu*) a *volost* to you.' Sviatoslav bowed down to Rostislav and accepted it with joy."[99]

"Bowing down" also signified recognition of a prince's authority, such as when Iziaslav with his army was passing Dorogobuzh during his war with George, and the "people of Dorogobuzh"—presumably, elite men on behalf of the community—"came to Iziaslav with Crosses and bowed down. Iziaslav [...] kissed them and gave them leave."[100] Similarly, regional princes are represented as "bowing down" to the new Kievan prince.[101] Thus, a range of situations in which "bowing down" appears in the chronicles is similar to occasions when homage was performed.

The two main differences in representations of "bowing down" and homage are that the former do not include references to hands, and that they do not use a specialized term reserved for this ceremony exclusively. "To bow down" is conveyed in East Slavonic by the verb *poklonitisia* that seems to signify various actions best captured by the modern English expression "to pay homage." For example, princes visiting a church are often said to "bow down" to the saint to whom the church is dedicated, such as "they went to Pereiaslavl and bowed down to St. Michael," that is, presumably, they visited the Pereiaslavl cathedral of St. Michael. Visiting one's father's grave is also described as "bowing down to the father's tomb."[102]

How exactly the "bowing down" was performed in a ceremony of creating hierarchical relations is unknown. Precise details of doing homage before the thirteenth century are also unknown, and it is likely that they varied from case to case. The textbook image of the homage ceremony is based on the famous description by Galbert of Burge, but Galbert's references to homage "all come amidst the most unusual political circumstances and are likely to have been crafted for the needs of the day," rather than representing a standard practice.[103] There is no description of any details of "bowing down" in Rusian sources, except for one chronicle passage that deserves to be discussed at some length.

This is the account of a scene that took place in the Galich principality after the Mongols first arrived there, but before Galich was incorporated in their empire. The Mongols sacked Galich territories on their way to Hungary, but this first time they did not stay long enough to establish their domination. Daniel of Galich fled before the Mongols and returned after they had left. His chronicler describes the breakdown of social order that Daniel encountered upon his return: non-princely nobles appropriated the prince's prerogatives; they recognized Daniel's authority only *pro forma*, but in reality "ruled (*derzhakhu*) all the land themselves." Daniel sent his man Jacob to one such noble, Dobroslav, who had taken control over a big part of the Galich principality, including

---

99 PSRL 2, 471. For another example of bowing down and receiving a *volost*, see PSRL 2, 496.
100 PSRL 2, 410.
101 George "the Long Arm" stated that he could not "bow down to a junior" prince to explain why he did not recognize Iziaslav Mstislavich as the Kievan prince, PSRL 2, 430. See also PSRL 2, 470.
102 PSRL 2, 383, 680.
103 Hyams, "Homage and Feudalism," 18, 21, 24–25.

Kolomyia, a region with rich salt mines that provided much of the Galich prince's income. Jacob delivered to Dobroslav Daniel's order to send the revenue from the salt trade to Galich. When Jacob was sitting with Dobroslav, two local men entered the room and "bowed down to him [Jacob], touching the ground (*do zemli*)." Jacob was "amazed" and asked for an explanation, "and Dobroslav said, 'I gave Kolomyia to them.'" When Jacob expressed his indignation at the unauthorized grant, Dobroslav only smiled.[104]

It appears that the insubordinate nobles mockingly acted out the ritual, or part of the ritual, that was normally performed by a person receiving a grant from a prince: they bowed down to Jacob as if he, on behalf of the prince, were giving Kolomyia to them. It was probably their way of breaking the news to Jacob that they were not going to send revenues from Kolomyia to Galich and to demonstrate their complete disregard for the prince's authority. Dobroslav and the two men had appropriated the prince's resources and were behaving in the manner of a playground bully who takes another child's toy by force and mocks him by saying, "Thank you for sharing this with me."

If this interpretation of the scene at Dobroslav's place is correct, the inference is that the "bowing down" that accompanied receiving a *volost* included touching the ground and was different from a gesture of respectful greeting. To this, it may only be added that the same chronicler, when describing the submission of Daniel to the Mongol khan Batu, repeats twice that Daniel bowed down to the khan "in their [Mongol] way," that was presumably different from the manner of bowing practised in Rus.[105] He, however, never explains the difference. The aspect of "bowing down" that is clearly seen from the sources is that it had to be performed face to face, unlike an oath that could be sworn without the physical presence of the other party. We usually see the person who "bows down" coming to the other party: a common phrase is "having come (*vyshed*), he bowed down."

In this respect, "bowing down" was similar to homage, which was normally performed on the lord's territory, apart from a special case of *hommage en marche*, when the two parties were almost equal and met on the border. In particular, to perform homage that signified entry into vassalic status, "the vassal characteristically came to seek his new lord," and the ceremony took place "on the lord's patch, in front of a crowd of the lord's intimate friends and supporters."[106] We see this in the account of Vladimir of Galich bowing down to Vsevolod, when the chronicler emphasizes the presence of Vsevolod's "brethren" at the ceremony.[107]

The role of "bowing down" for creating hierarchical relations is especially visible in the chronicle narrative describing how Vsevolod "the Big Nest" of Suzdalia becomes a "father and lord" to the five brothers Glebovichi, who were princes in the Riazan Land. First, the two youngest Glebovichi send Vsevolod a message: "You are our father, you are our lord. Our eldest brother Roman is taking our *volosts* from us by force [...] and he broke the oath

---

104 PSRL 2, 789–90.
105 PSRL 2, 807.
106 Hyams, "Homage and Feudalism," 33.
107 PSRL 2, 316.

on the Cross which he had sworn to you."[108] Vsevolod responds by going into the Riazan Land with his troops. Next, the chronicler tells us that the two brothers "came to meet him and bowed down (*sretosta s poklonom*), and Prince Vsevolod accepted them into love."[109] Apparently, by saying "You are our father, you are our lord," the younger Glebovichi, in fact, asked Vsevolod to be their "father and lord," in the same way as the words "I bow down to you," which Gleb mentioned above addressed to Iziaslav, signified Gleb's proposal to come and bow down before Iziaslav. After the proposal was accepted, Gleb performed the actual "bowing down." Similarly, Vsevolod accepts in principle the proposal to become "father and lord" sent through an envoy, but to realize this proposal, the parties must meet in person and perform the necessary ritual. The chronicler evidently refers to this ritual when he reports that the Glebovichi bowed down and Vsevolod "accepted them into love."

The story of "love" between Vsevolod and his Riazan "sons" deserves close attention. It is known better than most other cases of hierarchical interprincely relations, because it is reported in the section of the *Suzdalian* chronicle that includes relatively long stretches of uninterrupted narrative, apparently copied from a single source. The part of the narrative describing the events up to 1205 is present in all three redactions of the *Suzdalian* and thus its source must have existed before the redactions' divergence in the early thirteenth century.[110] Even though the source is rather partisan, it offers valuable information.

Vsevolod "the Big Nest" and the Glebovichi: Lord and Vassals?

After the two Glebovichi bowed down to Vsevolod and he "accepted them into love," he marched on their three older brothers and defeated them. The older Glebovichi had to swear an oath to Vsevolod "on all Vsevolod's will (*na vsei voli Vsevolozhi*)." Vsevolod's next act was similar to what Fantosme's Henry II planned to do after he "does his will" to Ralph de Fougères. As we remember, Henry would leave Ralph "all free within his own domain" if Ralph became his faithful man. Fantosme does not elaborate on the procedure by which Ralph would become Henry's *afiez* and at the same time would stay free in his own domain, but it is well known that a noble pledging service and loyalty to his lord often gave his land over to the lord and immediately received it back as the lord's grant. The classic writings on feudalism call this procedure *repris en fief*. Rusian sources also describe the situation when one prince "gives" to another the latter's own land. We have seen such cases in Chapter 1 when Monomakh "gave" Minsk to Gleb and Vsevolod Olgovich "gave" Volhynia to Iziaslav; as we remember, the recipients had already been princes of, respectively, Minsk and Volhynia when these lands were "given" to them.

---

108 PSRL 1, 387, under 1180. Previously, Roman Glebovich, along with other Riazan princes, was taken prisoner by Vsevolod during a military conflict and was then released "having kissed the Cross." PSRL 2, 606. See also PSRL 1, 383–86; PSRL 25, 89; N1L, 35.
109 PSRL 1, 387–88.
110 PSRL 1, 387–90, 400–6; see ibid. for the *Radzivill* redaction; PSRL 1, 430–34; PSRL 41,109–10, 116–19, 128, 130.

A similar *repris en fief* was performed with the lands of the Riazan princes, judging from the chronicler's report that Vsevolod returned home, "having properly arranged" the Glebovichi, and "having given their *volosts* to them, so that each received a *volost* according to his seniority."[111] Since we subsequently see the Glebovichi in the same Riazan Land where they had been before, the *volosts* that Vsevolod "gave" them were, indeed, their own. Evidently, they submitted their lands to Vsevolod and received them back from him.

How much of a "fief" did the Riazan prince's *volosts* become? The classic teaching on feudalism postulates the "union of fief and vassalage": the receiver of the fief becomes the grantor's "vassal," owing him service and loyalty; if the vassal fails in his obligations, the fief returns to the lord. The lord, on his part, not only grants the fief, but also offers his protection to the vassal. A key point in determining the "feudal" character of the relations between the giver and receiver of the grant is the degree of strictness and formality involved in their mutual obligations. A general connection between receiving a *volost* from a senior prince and performing service for him is surely present in the chronicles. However, most accounts are not detailed enough to see if the connection went beyond informal expectations typical of gift exchange and whether it came close to more formalized relations that Charles West finds in his high medieval sources. How negotiable were the "son's" obligations? Under what circumstances did a "father" revoke his grant? The account of Vsevolod and the Geblovichi sheds some light on these questions.

The report about Vsevolod giving the Glebovichi their *volosts* is found in the entry for 1180. From that time on, when the chronicler lists the princes fighting in Vsevolod's campaigns, we see the Glebovichi names.[112] On one occasion, when the members of Vsevolod's council are named, we see among them a junior Glebovich, and also princes of Murom, whom the chronicler represents as being "sent" by Vsevolod on various campaigns.[113] We do not know if Vsevolod was their "father" and if he granted the *volost* of Murom to them, because the chronicler mentions the Murom affairs only in passing. However, it is clear that both Murom and Riazan princes owed to Vsevolod what in Latin is called *auxilium et consilium* (aid and council), that is, what traditionally has been presented as the cornerstone of the vassal's duties. In the case of the Riazan princes, it is also clear that they provided aid and council in exchange for the grant of their *volosts*.

Vsevolod, on his part, acted as a protector of the younger Glebovichi during a conflict that broke out in the Riazan land in 1186. According to the entry for that year, the devil incited three older brothers to attack the two youngest. Vsevolod told the older brothers to stop their aggression, but they did not listen. Therefore, he sent 300 of his men to help the junior Glebovichi. This protection came at a high price. In the middle of the war between the two younger and three older brothers, one junior Glebovich had to

---

[111] "poriad stvoriv vsei brati rozdav im volosti ikh komuzhdo po stareishinstvu," PSRL 1, 387–88; PSRL 41, 110.

[112] PSRL 1, 389, 430; see also PSRL 2, 699.

[113] PSRL 1, 402, 430–31.

go to Vsevolod's capital city of Vladimir to attend Vsevolod's council, leaving his brother Sviatoslav to fight alone.[114]

The same situation is described in the *Conventum Hugonis*, where Hugh complains that he was forced to attend William's *placitum* during a war at home, in spite of his protestations that it was a bad time for him to leave his *castrum*. We do not know if the junior Glebovich tried to reason with his "father and lord" and to point out to him the risks involved in being away from his land in a time of war. What we do know is that Sviatoslav, when left alone to face his three older brothers, changed sides and went over to them, delivering to them Vsevolod's men who had been sent to help the two youngest Glebovichi. The account of these events again shows that *repris en fief* was a procedure well known in Rus. Sviatoslav "opened his stronghold (*otvori grad*)" to his older brothers who "entered and gave the stronghold to him. He swore an oath on the Cross to them, and they installed (*posadisha*) him in the same stronghold."[115]

Together, the four Glebovichi seized the wife, children, and men of their brother and plundered his men's property, while he was at the council in the city of Vladimir on Vsevolod's orders. The junior Glebovich thus suffered the same losses in the service of his "father and lord" as Hugh suffered at the service of his "senior" and "dominus," when his land was burned and plundered during his stay at William's *placitum*.[116] Neither of them had the option not to answer the lord's summons.

This is not the only episode which creates an impression that, had we had a document written from the perspective of the Glebovichi, it would probably have looked very much like the *Conventum*. The older Glebovichi argued that their fighting against their junior brother—and, consequently, against the contingent which Vsevolod had sent to help his "son"—did not constitute a breach of their obligations to Vsevolod. When they heard that Vsevolod was gathering an army to punish them for what they did to their junior brother who was at the council, they sent Vsevolod a message, calling him their father and lord and proclaiming their unwavering loyalty. They continued, "Do not be angry with us that we fought against our brother; [we did so] because he does not obey us. But as far as you are concerned, we bow down, and we release your men."[117]

Hugh used the same logic as the Riazan princes when he described to William his agreement with Count Fulk, who either had been Hugh's lord in the past, or who was his other lord simultaneously with William: "When I was Fulk's man, I told him that his men took from me what was rightfully mine (*rectum meum*) and that if I could take it back from them, I would do so; but I would [still] remain [just] as much in his fidelity."[118] Hugh argues that his attack on his lord's men does not constitute a breach of fidelity on his

---

114 PSRL 1, 402; PSRL 41, 117.
115 PSRL 1, 402; PSRL 41, 117.
116 PSRL 1, 402–3; PSRL 41, 117–18; *Conventum Hugonis*, 545.
117 PSRL 1, 403; PSRL 41, 118. On the expression used in the Glebovichi's message, "We will lay down our heads for you," see P. S. Stefanovich, "Kniaz i boiare: kliatva vernosti i pravo otezda," in *Drevniaia Rus*, ed. Gorskii et al., 176–81.
118 *Conventum Hugonis*, 546.

part, as long as he has a just reason and only attacks in order to take back what is rightly his. According to the *Conventum*, both Fulk and William agreed with Hugh's argument.[119]

We do not know what arguments the older Glebovichi used to justify their attack on the "disobedient brother" and to show that this did not constitute a breach of faith with their "father and lord" Vsevolod. However, their arguments must have been rather convincing, because Bishop Porphyrius of Chernigov apparently was on their side. When Vsevolod rejected their plea "not to be angry" and continued his preparations for a punitive expedition, the older Glebovichi turned to the bishop of Chernigov for help, just as Hugh turned to the bishop of Limoges to seek advice regarding his problems with William.[120] The chronicler, an admirer of Vsevolod, is very unhappy about Bishop Porphyrius's position regarding the conflict. He claims that, while acting as a mediator between the Glebovichi and Vsevolod, the bishop "perverted" the speech he was supposed to deliver (*inako rech izvorocha k nim*) and acted "not as a church hierarch, but as a traitor and a liar." Bishop Luke of Vsevolod's own Suzdalia also urged Vsevolod to reconcile with the Glebovichi, and he eventually "left it all to God and to the Holy Mother of God," did not confront Porphyrius about his alleged lying, and decided to accept the peace brokered by the Chernigov bishop.[121] Such behaviour by Porphyrius, Luke, and by Vsevolod himself, suggests that the older Glebovichi were able to present some arguments to justify their actions. Vsevolod remained their "father and lord," and they continued to keep their *volosts* from him for ten more years, until they committed another transgression. This time, the transgression was, indeed, serious: the Glebovichi were accused of treason.

In 1207, Vsevolod was gathering his forces for a campaign against the Olgovichi and summoned the Glebovichi, with their sons and other kinsmen. The junior brother who had been always loyal to Vsevolodovichi had died by that time. The other brothers, with their men, were on their way to Vsevolod, when he was informed that "the Riazan princes had an agreement with the Olgovichi directed against him, and they are coming to him with a deception (*na lste*)." Vsevolod with all his forces went towards the Glebovichi, and they met halfway. Vsevolod, "having kissed them, ordered them to go into a big tent" while he himself went into a small tent pitched nearby. The chronicler goes on to describe what looks like an established procedure, familiar to us from the account of the falling out between George the "Long Arm's" son Rostislav and Iziaslav. Unlike Rostislav, the Glebovichi received a proper hearing. Vsevolod sent to the big tent "Prince David of Murom and his man Michael Borisovich in order to expose them." David and Michael "were going back and forth" between the two tents for a long time, but the Riazan princes kept swearing that the accusation was not true. "However, their own nephews Gleb and Oleg Vladimirovichi arrived and exposed them. When the grand prince heard that the truth was revealed, he ordered to arrest (*izoimati*) them and their counselors and to bring them to [the city of] Vladimir."[122]

---

[119] *Conventum Hugonis*, 546.
[120] *Conventum Hugonis*, 545.
[121] PSRL 1, 404–5; PSRL 41, 118–19.
[122] PSRL 1, 430–31.

After that, Vsevolod entered the Riazan land with his troops, took the important stronghold of Pronsk, and gave it to Oleg Vladimirovich, one of the two junior Riazan princes who had testified against their uncles during the trial-like procedure in the tent. Next, Vsevolod placed his governors (*posadniki*) in all the strongholds of the perfidious Riazan princes, and then moved to Riazan itself. The townsmen sent envoys to bow down (*s poklonom*) to Vsevolod, beseeching him not to attack Riazan and swearing "to do all his will."[123] "Being merciful," Vsevolod cancelled the attack and sent his son to be the prince of Riazan. In the entry for the next year, 1208, the people of Riazan "broke their oath on the Cross to Vsevolod" and rose against his son. When Vsevolod arrived with his troops, they "sent to him an impertinent speech, according to their custom of disobedience (*buiuiu rech po svoemu obychaiu i nepokorstvu*)." Vsevolod punished them in the same way that William of the *Conventum* punished insubordinate men and/or lords of Aquitanian *castra*. William burned the *castrum* – which typically might be rebuilt later.[124] Vsevolod "ordered all the people to leave the town and to take their movable property with them (*s tovarom*)," burned Riazan, and brought its inhabitants to his city of Vladimir.[125] After Vsevolod's death in 1212, his son released the princes and the people of Riazan; they all "returned home" and rebuilt their town, which, up to the Mongol invasion of 1237, was a thriving urban centre.[126]

Let us now recapitulate the main developments in the relations between Vsevolod and the Glebovichi. The two younger Glebovichi seek Vsevolod's protection from their older brothers who lay claims to their lands; to receive this protection, they recognize Vsevolod as their "father and lord" and perform a special ritual that signifies their entry into hierarchical relations with him. The older brothers are forced to submit themselves to Vsevolod; he receives the supreme right to the lands of all the Glebovichi and gives these lands back to them. After that, the Glebovichi participate in his campaigns and his council. When four of them disobey Vsevolod in the course of their internal conflict, he plans to punish them, but after the interference of two bishops, reluctantly agrees that their behaviour towards their brother did not constitute a breach of loyalty to himself. When they communicate with Vsevolod's enemies, and when their breach of faith is established by due procedure, he revokes his grant, confiscates the *volosts* of the perfidious princes and grants them to those who serve him faithfully.

Change the personal names and toponymics, remove the word "father," and the whole story would be indistinguishable from an account of relations between a Western lord and his vassals. There is some negotiability in the Glebovichi's relations with Vsevolod— after all, what human relations are completely non-negotiable? However, the degree of leeway is much closer to the high medieval feudo-vassalic bond than to the informal relations between a Carolingian magnate and his followers. Thus, the Glebovichi had to go on Vsevolod's campaign against the Olgovichi, even though the oldest Glebovich

---

[123] PSRL 1, 432.
[124] *Conventum Hugonis*, 545; *Ademari Cabannensis Chronicon*, 156, 165, 181.
[125] PSRL 1, 434.
[126] PSRL 1, 434, 437, 440, 444.

was married to a daughter of the senior Olgovich, and Riazan had traditional ties with the Olgovichi's patrimonial Chernigov Land.[127] It was, actually, a small wonder that the Riazan princes wanted to go over to the Olgovichi. The fact that they could not simply refuse to participate in the campaign shows that they had clearly defined obligations; the loss of their lands after they failed in these obligations shows an equally clear connection between the land grant and the Glebovichi's service and loyalty to the grantor.

Revoked land grants figure in another relatively detailed narrative about relations between Vsevolod and other princes. However, in this case, Vsevolod was on the receiving end of the procedure: it was he who had received a *volost* and then had it taken back from him. This is another story that needs to be discussed at some length, because, in addition to providing more information about revocations of grants and mutual obligations between "fathers" and "sons," it allows us to see a case of layered tenure.

Vsevolod, Rurik, and Roman: Mutuality of Obligations and Layered Tenure

We have already touched on the chronicle report about Vsevolod becoming the senior of all the Monomakhovichi clan and demanding a *volost* from the Kievan prince Rurik. Vsevolod argued that his position as the senior Monomakhovich entitled him to a territory in the "Rus Land" in the narrow sense of the Middle Dnieper area which was under the direct control of the Kievan prince. As mentioned above, Vsevolod wanted to get the same five strongholds that Rurik had already granted to Roman. There can be little doubt that Vsevolod did not feel secure about his seniority over the strong and numerous southern, Dnieper-based Monomakhovichi. Apparently, he decided to strengthen his position by sowing discord among them. If this was his plan, it worked perfectly.

The chronicler explains that Rurik "wanted to be true to his oath on the Cross," which included a provision not to take the granted volost from Roman "in order to give it to someone else (*azh emu pod nim ne otdati nikomu zhe*)." This is the first time that we hear about Rurik's oath to Roman, and one of the few occasions when the chronicler quotes a specific clause of a sworn agreement. Evidently, generic statements that the parties promised to each other "love" and "well-wishing" do not necessarily cover the actual content of all oaths, some of which spelled out the sworn obligations more precisely. In the case of Rurik and Roman, all we know about their relations before Vsevolod began to create difficulties for them is that they referred to each other as "father" and "son." Evidently, there was a formal entry into their "father"–"son" relations, which included oaths and a grant, but the chronicle, our only source, never describes it.

After Rurik failed in all his attempts to convince Vsevolod to take some other territories, and after the metropolitan absolved him from his oath, Rurik contacted Roman and explained the situation to him. Roman graciously replied that he did not want to stay in the way of Rurik's "entering into love" with Vsevolod, and he agreed to cede the contested territory in exchange for another *volost* or for monetary compensation. Rurik

---

127 PSRL 1, 387; Dimnik, *The Dynasty of Chernigov*, 138, 184, 344.

transferred the five strongholds to Vsevolod, "and they established their mutual love by the oath on the Venerable Cross (*utverdishas krestom chestnym na vsei liubvi svoei*)."[128] This is all that we are told on this occasion, but later we find out that Vsevolod made a sworn promise to render military aid to Rurik. Soon after the establishment of "love," Rurik found himself in a conflict with a number of princes and sent envoys to Vsevolod, "telling him to mount his horse," which was a formulaic expression meaning "to go on a campaign." Vsevolod answered that he "was ready" to come and fight alongside Rurik, but then he lingered for a long time. Eventually, he joined the fighting, but soon made peace without consulting Rurik, and informed Rurik about the peace agreement only *post factum*.

Rurik's reaction to this news reveals that the grant of the five strongholds entailed specific obligations on Vsevolod's part. He addresses Vsevolod, "You swore an oath on the Cross to me that my enemy is your enemy, and you asked a share in the Rus Land from me. I gave you the best *volost*." Rurik then cites Vsevolod's promise to come and fight, his lingering, and his separate peace agreement, saying that this was not what he had in mind when he had told Vsevolod "to mount his horse (*tia esm i na konia vsadil*)." He concludes, "You fulfilled nothing of what you had promised and on what you had sworn your oath on the Cross." After listing these reasons for a revocation of his grant to Vsevolod, Rurik "took from him the strongholds that he had given to him, and gave them again to his own brethren."[129]

The account of Vsevolod's and Rurik's falling out reveals that their "love" was an interesting arrangement: Vsevolod was Rurik's superior in general, but he owed service to Rurik specifically for the *volost* that Rurik granted to him, even though he had forced Rurik to make the grant in the first place. There is a clearly defined connection between service and granted *volosts*: as a grantor, Rurik has the power to demand military aid from Vsevolod, who is otherwise Rurik's senior. Rurik's accusatory speech to Vsevolod is similar to the speech that Iziaslav made when he revoked his grant to George the "Long Arm"'s son Rostislav four decades earlier. On both occasions, the grantor cites the grantee's obligations: Rostislav had "to guard the Rus Land," that is, to secure the steppe border adjacent to a stronghold granted to him; Vsevolod had to fight against Ruriks's enemies as he would against his own. Both grantors stress their own generosity: Iziaslav gave Rostislav "what even your own father did not give you"; Rurik gave Vsevolod "the best *volost*." Finally, both speeches describe the grantees' violations that caused the revocation of the grant. These similarities suggest that the two accounts may have reflected an established procedure for dissolving contractual relations based on a *volost* grant in exchange for service.

It appears that Vsevolod's main goal in respect to Rurik was not to get lands from him, but to cause a dissolution of his relations with Roman. A grandson of Iziaslav Mstislavich and a son of Mistislav, Roman inherited their military talents and was one of the most powerful princes in the Dnieper region. Vsevolod must have been eager to

---

[128] PSRL 2, 683–85.
[129] PSRL 2, 699, 701–2.

break the "father"–"son" bond between Rurik and Roman when he insisted on getting exactly the same strongholds that had been granted to Roman. As we have seen, Roman still remained loyal to his "father" Rurik and relinquished the strongholds peacefully. Vsevolod then gave one of these strongholds, Torchesk, to Rurik's son. This was too much for Roman, who accused Rurik of conspiring with Vsevolod.

The chronicles show a consistent implication that there were some rules for the distribution of *volosts* and that the grantors were not completely free to decide who gets what territory. Grants had to be made "justly" and "rightfully." What constituted "right" and "justice" in this matter is a separate topic that need not concern us here. In this particular case, it was apparently Roman, and not Rurik's son, who had the right to receive Torchesk. After Vsevolod gave it to Rurik's son, Roman interpreted the whole story as an elaborate plot devised by Rurik and Vsevolod to benefit Rurik's son. He did not believe Rurik's assurances that he had acted in good faith, and he did not accept a *volost* offered to him in compensation. "Not wishing to have love" with Rurik, he entered into a sworn agreement with the Olgovichi.[130]

This account contains the most explicit reference to layered tenure, which otherwise is present in the sources implicitly. For example, the Riazan Glebovichi held all their lands as a grant from Vsevolod. At the same time, they had numerous junior princes under them. There is a clear implication in the chronicles that every prince of full age is entitled to a *volost*. When Andrew Bogoliubsky, upon becoming the Suzdalian prince, did not want to grant any lands to his nephews and younger brothers, he exiled them to Constantinople.[131] Otherwise, they would have gone and offered their service to another prince, as George the "Long Arm's" son did when his father allegedly did not give him a *volost*. The junior Riazan princes clearly had some lands that they must have received from the Glebovichi, but the chronicler does not refer explicitly to grants made by the Glebovichi to their subordinate princes from the land that the Glebovichi themselves were granted by Vsevolod. We have also seen Andrew Bogoliubsky "giving" Kiev to other princes, who then pass it to still others, but Kiev may have been a special case. There is also a reference to Vsevolod of Kiev "giving" Pereiaslavl to Viacheslav who then, with Vsevolod's permission (*smolviasia*), "gives" it to Iziaslav. However, this may have been a special case as well.[132]

Chroniclers mention in passing land property of non-princely nobles who perform honourable service to princes, but these tantalizing references are too brief and too few; they do not contain information about the origin and status of the land. The chronicle of the Galich principality mentions *volosts* granted to non-princely nobles on the eve of the Mongol invasion, but we do not know if this was a new practice that only emerged in the second quarter of the thirteenth century nor if such grants were ever made in other regions.[133] In short, it seems likely that princes made grants from land that was granted

---

130 PSRL 2, 685–86.
131 PSRL 2, 520.
132 PSRL 2, 312–13.
133 PSRL 2, 789.

to them, but there is no direct evidence for this practice, apart from the account about the complicated relations between Vsevolod, Rurik and Roman, to which we will now return.

The essence of the story is that Vsevolod receives five strongholds from Rurik, and then grants one of them, Torchesk, to Rurik's son. This creates problems for Rurik, but he evidently cannot simply take Torchesk back from his own son and give it to Roman again. A rather detailed report of an exchange between Roman and Rurik, devoted to the Torchesk situation, never mentions, or implies, this possibility.[134] In the end, Rurik took back from Vsevolod all the territories that he had granted to him, but as long as the grant as a whole was not revoked, he could not interfere with the next layer of tenure created by Vsevolod's decision to give Torchesk to another prince; nor could he interfere in the relations between Vsevolod and the receiver of Torchesk, even though it was his own son. For that matter, Vsevolod, the senior of all the Monomakhovichi and thus Rurik's superior, could not simply take possession of strongholds located in the territory under Rurik's direct control and could only receive them as Rurik's grant. The account of the "Torchesk affair" implies that all the princes involved have clearly delineated rights and limitations in regards to what they can, and cannot, do with various territories that are subject to a complicated, layered system of tenure. This system is based on mutual obligations, which are probably nowhere seen more clearly than in the story of the tumultuous relations between Rurik and Roman.

When Rurik found out about Roman's communication with the Olgovichi, to whom Roman promised military help against Rurik, he sent his men to "throw the charters of the Cross" in front of Roman, thus formally breaking their "father"–"son" relations. According to the chronicle, Roman turned for help to the Polish dukes, the sons of Casimir II. In reality, Roman must have contacted their mother, Casimir's widow, who acted as a regent, because the dukes were then small children. They concluded an agreement of mutual assistance: Roman was to help Casimir's sons against their uncle Mieszko, who sought to depose them; after that, they would help Roman against Rurik. Mieszko, however, crushed the joint forces of Roman and the young dukes; Roman was wounded, and many of his men died in battle. Thus, Roman found himself in a state of open hostility with Rurik at a time when he was recovering from wounds and his army had been decimated.[135] The only thing to do was to ask for mercy. Roman sent his envoys to Rurik and to Metropolitan Nicephorus with entreaties, "laying all the blame (*vina*) with himself," and asking the metropolitan to advocate for him. Nicephorus agreed to undertake a peace-making mission, and he accomplished it most successfully.

Rurik "forgave his anger" at Roman, "made him swear an oath on the Cross according to his will (*na vsei vole svoei*), and gave him Polonnyi and half of the Korsun district (*pol tortaka*)." A later reference to Roman's oath indicates that it included specific obligations—the chronicler cites his promise not to be in league with the Olgovichi anymore, but the loss of all the "charters of the Cross" makes it impossible to know more

---

134 PSRL 2, 685–86.
135 PSRL 2, 686–87.

about the content of this and other oaths. What the chronicler did record was Rurik's speech to his men about his plans to restore relations with Roman. This speech is probably the best expression of mutuality and reciprocity in "father"–"son" relations:

> If he is now entreating me and is repenting his offense (*vina*), I will accept him, and will make him swear an oath on the Cross, and will give him a grant (*nadelok*). If he keeps his word and has me as a father rightfully (*vo pravdu*) and wishes me well, then I will have him as a son, just as I had had him before and had wished him well.[136]

***

Accounts of agreements between Rusian princes include references to *volosts* granted and taken back, to obligations of service, loyalty, and obedience, and to hierarchical contractual relations created by oaths and by the ritual of "bowing down." These elements are not always present together, but formal agreements structured around a land grant and an obligation of service appear often enough to prompt a suggestion that Rus knew a type of personal bond that was similar in nature to what Western medievalists call "feudo-vassalic relations." The only element of the classic "feudal contract" absent from Rusian sources is a formal investiture into the granted property by means of a symbolic material object. If the words "I give you this *volost*," which princes often utter in the chronicles, were accompanied by the transfer of a symbolic object, this procedure did not make it into surviving written records.

Investiture is absent from Languedocienne sources as well; nonetheless, Hélène Débax's argument about the existence of *la féodalité languedocienne* is widely accepted.[137] It is based on her study of records of oaths sworn by Languedocienne aristocrats, which Débax divides into various categories such as "oaths of security," "feudo-vassalic oaths," and others, but she makes it clear that this classification is her own. The original documents do not contain any self-designation. They consist of descriptions of promises made by one person to another, and it is on the basis of the nature of these promises that Débax assigns some of them to the feudo-vassalic category.[138] In Catalonia, different types of agreements—those containing what "amounts to the details of the 'feudal contract'," settlements of disputes, treaties, alliances, and others—also composed a coherent group of documents that medieval scribes uniformly designated as *conveninentiae*. Again, the division of these documents into different categories on the basis of their content belongs to a modern scholar, who uses it as an analytical tool, while keeping in mind that "these categories are in no way absolute; many agreements do not do fit well under any of these headings, and there is a good deal of overlap among those that do."[139]

---

[136] PSRL 2, 687–88.

[137] Hélène Débax, "L'aristocratie languedocienne et la société féodale," in Bagge, Gelting, and Lindkvist, *Feudalism*, 98; Patzold, *Das Lehnswesen*, 66–68.

[138] Débax, *La féodalité languedocienne*, 100.

[139] Kosto, *Making Agreements*, 80, 85.

This chapter is an attempt to apply the methodology used in studies of records of oaths and agreements to narratives of interprincely relations: to classify agreements between princes on the basis of their content in accordance with modern analytical categories. Of course, no narrative, let alone one as fragmentary as Rusian chronicles, allows readers to see terms and conditions of an agreement with the same degree of clarity as the actual text of the agreement. Nonetheless, some accounts of interprincely relations do contain enough details that appear to fit rather well with the modern scholarly category of "feudo-vassalic."

The most idiosyncratic Rusian feature is the use of the terms "father" and "son." "Father" as "lord" has no direct parallels in Western sources. However, it corresponds to the well-attested perception of social bonds created by sworn agreements as "artificial kinship."[140] One of William's broken promises to Hugh was, "You will be my friend above everyone else except my son."[141] In high medieval Gascony, it was not uncommon for blood relatives to enter into formal agreements promising fidelity to one another, while agreements between non-relatives were infused by rhetoric of family bonding.[142] In Normandy, the killing of one's lord or vassal was punished "as if it were parricide."[143] An extremely interesting phenomenon probably related to the perception of a lord as "father" is attested to in Languedocien and Catalan oaths of fidelity. Like other medieval texts, they give personal names in the form "X, son of Y." Unlike almost any other text—including other documents from the same areas—they use mother's, and not father's, name for those swearing fidelity. Various explanations for this anomaly have been proposed, but Débax has convincingly argued that the most plausible one is that the lord took the place of father for the person who swore fidelity to him. The use of the maternal, instead of paternal, name excluded the biological father of the lord's man in order to present the lord as his "virtual" father.[144]

Interestingly, in Catalonia, matrilineal identification is more common in the records of oaths sworn by one party to the other than in the *convenientiae*, that is, texts of agreements concluded when the oaths were sworn. Kosto notes that "the *convenientia* carries with it the notion of bilateral agreement (even if this is not always the case), while the oath is purely unilateral." Consequently, "the *convenientia* deemphasizes the subordination of one party to the other, while this is what defines many oaths." He does not mention whether the use of the maternal name is equally present in oaths not defined by relations of subordination, but the difference between the two types of texts that he describes is suggestive. In addition to emphasizing subordination, oaths "are more

---

[140] For titles of works on "artificial kinship," see Hyams, "Homage and Feudalism," 38; Althoff, *Family, Friends, and Followers*, 6–64.

[141] "meusque eris amicus super omnes preter filio meo," *Conventum Hugonis*, 542.

[142] Benoît Cursente, "Entre parenté et fidélité: les 'amis' dans la Gascogne des Xie et XIIe siècles," in *Les sociétés méridionales à l'âge féodal: Espagne, Italie et sud de la France, Xe–XIIIes.: Hommage à Pierre Bonnasie*, ed. Hélène Débax (Toulouse: Editions Médiriennes, 1999), 285–92.

[143] Hyams, "Homage and Feudalism," 32.

[144] Débax, *La feodalite languedocienne*, 134–35.

likely than *convenientiae* to contain vernacular terms."[145] Can this indicate that the oral vernacular discourse of hierarchical relations included the view of the superior party as a "father"?

In any case, when viewed in light of the concept of "artificial kinship," the Rusian use of "father" and "son" is not as much at odds with the political discourse of the medieval West as it may seem at first glance. Rather, it appears that Rusian chronicles, once again, make explicit an aspect implicitly present in the Western sources.

---

145 Kosto, *Making Agreements*, 150–51.

CONCLUSIONS

THE LAST CHAPTER of this book ends with a story about the complicated relations of Rurik, Vsevolod, and Roman. Their social status is described in English as "princes," the term that, as argued in Chapter 1, serves as a conventional label for the upper social stratum of Rus, which consisted of royalty and aristocracy. We followed a break-up and subsequent repair of the bond of artificial kinship between Rurik and Roman, for which Russian chroniclers use the terms "father" and "son," and which this book presented as analogous to lordship of high medieval Western sources. Soon after Rurik and Roman restored their "father"–"son" relations, they fell out again.[1] We did not discuss this new development, because not much is known about it.

The thriller about fighting and peace-making, cunning machinations and faithfulness, sworn and broken oaths, and multiple transfers of the rights to Torchesk breaks off shortly before the end of the *Kievan Chronicle*, where it is found in the entries for the 1190s. Like the majority of Russian chronicles, these entries are in the vernacular East Slavonic and often use direct speech—in short, they are written in what may be deemed the "*Conventum Hugonis* style." This style changes suddenly in the entry for 1198/9, which includes a Church Slavonic eulogy to Rurik, probably composed as a separate text and at some point interpolated into the chronicle. This is the same Rurik who had difficulties with Vsevolod and Roman, but one hardly recognizes the figure from the accounts of princely wars, negotiations, and agreements, in which we have seen Rurik so actively involved. The Rurik of the entry for 1198/99 is a majestic monarch, belonging to the long line of the "autocrats holding the throne of Kiev" and ruling over what looks like a "normal" European kingdom.[2]

This is not how Rurik's country is usually viewed. Rus of scholarly literature, with some exceptions discussed above, is not a kingdom, does not belong to Europe, and follows a "special path" of social and political development. The contention of this book is that this view is largely a product of the nature of available sources and of differences in historiographical traditions. If we leave out the question of why the nineteenth-century founders of Russian and Ukrainian historiography opposed Rus to the West—a question that merits a separate study—and if we concentrate on differences between Rus and Latin Europe seen in the sources, the main difference would arguably lie in the sphere of culture, not in the social and political organizations of the two regions.

If sources rarely present Rus as an orderly monarchy, it is because few of them are fine literary works in the style of the eulogy for Rurik in the *Kievan* entry for 1198/99, and few are written in Church Slavonic, the language of the learned Byzantine tradition going back to imperial Rome. If medieval European kingdoms had "civil wars" at the time when "princely strife" was going on in Rus, it is not because the nature of the conflicts was that much different, but because the former were described by Latin scholars who were using the language of Livy and Suetonius. Classical heritage played a much greater

---

[1] PSRL 2, 697.
[2] PSRL 2, 708–15.

role in the West than it did in Rus; consequently, there is a big difference in the degree to which it shaped the historical writings of Rusian and Western *literati*. The reader is immediately struck by differences in style, language, and rhetorical strategies, and is left with a general impression that these writings describe societies that have very little in common. Few readers would go beyond this general impression: scholars of Rus are rarely engaged in a closer reading of Western primary sources with a goal other than looking for information on Rus; Western medievalists would not be able to read Rusian sources even if they wanted to, because few are translated into modern languages.

An interpretation of Latin and East Slavonic narratives offered in this book suggests that they not so much describe radically different societies, as emphasize different aspects of social and political organization. A close reading of Latin sources uncovers similarities with Rus, but these similarities are much more pronounced in vernacular texts and in the semi-vernacular *Conventum Hugonis*. The latter in particular displays striking parallels with Rusian chronicles, which suggests a similarity between oral political discourses reflected in these narratives. Vernacular sources, arguably connected with an oral discourse, of course, do not provide a direct, unmediated access to the realities of the past, but a legitimate question to ask is whether such sources may reflect some aspects of the medieval life not visible in more "learned" texts. In fact, a striking case of a connection between the language and the content was recently discovered in a set of documents from a later period, namely, the proceedings of the interrogation of the Templars in Caen in 1307.

The royal instructions concerning the arrest and interrogation were written in Latin and in French, as were records of the Templars' confessions. Only the French version contains an explicit reference to torture and mentions that the accused swore twice that the charges were false; the Latin documents "sanitized events," creating an impression that the interrogation consisted of nothing more than "an orderly, perhaps even tedious, two days of questioning, reasoning, and cajoling." Although "one might at first be tempted to imagine that the French document could have been written up as a sort of 'first draft' taken down on the fly," this was not the case: "the two acts are both 'formal' and 'final,' intended to be read and preserved as a record. Indeed, the French version [...] was almost certainly written after the Latin."[3]

Apparently, those who drafted the documents felt uncomfortable about describing messy and unpleasant aspects of the medieval judicial practice in Latin, but they had less compunction when writing in the vernacular. Of course, this one case cannot be extrapolated across time and space, but it does show that in the fourteenth century the choice of language could directly affect the content of a document; differences between high medieval Latin and vernacular narratives describing the same, or similar, events suggest that a connection between the sources' language and the content may have already existed in previous centuries. If it did, what are its implications for the debate on feudalism?

The question of the nature of sources has been an aspect of this debate since Barthélemy proposed his "feudal revelation" theory of the documentary change around

---

3 Sean L. Field, "Torture and Confession in the Templar Interrogations at Caen, 28–29 October 1307," *Speculum: A Journal of Medieval Studies* 91 (2016): 297–327, at 311–12, 314.

the year 1000, arguing that new practices of charter writing simply revealed features of the social order that hitherto had been left unrecorded. Not all were convinced; Charles West in particular pointed to methodological problems created by an assumption that "historians can bypass their sources to access directly some hidden underlying reality."[4]

Even if Barthélemy may have oversimplified relations between concepts and words,[5] his critique of the "feudal revolution" raised an important question of how to distinguish between a documentary and a social change in a diachronic study, or between variations in the type of historical evidence and "real" social differences in a synchronic one. A picture of our own society that would emerge from reading legal documents or a collection of contracts signed by its citizens on various occasions would surely be very different from an image of the same society that would be formed by watching the evening news.

Of course, to say that our perception of the past is affected by the nature of the available sources is to state the obvious. There is no historian who would not agree with this in principle; however, in practice, it is extremely hard to balance evidence coming from different types of sources. When Charles West sees high medieval social relations as much more formal and clearly defined than Stephen White and Fredric Cheyette do, who emphasize fluidity and ambiguity, is the difference in their concepts of medieval society partly explained by the difference in their source bases? What, if any, is the significance of the fact that White and Cheyette produced prolific studies of vernacular literature, while West has worked with Latin, and mostly diplomatic, sources? Is it possible to imagine a future synthesis of the themes related to the "feudal revolution" debate that would incorporate evidence from Latin and vernacular, diplomatic and literary, prose and poetical sources?

This work is in no way an attempt at such a synthesis. Such an ambitious undertaking would exceed by far the capabilities of the author, whose much more modest goal is to broaden the geographic and linguistic scope of the debate by bringing in Rusian material. The main argument of this book is that feudo-vassalic relations existed among Rusian princes. If this is so, if the interpretation of the chronicle accounts about "fathers" and "sons" offered in Chapter 4 convinced the reader, then feudo-vassalic relations were not an exclusively Western European phenomenon they are normally believed to be. One explanation for their existence in Rus would be to postulate an active interaction with Latin Europe leading to a borrowing of some Western practices and institutions. Christian Raffensperger has recently drawn attention to extensive marital ties between Rusian princes and the Western European elite and has suggested that women served as a conduit of cultural exchange that was more vivid than the existing sources allow us to see.[6] Indeed, there are some indications that cultural exchange between Rus and the West may be significantly more broad than is generally realized, but this is a subject for another study. On the other hand, the "father"–"son" relations has a native flavour that may be difficult to reconcile with a view of them as a borrowed foreign practice.

---

4 West, *Reframing the Feudal Revolution*, 180.

5 West, *Reframing the Feudal Revolution*, 180.

6 Raffensperger, *Reimagining Europe*.

There may be some pan-European processes at work that resulted in similar social developments across the continent.

In Latin Europe, the classical heritage was part of the process that led to the formation of the high and late medieval socio-political structures, although the role of academic scholars in the rise of the feudo-vassalic relations probably was not as drastic as assigned to them by Reynolds, who sees university-trained lawyers as almost single-handed creators of "feudalism." We have seen that recent scholarship presents the development of feudo-vassalic relations as a more gradual and organic process than the one depicted in *Fiefs and Vassals*. Nonetheless, high culture in the broad sense, which included monastic scholars, ecclesiastics, and scribes trained in Latin literacy, did contribute to the development towards more formal and better conceptualized relationships.

When the mutual obligations of the lord and his man were written down in Latin, all the parties involved were compelled to think hard about the precise character of these obligations. Even with the meaning of much classical legal terminology lost or blurred, the very structure of the language encouraged those drafting a Latin charter to strive for clearer expression, which, in turn, probably influenced the parties' understanding of their relations and, ultimately, their behaviour towards each other. By the same token, royal panegyrists, such as Suger, surely contributed to the rise of monarchy. Even though they did not portray accurately the actual royal power of their time, their elevated representations of the king helped to create the royal ideology which later sanctified the institutions of administrative kingship.

Much of this book draws a distinction between ideology and reality, between cultural and social history, but it is important to keep in mind that all such distinctions are artificial. A separation of representation from practice, present in my discussion of the Latin and vernacular sources, is no more than a heuristic device, which was employed because of the focus on social practices that, arguably, were common to Rus and the West. This study leaves out an important question about the role of the "learned" culture in the further evolution of these practices, because in respect to Rus this question may be unanswerable. An examination of the interaction between culture, ideology, and socio-political developments of any medieval region is a complex task, but when it comes to Rus, the complexity is almost insurmountable. The problem is that the period of an uninterrupted development documented by native written sources is simply too short. Western medievalists can observe centuries of social and cultural evolution before and after the Viking invasions which represent the only substantial outside disruption in the development of medieval Europe. The question of what impact the Vikings had on this development is debated, but it is clear that eventually they became part of European society, not the other way around. The Vikings in their relations to Western Europe may be compared to the Turkic steppe nomads in their relations to Rus: they raided its territories, they settled there on various conditions, but, apart from a relatively brief reign of Danish kings in England, they never created any overarching political structure that would bring these territories under their rule.

The Mongols, in contrast, incorporated Rus into their empire. Muscovy eventually emerged from the part of the Mongol Empire that encompassed former eastern Russian principalities. Thus, cultural influences that shaped the socio-political development of Muscovy included the Mongols, under whose gradually weakening overlordship its lands had remained for two and a half centuries; another important influence was the Byzantine Empire, whose symbolism and ideology was actively employed by the Moscovite elite. The legacy of pre-Mongol Rus, arguably, also played a part, but it is very difficult to differentiate it from other ingredients of this complex cultural amalgam. The amalgam was somewhat different, but no less complex, in the former western Rusian principalities which later became Ukraine and Belarus. These lands, after they had spent various amounts of time under the Mongol rule, became parts of Lithuania and, subsequently, of the Polish-Lithuanian Commonwealth. All these upheavals started with the Mongol conquest of the 1230s; given that the social and political organization of Rus is relatively well documented only in the twelfth century, this leaves us with scarcely more than a hundred-year period over which we may observe the evolution of social and political practices and their interaction with culture and ideology.

Another thing to keep in mind is that it is possible to talk about anything in Rus to be "relatively well-documented," only with a large emphasis on "relatively." The interpretation of the Rusian socio-political organization offered in this book is hypothetical, but, arguably, so are other, more conventional interpretations inasmuch as they depart from purely East Slavonic terminology. The upper stratum of the Rusian elite undoubtedly consisted of *kniazi*; a *kniaz* fought a lot with other *kniazi* and collected *dan* from the population of his *volost*—this much is a fact, not a hypothesis. However, anyone who wants to situate Rus in a broader historical context and to describe *kniazi* in external terms must rely on scarce sources that survive mostly in late copies. We have seen that *kniazi* have often been regarded as a dynasty; a more traditional approach blames the dynastic disorganization for the disintegration of Rus into petty principalities, while a strand in recent scholarship, associated primarily with Shepard and Franklin, presents the extended dynasty as an efficient instrument for ruling the diverse and constantly growing territories which had never had much unity in the first place. Alternatively, Ostrowski argues that Rus was an "aristocratic state," where *kniazi* were members of nobility, not a dynasty; Raffensperger sees Rus as a kingdom and *kniazi* as kings.

All these interpretations, just as the one found in the above chapters, although not based on the chronicles exclusively, make abundant use of them. In other words, all these interpretations would have been impossible without information from compilations, most of which currently exist in fifteenth-century copies. Such sources would undoubtedly strike a Western medievalist as unreliable. Abandoning any attempts to characterize social and political structures of Rus may be the only way to leave the realm of the hypothetical, but this hardly sounds like a realistic plan. Somehow, it does not feel right to begin the account of the socio-political development of most of Eastern Europe in the fifteenth century and to exclude a polity bigger than the German Empire from medieval history.

In addition, if we adopt an overly strict approach to what can constitute a source base for a legitimate historical study and abandon Rus as a hopeless case, where should we stop? Quantity and quality of Rusian sources, dismal by the standards of Western medievalists, would look enviable to a scholar of pre-Columbian America where piles of Maya books were famously destroyed by an overzealous Spanish bishop. Western medieval sources, in turn, are scant compared to those from later periods. Ultimately, historical records from any time and place are shards of broken mirrors; more precisely, shards of broken curved mirrors with varying angles of reflection.

The shards that are the sources used in this book reflect the same key elements in the social organization of the elite in Rus and in the West, such as ties of kinship and sworn agreements, with some of the latter arguably fitting the definition of feudo-vassalic. The question not discussed here is the relative significance of these elements. Historiography of Rus has always focused on the role of kinship in princely politics, often viewed as part of Rus's "special path." However, recent Western scholarship also stresses the importance of kinship. Particularly fruitful in this respect has been research of the German Empire. Althoff sees "no recognized hierarchy of different bonds" there: when multiple loyalties clashed, "on some occasions the bond of kinship might come out on top, on others the bond of friendship or lordship. What is clear [...] is that bonds of kinship, friendship and co-operation often proved rather more powerful than the bond which existed between a vassal and his lord."[7] Lyon, in his study of the sibling relationships among German nobles, emphasizes the necessity of "embracing the central role that family bonds played within medieval politics."[8]

Of course, concrete configurations of familial, contractual, and other cooperative and vertical relations differed from one medieval society to another. Lyon notes that sibling relationships "could create widely divergent political and territorial strategies among nobles" of Swabia, Bavaria, and Saxony;[9] there may be little doubt that the same is true of other regions inside and outside of the German Empire. When it comes to Rus, it may well be that the political significance of kinship there was stronger than it was elsewhere in Europe. More comparative studies are needed before we can be certain that this was, indeed, the case, but even if such studies show that the bond of kinship in Rus, to borrow Althoff's phrase, came out on top more often than it did in the West, would this necessarily exclude Rus from the medieval European civilization? After all, Rus also differed greatly from the Byzantine Empire and from the Orthodox polities of south-eastern Europe; nonetheless, the classic work by Obolensky presented all of them as parts of the Byzantine Commonwealth.

The goal of the present book is not to "move" Rus from the "Byzantine Commonwealth" to "Medieval Europe"; if the analysis offered here concentrates on commonalities between Rus and the West, it is not because they are inherently more important, but because they appear understudied and underappreciated, as compared with the Byzantine connections. Just as a medieval—or, for that matter, any other—person could participate in multiple relationships which did not have to be mutually exclusive, so Rus—or, for that matter, probably any other country—could be part of more than one cultural area. A representation of Rus as a regional variation of European society does not exclude other perspectives, but simply offers one more way to situate Rus in a wider historical context. This book revisits the view first expressed by the compiler of the *Primary Chronicle*, who placed his country in the "lot of Japheth" along with the Franks, Germans, and Angles, and it seeks to show that this Kievan monk probably was not wrong in doing so.

---

[7] Althoff, *Family, Friends, and Followers*, 162.
[8] Lyon, *Princely Brothers and Sisters*, 7.
[9] Lyon, *Princely Brothers and Sisters*, 13.

BIBLIOGRAPHY

Primary Sources

Chronicles Published in the Polnoe Sobranie Russkikh Letopisei

Ermolinskaia letopis. Edited by F. I. Pokrovskii. Polnoe sobranie russkikh letopisei. Vol. 23. St. Petersburg: Imperatorskaia Arkheograficheskaia Komissia, 1910. Reprinted with a new introduction by B. M. Kloss. Moscow: Iazyki slavianskikh kultur, 2004.

Letopis po Ipatevskomu spisku. Edited by A. A. Shakhmatov. Polnoe sobranie russkikh letopisei. Vol. 2. St. Petersburg: Imperatorskaia Arkheograficheskaia Komissia, 1908. Reprinted with a new introduction by B. M. Kloss as *Ipatevskaia*. Moscow: Iazyki slavianskikh kultur, 1998.

Letopis po Lavrentevskomu spisku. Edited by E. F. Karskii. Polnoe sobranie russkikh letopisei. Vol. 1. 2nd ed. Leningrad: Izdatelstvo Akademii Nauk SSSR, 1927. Reprinted with a new introduction by B. M. Kloss as *Lavrentievskaia*. Moscow: Iazyki slavianskikh kultur, 1997.

Letopisets Pereiaslavlia-Russkogo (Letopisets russkikh tsarei). Edited by B. A. Rybakov and V. I. Buganov. Polnoe sobranie russkikh letopisei. Vol. 41. Moscow: Arkheograficheskii tsentr, 1995.

Moskovskii letopisnyi svod kontsa XV veka. Edited by M. N. Tikhomirov. Polnoe sobranie russkikh letopisei. Vol. 25. Leningrad: Izdatelstvo Akademii Nauk SSSR, 1949. Reprinted Moscow: Iazyki slavianskikh kultur, 2004.

Novgorodskaia pervaia letopis starshego i mladshego izvodov. Edited by A. N. Nasonov. Polnoe sobranie russkikh letopisei. Vol. 3. Moscow: Izdatelstvo Akademii nauk SSSR, 1950.

Radzivillovskaia letopis. Edited by B. A. Rybakov. Polnoe sobranie russkikh letopisei. Vol. 38. Moscow: Izdatelstvo Akademii nauk, 1989.

Sofiiskaia pervaia letopis. Edited by P. G. Vasenko. Polnoe sobranie russkikh letopisei. Vol. 5. 2nd ed. Leningrad: Izdatelstvo Akademii nauk SSSR, 1925.

Other Editions of Rusian Chronicles

Galitsko-volynskaia letopis: Tekst, kommentarii, issledovanie. Edited by M. F. Kotliar, V. Iu. Franchuk, and A. G. Plakhonin. St. Petersburg: Aleteia, 2005.

Radzivillovskaia letopis. Tekst, issledovaniia, opisanie miniatiur. Edited by M. V. Kukushkina and G. M. Prokhorov. Moscow: Glagol, 1994–95.

The Old Rus' Kievan and Galician-Volhynian Chronicles: The Ostroz'kyj (Xlebnikov) and Cetvertyns'kyj (Pogodin) Codices. Edited by Omeljan Pritsak. Harvard Library of Early Ukrainian Literature, Text Series 8. Cambridge, MA: Harvard University Press, 1990.

The "Povest' vremennykh let": An Interlinear Collation and Paradosis. Edited by Donald Ostrowski, with David Birnbaum and Horace G. Lunt. Harvard Library of Early Ukrainian Literature, Text Series 10. Cambridge, MA: Harvard University Press, 2003.

The Russian Primary Chronicle: Laurentian Text. Translated by Samuel Hazzard Cross and Olgerd P. Sherbowitz-Wetzor. Cambridge, MA: Medieval Academy of America, 1953.

Birchbark Documents

Gr. 115. In *Novgorodskie gramoty na bereste: iz raskopok 1953-1954 gg.* Edited by A. V. Artsikhovskii, 48. Novgorodskie gramoty na bereste 3. Moscow: Nauka, 1958.
Gr. 155. In *Novgorodskie gramoty na bereste: iz raskopok 1955 g.* Edited by A. V. Artsikhovskii and V. I Borkovskii, 34-36. Novgorodskie gramoty na bereste 4. Moscow: Nauka, 1958.
Gr. 226. In *Novgorodskie gramoty na bereste: iz raskopok 1956-1957 gg.* Edited by A. V. Artsikhovskii and V. I Borkovskii, 49. Novgorodskie gramoty na bereste 5. Moscow: Nauka, 1963.
Gr. 550. In *Novgorodskie gramoty na bereste: iz raskopok 1977-1983 gg.* Edited by V. L. Ianin and A. A. Zalizniak, 23-24. Novgorodskie gramoty na bereste 8. Moscow: Nauka, 1986.
Gr. 603. In *Novgorodskie gramoty na bereste: iz raskopok 1977-1983 gg.* Edited by V. L. Ianin and A. A. Zalizniak, 66-67. Novgorodskie gramoty na bereste 8. Moscow: Nauka, 1986.
Gr. 664. In *Novgorodskie gramoty na bereste: iz raskopok 1984-1989 gg.* Edited by V. L. Ianin and A. A. Zalizniak, 54. Novgorodskie gramoty na bereste 9. Moscow: Nauka, 1993.
Gr. St. R.12. In *Novgorodskie gramoty na bereste: iz raskopok 1962-1976 gg.* Edited by A. V. Artsikhovskii, V. L. Ianin, and A. A. Zalizniak, 152-53. Novgorodskie gramoty na bereste 7. Moscow: Nauka, 1978.
Gr. St. R.17. In *Novgorodskie gramoty na bereste: iz raskopok 1984-1989 gg.* Edited by V. L. Ianin and A. A. Zalizniak, 105-6. Novgorodskie gramoty na bereste 9. Moscow: Nauka, 1993.

Other Primary Sources

Adémar de Chabannes. *Chronicon.* Edited by Bourgain, P. R. Landes, and G. Pon. *Ademari Cabannensis Chronicon.* Corpus Christianorum, Continuatio Mediaevalis 79. Turnhout: Brepols, 1999.
Annales Bertiniani. Edited by Félix Grat, Jeanne Vielliard, and Suzanne Clémencet. Paris: C. Klincksieck, 1964.
Chroniques des comtes d'Anjou et des seigneurs d'Amboise. Edited by Louis Halphen and René Poupardin. Paris: Libraire des Archives nationales et de la Société de l'Ecole des Chartes, 1913.
"Conventum inter Guillelmum Aquitanorum comitem et Hugonem Chiliarchum." Edited and translated by Jane Martindale. *English Historical Review* 84 (1969): 528-48.
Danil. *Zhite i khozhene Danila Russkyia zemli igumena.* Edited by G. M. Prokhorov. In *XII vek.* Edited by D. S. Likhachev, L. A. Dmitriev, A. A. Aleskeev, and N. V. Ponyrko. Biblioteka literatury Drevnei Rusi 4. St. Petersburg: Nauka, 1997. Available as an electronic text at http://lib.pushkinskijdom.ru/Default.aspx?tabid=4934

Danil Zatochenik. *Slovo Danila Zatochenika, ezhe napisa svoemu kniaziu, Iaroslavu Volodimerovichiu*. Edited by L. V. Sokolova. In *XII vek*. Edited by D. S. Likhachev, L. A. Dmitriev, A. A. Aleskeev, and N. V. Ponyrko. Biblioteka literatury Drevnei Rusi 4. St. Petersburg: Nauka, 1997. Available as an electronic text at http://lib.pushkinskijdom.ru/Default.aspx?tabid=4942

Die Kaiserchronik eines Regensburger Geistlichen. Edited by Edward Schröder. Monumenta Germaniae Historica, Scriptores Qui Vernacula Lingua Usi Sunt 1. Hanover: Hahnsche Buchhandlung, 1895.

Dudo of St-Quentin. *De moribus et actis primorum Normanniae ducum auctore Dudone Sancti Quintini decano*. Edited by Jules Lair. Caen: Le Blanc-Hardel, 1865.

Fulbert of Chartres. *Epistolae*. Edited and translated by F. Behrends. *The Letters and Poems of Fulbert of Chartres*. Oxford: Clarendon Press, 1976.

Johannis de Fordun. *Chronica Gentis Scotorum*. Edited by Felix James Henry Skene and William Forbes Skene. Edinburgh: Edmonstone and Douglas, 1872.

Jordan Fantosme. *Jordan Fantosme's Chronicle*. Edited by R. C. Johnston. New York: Oxford University Press, 1981.

Hilarion of Kiev. *Slovo o zakone i blagodati*. Edited by A. M. Moldovan. *"Slovo o zakone i blagodati" Ilariona*. Kiev: Naukova dumka, 1984.

The Laws of Rus': Tenth to Fifteenth Centuries. Edited and translated by Daniel H. Kaiser. Salt Lake City: Charles Schlacks Jr., 1992.

Nicephorus of Kiev. *Chista molitva tvoia: pouchenie i poslaniia drevnerusskim kniaziam Kievskogo mitropolita Nikifora*. Edited by G. S. Barankova. Moscow: Ikhtios, 2005.

Nestor of the Kievan Caves. *Zhitie prepodobnaago ottsa nashego Feodosiia*. Edited by O. V. Tvorogov. In *XI–XII veka*. Edited by S. D. Likhachev, L. A. Dmitriev, A. A. Aleskeev, and N. V. Ponyrko. Biblioteka literatury Drevnei Rusi 1. St. Petersburg: Nauka, 1997. Available as electronic text at http://lib.pushkinskijdom.ru/Default.aspx?tabid=4872#_ednref26

Poème anglo-normand sur l'Ancien Testament. Edited by Pierre Nobel. Nouvelle bibliothèque du Moyen Âge 37. Paris: H. Champion, 1996.

Robert of Torigni. *The Chronicle of Robert of Torigni, Abbot of the Monastery of St. Michael-in-Peril-of-the-Sea*. Edited by Richard Howlett. *Chronicles of the Reigns of Stephen, Henry II., and Richard I*. Vol. 4. Rerum Britannicarum Medii Aevi scriptores 82–84. London: Eyre and Spottiswoode, 1889.

"Russkaia pravda. Prostrannaia redaktsia." In *Zakonodatelstvo Drevnei Rusi*, edited by V. L. Ianin, 64–80. Rossiiskoe zakonodatelstvo X–XX vekov 1. Moscow: Iuridicheskaia literatura, 1984.

The Song of Roland: An Analytical Edition. Edited by Gerard J. Brault. University Park: Pennsylvania State University Press, 1978.

Svod zapisei pistsov, khudozhnikov i perepletchkov drevnerusskikh pergamennykh kodeksov XI–XIV vv. Edited by L. V. Stoliarova. Moscow: Nauka, 2000.

Theoderic of Echternach, *Vita Sanctae Hildegardis*. In *Jutta and Hildegard: The Biographical Sources*. Edited by Anna Silvas, 118–210. Turnhout: Brepols, 1998.

"Ustav kniazia Iaroslava o tserkovnykh sudakh." In *Drevnerusskie kniazheskie ustavy XI—XV vv.*, edited by Ia. N. Shchapov, 85–139. Moscow: Nauka, 1975.

"Ustav kniazia Vladimira o desiatinakh, sudakh i liudiakh tserkovnykh." In *Drevnerusskie kniazheskie ustavy XI—XV vv.*, edited by Ia. N. Shchapov, 12–84. Moscow: Nauka, 1975.

"Ustavnaia gramota novgorodskogo kniazia Sviatoslava Olgovicha tserkvi Sv. Sofii v Novgorode." In *Drevnerusskie kniazheskie ustavy XI—XV vv.*, edited by Ia. N. Shchapov, 147–48. Moscow: Nauka, 1975.

"Ustavnaiai i zhalovannaia gramota smolenskogo kniazia Rostislava Mstislavicha tserkvi Bogoroditsy i episkopu." In *Drevnerusskie kniazheskie ustavy XI—XV vv.*, edited by Ia. N. Shchapov, 140–45. Moscow: Nauka, 1975.

Vladimir Monomakh. Instruction. In *Letopis po Lavrentevskomu spisku*, edited by E. F. Karskii, 240–52. Polnoe sobranie russkikh letopisei. Vol. 1. 2nd ed. Leningrad: Izdatelstvo Akademii Nauk SSSR, 1927. Reprinted with a new introduction by B. M. Kloss as *Lavrentievskaia*. Moscow: Iazyki slavianskikh kultur, 1997.

Wace. *Le Roman de Rou de Wace*. Edited by A. J. Holden. Paris: Éditions A. and J. Picard, 1973.

William of Malmesbury. *Gesta Regum Anglorum: The History of the English Kings*. Edited and translated by R. A. B. Mynors, R. M. Thomson, and M. Winterbottom. 2 vols. Oxford: Clarendon Press, 1998.

———. *Historia Novella: The Contemporary History*. Edited by Edmund King, translated by K. R. Potter. Oxford: Clarendon Press, 1998.

William of Newburgh. *Historia Rerum Anglicarum Willelmi Parvi, Ordinis Sancti Augustini Canonici Regularis in Coenobio Beatae Mariae de Newburgh in Agro Eboracensi*. Edited by Hans Claude Hamilton. English Historical Society Publications 15. London: Sumptibus societatis, 1856.

Secondary Sources

Alekseev, A. A. "Koe-chto o perevodakh v Drevnei Pusi (po povodu stati Fr. Dzh. Tomsona 'Made in Russia')." *Trudy Otdela drevnerusski literatury* 49 (1999): 278–95.

———. "Po povodu stati G. G. Lanta 'Eshcho raz o mnimykh perevodakh v Drevnei Rusi.'" *Trudy Otdela drevnerusski literatury* 51 (1991): 442–45.

Alekseev, L. V. *Smolenskaia zemlia v IX–XIII vv. Ocherki istorii Smolenshchiny i Vostochnoi Belorussii*. Moscow: Nauka, 1980.

Althoff, Gerd. *Family, Friends, and Followers: Political and Social Bonds in Medieval Europe*. Translated by Christopher Carroll. New York: Cambridge University Press, 2004.

———. *Spielregeln der Politik im Mittelalter. Kommunikation in Frieden und Fehde*. Darmstadt: Primus, 1997.

Androshchuk, Fedir. "The Vikings in the East." In *The Viking World*, edited by Stefan Brink and Neil Price, 496–516. New York: Routledge, 2008.

Anglo-Norman Dictionary. Available as electronic text at www.anglo-norman.net/gate/.

Ashe, Laura. "The Anomalous King of Conquered England." In *Every Inch a King. Comparative Studies on Kings and Kingship in the Ancient and Medieval Worlds*, edited by Lynette Mitchell and Charles Melville, 174–94. Leiden: Brill, 2012.

———. *Fiction and History in England, 1066–1200*. Cambridge Studies in Medieval Literature 68. New York: Cambridge University Press, 2007.

Avanesov R. I., I. S. Ulukhanov, and V. B. Krysko, eds. *Slovar drevnerusskogo iazyka (XI–XIV vv.)*. 11 vols. Moscow: Russkii iazyk, 1988–2016.

Bachrach, B. S. "'Potius Rex quam Dux putabatur': Some Observations Concerning Adémar of Chabannes' Panegyric on Duke William the Great." *The Haskins Society Journal* 1 (1989): 11–21.

Bagge, Sverre and Sæbjørg Walaker Nordeide. "The Kingdom of Norway." In *Christianization and the Rise of Christian Monarchy: Scandinavia, Central Europe and Rus' c. 900–1200*, edited by Nora Berend, 121–66. New York: Cambridge University Press, 2007.

Bagge, Sverre, Michael H. Gelting, and Thomas Lindkvist, eds. *Feudalism: New Landscapes of Debate*. Turnhout: Brepols, 2011.

Baker, John, Stuart Brookes, and Andrew Reynolds, eds. *Landscapes of Defence in Early Medieval Europe*. Turnhout: Brepols, 2013.

Baldwin, John. "Crown and Government." In *The New Cambridge Medieval History*, edited by David Luscombe and Jonathan Riley-Smith, 510–29. Vol. 4. Cambridge: Cambridge University Press, 2004.

Barrière, Bernadette. *Limousin médiéval: Le temps des créations. Occupation du sol, monde laïc, espace cistercien. Recueil d'articles*. Limoges: Presses universitaires de Limoge, 2006.

Barthélemy, Dominique. "Autour d'un récit de pactes ('Conventum Hugonis'): La Seigneurie châtelaine et le féodalisme, en France au XIe siècle." *Settimane di studio/Centro Italiano di studi sull' Alto Medioevo* 47 (2000): 447–96.

——. "Une crise de l'écrit? Observations sur des actes de Saint-Aubin d'Angers (XIe siècle)." *Bibliothèque de l'École des chartes* 155 (1997): 95–117.

——. "Note sur le titre seigneurial, en France, au XIè siècle." *Archivum Latinitatis Medii Aevi* (54) 1996: 131–58.

——. *The Serf, the Knight, and the Historian*. Translated by Graham Robert Edwards. Ithaca: Cornell University Press, 2009.

Barton, Richard E. *Lordship in the County of Maine, c.890–1160*. Woodbridge: Boydell Press, 2004.

Bauduin, Pierre, and Alexander Musin, eds. *Vers l'Orient et vers l'Occident: Regards croisés sur les dynamiques et les transferts culturels des Vikings à la Rous ancienne*. Caen: Presses universitaires de Caen, 2014.

Bennett, Philip E. "La Chronique de Jordan Fantosme: épique et public lettré au XIIe siècle." *Cahiers de civilisation médiévale* 40 (1997): 37–56.

Berend, Nora, Przemysław Urbańczyk, and Przemysław Wiszewski. *Central Europe in the High Middle Ages: Bohemia, Hungary and Poland, c.900–c.1300*. Cambridge: Cambridge University Press, 2013.

Berezhkov, N. G. *Khronologiia russkogo letopisaniia*. Moscow: Izdatelstvo Akademii nauk SSSR, 1963.

Birnbaum, Henrik. *Aspects of the Slavic Middle Ages and Slavic Renaissance Culture*. New York: Peter Lang, 1992.

Bisson, Thomas. *The Crisis of the Twelfth Century: Power, Lordship, and the Origins of European Government*. Princeton: Princeton University Press, 2009.

—. "The 'Feudal Revolution'." *Past and Present* 142 (1994): 6–42.
Bloch, Marc. *Feudal Society*. Translated by L. A. Manyon. Chicago: University of Chicago Press, 1961.
Bogatova G. A., S. G. Barhudarov, G. A. Bogatova, F. P. Filin, V. B. Krysko, and D. N. Shmelev, eds. *Slovar Russkogo iazyka XI—XVII vv.* 26 vols. Moscow: Nauka, 1975–present.
Bourchard, Constance Brittain. "The Kingdom of the Franks to 1108." In *The New Cambridge Medieval History*, edited by David Luscombe and Jonathan Riley-Smith, 120–53. Vol. 4. Pt. 2. Cambridge: Cambridge University Press, 2004.
Brandt, William J. *The Shape of Medieval History: Studies in Modes of Perception*. New Haven: Yale University Press, 1966.
Brink, Stefan, and Neil Price. *The Viking World*. Abingdon: Routledge, 2009.
Brown, Elizabeth A. R. Review of *Feudalism: New Landscapes of Debate*, edited by Sverre Bagge, Michael H. Gelting, and Thomas Lindkvist. *The Medieval Review* 6 (2012). Available as electronic text at https://scholarworks.iu.edu/dspace/bitstream/handle/2022/14548/12.06.10.html?sequence=1
——. "The Tyranny of a Construct: Feudalism and Historians of Medieval Europe." *American Historical Review* 79 (1974): 1063–88.
Brown, Reginald Allen. *English Castles*. Woodbridge: Boydell Press, 1976.
Brown, Warren C., and Piotr Gorecki, eds. *Conflict in Medieval Europe: Changing Perspectives on Society and Culture*. Burlington: Ashgate, 2003.
Bugoslavskii, Sergei. *Tekstologiia Drevnei Rusi*. Moscow: Iazyki slavianskikh kultur, 2006.
Bulanin, D. M. *Antichnye traditsii v drevnerusskoi literature XI–XVI vv.* Slavistische Beiträge 278. Munich: Otto Sagner, 1991.
Butler, Francis. *Enlightener of Rus': The Image of Vladimir Sviatoslavich across the Centuries*. Bloomington: Slavica, 2002.
Butler, Francis. "Ol'Ga's Conversion and the Construction of Chronicle Narrative." *Russian Review* 67 (2008): 230–42.
Bur, Michel. "The Seigneuries." In *The New Cambridge Medieval History*, edited by David Luscombe and Jonathan Riley-Smith, 530–48. Vol. 4. Pt. 2. Cambridge: Cambridge University Press, 2004.
Canning, Joseph. *A History of Medieval Political Thought: 300–1450*. New York: Routledge, 2005.
Cawley, Charles. *Medieval Lands: A Prosopography of Medieval European Noble and Royal Families*, at http://fmg.ac/Projects/MedLands/index.htm
Cherepnin, L. V. *Novgorodskie berestianye gramoty kak istoricheskii istochnik*. Moscow: Nauka, 1969.
——. "Rus: Spornye voprosy istorii feodalnoi zemelnoi sobstvennosti v IX–XV vv." In *Puti razvitiia feodalisma*, edited by A. P. Novoseltsev, V. T. Pashuto, and L. V. Cherepnin. 126–251. Moscow: Nauka, 1972.
Cheyette, Fredric L. "'Feudalism': A Memoir and an Assessment." In *Feud, Violence and Practice: Essays in Medieval Studies in Honor of Stephen D. White*, edited by Belle S. Tuten and Tracey L. Billado, 119–34. Burlington: Ashgate, 2010.
——. "Georges Duby's Mâconnais after Fifty Years: Reading It Then and Now." *Journal of Medieval History* 28 (2002): 291–317.

———. Review of *La féodalité languedocienne aux XI–XII siécles: serments, sommages et fiefs dans le Languedoc des Trencavel* by Hélène Débax, *The Medieval Review* 12 (2004), at https://scholarworks.iu.edu/dspace/bitstream/handle/2022/5661/04.12.14.html?sequence=1.

Cheyette, Fredric, and Howell Chickering. "Love, Anger, and Peace: Social Practice and Poetic Play in the Ending of *Yvain*." *Speculum* 80 (2005): 75–117.

Clanchy, M. T. *England and Its Rulers: 1066–1307*. 3rd ed. Malden: Blackwell, 2006.

Coulson, Charles L. H. *Castles in Medieval Society: Fortresses in England, France, and Ireland in the Central Middle Ages*. Oxford: Oxford University Press, 2003.

Creighton, O. H. *Castles and Landscapes*. New York: Continuum, 2002.

Cursente, Benoît. "Entre parenté et fidélité: les 'amis' dans la Gascogne des XIe et XIIe siècles." In *Les sociétés méridionales à l'âge féodal: Espagne, Italie et sud de la France, Xe–XIIIe s.: Hommage à Pierre Bonnasie*, edited by Hélène Débax, 285–92. Toulouse: Editions Méridiennes, 1999.

Damian-Grint, Peter. *The New Historians of the Twelfth-Century Renaissance: Inventing Vernacular Authority*. New York: Boydell Press, 1999.

Davies, Rees. "The Medieval State: The Tyranny of a Concept?" *Journal of Historical Sociology* 16 (2003): 280–300.

Débax, Hélène. *La féodalité languedocienne aux XIe–XIIe siècles: serments, sommages et fiefs dans le Languedoc des Trencavel*. Toulouse: Presses universitaires du Mirail, 2003.

———. *La seigneurie collective: Pairs, pariers, paratge, les coseigneurs du XIe au XIIe siècle*. Rennes: Presses Universitaires de Rennes, 2012.

———. "L'aristocratie languedocienne et la société féodale." In *Feudalism: New Landscapes of Debate*, edited by Sverre Bagge, Michael H. Gelting, and Thomas Lindkvist. Turnhout: Brepols, 2011.

Dendorfer, Jürgen, and Roman Deutinger, eds. *Das Lehnswesen im Hochmittelalter. Forschungskonstrukte—Quellenbefunde—Deutungsrelevanz*. Ostfildern: Thorbecke, 2010.

Dimnik, Martin. *The Dynasty of Chernigov, 1146–1246*. Cambridge: Cambridge University Press, 2003.

———. "The Title "Grand Prince" in Kievan Rus'." *Mediaeval Studies* 66 (2004): 253–312.

Dubrovskii, I. V., P. Iu. Uvarov, A. Iu. Sogomonov, and A. L. Iastrebitskaia. *Konstruirivanie sotsialnogo. Evropa. V–XVI vv*. Moscow: Editorial URSS, 2001.

Duffy, Seán. "Henry II and England's Insular Neighbours." In *Henry II: New Interpretations*, edited by Christopher Harper-Bill and Nicholas Vincent, 129–53. Woodbridge: Boydell Press, 2007.

Duby, Georges. *The Chivalrous Society*. Translated by Cynthia Postan. Los Angeles: University of California Press, 1977.

———. *La société aux XIe et XIIe siècles dans la région mâconnaise*. 2nd ed. Paris: Éditions de l'École des hautes études en sciences sociales, 1971. First published in 1953, reprinted in 1988.

Dunphy, Graeme. "Historical Writing in and after the Old High German Period." In *German Literature of the Early Middle Ages*, edited by Brian Murdock, 201–26. Camden House History of German Literature 2. Camden: Boydell and Brewer, 2004.

———. "On the Function of the Disputations in the *Kaiserchronik*." *The Medieval Chronicle* 5 (2009): 77–86.
Everard, J. A. *Brittany and the Angevins: Province and Empire 1158-1203*. Cambridge: Cambridge University Press, 2000.
Field, Sean L. "Torture and Confession in the Templar Interrogations at Caen, 28-29 October 1307." *Speculum: A Journal of Medieval Studies* 91 (2016): 297–327.
Fouracre, Paul. "The Use of the Term Beneficium in Frankish sources: A Society Based on Favours?" In *The Languages of Gift in the Early Middle Ages*, edited by Wendy Davies, 62–88. Cambridge: Cambridge University Press, 2010.
Franklin, Simon. "Literacy and Documentation in Early Medieval Russia." *Speculum* 60 (1985): 1–38.
———. "On Meanings, Function and Paradigms of Law in Early Rus'." *Russian History/Histoire Russe* 34 (2007): 63–81.
———. "Po povodu 'Intellektualnogo molchaniia' Drevnei Rusi (o sbornike trudov F. J. Tomsona)." *Russia Mediaevalis* 10 (2001): 262–70.
———. *Sermons and Rhetoric of Kievan Rus'*. Harvard Library of Early Ukrainian Literature, Translation Series 5. Cambridge, MA: Harvard University Press, 1991.
———. "Some Apocryphal Sources of Kievan Rus Historiography." *Oxford Slavonic Papers* 15 (1982): 3–27.
———. *Writing, Society and Culture in Early Rus, c. 950-1300*. Cambridge: Cambridge University Press, 2002.
Franklin, Simon and Jonathan Shepard. *The Emergence of Rus, 750-1200*. New York: Longman, 1996.
Froianov, I. Ia. *Kievskaia Rus*. Leningrad: Izdatelstvo Leningradskogo Universiteta, 1980.
———. *Rabstvo i dannichestvo u vostochnykh slavian: VI–X vv*. St. Petersburg: Izdatelstvo Sankt-Peterburgskogo Universiteta, 1996.
Galkova, I. G., ed. *Feodalizm: poniatie i realii*. Moscow: Institut vseobshchei istorii RAN, 2008.
Galloway, Andrew. "Writing History in England." In *The Cambridge History of Medieval English Literature*, edited by David Wallace, 255–83. Cambridge: Cambridge University Press, 1999.
García de la Puente, Inés. "The Indo-European Heritage in the *Povest' Vremennykh Let*." In *Papers of the First Biennial Conference of the Association for the Study of Eastern Christian History and Culture*, edited by Russell E. Martin and Jennifer B. Spock, 49–62. Columbus: Ohio State University Press, 2009.
———. "The Revenge of the Princess: Some Considerations about Heroines in the PVL and in Other Indo-European Literatures." In *Medieval Slavonic Studies: New Perspectives for Research*, edited by Juan Antonio Alvarez-Pedroza and Susana Torres Prieto, 193–204. Paris: Institut d'études slaves, 2009.
Garnier, Claudia. *Amicus amicis, inimicus inimicis: Politische Freundschaft und fürstliche Netzwerke im 13. Jahrhundert*. Monographien zur Geschichte des Mittelalters 46. Stuttgart: Anton Hiersemann, 2000.
Gaunt, Simon, and Sarah Kay, eds. *The Cambridge Companion to Medieval French Literature*. Cambridge: Cambridge University Press, 2008.

Gelting, Michael H. "The Kingdom of Denmark." In *Christianization and the Rise of Christian Monarchy: Scandinavia, Central Europe and Rus' c. 900–1200*, edited by Nora Berend, 73–120. New York: Cambridge University Press, 2007.

Gimon, T. V. "Drevnerusskie sudebnye dokumenty XIII-XIV vekov." In *Pismo i povsednevnost*, edited by A. O. Chubarian, 18–48. Moscow: IVI RAN, 2016.

Gippius, A. A. "Galitskie akty XIII v. iz tserkvi sv. Panteleimona." In *Pismennost Galitsko-Volynskogo kniazhestva: Istoriko-filologicheskie issledovania*, edited by Jitka Komendová, 49–64. Olomouc: Univerzita Palakeho v Olomouci, 2016.

Given-Wilson, Chris. *Chronicles: The Writing of History in Medieval England*. New York: Hambledon, 2004.

Goetz, Hans-Werner. "The Perception of 'Power' and 'State' in the Early Middle Ages: The Case of the Astronomer's 'Life of Louis the Pious'." In *Representations of Power in Medieval Germany: 800–1500*, edited by Björn Weiler and Simon MacLean, 15–36. Turnhout: Brepols, 2006.

Goldstein, R. James. *The Matter of Scotland: Historical Narrative in Medieval Scotland*. Lincoln: University of Nebraska Press, 1993.

Gorskii, A. A. *Drevnerusskaia Druzhina*. Moscow: Prometei, 1989.

———. "Ob evoliutsii titulatury verkhovnogo pravitelia Drevnei Rusi (domongloskii period)." In *Rimsko-Konstantinopolskoe nasledie na Rusi: Ideia vlasti i politicheskaia praktika. IX Mezhdunarodnyi seminar istoricheskikh issledovanii "Ot Rima k Tret'emy Rimu," Moskva, 1989*, edited by A. N., Sakharov, 97–102. Moscow: Rossiiskaia akademiia nauk, Institut Rossiiskoi istorii, 1995.

———. "O 'feodalizme': 'russkom' i ne tolko." *Srednie veka* 69 (2008): 9–26.

———. "Poniatie 'suzdalskii' v politicheskom leksikone XII–XIV vekov," 27–32. In *Na poroge tysiachetiletiia. Suzdal v istorii i culture Rossii: k 990-letiiu pervogo upominaniia Suzdalia v drevnerusskikh letopisiakh*, edited by M. E. Rodina. Vladimir: GVSMZ, 2015.

———. *Russkoe Srednevekov'e*. Moscow: Astrel, 2009.

———. "Zemli i volosti." In *Drevniaia Rus: Ocherki politicheskogo i sotsialnogo stroia*, edited by A. A. Gorskii, V. A. Kuchkin, P. V. Lukin, and P. S. Stefanovich, 9–32. Moscow: Indrik, 2008.

Gurevich, A. J. *Categories of Medieval Culture*. Translated by G. L. Campbell. Boston: Routledge and Kegan Paul, 1985.

Halbach, Uwe. *Der russische Fürstenhof vor dem 16. Jahrhundert: Eine vergleichende Untersuchung zur politischen Lexikologie und Verfassungsgeschichte der alten Rus'*. Stuttgart: Steiner, 1985.

Hallam, Elizabeth M., and Judith Everard. *Capetian France: 987–1328*. 2nd ed. Harlow: Pearson Education, 2001.

Halperin, Charles. "Novgorod and the 'Novgorodian Land'." *Cahiers du monde russe* 40 (1999): 345–63.

Harper-Bill, Christopher, and Nicholas Vincent, eds. *Henry II: New Interpretations*. Woodbridge: Boydell, 2007.

Heirbaut, Dirk. "Not European Feudalism, But Flemish Feudalism: A New Reading of Galbert of Bruges's Data on Feudalism in the Context of Early Twelfth-Century Flanders." In *Galbert of Bruges and the Historiography of Medieval Flanders*, edited by

Jeff Rider and Alan V. Murray, 56–88. Washington, DC: Catholic University of America Press, 2009.

Helmerichs, Robert. "Princeps, Comes, Dux Normannorum: Early Rollonid Designators and their Significance." *Haskins Society Journal* 9 (1997): 57–77.

Hill, John. *The Anglo-Saxon Warrior Ethic: Reconstructing Lordship in Early English Literature*. Gainesville: University Press of Florida, 2000.

Hosking, Geoffrey. *Russia and the Russians: A History*. 2nd ed. Cambridge, MA: Belknap Press, 2011.

Hrushevskyi, Mykhailo. *Istoriia Ukrainy-Rusi*. Lviv: Naukovo Tovaristvo imeni Shevchnka, 1905.

———. *Khronologiia podii Galitsko-Volynskogo litopisu*. Lviv: Zapiski Naukovogo tovaristva imeni Shevchenka, 1901.

Hyams, Paul R. "Homage and Feudalism: A Judicious Separation." In *Die Gegenwart des Feudalismus/Présence du féodalisme et présent de la féodalité/The Presence of Feudalism*, edited by Natalie Fyrde, Pierre Monnet, and Otto Gerhard Oexle, 13–50. Veröffentlichungen des Max-Planck-Instituts für Geschichte 173. Göttingen: Vandenhoeck and Ruprecht, 2002.

———. Introduction to the *Agreement between Count William V of Aquitaine and Hugh IV of Lusignan*, at www.fordham.edu/halsall/source/agreement.asp

———. "Was There Really Such a Thing as Feud in the High Middle Ages?" In *Vengeance in the Middle Ages: Emotion, Religion and Feud*, edited by Susanna A. Throop and Paul R. Hyams, 151–75. Farnham: Ashgate, 2010.

Ianin, V. L. *Denezhno-vesovye sistemy russkogo srednevekovia: Domongolskii period*. Moscow: Nauka, 1956.

———. *Ia poslal tebe berestu*. Moscow: Izdatelstvo MGU, 1975.

Ianin, V. L. and A. A. Zalizniak. *Novgorodskie gramoty na bereste: iz raskopok 1990–1996. Paleografiia berestianykh gramot i ikh vnestratigraficheskoe datirovanie*. Moscow: Nauka, 2000.

Iasnovska, Liudmila. "Davnioruski starozhitnosti Novgorod-Siverskogo Podesennia." *Siverianskyi litopys: vseukrainskyi naukovyi zhurnal* 11 (2005): 9–26.

Ingham, Norman W. "Genre characteristic of the Kievan Lives of Princes in Slavic and European Perspective." In *American Contributions to the Ninth International Congress of Slavists (Kiev, September 1983)*, edited by P. Debreczeny, 223–38. Vol. 2: *Literature, Poetics, History*. Columbus: Slavica, 1983.

———. "The Martyred Princes and the Question of Slavic Cultural Continuity in the Early Middle Ages." In *Medieval Russian Culture*, edited by Henrik Birnbaum and Micahel Flier, 31–53. Vol. 1. California Slavic Studies 12. Berkeley: University of California Press, 1984.

———. "The Sovereign as Martyr, East and West." *The Slavic and East European Journal* 17 (1973): 1–17.

Innes, Matthew. *State and Society in the Early Middle Ages: The Middle Rhine Valley, 400–1000*. Cambridge: Cambridge University Press, 2006.

Inokov, A. A. "Vsevolod Olgovich—poslednii obedinitel domongolskoi Rusi." *Istoricheskoe obozrenie* 12 (2011): 23–57.

Jarrett, Jonathan, and Allan Scott McKinley, eds. *Problems and Possibilities of Early Medieval Charters*. Turnhout: Brepols, 2013.

Jesse, W. Scott. *Robert the Burgundian and the Counts of Anjou, ca. 1025–1098*. Washington, DC: Catholic University of America Press, 2000.

Jones, George Fenwick. *The Ethos of the Song of Roland*. Baltimore: Johns Hopkins University Press, 1963.

Jordan, William Chester. *Europe in the High Middle Ages*. New York: Penguin Books, 2004.

———. " 'Europe' in the Middle Ages." In *The Idea of Europe: From Antiquity to the European Union*, edited by Anthony Pagden. New York: Cambridge University Press, 2002.

Kafengauz, B. B. "Zametki o novgorodskikh berestianykh gramotakh." *Istoriia SSSR* 1 (1960): 168–74.

Kaiser, Daniel H. *The Growth of the Law in Medieval Russia*. Princeton: Princeton University Press, 1980.

Karamzin, N. M. *Istoriia gosudarstva rossiiskogo v dvenadtsati tomakh*. Moscow: Nauka, 1989.

———. *Letters of a Russian Traveler*. Translated by Anderw Kahn and Jonathan Mallinson. Oxford: Voltaire Foundation, 2003.

King, David. *Castellarium Anglicanum*. Millwood: Kraus International Publishing, 1983.

Kobylin, Igor. *Fenomen totalitarizma v kontekste evropeiskoi kultury*. Available as electronic text at www.dslib.net/religio-vedenie/fenomen-totalitarizma-v-kontekste-evropejskoj-kultury.html

Kollmann, Nancy Shields. *By Honor Bound: State and Society in Early Modern Russia*. Ithaca: Cornell University Press, 1999.

———. "Collateral Succession in Kievan Rus'." *Harvard Ukrainian Studies* 14 (1990): 377–88.

Koniavskaia, E. L. "Letopisnye 'rostovtsy', 'suzdaltsy' i 'vladimirtsy' vo vremia Iuriia Dolgorukogo i Andreia Bogoliubskogo." *Drevniaia Rus: Voprosy medievistiki* 58 (2014): 37–44.

———. "Suzdalskaia zemlia ot Iuriia Dolgorukogo do Aleksandra Nevskogo (po rannim pismennym istochnikam." In *Na poroge tysiachetiletiia. Suzdal v istorii i culture Rossii: k 990-letiiu pervogo upominaniia Suzdalia v drevnerusskikh letopisiakh*, edited by M. E. Rodina, 27–32. Vladimir: GBSMHZ, 2015.

Kosto, Adam J. *Making Agreements in Medieval Catalonia: Power, Order, and the Written Word, 1000–1200*. Cambridge: Cambridge University Press, 2007.

Kotliar, N. F. "K voprosu o prichinakh udelnoi razdroblennosti na Rusi." *Drevniaia Rus: Voprosy Medievistiki* 43 (2011): 5–17.

———. "Nastuplenie udelnoi razdroblennosti na Rusi (kniazia-izgoi)." *Ruthenica* 10 (2011): 69–77.

Koval, V. Iu. "Malye goroda: neulovimaia kategoriia." Forthcoming.

Kovalenko, V. P., and R. S. Orlov, "Raboty Novgorod-Severskoi ekspeditsii." In *Archeologicheskie otkrytiia 1979 goda*, edited by B. A. Rybakov, 281–83. Moscow: Nauka, 1980.

Kuchkin, V. A. *Formirovanie gosudarstvennoi territorii severo-vostochnoi Rusi v X–XIV vv*. Moscow: Nauka, 1984.

———. "'Russkaia zemlia' po letopisnym dannym XI–pervoi treti XIII v." In *Drevneishie gosudarstva Vostochnoi Evropy: Materialy i issledovaniia, 1992–1993 gody*, edited by A. P. Novoseltsev, 74–100. Moscow: Nauka, 1995.

Kuza, A. V. *Malye goroda Drevnei Rusi*. Moscow: Nauka, 1989.

Kuzmin, A. G. *Kreshchenie Kievskoi Rusi*. Moscow: Algoritm, 2012.

Lavrenchenko, M. L. "'Priiateli' russkikh kniazei (po tekstam letopisei za XII vek)." *Slavianovedenie* 2 (2015): 96–108.

Le Goff, Jacques. *The Birth of Europe*. Translated by Janet Lloyd. Malden: Blackwell, 2005.

Lenhoff, Gail. *The Martyred Princes Boris and Gleb: A Sociocultural Study of the Cult and the Texts*. UCLA Slavic Studies 19. Columbus: Slavica, 1989.

Likhachev, D. S., ed. *Slovar knizhnikov i knizhnosti Drevnei Rusi (XI–XVI veka)*. St. Petersburg: Nauka, 1987–2004.

Lobban, Michael. "Sociology, History, and the 'Internal' Study of Law." In *Law, Society and Community: Socio-Legal Essays in Honour of Roger Cotterrel*, edited by Richard Nobles and David Schiff, 39–60. New York: Routledge, 2016.

Lodge, Anthony. "Literature and History in the Chronicle of Jordan Fantosme." *French Studies* 44 (1990): 257–70.

Lotman, Yu. M. *Izbrannye statii*. 3 vols. Tallinn: Alexandra, 1993.

Lukin, P. V. *Novgorodskoe veche*. Moscow: Indrik, 2014.

———. "Veche: Sotsialnyi sostav." In *Drevniaia Rus: Ocherki politicheskogo i sotsialnogo stroia*, edited by A. A. Gorskii, V. A. Kuchkin, P. V. Lukin, and P. S. Stefanovich, 33–147. Moscow: Indrik, 2008.

Lunt, G. G. "Eshcho raz o mnimykh perevodakh v Drevnei Rusi (po povodu stati A. A. Alekseeva)." *Trudy Otdela drevnerusski literatury* 51 (1999): 435–41.

Luscombe, David, and Jonathan Riley-Smith, eds. *The New Cambridge Medieval History. Vol. 4, c.1024–c.1198*. Cambridge: Cambridge University Press, 2004.

Lyon, Jonathan R. *Princely Brothers and Sisters: The Sibling Bond in German Politics, 1100–1250*. Ithaca: Cornell University Press, 2013.

Malegam, Jehangir. *The Sleep of Behemoth: Disputing Peace and Violence in Medieval Europe, 1000–1200*. Ithaca: Cornell University Press, 2013.

Manion, Lee. "Sovereign Recognition: Contesting Political Claims in the *Alliterative Morte Arthure* and *The Awntyrs off Arthur*." In *Law and Sovereignty in the Middle Ages and the Renaissance*, edited by R. S. Sturges, 69–91. Turnhout: Brepols, 2011.

Matthews, Alastair. *The "Kaiserchronik": A Medieval Narrative*. Oxford University Press, 2012.

Martin, Janet. *Medieval Russia, 980–1584*. 2nd ed. New York: Cambridge University Press, 2007.

———. *Treasure of the Land of Darkness: The Fur Trade and its Significance for Medieval Russia*. New York: Cambridge University Press, 2004.

Martindale, Jane. *Status, Authority and Regional Power: Aquitaine and France, 9th to 12th Centuries*, Variorum Collected Studies Series. Brookfield: Ashgate, 1997.

Mavrodin, V. M. *Narodnye vosstaniia v Kievskoi Rusi XI–XIII vv*. Moscow: Sotsekgiz, 1961.

Melnichuk, V. A. "Letopisanie dvukh vetvei dinastii Olgovichei v sostave Kievskogo svoda XII veka: tekst i kontekst." *Izvestiia Uralskogo federalnogo universiteta: Gumanitarnye nauki* 105 (2012): 170–79.

Mikhailova, Yulia. " 'He Sighed from His Heart and Began to Gather Soldiers': Emotions in Rusian Political Narratives." Forthcoming in *Studia Slavica et Balcanica Petropolitana*.

———. "O nekotorykh napravleniiakh v sovremennoi medievistike i ikh znachimosti dlia izucheniia Drevnei Rusi." In *Srednevekovia Rus* 12, edited by Anton Gorskii, 65–94. Moscow: Indrik, 2016.

Mikhailova, Yulia, and David Prestel. "Cross Kissing: Keeping One's Word in Twelfth-Century Rus." *Slavic Review* 70 (2011): 1–22.

Miliutenko, N. I. *Sviatye kniazia-mucheniki Boris i Gleb*. St. Petersburg: Izdatelstvo Olega Abyshko, 2006.

Morgunov, Iu. Iu. *Drevo-zamlianye ukrepleniia iuzhnoi Rusi X–XIII vekov*. Moscow: Nauka, 2009.

———. *Letopisnyi gorod Sneporod i ego okruga, X–XIII veka*. St. Petersburg: Institut Archeologii Rossiiskoi Akademii Nauk, 2012.

Nalivaiko, Dmitro. *Ochima Zakhodu: Retseptsiia Ukrainy v zakhidnoi Evropi XI–XVIII st.* Kiev: Osnovy, 1998.

Nasonov, A. N. *Istoriia russkogo letopisaniia XI–nachala XIII veka*. Moscow: Nauka, 1969.

———. *"Russkaia zemlia" i obrazovanie territorii drevnerusskogo gosudarstva: Istoriko-geograficheskoe issledovanie*. Moscow: Nauka, 1951.

Nazarenko, A. V. *Drevniaia Rus i slaviane*. Moscow: Universitet Dmitriia Pozharskogo, 2009.

———. *Drevniaia Rus na mezhdunarodnykh putiakh: Mezhdistsiplinarnye ocherki kulturnykh, torgovykh, politicheskikh sviazei IX–XII vekov*. Moscow: Iazyki russkoi kultury, 2001.

———. *Nemetskie latinoiazychnye istochniki IX–XI vekov: Teksty, perevod, kommentarii*. Moscow: Nauka, 1993.

———. "Nesostoiavshaiasia mitropolia (ob odnom iz tserkovno-politicheskikh proektov Andreia Bogoliubskogo)." In *"Khvalam dostoinyi …": Andrei Bogoliubskii v russkoi istorii i culture*, edited by M. E. Rodina, 12–35. Vladimir: GVSMZ, 2013.

———. "Poriadok prestolonaslediia na Rusi X–XII vv.: nasledstvennye razdely, seniorat i popytki designatsii (tipologicheskie nabliudeniia)." In *Iz istorii russkoi kultury*, 500–519, edited by V. Ia. Petrukhin. Vol. 1: *Drevniaia Rus*. Moscow: Iazyki russkoi kultury, 2000.

———. "Rodovoi siuzerinetet Rurikovichei nad Rus'iu (X–XI vv.)." In *Drevnie gosudarstva na territorii SSSR, 1985 god*, edited by A. P. Novoseltsev, 149–57. Moscow: Nauka, 1986.

Nelson, Janet L. "Kingship and Royal Government." In *The New Cambridge Medieval History*, edited by Rosamund McKitterick, 383–431. Vol. 2. New York: Cambridge University Press, 1995.

———. *Politics and Ritual in Early Medieval Europe*. Oxford: Hambledon, 1986.

———. "Rulers and Government." In *The New Cambridge Medieval History*, edited by Timothy Reuter. Vol. 3. Cambridge: Cambridge University Press, 1999.

Niermeyer, J. F. *Mediae Latinitatis Lexicon Minus*. Leiden: Brill, 1976.

Nikolskaia, T. N. *Zemlia viatichei: K istorii naseleniia basseina verkhnei i srednei Oki v IX–XIII vv.* Moscow: Nauka, 1981.
Noonan, Thomas. "The Monetary History of Kiev in the Pre-Mongolian Period." *Harvard Ukrainian Studies* 11 (1987): 383–443.
Nosov, E. N., V. M. Goriunova, and A. B. Plokhov, *Gorodishche pod Novgorodom i poseleniia Severnogo Priilmenia: Novye materialy i issledovaniia.* St. Petersburg: Dmitrii Bulanin, 2005.
Novoseltsev, A. P., ed. *Drevneishie gosudarstva Vostochnoi Evropy: Materialy i issledovaniia, 1992–1993 gody.* Moscow: Nauka, 1995.
Novoseltsev, A. P., V. T. Pashuto, and V. L. Cherepnin. *Drevnerusskoe gosudarstvo i ego mezhdunarodnoe znachenie.* Moscow: Nauka, 1965.
Obolensky, Dimitri. *The Byzantine Commonwealth: Eastern Europe, 500–1453.* New York: Praeger, 1971.
Oksanen, Eljas. *Flanders and the Anglo-Norman World, 1066–1216.* Cambridge: Cambridge University Press, 2012.
Ostrowski, Donald. "Identifying Psalmic Quotations in the PVL." In *The "Povest' vremennykh let": An Interlinear Collation and Paradosis*, edited by Donald Ostrowski, with David Birnbaum and Horace G. Lunt, 217–50. Harvard Library of Early Ukrainian Literature, Text Series 10. Cambridge, MA: Harvard University Press, 2003.
———. "Systems of Succession in Rus' and Steppe Societies." *Ruthenica* 11 (2012): 29–58.
Painter, Sidney. "Castellans of the Plain of Poitou in the Eleventh and Twelfth Centuries." *Speculum* 31 (1956): 243–57.
Pashuto, V. T. *Vneshniaia politika Drevnei Rusi.* Moscow: Nauka, 1968.
Patzold, Steffen. "Königserhebungen zwischen Erbrecht und Wahlrecht? Throngfolge und Rechtmentalität um das Jahr 1000." *Deutsches Archiv für Erforschung des des Mittelalters* 58 (2002): 467–501.
———. *Das Lehnswesen.* Munich: Beck, 2012.
Paul, Nicholas L. "The Chronicle of Fulk le Réchin: A Reassessment." *The Haskins Society Journal: Studies in Medieval History* 18 (2006): 19–35.
Pavlov-Silvanskii, N. P. *Feodalizm v udelnoi Rusi.* St. Petersburg: Tipografia M. M. Stasiulevicha, 1910. Reprinted in Russian Reprint Series 21. The Hague: Europe Printing, 1966.
Petrukhin, V. Ia. "Drevniaia Rus: Narod. Kniazia. Religiia." In *Iz istorii russkoi kultury*, edited by V. Ia. Petrukhin, 13–402. Vol. 1: *Drevniaia Rus.* Moscow: Iazyki russkoi kultury, 2000.
———. "Legenda of prizvanii variagov i Baltiiskii region." *Drevniaia Rus: Voprosy medievistiki* 32 (2008): 41–46.
Petrukhin, V. Ia. and T. A. Pushkina. "K predystorii Drevnerusskogo goroda." *Istoriia SSSR* 4 (1979): 100–112.
Plokhy, Serhii. *The Origins of the Slavic Nations: Premodern Identities in Russia, Ukraine, and Belarus.* Cambridge: Cambridge University Press, 2006.
Poe, Marshall T. *The Russian Moment in World History.* Princeton: Princeton University Press, 2003.

Poly, Jean-Pierre and Eric Bournazel. *The Feudal Transformation: 900–1200*. Translated by Caroline Higgitt. New York: Holmes and Meier, 1991.

——. *La mutation féodale, Xe–XIIe siècles*. Paris: Presses universitaires de France, 1980.

Prestel, David. "Plody providentia: iazycheskaia i sviashchennaia istoriia v Povesti vremennykh let." *Rossica Antiqua* 4 (2011): 23–42.

Priselkov, M. D. *Istoriia russkogo letopisaniia XI–XV vv*. Leningrad: Izdatelstvo Leningradskogo Gosudarstvennogo Universiteta, 1940.

Pritsak, Omeljan. *The Origins of Rus*. Cambridge, MA: Harvard University Press, 1981.

Raffensperger, Christian. *The Kingdom of Rus'*. Kalamazoo: Medieval Institute Publications, 2017.

——. *Reimagining Europe: Kievan Rus' in the Medieval World*. Harvard Historical Studies 177. Cambridge, MA: Harvard University Press, 2012.

Rapov, O. M. *Kniazhaskie vladeniia na Rusi v X—pervoi polovine XIII v*. Moscow: Izdatelstvo MGU, 1977.

Reuter, Timothy. "Debate: The 'Feudal Revolution' III." *Past and Present* 155 (1997): 177–95.

——. "The Medieval Nobility in Twentieth-Century Historiography." In *Companion to Historiography*, edited by Michael Bentley, 177–202. New York: Routledge, 2006.

——. *Medieval Polities and Modern Mentalities*. New York: Cambridge University Press, 2006.

Reynolds, Susan. *Fiefs and Vassals: The Medieval Evidence Reinterpreted*. New York: Oxford University Press, 1994.

——. "*Fiefs and Vassals* after Twelve Years." In *Feudalism: New Landscapes of Debate*, edited by Sverre Bagge, Michael H. Gelting, and Thomas Lindkvist, 15–26. Turnhout: Brepols, 2011.

——. "Government and Community." In *The New Cambridge Medieval History*, edited by David Luscombe and Jonathan Riley-Smith, 86–111. Vol. 4. Cambridge: Cambridge University Press, 2004.

——. *Kingdoms and Communities in Western Europe, 900–1300*. Oxford: Clarendon Press, 1984.

——. "There were States in Medieval Europe: A Response to Rees Davies." *Journal of Historical Sociology* 16 (2003): 550–55.

Riasanovsky, Nicholas V., and Mark D. Steinberg. *A History of Russia*. 8th ed. Oxford: Oxford University Press, 2010.

Roach, Levi. *Kingship and Consent in Anglo-Saxon England, 871–978*. Cambridge: Cambridge University Press, 2013.

——. "Submission and Homage: Feudo-Vassalic Relations and the Settlement of Disputes in Ottonian Germany." *History* 97 (2012): 356–57.

Rosenwein, Barbara, ed. *Anger's Past: The Social Uses of an Emotion in the Middle Ages*. Ithaca: Cornell University Press, 1998.

——. "Eros and Clio: Emotional Paradigms in Medieval Historiography." In *Mediävistik im 21. Jahrhundert; Stand und Perspektiven der internationalen und interdisziplinaren Mittelalterforschung*, edited by Hans-Werner Goetz and Jörg Jarnut, 427–41. Munich: Fink, 2003.

Rossignol, Sébastien. "Die Burgen der Slawen in der lateinischen Überlieferung des 9. bis 11. Jahrhunderts." In *Siedlungsstrukturen und Burgenim westslawischen Raum. Beiträge der Sektion zur slawischen Frühgeschichteder 17. Jahrestagung des Mittel- und OstdeutschenVerbandes für Altertumsforschungin Halle an der Saale, 19. bis 21. März 2007*, edited by Felix Biermann, Thomas Kersting, and Anne Klammt, 31–38. Langenweissbach: Beier and Beran, 2009.

———. "*Civitas* in Early Medieval Central Europe—Stronghold or District?" *Medieval History Journal* 14 (2011): 71–99.

Rubel, Alexander. "Caesar und Karl der Große in der Kaiserchronik. Typologische Struktur und die translatio imperii ad Francos." *Antike und Abendland* 47 (2001): 146–63.

Ryan, Magnus. "The Oath of Fealty and the Lawyers." In *Political Thought and the Realities of Power in the Middle Ages*, edited by Joseph Canning and Otto Gerhard Oexle, 211–28. Veröffentlichungen des Max-Planck-Instituts für Geschichte, 147. Göttingen: Vandenhoeck and Ruprecht, 1998.

Sakharov, A. N., V. V. Fomin, N. N. Ilina, A. G. Kuzmin, L. P. Grot, and S. V. Perevezentsev. *Izgnanie normannov is russkoi istorii*. Moscow: Russkaia panorama, 2010.

Sawyer, Birgit and Peter Sawyer. *Medieval Scandinavia: From Conversion to Reformation, Circa 800–1500*. Minneapolis: University of Minnesota Press, 1993.

Sawyer, Peter. "Scandinavia in the Eleventh and Twelfth Centuries." In *The New Cambridge Medieval History*, edited by David Luscombe and Jonathan Riley-Smith, 290–303. Vol. 4. Cambridge: Cambridge University Press, 1999.

Sedov, V. V. "Nekotorye voprosy geografii Smolenskoi zemli (po materialam ekspeditsii 1960 g.)." *Kratkie soobshcheniia Instituta arkheologii* 90 (1962): 12–23.

———. *Selskie poseleniia tsentralnykh raionov Smolenskoi zemli (VIII–XV vv.)*. Materialy i issledovaniia po arkheologii SSSR 92. Moscow: Izdatelstvo Akademii Nauk SSSR, 1960.

Shchapov, Ia. N., ed. *Pismennye pamiatniki istorii Drevnei Rusi: letopisi, povesti, khozhdeniia, poucheniia, zhitiia, poslaniia: annotirovannyi katalog-spravochnik*. St. Petersburg: Russko-Baltiiskii informatsionnyi tsentr "BLITS," 2003.

Shepard, Jonathan. "Adventus, Arrivistes and Rites of Rulership in Byzantium and France in the Tenth and Eleventh Century." In *Court Ceremonies and Rituals of Power in Byzantium and the Medieval Mediterranean*, edited by Alexander Beihammer, Stavroula Constantinou, and Maria Parani, 337–71. Leiden: Brill, 2013.

———. "Crowns from the Basileus, Crowns from Heaven." In *Byzantium, New Peoples, New Powers: The Byzantino-Slav Contact Zone*, edited by Miliana Kaĭmakamova, Maciej Salamon, and Małgorzata Smorąg Różyck, 139–59. Cracow: Towarzystwo Wydawnicze Historia Iagellonica, 2007.

———. "Orthodoxy and Northern Peoples: Goods, Gods and Guidelines." In *A Companion to Byzantium*, edited by Liz James, 171–86. Malden: Wiley-Blackwell, 2010.

———. "Rus'." In *Christianization and the Rise of Christian Monarchy: Scandinavia, Central Europe and Rus' c.900–1200*, edited by Nora Berend, 369–416. New York: Cambridge University Press, 2007.

———. "Slav Christianities, 800-1100." In *The Cambridge History of Christianity. Vol. 3. Early Medieval Christianities, c.600–c.1100*, edited by Thomas F. X. Noble and Julia M. H. Smith, 130-58. Cambridge: Cambridge University Press, 2008.

———. "The Viking Rus and Byzantium." In *The Viking World*, edited by Stefan Brink and Neil Price, 496–516. New York: Routledge, 2008.

Simpson, James R. "Feudalism and Kingship." In *The Cambridge Companion to Medieval French Literature*, edited by Simon Gaunt and Sarah Kay, 197–209. Cambridge: Cambridge University Press, 2008.

Soloviev, S. M. *Sochinenia*, Moscow: Golos, 1993–98.

Starodubtsev, G. Iu. "Gochevskii kompleks (letopisnyi Rimov)–gorod XI–XIV vv. na iugo-vostoke Rusi." *Sumska Starovina* 26–27 (2009): 166–71.

Stefanovich, P. S. *Boiare, otroki, druzhiny: Voenno-politicheskaia elita Rusi v X–XI vv.* Moscow: Indrik, 2012.

———. "Boiarstvo i tserkov v domongolskoi Rusi." *Voprosy istorii* 7 (2002): 41–59.

———. "'Bolshaia druzhina' v Drevnei Rusi." *Srednie veka: Issledovaniia po istorii Srednevekovia i rannego Novogo vremeni* 73 (2011): 27–57.

———. "Drevnerusskoe poniatie chesti po pamiatnikam literatury domongolskoi Rusi." *Drevniaia Rus: Voprosy medievistiki* 15 (2004): 63–87.

———. "Der Eid des Adels gegenüber dem Herrscher im mittelalterlichen Russland." *Jahrbücher für Geschichte Osteuropas* 53 (2005): 497–505.

———. "Kniaz i boiare: kliatva vernosti i pravo otezda." In *Drevniaia Rus: Ocherki politicheskogo i sotsialnogo stroia*, edited by A. A. Gorskii, V. A. Kuchkin, P. V. Lukin, and P. S. Stefanovich, 148–269. Moscow: Indrik, 2008.

———. "Krestotselovanie i otnoshenie k nemu tserkvi v Drevnei Rusi." In *Srednevekovaia Rus* 5, edited by A. A. Gorskii, 86–113. Moscow: Indrik, 2004.

———. "Poliudie po letopisnym dannym 1154–1200 g." *Drevniaia Rus: Voprosy medievistiki* 62 (2015): 97–103.

———. "'Vernost' v otnosheniiakh kniazia i druzhiny na Rusi XII–XIII v." *Drevniaia Rus: Voprosy medievistiki* 37 (2009): 72–82.

Strakhova, Olga B. Review of *The Reception of Byzantine Culture in Mediaeval Russia* by F. J. Thomson. *Russia Mediaevalis* 10 (2001): 245–61.

Sverdlov, M. B. *Domongolskaia Rus: Kniazia i kniazheskaia vlast' na Rusi VI–pervoi treti XIII vv*. St. Petersburg: Akademicheskii proekt, 2003.

Thomson, Francis J. "'Made in Russia.' A Survey of the Translations Allegedly Made in Kievan Russia." In *Millenium Russiae Christianae: Tausend Jahre Christliches Russland*, edited by Gerhard Birkfellner, 295–354. Cologne: Bőhlau, 1993.

———. *The Reception of Byzantine Culture in Mediaeval Russia*. Brookfield: Ashgate, 1999.

Tikhomirov, M. N. *Krestianskie i gorodskie vosstaniia na Rusi X–XIII vv*. Moscow: Gosudarstvennoe izdatelstvo politicheskoi literatury, 1955.

Tolochko, O. "Notes on the *Radziwiłł Codex*." *Studi Slavistici* 10 (2013): 29–42.

Tolochko, P. P. *Kniaz' v Drevnei Rusi: vlast', sobstvennost', ideologiia*. Kiev: Naukova dumka, 1992.

———. *Russkie letopisi i letopistsy X–XII vv*. St. Petersburg: Aleteia, 2003.

Tolstoy, A. K. *Sobranie sochinenii*. Moscow: Izdatelstvo khudozhestvennoi literatury, 1963.
Tvorogov, O. V. *Drevniaia Rus: Sobytiia i liudi*. St. Petersburg: Nauka, 1994.
Uspenskii, B. A. *Iazykovaia situatsia Kievskoi Rusi i ee znachenie dlia istorii russkogo literaturnogo iazyka*. Moscow: Nauka, 1983.
Van Eickels, Klaus. "'Homagium' and 'Amicitia': Rituals of Peace and their Significance in the Anglo-French Negotiations of the Twelfth Century." *Francia* 24 (1997): 133–40.
Vediushkina, I. V. "'Rus' i 'Russkaia zemlia' v Povesti vremennykh let i letopisnykh statiiakh vtoroi treti XII—pervoi treti XIII v." In *Drevneishie gosudarstva Vostochnoi Evropy: Materialy i issledovaniia, 1992-1993 gody*, edited by A. P. Novoseltsev, 101–16. Moscow: Nauka, 1995.
Venckeleer, Theo. "Faut-il traduire VASSAL par vassal?" In *Mélanges de linguistique, de littérature et de philologie médiévales, offert à J. R. Smeets*, edited by Q. I. M. Mok, J. R. Smeets, Ina Spiele, and P. E. R. Verhuyck, 303–16. Leiden: Université de Leiden, 1982.
Verbruggen, J. F. "Note sur le sens des mots castrum, castellum, et quelques autres expressions qui désignent des fortifications." *Revue belge de philologie et d'histoire* 28 (1950): 147–55.
Vernadsky, George. *Kievan Russia*. New Haven: Yale University Press, 1948, reprinted 1972.
Vilkul, T. L. "O proiskhozhdenii obshchego teksta Ipatevskoi i Lavrentevskoi letopisi za XII vek (predvaritelnye zametki)." *Palaeoslavica* 13 (2005): 31–37.
Vodoff, Wladimir. "Remarques sur la valeur du terme le 'tsar' appliqué aux princes russes avant le milieu du XV siècle." *Oxford Slavonic Papers* 11 (1978): 1–41.
——. "La titulature des princes russes du Xe au début du XIIe siècle et les relations extérieures de la Russie kiévienne." *Revue des études slaves* 55 (1983): 139–50.
——. "La titulature princièr en Russie du XIe au début du XVIe siècle: Questions de critique des sources." *Jahrbücher für Geschichte Osteuropas* 35 (1987): 1–35.
Vukovich, Alexandra. "The Enthronement Rituals of the Princes of Vladimir-Suzdal in the 12th and 13th centuries." *FORUM University of Edinburgh Postgraduate Journal of Culture and the Arts* 17 (2013), at www.forumjournal.org/article/view/704/978
Warner, David A. "Reading Ottonian History: The *Sonderweg* and Other Myths." In *Challenging the Boundaries of Medieval History: The Legacy of Timothy Reuter*, edited by Patricia Skinner, 81–114. Turnhout: Brepols, 2009.
——. "Rituals, Kingship and Rebellion in Medieval Germany." *History Compass* 8/10 (2010): 1209–20.
West, Charles. "Lordship in Ninth-Century Francia: The Case of Bishop Hincmar of Laon and his Followers." *Past and Present* 226 (2014): 3–40.
——. *Reframing the Feudal Revolution: Political and Social Transformation between Marne and Moselle, c.800–c.1100*. Cambridge: Cambridge University Press, 2013.
Wheatley, Abigail. *The Idea of the Castle in Medieval England*. Woodbridge: York Medieval Press, 2004.
White, Monica. *Military Saints in Byzantium and Rus, 900–1200*. Cambridge: Cambridge University Press, 2013.

White, Stephen. "A Crisis of Fidelity in c. 1000?" In *Building Legitimacy: Political Discourses and Forms of Legitimacy in Medieval Societies*, edited by Isabel Alfonso, Hugh Kennedy, and Julio Escalona, 27–49. Boston: Brill, 2004.
——. "Debate: The 'Feudal Revolution'." *Past and Present* 152 (1996): 205–23.
——. "The Discourse of Inheritance in Twelfth-Century France: Alternative Models of the Fief in Raoul de Cambrai." In *Law and Government in Medieval England and Normandy*, edited by George Garnett and John Hudson, 173–97. New York: Cambridge University Press, 1994.
——. "Giving Fiefs and Honor: Largess, Avarice, and the Problem of 'Feudalism' in Alexander's Testament." In *The Medieval French Alexander*, edited by Sara Sturm-Maddox and Donald Maddox, 127–42. New York: State University of New York Press, 2002.
——. "Stratégie rhétorique dans la Conventio de Hugues de Lusignan." *Histoire et société: mélanges offerts à Georges Duby*, edited by Georges Duby, 147–57. Aix-en-Provence: Publications de l'Université de Provence, 1992.
Wickham, Christopher. *The Inheritance of Rome: Illuminating the Dark Ages 400–1000*. New York: Penguin, 2009.
——. "The 'Feudal Revolution' and the Origins of Italian City Communes." *Transactions of the Royal Historical Society* 24 (2014): 29–55.
——. *Medieval Europe*. New Haven: Yale University Press, 2016.
Worth, Dean S. "([Church] Slavonic) Writing in Kievan Rus'." In *Christianity and the Eastern Slavs*, edited by Boris Gasparov and Olga Raevsky-Hughes, 141–53. Berkeley: University of California Press, 1993.
——. "Was There a 'Literary Language' in Kievan Rus'?" *The Russian Review* 34 (1975): 1–9.
Zaitsev, A. K. *Chernigovskoe kniazhestvo X–XIII vv*. Moscow: Kvadriga, 2009.
Zalianiak, A. A. *Drevnenovgorodskii dialekt*. Moscow: Nauka, 1995.

INDEX

Adémar of Chabannes, 4, 102, 106, 172, 186
Ademari Cabanensis Chronicon see Adémar of Chabannes
Aimery, an Aquitanian noble mentioned in the *Conventum Hugonis*, 105–7
Africa, 132
Alnwick, battle of, 87
Althoff, Gerd, 22, 58–59, 81, 103, 154, 155, 158, 159–61, 192, 200
America, pre-Columbian, 199
amicitia, 159–60, 163; *see also* "love" as a political term
Andrew Bogoliubsky of Suzdalia, x, 19, 24, 26, 48, 56, 79, 101, 133, 189
 relations with the Rostislavichi of Smolensk, 101, 118, 169–74, 176
 and the sack of Kiev in 1169, 19, 79, 169
Andrew Vladimirovich of Pereiaslavl, 44, 74–76, 102–3, 108, 149–50, 156–57
Angles, 1, 200
Anglo-Norman
 castle, 134
 kings, 26, 82; *see also* William the Conqueror; Henry II; Henry the Young King; Stephen of Blois
 as a language of history-writing, 5–6; *see also Jordan Fantosme's Chronicle*
 political terminology in literary sources, 84, 150, 174, 176
 a variety of Old French, 5, 90; *see also* vernacular languages and sources in
Anjou, 50, 59–60, 106, 145, 150
Anglo-Saxon Chronicle, 5
Anna Iaroslavna, 16, 38
Annals of St. Bertin, 16
antiquity *see* classical cultural heritage
"anti-Normannists," 113
apocryphal texts, 99
Aquitaine, 4, 6, 51–53, 60, 83, 102, 105–9, 120–21, 175; *see also Conventum Hugonis*; Hugh IV of Lusignan; William V of Aquitaine
aristocracy, 7, 12, 46, 51, 89, 107, 114, 120, 125–27, 153, 163, 171, 177–78, 191, 195
 and "aristocratic state," 34–36, 46, 93, 199
 culture of, 90–93, 94, 102–4, 109
 relations with royalty in Latin Europe, 30–34, 56, 63, 69, 70–72, 93, 102, 127
 Rusian princes as, 12, 35, 45, 69, 70, 92–93, 102–3, 111, 114, 132, 174
Ashe, Laura, 18, 24, 88, 90–93, 149
Asia, 1
Azov Sea, 171
autocrat, as a designation for Rusian princes, 25, 36–37, 62, 92, 97–98, 195

Baldwin I of Jerusalem, 17
Baldwin IX of Flanders, Latin Emperor of Constantinople, 150
Balkans 3, 96
Baltic, 140
bannum, ban, 126, 133, 142, 151
banal lordship, 15, 125–27, 142–51
Batu, Mongol khan, 140, 181
Barbarossa, Frederick, 157, 160, 167
Barthélemy, Dominique, 10, 32–33, 51, 52, 97, 105, 110, 139, 145, 149, 196–97
Bath, bishop of, 131–32
Bavaria, 5, 200
Beaumont family, 59
Becket, Thomas, 87, 90
Béla III of Hungary, 168
Belarus, 1, 2, 16, 57, 72, 140, 199
Belgorod, 169–70, 173
Berengar of Italy, 26
Berlad, 171

Bernard, an Aquitanian noble mentioned in the *Conventum Hugonis*, 52–53, 105, 163
Bernard of Italy, 46
birchbark documents, 40, 131, 142–44
Bisson, Thomas, 10, 29, 31, 33
Bloch, Marc, 7–8, 104, 153
Boris and Gleb, 98, 99–102, 149
bowing down, ritual of, 57, 61, 64, 80, 98, 156, 168, 178–82, 184, 186, 191
boyars, 11, 22, 27, 48, 124, 141
Brittany, Bretons, 56, 83, 94, 164–65, 174
Brown, Elizabeth, 8, 13, 14, 154
Burgundy, 9, 46, 56, 63, 126
Burundai, a Mongol general, 140
Byzantium, 1–2, 16, 21, 25, 26–27, 36, 39, 95, 96–101, 141, 150, 195, 199, 200
Byzantine Commonwealth, 1–3, 7, 15, 200
Byzantine emperor, 2, 25, 38, 96–98, 151

Caen, 196
Canterbury, 87
Capetians, 46, 47, 53–54, 56, 90
Carolingians, 9, 10–11, 26, 31–33, 46, 47, 51, 59, 127, 153, 155, 162, 166, 186
castles, 13, 52, 53, 83, 90–91, 103, 120–21, 123, 124, 133–40, 141, 142, 145–46, 150–51; *see also castrum*; *gorod*
castrum, 51–53, 103, 105–7, 109, 110, 120–21, 137–39, 145, 150, 184, 186; *see also* castles
Casimir II of Poland, 150, 190
Caspian Sea, 21, 115
Catholics, 1; *see also* "Latins" in Rusian sources
Catalonia, 191–92
Catullus, 160
chaganus see kagan
chansons de geste, 92
chanson de la Croisade, 160
Charlemagne, 1, 163
Charles the Simple, 46
charters, 34, 48, 65, 103, 104, 125–28, 130–31, 143, 144, 146, 158, 165, 197, 198; *see also* Smolensk, bishopric foundational charter of
"of the Cross," 65, 104, 157–58, 176, 178, 190
Cheyette, Fredric, 6, 8, 10, 14, 31, 159, 160, 197
Chizé, *castrum* of, 105
Christendom, 1, 2, 25
Christianity, 1, 2, 3, 5, 16, 28, 34, 36, 45, 82, 98, 128, 130
Church Slavonic, 3, 95–98, 195
Civray, *castrum* of, 51–53, 105
Cicero, 90, 96
classical cultural heritage, 3, 27, 54, 91–92, 96, 98, 159–60, 165, 195, 198; *see also* Greek language; Latin language; Rome; Roman law
Clement, metropolitan of Kiev (Klim Smoliatich), 55
comitatus, 50–51, 121, 124–26
communities
  role of in princely succession in Rus, 20–22, 79
  consent of to be governed, 31, 49–50
  justice and dispute-resolution in, 131–32, 151
  participation in politics and relations with lords and rulers, 41, 42, 48, 53, 56, 65, 67–68, 79, 82, 98, 118, 130–32, 151, 158, 159, 180
  of the realm, 57, 73–74, 77, 93–95
Constantine I the "Great," Roman emperor, 150
Constantine Vsevolodovich, x, 98–99
Constantinople, 1, 2, 55, 141, 189
  patriarch of, 55–56
Conventum Hugonis, 4, 51–53, 105–11, 120–21, 145, 147, 150, 160, 163, 172, 174–75, 184–86, 192, 195–96
Constitutional-Democratic party, Russia, 8
coseigneurie, 103–4
Coulson, Charles, 121, 137–39
Couronnement de Louis, 90
Cross-kissing *see* oaths on the Cross
crusades
  Albigensian, 104
  Fourth, 1, 150
Cumans, 28, 61–64, 69, 81

dan, 113, 115–18, 121, 127–28, 133, 140–41, 144, 146–48, 151, 199; *see also* princes of Rus; translation
Daniel Romanovich of Galich, x, 140, 180–81
Danube, 171
David, biblical, 150
David, brother of William of Scotland, 88
David of Murom (patronymic unknown), 185
David Igorevich of Volhynia, 35, 120
David Rostislavich of Smolensk, x, 61, 63, 144, 169–70; *see also* Rostislavichi of Smolensk
Davidovichi, a princely clan, ix
Davidovichi, Iziaslav and Vladimir, 122–23, 127, 134; *see also* Iziaslav Davidovich of Chernigov
Débax, Hélène, 103–4, 111, 121, 151, 157, 159, 160, 164, 178, 191–92
democracy, 8
Derevlian land, Derevlians, 115–16
disintegration, a concept in historiography of Rus, 17–20, 25, 30–31, 44, 45, 62, 79, 93, 97, 199
Dimnik, Martin, 21, 24, 61, 77, 79, 187
Dnieper, 16, 19, 23, 37–38, 62, 64, 75, 79, 100, 166, 171–72, 187–88
druzhina, 22, 38
Dobroslav, a noble in the Galician-Volhynian principality, 180–81
Dorogobuzh, 180
Dorogychin, 134, 150–51
Duby, Georges, 9–10, 126–27, 164
Dudo of Saint-Quentin, 35, 94–95
Duncan, a Scottish earl, 176–77

Ecclesiastical History see Orderic Vitalis
East (as a cultural construct), 1
East European Plain, 24
East Slavonic, 3, 16, 39, 53, 70, 73, 88, 95–97, 106, 108, 110, 115, 138, 149, 151, 166, 176, 180, 195–96, 199; *see also* vernacular languages and sources
Eleanor of Aquitaine, Queen of England, 84

England, vii, 5–6, 12, 18, 23–24, 26, 29, 59, 79, 82–90, 93, 134, 138, 157, 164, 198
enthronement, 27–28
Erik dynasty, Sweden, 23–24
Europe 1–3, 7, 11, 16, 29, 195, 201
  Carolingian, 46
  continental, 4
  Eastern, 1, 199, 200
  Latin, 2, 4, 5, 15, 29, 70–72, 82, 95, 109, 142, 151, 153, 195, 198
  medieval, 1–2, 6, 15, 18, 23, 24, 26–27, 32–34, 38, 45–47, 54–55, 59, 69, 70, 73, 79, 96–97, 103–4, 111, 137, 155, 161, 195, 197–98, 200
  Western, 1, 3, 7, 10, 30, 46, 59, 197–98; *see also* West (as a cultural construct)

fealty, oath of, 13, 161–62, 165, 175
feudal anarchy, 30
feudal construct, 8, 10, 13–14, 17, 32–33, 95, 155 *see also* feudalism, debate on
feudal contract, 7–9, 153–54, 161, 191
feudal mutation *see* feudal revolution
feudal pyramid, 32
feudal revolution, 9–10, 32, 97, 125–27, 141, 154, 197
feudal zone of Europe, 7, 104
feudalism
  "broad" vs. "narrow" definition of, 6–7, 153, 161
  debate on, 6–11, 32, 110, 114, 153–55, 161–62, 196–97; *see also* feudal construct
  as a legal system, 6, 32, 110, 153, 161
  Marxist definition of, 6
  as a Veberian ideal type, 7
  whether it existed in Rus, 6–7, 11, 114, 182, 191–92, 200
feudalization of offices, 58
feudo-vassalic relations, 8, 10–11, 103, 153–55, 161–63, 165, 167, 172, 178, 183, 186, 191–92, 197–98, 200
fief (excluding occurrences in titles of scholarly works), 6–10, 13, 92, 115, 141, 153, 161–63, 165, 174, 182–83, 184; *see also honor*; land grants; *repris en fief*; *volost*

Fiefs and Vassals see feudalism, debate on; Reynolds, Susan
Flanders, 83–84, 94–95, 110, 150, 157
formulaic expressions, 61, 65, 69, 95, 99, 163, 168, 174, 175, 188
Franklin, Simon, 3, 16, 18–20, 22–25, 36–37, 40, 44, 48, 54–55, 62, 64, 96–99, 115–18, 131, 157, 199
Frederick Barbarossa *see* Barbarossa, Frederick
Fulbert of Chartres, 164, 175
Fulk le Réchin of Anjou, 59, 150
Fulk Nerra of Anjou, 105–6, 120, 184–85
Finnic peoples, 113
Francia, France, Franks, 1, 4, 9–10, 16–17, 24, 26–28, 22, 33, 35, 45–46, 49, 51, 53–54, 56, 59, 64, 83–86, 103–4, 111, 121, 138, 145, 162, 164–65, 192

Galbert of Burge, 180
Galich, 42, 60–61, 64–65, 116–17, 140, 144, 167–68, 176–81, 189
Galician-Volhynian Chronicle, 40, 42, 140
Galician-Volhynian principality, 40; *see also* Galich; Volhynia; Vladimir-in-Volhynia
Ganshof, François-Louis, 6–8, 110, 161
Geoffrey, an Aquitanian noble mentioned in the *Conventum Hugonis* 107
George the "Long Arm" (Yury Vladimirovich Dolgoruky) of Suzdal, Kievan prince (1154–1157), x, 43–44, 60, 61, 66–68, 78–80, 82, 86, 133, 158, 168, 173, 175, 178–80, 185, 188
Germany, German Empire, Germans, 1, 5–6, 8, 13, 15, 23, 26, 29–31, 35, 54, 56–58, 69, 72, 103, 126, 138–39, 154, 159, 199–200
Gesta Regum Anglorum see William of Malmesbury
Géza II of Hungary, 60–61
Gleb Iurevich, Kievan prince (1170–1171), x, 169, 178–79, 182
Gleb Vladimirovich, 185
Gleb Vseslavich of Minsk, xi, 57–58, 60
Glebovichi of Riazan, 181–87, 189
Gloucester, 91, 134

Godfrey of Bouillon, 5
gorod, 47, 103, 119, 133–40, 144–46, 147–48, 173
Gorskii, Anton, 21, 41, 47–48, 73, 114, 161, 184
Grand Prince, 21, 24, 37, 185
Greece, Greeks, 73, 97, 141, 150
Greek language, 3, 96, 97
Greek Orthodox, 1–2, 3, 200
grivna, 118, 120, 143–44, 167
Gurevich, Aron, 7
Guy, a Norman noble mentioned by William of Malmesbury, 90–91

Ham, biblical, 1
Helias I of Maine, 50–51, 124–26
Henry I of England, 26
Henry I of France, 16, 18
Henry I the "Fowler" of East Francia, 158
Henry II of England, 82–90, 149, 164–65, 174, 176–77, 182
Henry IV, emperor, 5
Henry VIII of England, 138
Henry the "Lion" of Saxony and Bavaria, 57, 60
Henry the Young King of England, 79, 82–85, 150, 164, 176
Herbert the "Wake Dog" of Maine, 50–51
Hilarion (Ilarion), metropolitan of Rus, 36–37, 55, 97
Hildegard of Bingen, 52
Hincmar, bishop of Laon, 10, 33, 162, 163, 171
Historia Novella, 91
homage, 7–10, 13, 26, 85, 91, 154–55, 161–65, 177–81, 192
hommage de pais, 179
honor, 82, 84–86, 93, 141, 148–50, 174; *see also* fief; land grants; *volost*
honur see honor
Hugh V of Maine, 50–51, 124–25
Hugh Capet, 47
Hugh IV of Lusignan, 4, 51–53, 105–8, 111, 120, 145, 147, 150, 160, 163, 172, 175–76, 184–85, 192; *see also Conventum Hugonis*

Hungary, Hungarians, 1, 38, 45, 60, 167–68, 180
Hyams, Paul, 4, 14, 109, 178–81, 192
Hypatian Codex, 46, 42, 43, 69, 119

Iaropolk Vladimirovich, Kievan prince (1132–1139), x, 18, 43–44, 58, 66, 74
Iaropolk Rostislavich, grandson of George the "Long Arm," Kievan prince jointly with Vsevolod the "Big Nest" (1173), x, 48, 170
Iaroslav the "Wise"(Iaroslav Vladimirovich), Kievan prince (1019–1054), viii, 17–18, 20, 25, 36–39, 64, 97, 100, 130
  as "autocrat," 24, 36–37, 62, 97
  conflict with his brother Mstislav, 37–38, 100
  daughter's marriage to Henry I of France, 16, 38
  progeny of, 18, 45–46
  as *rex russorum*, 16–17, 38
  "Testament" of, 94
  title translated as archduke, 16–17
Iaroslav Vladimirovich of Galich, viii, 61
Ignatius, an official in Galich, 144
Igor, Kievan prince (first half of the tenth century), vi, viii, 115–16
Igor Olgovich of Chernigov, Kievan prince (1147), ix, 42–43, 47, 62, 76, 77, 122–23, 128
  village of (*Igorevo seltso*), 123
Igor Sviatoslavich of Novgorod-Severskii, 62, 81, 89
Ilarion *see* Hilarion
Instruction by Vladimir Monomakh, 40, 47, 97, 132
Ipatevskaia letopis see Hypatian Codex
Israel, 150
Iziaslav Davidovich of Chernigov, Kievan prince (1155–1161), ix, 28, 119; *see also* Davidovichi, Izaiaslav and Vladimir
Iziaslav Mstislavich of Volhynia, Kievan prince (1146–1154), x, 43, 44, 48, 58, 60–61, 64, 75–82, 88, 108, 122–24, 127, 134, 156, 168–69, 173, 175, 178–79, 180, 182, 185, 188, 189
  "duumvirate" with Viacheslav Vladimirovich (1151–1154), 79–80, 81–82, 179
  sister of, 48

Jacob, biblical, 99
Jacob, a man of Daniel Romanovich of Galich, 180–81
Japheth, biblical, 1, 200
Jatvingians, 140
Jerusalem, 17
Jews, 22
Jewish War, 41
Jordan Fantosme's Chronicle, 5, 82, 84–90, 93–95, 104, 110–11, 149–50, 159, 163–65, 174, 176–77, 182
Jordan, William Chester, 1, 92
Joscelin, an Aquitanian noble mentioned in the *Conventum Hugonis*, 45
Josephus *see Jewish War*
Judea, 150

kagan, the title of the ruler of Khazaria, 21
Kaiser, Daniel, 117–18, 128, 130–32
Kaiserchronik, 5–6
Kasogs, 38
Khazaria, Khazars, 21, 38, 115
Kiev, Kievans, 1, 16, 18, 23, 28, 37–38, 43–47, 54, 55, 57, 60–69, 72, 74–82, 88, 94, 97, 100, 101, 113, 116, 118, 119, 122, 128, 157, 158, 166, 167, 169–74, 178–79, 189, 195; *see also* Kievan prince
  1113 uprising in, 18, 22
  1169 sack of, 19, 101, 116, 118
  seat of the metropolitan, 55–56
Kievan Caves monastery, 117
Kievan Chronicle, 40, 42–44, 45, 48, 57, 66, 68, 69, 106, 117, 119, 122, 128, 134, 156, 157, 158, 169, 172–73, 195
Kievan prince, 19, 28, 31, 36–39, 45–46, 57–70, 74, 77–82, 88, 92, 97–98
  as a local lord on par with other princes, 19, 35, 38, 45, 54, 66

Kievan prince (cont.)
  as a monarch, 19, 20, 24–25, 34, 38, 57, 60–65, 68–70, 73, 79, 88, 96–97, 102, 158, 195
  legitimacy of, 28, 77–82
  personal domain of, 58, 64, 75, 77, 79
  relations with the Suzdalian prince, 19, 24, 26, 42, 56, 65, 79, 101, 158, 166–67, 169–74, 187–90
  relations with other princes, 19, 37, 48, 57–66, 68, 71, 74–76, 92, 94, 102, 108–9, 114, 158
  relations with the metropolitan, 28, 55–56, 190
  title of, 21, 24, 37; *see also* autocrat; Grand Prince
  as a warlord, 38, 98
kingship, 15–17, 23–24, 26–35, 46–47, 50, 53–57, 63, 64, 71–74, 79, 82–93, 95
  administrative, 29–30, 73, 114
  and aristocracy, 30–34, 54–57, 59–60, 69–72, 89–91, 102–3, 104, 114, 127, 150, 158
  hierarchy of kings, 26, 177
  in Rus, 3, 15–25, 27–29, 31, 34–39, 45–47, 54–72, 73–79, 98–99; *see also* Kievan prince
  ideology of, 28, 70, 77, 93, 96–98, 102
  personal, 29, 54–56, 70
  rituals of, 26–27
  sacred, 28
  in vernacular literature, 92–93, 103
  without coronation or anointing, 26–27, 70
kinship, 11, 46, 48, 80, 84–86, 88, 154, 164–65, 171–72, 192, 200; *see also* princes of Rus
  artificial, 48, 80, 171, 192–93, 195
Klim Smoliatich *see* Clement, metropolitan of Kiev
kniaz, 11, 16–21, 26–27, 29, 37, 47, 49, 53, 61, 69–70, 74, 95, 100, 114, 117–18, 127–28, 130–31, 133, 144, 147, 151, 160, 173, 184, 199
konung, 19, 29
Kolomyia, 181

Korachev, 173
Korsun, 190
Kosto, Adam, 10, 14, 33, 191–93
Kostroma, 40

La Manse, 126
land grants, 6, 8–9, 49, 51–52, 58, 60, 76, 84, 85, 88, 92, 106–8, 118, 166–70, 180–81, 184, 187–89; *see also* fief; honor; volost
Languedoc, 103–4, 121, 157, 159–60, 164, 178, 191
Laon, 10, 33, 162–63, 171
Latin
  Christians, 1, 2; *see also* Catholics
  Europe *see* Europe, Latin
  language and sources in, 2–6, 13–14, 16–17, 34, 53, 70, 73–74, 84, 89–92, 95–96, 102, 104, 106–7, 109–11, 115–16, 120, 126, 138–39, 144, 148–49, 159–60, 163–65, 166, 175, 183, 195–98
"Latins" in Rusian sources, 116, 150
Laurentian Chronicle, 36, 39–41
Laurentius, 39, 41, 156
Lavrentevskaia letopis see Laurentian Chronicle
legal codes, 36, 130, 131–32
Lehnswesen, 8
Leszek the "White" of Poland, 150
Life of Thomas Becket, 90
Liakh, a person mentioned in a court case, 144
Liguria, 50–51
Limoges, bishop of, 51, 185
Lithuania, 140, 199
literati, 3, 39, 91, 96, 99
Liubech conference, 17–18, 21, 35, 39
Loire, 110
lordship, 32–33, 45, 59, 103–4, 121, 125–27, 139, 142, 155, 162–65, 195, 200
  banal, 15, 125–27, 142, 151
Lotharingia, 127
Louis VII of France, 54, 83, 85
Louis the "Pious," 25, 31, 90
"love" as a political term, 65, 79–82, 84–86, 88, 93–94, 108, 158–60,

163–65, 171, 173–74, 182, 187–89; see also amicitia
brotherly, in Rusian political culture (*bratoliubie*), 99–100, 102, 104–5
Luke, Bishop of Suzdalia, 185
Lyon, Jonathan, 103, 200

Mâcon, 10, 126
Magna Carta, 7
Maine, 50–51, 53, 60, 121, 124, 126
Marsile, a character in the *Song of Roland*, 163
Maya, 199
Malval, *castrum* of, 105
Marne, 125
Martin, Janet, 19, 23, 116, 128
Martindale, Jane, 4, 52, 105–6, 109, 111, 120–21, 175
Matilda, empress, claimant to the English throne, 79, 91
Merovingians, 26–28, 45, 70
Metropolitan of Rus, 27–28, 36, 55–56, 97, 117, 166–67, 187, 190
Michael Borisovich, a man of David of Murom, 185
Michael Iurievich (Mikhalko) of Vladimir (1174–1176), 48
Michesk, 116
Middle High German, 5
Mieszko the "Old" of Poland, 150, 190
Minsk, xi, 57–58, 60, 182
models
    cultural, 49–50, 162
    theoretical, 14, 25, 36, 71–72, 90, 153, 162, 199; *see also* disintegration, a concept in historiography of Rus; feudal construct; feudalism; translation
monarchy *see* kingship
Mongol conquest of Rus, 4, 18, 19, 20, 31, 39, 47, 140, 141, 180–81, 186, 198–99
Monomakhovichi dynasty, Rus, x, 18, 24, 45–48, 55, 61, 63–64, 66–67, 69, 74, 77–81, 108, 119, 166–68, 176, 187, 190
Moselle, 125
Mstislav Iziaslavich, Kievan prince (1167–1169), x, 23, 28, 55, 61, 78–79, 158
Mstislav Mstislavich Udatnyi of Galich, 144

Mstislav Rostislavich, grandson of George the "Long Arm," x, 48
Mstislav Rostislavich, of the Smolensk princely dynasty, x, 169, 171
Mstislav Vladimirovich of Tmutarokan and Chernigov, viii, 37–38, 100
Mstislav Vladimirovich (Mstislav the "Great"), Kievan prince (1125–1132), x, 18, 57, 58, 60, 66, 70, 74, 76
    daughter of, 66
Murom, 140, 183, 185
Muscovy, 2, 17, 198–99
"mutation of the year 1000" *see* feudal revolution

nationalism, 72
Nazarenko, Alexander, 2, 17, 21, 23, 45, 56
Nelson, Janet, 15, 24, 27–28, 54–56
Nicephorus I, metropolitan of Rus, 97–99, 117
Nicephorus II, metropolitan of Rus, 190
Noah, biblical, 1
Norman Conquest of England, 5, 29, 164; *see also* Anglo-Norman
Norman kingdom of Sicily, 29
Normandy, 35, 49–50, 60, 87, 90, 92, 94–95, 116, 177, 192
Normans, 1, 35, 50, 94, 95, 125, 134, 177
Northumberland, 83, 85–88, 164, 176
Novgorod, Novgorodians, 19–20, 37–39, 42–43, 48, 65–68, 72, 81, 98–99, 128–31, 133, 142–43, 158
    bishop of, 68, 131
Novgorod-Severskii, 62, 81, 122–23, 127, 148, 173
Novgorodian First Chronicle, 39, 66–68

oaths on the Cross, 44, 48, 49, 80, 108, 109, 123, 148, 155–59, 160, 167–70, 176–78, 180–82, 184, 187–88, 190–91; *see also* charters, "of the Cross"
Obolensky, Dimitri, 1, 200
Occitan, 4, 103–4, 111; *see also* vernacular
Odo, king of West Francia, 47
Old English, 5
Old French, 5, 90, 92, 149; *see also* vernacular
Old Russian *see* East Slavonic

Old Ukrainian *see* East Slavonic
Oleg, Kievan prince (late ninth–early tenth century?), 140
Oleg Sviatoslavich, the founder of the Olgovichi dynasty, ix, 18, 45
Oleg Sviatoslavich of Starodub, ix, 108
Oleg Vladimirovich, 185–86
Olgovichi dynasty, Rus, ix, 18, 24, 43–47, 48, 55, 58, 61, 63, 64, 66–67, 74, 77, 78, 81, 119, 148, 166, 167, 176, 185–87, 189–90
Orderic Vitalis, 50–51, 53, 121, 124–26, 138
Orleans, 53
Ostromir, governor of Novgorod, 37
Ostrowski, Donald, 1, 15, 19, 21, 23–24, 26, 34–36, 44–46, 99, 199
Otto I the "Great", 26, 58–59
Ottonians, 8, 14, 23, 29–31, 71–72, 154

paratge, 103–5
Paris, 53, 60, 63
Parthenay, *castrum* of, 145, 150
Pashuto, V. P., 11–12, 114
patristic literature, 90, 92, 96, 98
Patzinaks *see* Pechenegs
Pavlov-Silvansky, N. P., 2, 8
Pechenegs, 62
Pereiaslavl, 43–44, 58, 62–63, 69, 74–76, 102, 108, 135, 149, 156–57, 180, 189
Pereislavl-Zalessky, 41
Peter, an Aquitanian noble mentioned in the *Conventum Hugonis*, 145
Philip I of France, 59–60
Philip of Flanders, 85
Pinesk, 179
Plantagenet dynasty, 82
Plato, 92
Poe, Marshall, 1
poesté, 148–49, 165, 174
Poitou, 138–39, 145
Poland, Poles, 1, 19, 45, 69, 140, 150–51
Polonnyi, 190
Polotsk, xi, 16, 37, 57–58, 60, 167
Polovtsians *see* Cumans
Polycarp of the Kievan Caves monastery, 117
Pontius Pilate, biblical, 90

Porcien, 125
Porphyrius, Bishop of Chernigov, 185
posadnik, 123, 128, 140, 145, 146–47, 186
Primary Chronicle, viii, 1, 34–36, 39–40, 62, 73, 99–100, 113–15, 120, 128, 130, 140, 200
primogeniture, 24, 99; *see also* succession
princes of Rus, 11, 15–25, 27–50, 54–82, 84, 87, 88, 91–104, 108–25, 127–33, 140–52, 155–60, 164, 166–76, 178–93, 199
  as aristocrats, 34–35, 45–46, 102, 111, 114, 140, 199
  as "brethren," 48, 99, 172
  co-ruling groups among, 82, 101, 103, 151, 170; *see also* Rostislavichi of Smolensk; Glebovichi of Riazan
  and *dan*, 113, 115–18, 121, 127, 133, 140, 147–48
  "duumvirates" of, 78–82, 179
  as a dynasty, 25, 34, 46, 98, 199; *see also* Rurikids
  as a "family concern," 18, 51
  "father–son" relations among, 48, 79–80, 99, 167–74, 176, 178–79, 181–87, 190–93, 197–98
  hierarchical relations among, 11, 19, 23, 48, 57–69, 75–78, 89, 166–76, 178–93
  "junior" and "senior," 19, 77–78, 89, 166–67, 187–89
  and justice, 113, 117, 127–33, 144
  as kings *see* kingship in Rus
  as members of a kin-group, 11, 18, 25, 45, 48, 66, 101, 172
  and their monopoly on strongholds, 133–34, 144–46
  as royalty and aristocracy, 11, 29, 46, 63–65, 70–71, 102
  succession of, 18, 22–23, 25, 74, 94, 100
  two main dynasties of, 18, 45–47; *see also* Olgovichi; Monomakhovichi
Pronsk, 186
public/private dichotomy, 9, 30–33, 51, 72–73, 90, 126–27, 137–38, 150, 153
Putivl, 122–24, 127, 134

Radziwill Codex, 41
Raffensperger, Christian, 2, 16–17, 34, 38, 197, 199
Ralph de Fougères, 165, 174, 182
Raoul de Cambrai, 49, 103
Ratsha, an official in Kiev, 128
Regensburg, 5
regnum, 16–17, 26, 34, 60, 73, 93–95
Reich *see* Germany, German Empire, Germans
repris en fief, 182–83, 184
res publica, 73–74, 95
Reuter, Timothy, 14–15, 24, 29–30, 54, 70, 90
rex, 15–17, 38, 83, 102, 106
Reynolds, Susan, 6–10, 13–14, 31, 32, 56–57, 60, 73–74, 93–95, 114, 153–55, 162–63, 166, 198
Rheims, 125
Riazan, ix, 100–1, 181–87, 189
Roach, Levi, 8–10, 23, 26–27, 30, 33–34, 46, 67, 127, 154–55, 162, 199
Robert of Gloucester, 91
Robert of Torigni, 82–86, 89–90
Robertins *see* Capetians
Rollo, 94
Rollonid dynasty, Normandy, 35
Roman Glebovich of Riazan, ix, 181–82
Roman Mstislavich of Galich, x, 119–20, 166–67, 187–91, 195
Roman Rostislavich of Smolensk, Kievan prince (1171–1176), x, 61–62, 156, 169–72, 174; *see also* Rostislavichi of Smolensk
romances, 90, 93
Roman de Rou see Wace
Rome, Romans, 1, 27, 54, 92, 96, 165; *see also* classical heritage
Roman law, 10
Rostislav Iurevich, son of George the "Long Arm," x, 66–68, 82, 86, 168, 175, 185, 188–89
Rostislav Mstislavich of Smolensk, Kievan prince (1159–1167), x, 55, 76, 78–80, 108–9, 117–18, 127, 131, 133, 144, 156, 167, 173, 179–80; *see also* Smolensk, bishopric foundational charter of
Rostislav Rurikovich, x, 146
Rostislavichi of Riazan (Andrew and Gleb), ix
Rostislavichi of Smolensk, 101, 118, 169–74, 176; *see also* David Rostislavich of Smolensk; Mstislav Rostislavich of Smolensk; Roman Rostislavich of Smolensk; Rurik Rostislavich of Smolensk
Rostislavichi, Iaropolk and Mstislav, x, 48–50, 52, 53, 124, 128
Rostov, 140
royalty *see* kingship
"rules of play" *see Spielregeln*
Rurik, the purported founder of the princely dynasty of Rus, 15, 45–46, 51, 113
Rurik Rostislavich of Smolensk, Kievan prince (1194–1210), x, 42, 63, 64, 97–98, 119–20, 146, 166–68, 170, 187–91, 195; *see also* Rostislavichi of Smoilensk
Rurikids, 15–16, 18, 21, 23–27, 34, 45–46, 113
Rus Land, 28, 36, 69, 73–75, 77, 80–81, 88, 93–94, 100, 168–69, 173–74, 179
as a territory on the Middle Dnieper, 37, 64, 168–69, 170–71, 187, 188
Rusian
language *see* East Slavonic
versus Russian, 2
Russia, 1–3, 7–8, 17, 19, 40, 44, 48, 72, 97, 113, 122

St. Boris *see* Boris and Gleb
St. Gleb *see* Boris and Gleb
St. Hypatius monastery, Russia, 40
St. Lawrence church, England, 87
St. Panteleimon church, Galich, 144
St. Thierry monastery, France, 125
St. Thomas *see* Becket, Thomas
Salian kings, 23
Sallust, 90–91, 96, 98
Sancho VI of Gascony, 106
Sappho, 160
Saxony, 57, 200
Scandinavia, Scandinavians, 1, 15, 23, 27, 29, 38, 113; *see also* Varangians

Scotland, 26–28, 70, 84–87, 164, 176–77
Scripture, 41, 96, 98–99
seigneurie banale see banal lordship
Sermon on Law and Grace, 36, 97
Shem, biblical, 1
Shepard, Jonathan, 2–3, 15–16, 18–28, 34, 36–37, 45, 48, 56, 62, 64, 97–98, 101, 116, 129–31, 199
Sicily, 29
Smolensk, 19, 55, 61, 63–64, 75–76, 80, 117–18, 120, 127–28, 131, 133, 135, 143, 144, 146–48, 169–71, 173–74, 179; *see also* Rostislavichi of Smolensk
  bishopric foundational charter of, 117–18, 120, 127–28, 131, 146–48
Sneporod, 134–35
Snovsk, 173
Song of Roland, 163
Sonderweg see "special path"
Soviet Union, 12
"special path," 1, 29–30, 31, 111, 195, 200
Spielregeln, 22–23
Stephen of Blois, king of England, 79, 91
strips regia, 27
succession
  in England, 18, 24, 83
  in France, 24
  in the German Empire, 23, 59
  in Maine, 50–51
  "rota" system of in Rus, 21
  in Rus *see* princes of Rus, succession of
  in Scandinavia, 23–24
Suetonius, 90–91, 96, 98, 195
Suger of St. Denis, 56, 63, 198
Suzdal, x, 39, 41, 48
Suzdalia, x, 19, 21, 24, 26, 27, 40–42, 48–52, 65–66, 72, 78–79, 98, 101, 116, 118, 128, 133, 146, 166, 168–69, 181, 185
Suzdalian Chronicle, 40–41, 53, 62–63, 98, 124, 169, 182
Swabia, 200
Sverker dynasty, Sweden, 23
Sviatopolk the "Cain-like" (Sviatopolk the "Accursed," Sviatopolk Vladimirovich), Kievan prince (1015–1019), viii, 99–100, 102, 149–50
Sviatopolk Iziaslavich, 18, 21–22, 35

Sviatopolk Mstislavich, x, 48, 66–68
Sviatoslav Igorevich, Kievan prince (d. 972), viii, 27, 99, 100
Sviatoslav Glebovich, ix, 184; *see also* Glebovichi of Riazan
Sviatoslav Olgovich of Chernigov, ix, 66–67, 76, 108–9, 119, 122–24, 128, 130, 134, 147–48, 164, 173, 175
Sviatoslav Vladimirovich, ix, 99
Sviatoslav Vsevolodovich of Chernigov, Kievan prince (1176–1194), ix, 61, 62–65, 70, 81, 89, 179–80
Sweden, Swedes, 1, 16, 23

Templars, process of, 196
terre, 84–85, 89, 93, 95
Thomson, Francis, 3, 97
Thouars, *castrum* of, 53
tiun, 77, 146–47
Tmutarokan, 37
Tolochko, P. P., 11–12, 20–21, 27, 41, 43, 47, 114
Tolstoy, Aleksei K., 20
Torchesk, 146, 189–90, 195
Toropichi, 118
translation
  of *castrum*, 103, 137
  of *dan*, 115–18
  of *Conventum Hugonis*, 52, 120, 175–76
  of *gorod*, 133–37, 140, 146
  of historical terms, 13, 19, 29, 95, 115–16, 136, 149, 175–76; *see also castrum; fief; honor; regnum; terre*
  of *kniaz*, 16, 17, 19, 21, 29, 151
  of *konung*, 19, 29
  of medieval Slavonic terms into modern languages, 14–15, 17, 21, 72, 115, 132, 136, 157, 175–77; *see also dan; gorod; kniaz; volost; zemlia*
troubadour poetry, 105
Tudor, an official in Kiev, 128
Turov, 179

Ukraine, 1–2, 12, 19, 72, 113, 199

Varangians, 38, 113, 115, 117, 128; *see also* Scandinavians
Vasilko Rostislavich of Terebovl, viii, 35, 39
vassal, 6–7, 9, 13, 32, 153, 161–62, 181, 183, 192, 199
vassalage, 7, 8, 153, 161–62, 183
velikii kniaz see Grand Prince
Vermondois, count of, 46
vernacular languages and sources, 2–6, 13, 89–90, 92–96, 103–5, 109, 111, 149, 159–60, 161, 163–65, 174–75, 177, 194–98; *see also* Anglo-Norman; East Slavonic; Occitan; Old French
Viacheslav Vladimirovich, Kievan prince (1139, 1151–1154, jointly with Iziaslav Mstislavich and Rostislav Mstislavich), x, 44, 74, 76–82, 149, 179, 189; *see also* princes of Rus, "duumvirates" of
vira, 128–29, 143
Vladimir, town in Suzdalia, 24, 41, 42, 48–50, 56, 124, 133, 146, 184, 185, 186
Vladimir-in-Volhynia, 58, 75, 108
Vladimir Glebovich of Pereiaslavl, x, 63
Vladimir Iaroslavich of Galich, 167–68
Vladimir Monomakh, Kievan prince (1113–1125), x, 18, 21, 35, 36, 40, 45, 47, 57–58, 60, 74, 97, 117, 132
Vladimir Sviatoslavich (St. Vladimir), Kievan prince (978–1015), viii, 16, 36, 97, 99, 100, 128–30, 141–42
Vladimir Volodarevich of Galich (Volodimerko), viii, 60–61, 64–65, 116–17, 157–58, 176, 178–79, 181
Volga, 21, 115
Volhynia, x, 40, 42, 58, 60, 75, 182; *see also* Vladimir-in-Volhynia
volost, 47–49, 60–61, 74–77, 79, 82, 86, 88, 92, 94, 103, 106, 108, 116–24, 127, 133–35, 139, 141, 146–51, 166–69, 173–75, 179–80, 183, 185–91, 199
  as power or authority, 47, 148–50
  as a princely holding, 49, 74–75, 76, 82, 103, 108, 116–24, 127, 133, 133–35, 141, 146–48

  as fief, 92, 151, 168–69, 174, 179–80, 183–87, 189–91
vlast as a variant spelling, 47, 149
Rus as a collection of, 47, 74, 77
polysemy of, 49, 75, 149–50
Vorotinesk, 173
Vsevolod Glebovich, ix
Vsevolod Iurevich (Vsevolod the "Big Nest") of Suzdalia (1176–1212), Kievan prince (1173, jointly with Iaropolk Rostislavich), x, 42, 98, 124, 146, 166–68, 170, 181–93
Vsevolod Olgovich of Chernigov, Kievan prince (1139–1146), ix, 44, 58, 64–70, 73–77, 102–3, 108, 122, 128, 134–35, 149–50, 156–58, 176, 178–79, 181, 182
  daughter of, 69
Vsevolod Mstislavich, x, 43–44, 130
Vyr, 119
Vyshegorod, 77, 169–70, 173

Wace, author of *Roman de Rou*, 174
Warwick, earls of, 59
West (as a cultural construct), 1–4, 6, 8, 11–12, 14–15, 17, 25, 29–31, 65, 71–72, 77, 96, 98, 102–5, 110–11, 114, 121, 132, 136, 142, 145, 151, 159–60, 171, 174–75, 186, 191–93; *see also* Europe, Latin; Europe, Western
West, Charles, 9–10, 33, 125–27, 133, 141, 151, 154–55, 162–63, 165–66, 171, 178–79, 183, 197
William I the "Longsword" of Normandy, 35
William V of Aquitaine, 4, 51–53, 102, 105–9, 120, 145, 150, 163, 172, 175–76, 184–86, 192; *see also* *Conventum Hugonis*
William of Malmesbury, 26, 90–92, 177
William of Newburgh, 83–84, 86, 89–90
William the "Conqueror," 90
William the "Lion" of Scotland, 84–88, 164, 176–77
White, Monica, 100, 101
White, Stephen, 6, 10, 49, 109, 161, 164–65, 197
Wladyslaw II of Poland, 69

zemlia 73, 93, 95